ANNUAL EDITIONS

Adolescent Psychology

Seventh Edition

EDITOR

Fred E. Stickle
Western Kentucky University

Fred E. Stickle received his BS degree from Cedarville University where he majored in Social Science Secondary Education. He completed his graduate study in counseling at Wright State University (MS) and Iowa State University (PhD). He is currently a professor at Western Kentucky University where he teaches adolescent counseling. Dr. Stickle also maintains a private practice where he provides counseling for adolescents and their families.

The McGraw-Hill Companies

Connect
Learn
Succeed™

ANNUAL EDITIONS: ADOLESCENT PSYCHOLOGY, SEVENTH EDITION

Annual Editions® is a registered trademark of The McGraw-Hill Companies, Inc.

Annual Editions is published by the **Contemporary Learning Series** group within the McGraw-Hill Higher Education division.

1 2 3 4 5 6 7 8 9 0 QWD/QWD 0 9

ISBN 978–0–07–812775–5
MHID 0–07–812775–0
ISSN 1094–2610

Managing Editor: *Larry Loeppke*
Senior Managing Editor: *Faye Schilling*
Developmental Editor: *Debra A. Henricks*
Editorial Coordinator: *Mary Foust*
Editorial Assistant: *Cindy Hedley*
Production Service Assistant: *Rita Hingtgen*
Permissions Coordinator: *Lenny Behnke*
Senior Marketing Manager: *Julie Keck*
Marketing Communications Specialist: *Mary Klein*
Marketing Coordinator: *Alice Link*
Project Manager: *Joyce Watters*
Design Specialist: *Tara McDermott*
Cover Graphics: *Kristine Jubeck*

Compositor: Laserwords Private Limited
Cover Image: © Corbis/RF (both)

Library in Congress Cataloging-in-Publication Data
Main entry under title: Annual Editions: Adolescent Psychology. 2010/2011.
  1. Adolescent Psychology—Periodicals. I. Stickle, Fred E., Title: Adolescent Psychology.
658'.05

www.mhhe.com

Editors/Academic Advisory Board

Members of the Academic Advisory Board are instrumental in the final selection of articles for each edition of ANNUAL EDITIONS. Their review of articles for content, level, and appropriateness provides critical direction to the editors and staff. We think that you will find their careful consideration well reflected in this volume.

ANNUAL EDITIONS: Adolescent Psychology
7th Edition

EDITOR

Fred E. Stickle
Western Kentucky University

Preface

In publishing ANNUAL EDITIONS we recognize the enormous role played by the magazines, newspapers, and journals of the public press in providing current, first-rate educational information in a broad spectrum of interest areas. Many of these articles are appropriate for students, researchers, and professionals seeking accurate, current material to help bridge the gap between principles and theories and the real world. These articles, however, become more useful for study when those of lasting value are carefully collected, organized, indexed, and reproduced in a low-cost format, which provides easy and permanent access when the material is needed. That is the role played by ANNUAL EDITIONS.

The word adolescence is Latin in origin, derived from the verb adolescere, which means to grow into adulthood. Growing into maturity involves change. Most would argue that, except for infancy, adolescence is the most change-filled period of life. The traditional definition was based largely on physical growth, as evident in the marked increase in height and weight.

Most researchers define the period of life between age 10 and 20 as adolescence. It is a period of transition in which a person moves from the immaturity of childhood into the maturity of adulthood. There is a growing realization that characteristics of adolescent behaviors do not result simply from the physical changes, but include a variety of psychological and social factors. Environmental settings such as family, peer, and school influence the development and the numerous and dynamic changes that take place.

It is commonplace to hear a discussion concerning adolescence as the story years with new crazes and fads or the problems of teenagers involving crime or sexuality.

However, there are many strengths and even advantages to the teenage years.

This anthology of readings will help you understand the bases of the developmental changes young people experience and appropriate aspects of individuals, families, communities, and cultures that give richness to adolescent development. The selection of articles will include opinions of various authors. You may agree with some and disagree with others. Some may even spur classroom debate.

Fred E. Stickle

Fred E. Stickle
Editor

Contents

UNIT 1
Perspective on Adolescent Development

UNIT 2
Developmental Changes of Adolescents:
Physical, Cognitive, and Social

The concepts in bold italics are developed in the article. For further expansion, please refer to the Topic Guide.

UNIT 3
Relationships of Adolescents: Family, Peers, Intimacy, and Sexuality

The concepts in bold italics are developed in the article. For further expansion, please refer to the Topic Guide.

UNIT 4
The Contexts of Adolescents in Society: School, Work, and Diversity

The concepts in bold italics are developed in the article. For further expansion, please refer to the Topic Guide.

UNIT 5
Problem Behaviors and Challenges of Adolescents

The concepts in bold italics are developed in the article. For further expansion, please refer to the Topic Guide.

The concepts in bold italics are developed in the article. For further expansion, please refer to the Topic Guide.

Correlation Guide

The *Annual Editions* series provides students with convenient, inexpensive access to current, carefully selected articles from the public press. **Annual Editions: Adolescent Psychology, 7/e** is an easy-to-use reader that presents articles on important topics such as *development, mental health, socialization,* and many more. For more information on *Annual Editions* and other *McGraw-Hill Contemporary Learning Series* titles, visit www.mhhe.com/cls.

This convenient guide matches the units in **Annual Editions: Adolescent Psychology, 7/e** with the corresponding chapters in one of our best-selling McGraw-Hill Psychology textbooks by Santrock.

Annual Editions: Adolescent Psychology, 7/e	Adolescence, 13/e by Santrock
Unit 1: Perspective on Adolescent Development	**Chapter 1:** Introduction **Chapter 7:** Moral Development, Values, and Religion
Unit 2: Developmental Changes of Adolescents: Physical, Cognitive, and Social	**Chapter 2:** Puberty, Health, and Biological Foundations **Chapter 3:** The Brain and Cognitive Development **Chapter 4:** The Self, Identity, Emotion, and Personality **Chapter 5:** Gender
Unit 3: Relationships of Adolescents: Family, Peers, Intimacy, and Sexuality	**Chapter 6:** Sexuality **Chapter 8:** Families **Chapter 9:** Peers, Romantic Relationships, and Life Styles
Unit 4: The Contexts of Adolescents in Society: School, Work, and Diversity	**Chapter 7:** Moral Development, Values, and Religion **Chapter 10:** Schools **Chapter 11:** Achievement, Work, and Careers **Chapter 12:** Culture
Unit 5: Problem Behaviors and Challenges of Adolescents	**Chapter 13:** Problems in Adolescence and Emerging Adulthood

Topic Guide

This topic guide suggests how the selections in this book relate to the subjects covered in your course. You may want to use the topics listed on these pages to search the web more easily.

On the following pages a number of websites have been gathered specifically for this book. They are arranged to reflect the units of this Annual Editions reader. You can link to these sites by going to *http://www.mhcls.com.*

All the articles that relate to each topic are listed below the bold-faced term.

Internet References

The following Internet sites have been selected to support the articles found in this reader. These sites were available at the time of publication. However, because websites often change their structure and content, the information listed may no longer be available. We invite you to visit http://www.mhcls.com for easy access to these sites.

Annual Editions: Adolescent Psychology

General Sources

ADOL: Adolescence Directory Online
http://site.educ.indiana.edu/aboutus/AdolescenceDirectoryonLine
ADOL/tabid/4785/Default.aspx

This site is intended to be a clearinghouse of links to websites related to adolescent issues. Topics range from mental health issues to conflict and violence.

Questions and Answers about Child and Adolescent Psychiatry
http://www.aacap.org/cs/root/about_us/about_us

The American Academy of Child & Adolescent Psychiatry attempts to answer questions related to feelings and behaviors that cause disruption in the lives of children and young adults and the people around them.

Search Institute
http://www.search-institute.org

The Search Institute has the mission of providing leadership, knowledge, and resources to promote healthy children, youth, and communities. They are the creators of the "40 Developmental Assets."

UNIT 1: Perspective on Adolescent Development

American Youth Policy Forum
www.aypf.org

The goal of the American Youth Policy Forum is to provide learning opportunities to policymakers, practitioners, and researchers on youth issues. The Forum has three overlapping themes: education; youth development and community involvement; and preparation for careers.

Facts for Families
http://www.aacap.org/page.ww?section=Facts+for+Families&name=Facts+for+Families

The American Academy of Child and Adolescent Psychiatry provides concise, up-to-date information on issues that affect teenagers and their families. Fifty-six fact sheets include teenagers' issues, such as coping with life, sad feelings, inability to sleep, or not getting along with family and friends.

National Youth Development Information Center
www.nydic.org

The mission of the National Youth Development Information Center is to provide "practice-related information about youth development to national and local youth-serving organizations." This website provides a variety of resources including information about the basics of Positive Youth Development, links to reports by other organizations, funding information, and other resources.

UNIT 2: Developmental Changes of Adolescents: Physical, Cognitive, and Social

ADOL: Adolescence Directory On-Line
http://site.educ.indiana.edu/aboutus/AdolescenceDirectoryonLine
ADOL/tabid/4785/Default.aspx

This is an electronic guide to information on adolescent issues. Some of the issues concern conflict and violence, peer meditation, mental health problems, and health issues.

At-Risk Children and Youth
http://www.ncrel.org/sdrs/areas/at0cont.htm

North Central Regional Educational Laboratory (NCREL) offers this list of resources. Critical issues include rethinking learning for students at risk, linking at-risk students to integrated services, providing effective schooling for students at risk, and using technology to enhance engaged learning.

Educational Forum on Adolescent Health: Youth Bullying
http://www.ama-assn.org/ama1/pub/upload/mm/39/youthbullying.pdf

This is a comprehensive resource providing definitions, prevalence, conditions surrounding bullying, characteristics of bullies and victims, the effects of bullying on the victim, and prevention and intervention strategies.

Teens Health
http://www.teenshealth.org

This website provides portals for parents, kids, and teens. Information on this site ranges from the mind and body, to safety and life after high school.

Teens in Distress Series: Adolescent Stress and Depression
http://www.extension.umn.edu/distribution/youthdevelopment/DA3083.html

Included in this website is a discussion about troubled and high-risk youth in relation to stress.

UNIT 3: Relationships of Adolescents: Family, Peers, Intimacy, and Sexuality

American Sexual Behavior
http://www.norc.uchicago.edu/online/sex.pdf

This article, "American Sexual Behavior," discusses trends, sociodemographics, and risky behavior.

CDC National AIDS Clearinghouse
http://www.cdcnpin.org/

This complete source on AIDS includes "Respect Yourself, Protect Yourself," a public service announcement that targets youth.

CYFERNET: Cooperative Extension System's Children, Youth, and Family Information Service
http://www.cyfernet.org/

CYFERNET provides hundreds of complete online publications featuring practical, research-based information in six major areas.

Internet References

Family Violence Prevention Fund
www.endabuse.org

This website is the source of a number of innovative projects to end violence. Coaching Boys into Men (www.endabuse.org/cbim) is a national campaign to prevent violence by teaching young men to respect women. Building Partnerships Initiative to End Men's Violence (www.endabuse.org/bpi) is a national collaborative to inspire men to take a stand against violence perpetrated by men, and to play an active role in promoting healthy, vibrant relationships.

Girls Inc.
http://www.girlsinc.org

The Girls Inc. website provides information for both teen girls and adults. Fact sheets on this site include information on sexuality, sexual health, HIV, STDs, AIDS, and sexual harassment.

Help for Parents of Teenagers
http://www.bygpub.com/parents/

In addition to discussing the book, *The Teenager's Guide to the Real World,* and how it can help parents, this site lists other book sources and websites for parents and teens.

National Council of Juvenile and Family Court Judges
http://www.ncifci.org

The Family Violence Department of the National Council of Juvenile and Family Court Judges provides a number of their publications online.

Stepfamily Association of America
http://www.stepfam.org

The problems that surround step-parenting and stepchildren are discussed at this site. Just click on Facts and Figures and then on FAQs to reach many aspects of adolescent adjustments based on the type of family in which they live.

Welcome to about Health
http://www.abouthealth.com/

This health site includes information about sexuality, HIV, AIDS, peer pressure, and other information to help adolescents. Sites include In Our Own Words: Teens & AIDS, Risky Times, and links to other sites.

UNIT 4: The Contexts of Adolescents in Society: School, Work, and Diversity

Afterschool Alliance
http://www.afterschoolalliance.org

The Afterschool Alliance is dedicated to raising awareness of the importance of after school programs.

National Institute on Out-Of-School Time
www.niost.org

The mission of the National Institute on Out-Of-School Time (NIOST) is to ensure that all youth and families have access to high quality programs, activities, and opportunities during non-school hours.

Public Education Network
www.publiceducation.org

The mission of the Public Education Network is to "build public demand and mobilize resources for quality public education for children through a national constituency of local education funds and individuals."

Public/Private Ventures
www.ppv.org

Public/Private Ventures is a nonprofit research organization committed to improving the effectiveness of social policies, programs, and community initiatives, especially those that affect youth and young adults. Their research areas include after-school programs, mentoring, high-risk youth, and education.

School Stress
http://www.kqed.org/w/ymc/stress/index.html

Created by youth attending high school, this site is written primarily to help other teens deal with school stress.

What Kids Can Do
www.whatkidscando.org

A national nonprofit organization, What Kids Can Do works to document the value of young people working with adults on projects that combine learning with public purpose.

UNIT 5: Problem Behaviors and Challenges of Adolescents

Anorexia Nervosa and Related Eating Disorders (ANRED)
http://www.anred.com

ANRED is a non-profit organization that provides information about anorexia, bulimia, and other lesser-known eating disorders and athletes, pregnancy, diabetes, and other issues.

Center for Change
http://www.centerforchange.com

Their website includes a number of free resources, mostly in the form of articles written by center staff.

Focus Adolescent Services: Alcohol and Teen Drinking
http://www.focusas.com/Alcohol.html

Focus Adolescent Services is an Internet clearinghouse of information and resources to help and support families with troubled and at-risk teens.

Higher Education Center for Alcohol and Other Drug Prevention
http://www.edc.org/hec/

This U.S. Department of Education site has interactive discussion forums and a Just for Students section.

Justice Information Center (NCJRS): Drug Policy Information
http://www.ncjrs.org/drgswww.html

National and international world wide websites on drug policy information are provided on this NCJRS site.

MentalHelp.Net
http://eatingdisorders.mentalhelp.net/

This is a very complete list of Web References on eating disorders, including anorexia, bulimia, and obesity.

National Center on Addiction and Substance Abuse at Columbia University
http://www.casacolumbia.org

The mission of the National Center on Addiction and Substance Abuse (CASA) is to "inform Americans about the economic and social costs of substance abuse."

Internet References

National Center for Missing and Exploited Children

www.ncmec.org

This website offers a number of important resources on the topic of sexual exploitation of children, including information about child pornography, sex tourism of children, and online enticement of children for sexual acts.

National Clearinghouse for Alcohol and Drug Information

http://www.health.org/

This is an excellent general site for information on drug and alcohol facts that relates to adolescence and the issues of peer pressure and youth culture.

National Institute of Mental Health

http://www.nimh.nih.gov/

This site is a gateway to resources provided by the National Institute of Mental Health.

National Sexual Violence Resource Center

www.nsvrc.org

The National Sexual Violence Resource Center collects and disseminates a wide range of resources on sexual violence, including statistics, research, and training curricula, as well as a searchable database of organizations.

National Youth Violence Prevention Resource Center

http://www.safeyouth.org

The National Youth Violence Prevention Resource Center is sponsored by the Centers for Disease Control and Prevention and the Federal Working Group on Youth Violence.

RAINN

www.rainn.org

RAINN (standing for Rape, Abuse & Incest National Network) provides a comprehensive website which provides crisis information, information about different types of sexual violence, common reactions following sexual violence, and how to assist a friend who has been sexually assaulted.

Suicide Awareness: Voices of Education

http://www.save.org/

This is one of the Internet's most popular sites that address the issue of suicide. It provides detailed information on suicide along with material from the organization's many education sessions.

Youth Suicide League

http://www.unicef.org/pon96/insuicid.htm

This UNESCO website provides international suicide rates of young adults in selected countries.

UNIT 1

Perspective on Adolescent Development

Unit Selections

1. **Trashing Teens,** Hura Estroff Marons
2. **Profile in Caring,** Kirsten Wier
3. **A Peaceful Adolescence,** Barbara Kantrowitz and Karen Springen
4. **Something to Talk About,** Ashley Jones
5. **Youth Participation: From Myths to Effective Practice,** Jennifer L. O'Donoghue, Ben Kirshner, and Milbrey McLaughlin

Key Points to Consider

- From where do most of teens' problems stem?

- What are the reasons teens give for becoming involved in volunteerism?

- What practices unite parents and teens?

- What helps teens today to become connected?

- What does youth participation mean today?

Student Website
www.mhcls.com

Internet References

American Youth Policy Forum
   www.aypf.org.
Facts for Families
   http://www.aacap.org/page.ww?section=Facts+for+Families&name=Facts+for+Families
National Youth Development Information Center
   www.nydic.org

Exactly what characterizes adolescence is not clearly established. G. Stanley Hall, who is credited with founding the scientific study of adolescence in the early part of the 1900s, saw adolescence as corresponding roughly with the teen years. He believed individuals of this age had great potential but also experienced extreme mood swings. He labeled adolescence as a period of "storm and stress." Because of their labile emotions, Hall believed that adolescents were typically maladjusted. But what did he believe was the cause of this storm and stress? He essentially believed the cause was biological. Hall's views had a profound effect on the subsequent study of adolescence. Biological factors that underlie adolescence and direct the transition from childhood to adulthood have been repeatedly studied and refined.

Historically, other researchers hold very different views on the causes and characteristics of adolescence. For example, Erik Erikson (1902–1994), a psychologist interested in how people formed normal or abnormal personalities, believed that adolescence was a key period in development. He theorized that during adolescence individuals develop their identity. Just as Hall did, Erikson believed that there was some biological basis underlying development. Unlike Hall, however, Erikson emphasized the role society plays in the formation of the individual. Erikson proposed that adolescents must confront a number of conflicts (for example, understanding gender roles and understanding oneself as male or female) in order to develop an identity. The form of these conflicts and the problems the adolescent faced coping with them were influenced by the individual's culture. If adolescents were successful in meeting the conflicts, they would develop a healthy identity; if unsuccessful, they would suffer role diffusion or a negative identity. Similar to Hall, Erikson saw adolescence as a period where the individual's sense of self is disrupted, so it was typical for adolescents to be disturbed. Today, Erikson's ideas on identity formation are still influential. The stereotype that all adolescents suffer because of psychological problems has been called into question.

Margaret Mead, an anthropologist who started studying adolescents in the 1920s, presented a perspective on adolescence that differs from both Hall's and Erikson's. She concluded that culture, rather than biology, was the underlying cause of the transitional stage between childhood and adulthood. In cultures that held the same expectations for children as for adults, the transition from childhood to adulthood was smooth; there was no need for a clearly demarcated period where one was neither child nor adult. In addition, adolescence did not have to be a period of storm and stress or of psychological problems. Although some of Mead's work has since been criticized, many of her ideas remain influential. Today's psychologists concur with Mead that adolescence need not be a time of psychological maladjustment. Modern anthropologists agree that biology alone does not define adolescence. Rather, the socio-cultural environment in which an individual is raised affects how adolescence is manifested and characterized.

A cogent question is, what social and cultural factors lead to the development of adolescence in our society? Modern scholars believe that adolescence as we know it today did not even exist until the end of the 1800s. During the end of the nineteenth century and the beginning of the twentieth century, societal changes caused the stage of adolescence to be "invented." In this period, job opportunities for young people doing either farm labor or apprenticeships in

© Thinkstock/Jupiterimages

factories were decreasing. For middle-class children, the value of staying in school in order to get a good job was stressed. Since there were fewer job opportunities, young people were less likely to be financially independent and had to rely on their families. By the beginning of the twentieth century, legislation ensuring that adolescents could not assume adult status was passed, child labor laws restricted how much time young people could work and compulsory education laws required adolescents to stay in school. In the 1930s, for the first time in this country's history, the majority of high school age individuals were enrolled in school. The teenagers were physically mature people who were dependent on their parents—they were neither children nor adults.

The articles in this unit focus on the images of adolescence in our culture. The first article explains that teens are more competent than our society assumes. Many youth are volunteers as explained by Kirsten Weir. Springen presents evidence that adolescents and families can have a peaceful friendship. Many youth today are more connected than ever. The last article defines youth participation and provides a review of the major myths surrounding youth participation.

Trashing Teens

We are throwing away 20 million young people, psychologist Robert Epstein argues in a provocative new book, *The Case against Adolescence.* Teens are far more competent than we assume, and most of their problems stem from restrictions placed on them. Epstein spoke to Hura Estroff Marons about the legal and emotional constraints on american youth.

HURA ESTROFF MARONS

Why Do You Believe That Adolescence Is an Artificial Extension of Childhood?

In every mammalian species, immediately upon reaching puberty, animals function as adults, often having offspring. We call our offspring "children" well past puberty. The trend started a hundred years ago and now extends childhood well into the 20s. The age at which Americans reach adulthood is increasing—30 is the new 20—and most Americans now believe a person isn't an adult until age 26.

The whole culture collaborates in artificially extending childhood, primarily through the school system and restrictions on labor. The two systems evolved together in the late 19th-century; the advocates of compulsory-education laws also pushed for child-labor laws, restricting the ways young people could work, in part to protect them from the abuses of the new factories. The juvenile justice system came into being at the same time. All of these systems isolate teens from adults, often in problematic ways.

Our current education system was created in the late 1800s and early 1900s, and was modeled after the new factories of the industrial revolution. Public schools, set up to supply the factories with a skilled labor force, crammed education into a relatively small number of years. We have tried to pack more and more in while extending schooling up to age 24 or 25, for some segments of the population. In general, such an approach still reflects factory thinking—get your education now and get it efficiently, in classrooms in lockstep fashion. Unfortunately, most people learn in those classrooms to hate education for the rest of their lives.

The factory system doesn't work in the modern world, because two years after graduation, whatever you learned is out of date. We need education spread over a lifetime, not jammed into the early years—except for such basics as reading, writing, and perhaps citizenship. Past puberty, education needs to be combined in interesting and creative ways with work. The factory school system no longer makes sense.

The factory system of education, in place for more than a hundred years, doesn't work today; two years after graduation, information is out of date.

What Are Some Likely Consequences of Extending One's Childhood?

Imagine what it would feel like—or think back to what it felt like—when your body and mind are telling you you're an adult while the adults around you keep insisting you're a child. This infantilization makes many young people angry or depressed, with their distress carrying over into their families and contributing to our high divorce rate. It's hard to keep a marriage together when there is constant conflict with teens.

We have completely isolated young people from adults and created a peer culture. We stick them in school and keep them from working in any meaningful way, and if they do something wrong we put them in a pen with other "children." In most non-industrialized societies, young people are integrated into adult society as soon as they are capable, and there is no sign of teen turmoil. Many cultures do not even have a term for adolescence. But we not only created this stage of life: We declared it inevitable. In 1904, American psychologist G. Stanley Hall said it was programmed by evolution. He was wrong.

How Is Adolescent Behavior Shaped by Societal Strictures?

One effect is the creation of a new segment of society just waiting to consume, especially if given money to spend. There are now massive industries—music, clothing, makeup—that revolve around this artificial segment of society and keep it going, with teens spending upward of $200 billion a year almost entirely on trivia.

The Adolescent Squeeze

Before 1850, laws restricting the behavior of teens were few and far between. Compulsory education laws evolved in tandem with laws restricting labor by young people. Beginning in 1960, the number of laws infantilizing adolescents accelerated dramatically. You may have had a paper route when you were 12, but your children can't.

- **1600s** **1641** Massachusetts law prohibits people under 16 from "smiting" their parents

- **1800s**
  1836 Massachusetts passes first law requiring minimal schooling for people under 15 working in factories
  1848 Pennsylvania sets 12 as minimum work age for some jobs
  1852 Massachusetts passes first universal compulsory education law in U.S., requires three months of schooling for all young people ages 8–14
  1880s Some states pass laws restricting various behaviors by young people: smoking, singing on the streets, prostitution, "incorrigible" behavior
  1881 American Federation of Labor calls on states to ban people under 14 from working
  1898 World's first juvenile court established in Illinois—constitutional rights of minors effectively taken away

- **1900s**
  1903 Illinois requires school attendance and restricts youth labor
  1918 All states have compulsory education laws in place
  1933 First federal law restricting drinking by young people
  1936 & 1938 First successful federal laws restricting labor by young people, establishing 16 and 18 as minimum ages for work; still in effect
  1940 Most states have laws in place restricting driving by people under 16
  1968 Supreme Court upholds states' right to prohibit sale of obscene materials to minors
  1968 Movie rating system established to restrict young people from certain films
  1970s Supreme Court upholds laws restricting young women's right to abortion
  1970s Dramatic increase in involuntary electroshock therapy (ECT) of teens
  1980s Many cities and states pass laws restricting teens' access to arcades and other places of amusement; Supreme Court upholds such laws in 1989
  1980s Courts uphold states' right to prohibit sale of lottery tickets to minors
  1980 to 1998 Rate of involuntary commitment of minors to mental institutions increases 300–400 percent
  1984 First national law effectively raising drinking age to 21
  1988 Supreme Court denies freedom of press to school newspapers
  1989 Missouri court upholds schools' right to prohibit dancing
  1989 Court rules school in Florida can ban salacious works by Chaucer and Aristophanes
  1990s Curfew laws for young people sweep cities and states
  1990s Dramatic increase in use of security systems in schools
  1992 Federal law prohibits sale of tobacco products to minors
  1997 New federal law makes easier involuntary commitment of teens

- **2000+**
  2000+ New laws restricting minors' rights to get tattoos, piercings, and to enter tanning salons spread through U.S.
  2000+ Tougher driving laws sweeping through states: full driving rights obtained gradually over a period of years
  2000+ Dramatic increase in zero-tolerance laws in schools, resulting in suspensions or dismissals for throwing spitballs, making gun gestures with hand, etc.
  2000+ New procedures and laws making it easier to prosecute minors as adults
  CURRENTLY SPREADING NATIONWIDE:
  - New rules prohibiting cell phones in schools or use of cell phones by minors while driving
  - Libraries and schools block access to Internet material by minors
  - New dress code rules in schools
  - New rules restricting wearing of potentially offensive clothing or accessories in schools
  - New laws prohibiting teens from attending parties where alcohol is served (even if they're not drinking)
  - New laws restricting teens' access to shopping malls
  - Tracking devices routinely installed in cell phones and cars of teens
  - New availability of home drug tests for teens
  - New laws prohibiting minors from driving with any alcohol in bloodstream (zero-tolerance)
  - Proposals for longer school days, longer school year, and addition of grades 13 and 14 to school curriculum under discussion

Ironically, because minors have only limited property rights, they don't have complete control over what they have bought. Think how bizarre that is. If you, as an adult, spend money and bring home a toy, it's your toy and no one can take it away from you. But with a 14-year-old, it's not really his or her toy. Young people can't own things, can't sign contracts, and they can't do anything meaningful without parental permission—permission that can be withdrawn at any time. They can't marry, can't have sex, can't legally drink. The list goes on. They are restricted and infantilized to an extraordinary extent.

In recent surveys I've found that American teens are subjected to more than 10 times as many restrictions as mainstream adults, twice as many restrictions as active-duty U.S. Marines, and even twice as many as incarcerated felons. Psychologist Diane Dumas and I also found a correlation between infantilization and psychological dysfunction. The more young people are infantilized, the more psychopathology they show.

What's more, since 1960, restrictions on teens have been accelerating. Young people are restricted in ways no adult would be—for example, in some states they are prohibited from entering tanning salons or getting tattoos.

You Believe in the Inherent Competence of Teens. What's Your Evidence?

Dumas and I worked out what makes an adult an adult. We came up with 14 areas of competency—such as interpersonal skills, handling responsibility, leadership—and administered tests to adults and teens in several cities around the country. We found that teens were as competent or nearly as competent as adults in all 14 areas. But when adults estimate how teens *will* score, their estimates are dramatically below what the teens actually score.

Other long-standing data show that teens are at least as competent as adults. IQ is a quotient that indicates where you stand relative to other people your age; that stays stable. But raw scores of intelligence peak around age 14-15 and shrink thereafter. Scores on virtually all tests of memory peak between ages 13 and 15. Perceptual abilities all peak at that age. Brain size peaks at 14. Incidental memory—what you remember by accident, and not due to mnemonics—is remarkably good in early to mid teens and practically nonexistent by the 50s and 60s.

If Teens Are So Competent, Why Do They Not Show It?

What teens do is a small fraction of what they are capable of doing. If you mistreat or restrict them, performance suffers and is extremely misleading.

The teens put before us as examples by, say, the music industry tend to be highly incompetent. Teens encourage each other to perform incompetently. One of the anthems of modern pop, "Smells Like Teen Spirit" by Nirvana, is all about how we need to behave like we're stupid.

Teens in America are in touch with their peers on average 65 hours a week, compared to about four hours a week in preindustrial cultures. In this country, teens learn virtually everything they know from other teens, who are in turn highly influenced by certain aggressive industries. This makes no sense. Teens should be learning from the people they are about to become. When young people exit the education system and are dumped into the real world, which is not the world of Britney Spears, they have no idea what's going on and have to spend considerable time figuring it out.

There are at least 20 million young people between 17 and 20, and if they are as competent as I think they are, we are just throwing them away.

Do You Believe That Young People Are Capable of Maintaining Long-Term Relationships and Capable of Moral Reasoning?

Everyone who has looked at the issue has found that teens can experience the love that adults experience. The only difference is that they change partners more, because they are warehoused together, told it's puppy love and not real, and are unable to marry without permission. The assumption is they are not capable. But many distinguished couples today—Jimmy and Rosalynn Carter, George and Barbara Bush—married young and have very successful long-term relationships.

According to census data, the divorce rate of males marrying in their teens is lower than that of males marrying in their 20s. Overall the divorce rate of people marrying in their teens is a little higher. Does that mean we should prohibit them from marrying? That's absurd. We should aim to reverse that, telling young people the truth: that they are capable of creating long-term stable relationships. They might fail—but adults do every day, too.

The "friends with benefits" phenomenon is a by-product of isolating adolescents, warehousing them together, and delivering messages that they are incapable of long-term relationships. Obviously they have strong sexual urges and act on them in ways that are irresponsible. We can change that by letting them know they are capable of having more than a hookup.

Studies show that we reach the highest levels of moral reasoning while we're still in our teens. Those capabilities parallel higher-order cognitive reasoning abilities, which peak fairly early. Across the board, teens are far more capable than we think they are.

What's the Worst Part of the Current Way We Treat Teens?

The adversarial relationship between parents and offspring is terrible; it hurts both parents and young people. It tears some people to shreds; they don't understand why it is happening and can't get out of it. They don't realize they are caught in a machine that's driving them apart from their offspring—and it's unnecessary.

What Can Be Done?

I believe that young people should have more options—the option to work, marry, own property, sign contracts, start businesses, make decisions about health care and abortions, live on their own—every right, privilege, or responsibility an adult has. I advocate a competency-based system that focuses on the abilities of the individual. For some it will mean more time in school combined with work, for others it will mean that at age 13 or 15 they can set up an Internet business. Others will enter the workforce and become some sort of apprentice. The exploitative factories are long gone; competent young people deserve the chance to compete where it counts, and many will surprise us.

It's a simple matter to develop competency tests to determine what rights a young person should be given, just as we now have competency tests for driving. When you offer significant rights for passing such a test, it's highly motivating; people who can't pass a high-school history test will never give up trying to pass the written test at the DMV, and they'll virtually always succeed. We need to offer a variety of tests, including a comprehensive test to allow someone to become emancipated without the need for court action. When we dangle significant rewards in front of our young people—including the right to be treated like an adult—many will set aside the trivia of teen culture and work hard to join the adult world.

Are You Saying That Teens Should Have More Freedom?

No, they already have too much freedom—they are free to spend, to be disrespectful, to stay out all night, to have sex and take drugs. But they're not free to join the adult world, and that's what needs to change.

Unfortunately, the current systems are so entrenched that parents can do little to counter infantilization. No one parent can confer property rights, even though they would be highly motivating. Too often, giving children more responsibility translates into giving them household chores, which just causes more tension and conflict. We have to think beyond chores to meaningful responsibility—responsibility tied to significant rights.

> **Too often, giving young people more responsibility translates into giving them more household chores, which only creates more conflict with adults.**

With a competency-based system in place, our focus will start to change. We'll become more conscious of the remarkable things teens can do rather than on culture-driven misbehavior. With luck, we might even be able to abolish adolescence.

Profile in Caring

Kirsten Weir

B etween school, sports, clubs and friends, today's teens have plenty to keep them busy. But that doesn't stop many young people from adding a volunteer job to their to-do lists.

There are lots of reasons to volunteer. Young people involved in community service are more likely to get good grades, graduate from high school, and go to college, says Steve Culbertson, president of Youth Service America (YSA). They're less likely to use drugs or turn to violence. Volunteering also leads to better physical and mental health, according to a recent study by the Corporation for National and Community Service.

An online study by the companies Cone Inc. and AMP Insights found that 61 percent of 13- to 25-year-olds feel personally responsible for making a difference in the world. Eighty-one percent of them volunteered within the past year.

"In the last two decades," Culbertson told Current Health, "the number of teenagers volunteering has doubled in the United States. Kids [today] are exposed much more to the problems of the world and [are] more likely to help." Read on for stories of four teens who make community service a part of their routines. As they have learned, volunteering is fun and loaded with benefits—both for volunteers and their communities.

Community Building

Last summer, 16-year-old Arizona native Leena Patel traveled to North Carolina for a 13-day volunteer mission. As part of a team of 14 teens, Leena helped build homes through Habitat for Humanity, an organization that serves families who need safe, affordable housing.

Working eight hours every day, Leena's team built homes for four families. "I had never done construction before," Leena says. She quickly learned to install doors and windows, attach baseboards, and put up vinyl siding. After all her hard work, the biggest reward was meeting the families that would live in the homes. "They were so genuine and so thankful," she says. "I didn't expect them to be just like me."

Leena is no stranger to volunteer work. At home, she volunteers for the American Cancer Society's Relay for Life, as well as several local community organizations. "I think volunteering really builds your character," she says. "It's a good way to learn about the world and the people in it, and it makes you grateful for what you have."

"A lot of people don't see the importance of volunteering," Leena adds. "I'm busy, but I'm trying to make it a part of my life."

Birds on the Brain

Kaleigh Gerlich has a cool volunteer job—literally. She's a penguin keeper's assistant at the Denver Zoo. The 18-year-old has volunteered at the zoo for more than two years. "People always think it's crazy; they say the penguins smell like fish," she says. "But they're just so much fun. They have the greatest personalities!"

Gerlich works at the zoo every Sunday during the school year. She cleans the penguin enclosures and prepares food for penguins and other birds. In the summer, Gerlich spends even more time at the zoo: Last summer, she logged 150 volunteer hours. As a teen leader, Gerlich helped coordinate other teen volunteers and pitched in with office work.

Gerlich hopes to study aerospace engineering and become an astronaut someday. However, she plans to keep working at the zoo as long as she can. "If I stay in Colorado for college, I hope to intern at the zoo," Gerlich says. "It's so much fun and so different from everything else I do."

She explains that community service has also helped her relate better to other people—especially adults. "Sometimes as a teen, I feel there's a generation gap of values and beliefs," Gerlich says. "Volunteering is like a bridge—it really unites people and helps you relate to one another because you're interested in the same things."

Hospital Helper

Paige Golinske, 16, is a people person. For the past three years, she has worked with many people at Crittenton Hospital, in Rochester, Mich. As a member of the Crittenteen program, Paige has helped out all over the hospital. She has done everything from changing bed linens to working in the medical records department. Now Paige works at the front desk—a job she loves because she gets to interact with visitors and patients. "I answer the phone, help people find the room of the person they're visiting, and I also deliver flowers," she says.

Paige's interest in community service goes way back. In elementary school, she volunteered with a school program called Can-Do Kids. The group cleaned up parks and put together care packages to send to schools in developing countries. In middle school, she worked as a peer mentor. Paige says her mom's commitment to community service inspired her: "My interest in volunteering came from my mom's influence. And I've always wanted to help people."

Paige notes that people are often surprised when she tells them that she's not planning a career in medicine. Still, her job has helped her develop a variety of skills that she could put to use in almost any field. "A hospital is a great place to volunteer," she says. "There are a lot of different opportunities for lots of different types of people."

Paige plans to continue her community service as an adult, but for now, she's content working each week at the hospital. "I think volunteering is really important," she says. "If more teens volunteered, I think the world would be a better place."

Bake a Difference

Daniel Feldman, 16, of Linwood, N.J., has a big goal: ending child hunger in the United States. It's not far-fetched for someone who practically grew up volunteering. Since the age of 7, Daniel has helped out with Peer Partners, a youth volunteer organization his sister founded. He first became interested in child hunger when he saw an ad for the Great American Bake Sale, a project that invites people across the country to hold bake sales to raise money for Share Our Strength, an organization dedicated to fighting child hunger.

Daniel decided to take part in the challenge. He held a bake sale and raised more than $2,000. Along the way, he learned that 13 million American children are at risk of going hungry. "I always had enough food, and I didn't think that other kids in America could be hungry," he says. "I got hooked [on the cause] because people were suffering."

After his first bake sale success, Daniel started his own organization, Kids Feeding Kids. The group holds bake sales, plant sales, and other community fund-raisers to fight child hunger. In the past three years, Kids Feeding Kids has raised nearly $30,000. "Child hunger is hurting our future," Daniel says. "It just made sense to give back to the community."

He hopes to end up with a degree in law or engineering and credits his volunteer work with giving him building blocks for future success. Those experiences "have already allowed me to develop my leadership skills by improving my thinking, problem-solving, and reasoning abilities," Daniel explains. They also sparked his "passion to help others in need."

Daniel hopes that the success of his groups will inspire others. "Find a cause you think is worthy and go for it," he says. "The smallest things can make the biggest difference."

A Peaceful Adolescence

The teen years don't have to be a time of family storm and stress. Most kids do just fine and now psychologists are finding out why that is.

BARBARA KANTROWITZ AND KAREN SPRINGEN

At 17, Amanda Hund is a straight-A student who loves competing in horse shows. The high school junior from Willmar, Minn., belongs to her school's band, orchestra and choir. She regularly volunteers through her church and recently spent a week working in an orphanage in Jamaica. Usually, however, she's closer to home, where her family eats dinner together every night. She also has a weekly breakfast date with her father, a doctor, at a local coffee shop. Amanda credits her parents for her relatively easy ride through adolescence. "My parents didn't sweat the small stuff," she says. "They were always very open. You could ask any question."

Is the Hund family for real? Didn't they get the memo that says teens and their parents are supposed to be at odds until . . . well, until forever? Actually, they're very much for real, and according to scientists who study the transition to adulthood, they represent the average family's experience more accurately than all those scary TV movies about out-of-control teens. "Research shows that most young people go through adolescence having good relationships with their parents, adopting attitudes and values consistent with their parents' and end up getting out of the adolescent period and becoming good citizens," says Richard Lerner, Bergstrom chair of applied developmental science at Tufts University. This shouldn't be news—but it is, largely because of widespread misunderstanding of what happens during the teen years. It's a time of transition, just like the first year of parenthood or menopause. And although there are dramatic hormonal and physical changes during this period, catastrophe is certainly not preordained. A lot depends on youngsters' innate natures combined with the emotional and social support they get from the adults around them. In other words, parents do matter.

The roots of misconceptions about teenagers go back to the way psychologists framed the field of adolescent development a century ago. They were primarily looking for explanations of why things went wrong. Before long, the idea that this phase was a period of storm and stress made its way into the popular consciousness. But in the last 15 years, developmental scientists have begun to re-examine these assumptions. Instead of focusing on kids who battle their way through the teen years, they're studying the dynamics of success.

At the head of the pack are Lerner and his colleagues, who are in the midst of a major project that many other researchers are following closely. It's a six-year longitudinal study of exactly what it takes to turn out OK and what adults can do to nurture those behaviors. "Parents and sometimes kids themselves often talk about positive development as the absence of bad," says Lerner. "What we're trying to do is present a different vision and a different vocabulary for young people and parents."

The first conclusions from the 4-H Study of Positive Youth Development, published in the February issue of The Journal of Early Adolescence, show that there are quantifiable personality traits possessed by all adolescents who manage to get to adulthood without major problems. Psychologists have labeled these traits "the 5 Cs": competence, confidence, connection, character and caring. These characteristics theoretically lead to a sixth C, contribution (similar to civic engagement). The nomenclature grows out of observations in recent years by a number of clinicians, Lerner says, but his study is the first time researchers have measured how these characteristics influence successful growth.

The 5 Cs are interconnected, not isolated traits, Lerner says. For example, competence refers not just to academic ability but also to social and vocational skills. Confidence includes self-esteem as well as the belief that you can make a difference in the world. The value of the study, Lerner says, is that when it is completed next year, researchers will have a way to quantify these characteristics and eventually determine what specific social and educational programs foster them.

During these years, parents should stay involved as they help kids move on.

In the meantime, parents can learn a lot from this rethinking of the teen years. Don't automatically assume that your kids become alien beings when they leave middle school. They still care what their parents think and they still need love and guidance—although in a different form. Temple University psychology professor Laurence Steinberg, author of "The Ten Basic Principles of Good Parenting," compares raising kids to building a boat that you eventually launch. Parents have to build a strong underpinning so their kids are equipped to face whatever's ahead. In the teen years, that means staying involved as you slowly let go. "One of the things that's natural in adolescence is that kids are going to pull away from their parents as they become increasingly interested in peers," says Steinberg. "It's important for parents to hang in there, for them not to pull back in response to that."

Communication is critical. "Stay in touch with your kids and make sure they feel valued and appreciated," advises Suniya Luthar, professor of clinical and developmental psychology at Columbia University. Even if they roll their eyes when you try to hug them, they still need direct displays of affection, she says. They also need help figuring out goals and limits. Parents should monitor their kids' activities and get to know their friends. Luthar says parents should still be disciplinarians and set standards such as curfews. Then teens need to know that infractions will be met with consistent consequences.

Adolescents are often critical of their parents but they're also watching them closely for clues on how to function in the outside world. Daniel Perkins, associate professor of family and youth resiliency at Penn State, says he and his wife take their twins to the local Ronald McDonald House and serve dinner to say thank you for time the family spent there when the children had health problems after birth. "What we've done already is set up the notion that we were blessed and need to give back, even if it's in a small way." That kind of example sets a standard youngsters remember, even if it seems like they're not paying attention.

Parents should provide opportunities for kids to explore the world and even find a calling. Teens who have a passion for something are more likely to thrive. "They have a sense of purpose beyond day-to-day teenage life," says David Marcus, author of "What It Takes to Pull Me Through." Often, he says, kids who were enthusiastic about something in middle school lose enthusiasm in high school because the competition gets tougher and they're not as confident. Parents need to step in and help young people find other outlets. The best way to do that is to regularly spend uninterrupted time with teens (no cell phones). Kids also need to feel connected to other adults they trust and to their communities. Teens who get into trouble are "drifting," he says. "They don't have a web of people watching out for them."

Teens should build support webs of friends and adults.

At some point during these years, teen-agers should also be learning to build their own support networks—a skill that will be even more important when they're on their own. Connie Flanagan, a professor of youth civic development at Penn State, examines how kids look out for one another. "What we're interested in is how they help one another avoid harm," she says. In one of her focus groups, some teenage girls mentioned that they decided none would drink from an open can at a party because they wouldn't know for sure what they were drinking. "Even though you are experimenting, you're essentially doing it in a way that you protect one another," Flanagan says. Kids who don't make those kinds of connections are more likely to get in trouble because there's no one their own age or older to stop them from going too far. Like any other stage of life, adolescence can be tough. But teens and families can get through it—as long as they stick together.

With Julie Scelfo

Something to Talk About

Humans, by nature, are social beings. Teenagers, by nature, are social machines.

ASHLEY JONES

The advent of online social networking giants Facebook and MySpace—among others—has reshaped the face of a mainstay within teenage culture: socializing. A new study released by the Pew Internet & American Life Project, "Teens and Social Media," shows that teens today are more connected than ever, and with the help of the web, they will become even more intertwined.

During my teenage years, my friends and I communicated with one another the old-fashioned ways: face-to-face and via a landline phone. Content creation and sharing came in the form of writing and passing notes to each other in class. It wasn't even that common for teens to own a personal cell phone—and this was the mid-to-late '90s.

Nowadays, teenagers are creating and sharing content and posting comments online at incredibly high rates. This study, the most recent in a string of teen-focused reports conducted by Pew, focuses on the difference in teens' online participation compared to that of adults. Mary Madden, a senior research specialist at Pew and one of the writers of this report, says, "We decided to focus on social media in this survey because we saw a really big difference in teens' online participation compared to adults."

That discrepancy is obvious when you look at the numbers. As the 90:9:1 adage goes, a whopping 90% of online adults are merely lurkers, and only 10% actually contribute to the Web 2.0 movement. In contrast, according to the report's findings, 64% of online teens have participated in a content-creating activity on the Internet, up from 57% of online teens in 2004.

Most of the content creation among teens today occurs on social networking websites like the aforementioned Facebook or MySpace. In fact, according to the study, 55% of online teens ages 12–17 have a profile on a social networking site. Madden says, "This survey discusses the conversational portion of social media. We found that teens want feedback, and they can get that feedback on social networking sites."

When it comes to social networking sites, feedback comes in many forms. Wall posts, photo albums, comments, blogging, and video posts are among the most popular, and the report from Pew finds that not only are teens in general using social networking sites to interact, but the type of online interaction varies depending on gender.

The study indicates that teenage girls as a whole are more likely to be content creators than are teenage boys (55 % and 45%, respectively). In this case, Pew defines content creators as "online teens who have created or worked on a blog or webpage, shared original creative content, or remixed content they found online into a new creation." The differences continue as methods of content creation are broken down.

For instance, teenage girls are blogging. The study states that 35% of all online teen girls blog, compared to only 20% of teen boys, and that "virtually all of the growth in teen blogging between 2004 and 2006 is due to the increased activity of girls." Furthermore, older teen girls are more likely to blog than older teen boys (38% versus 18%), but younger teen girls are now outpacing older teen boys in the blogosphere: 32% of girls ages 12–14 blog compared to 18% of boys ages 15–17. Madden says, "Girls have always demonstrated a more aggressive adoption of online messaging in general. Prior to Web 2.0, it was instant messaging, and now it is seen in the forms of writing on friends' walls and blogging. It seems that girls are more focused on verbal expression."

In contrast, teenage boys are posting video files more readily than girls. While the study states that 57% of all online teens watch videos online, teenage boys are twice as likely as girls to post video files (19% versus 10%). "There is a fascination with visual media, especially among boys, today," says Madden.

It also appears that all online teenagers have a comment about something: 89% of teens who post photos online say that people comment at least "sometimes" about the photos they post, and 37% of those teenagers say that their audience comments on their photos "most of the time." Further, 72% of teen video posters report receiving comments "sometimes," and 24% say that people comment "most of the time."

What all of these numbers seem to suggest is that teenagers today are super-connected communicators. A huge aspect of adolescence is socialization, the need to feel like a part of a larger group, and social networking sites make achieving that sense of belonging easier. "I think teens are more open to exploring and trying out these new tools," posits Madden. "They just want to feel connected, maintain ties, and receive feedback from friends."

From *EContent*, March 2008, pp. 10–11. Copyright © 2008 by Information Today, Inc. Reprinted by permission.

Youth Participation
From Myths to Effective Practice

Jennifer L. O'Donoghue, MPA, Ben Kirshner, PhD, and Milbrey McLaughlin, PhD

Five youth from the San Francisco Bay Area recently joined 25 other young people and over 100 adults at an international conference on the United Nations Convention on the Rights of the Child. "It was the most un-youth-friendly place," explained one young woman. "Every day we woke up early and spent hours listening to adults lecture about the experiences of youth. There was no time for us to talk to anyone, no time to move around, and when we tried to tell them about our feelings, they didn't really listen. Nothing really changed—until the last day when we finally got to do our presentation. One of the adults tried to come up and facilitate our question-and-answer period, and we just said, 'No, thank you. We're prepared to do this for ourselves. Sit down please.' I don't think the adults really got it until then."[1]

The concept of youth participation, whether under the name of youth voice, decision making, empowerment, engagement, or participation, has become a hot topic. The United Nations Convention on the Rights of the Child (CRC), the most widely ratified treaty in history, made participation a fundamental right of all young people. Advocates and researchers of youth development point to the developmental benefits of youth involvement in decision making and public engagement. (see for example Hart, 1992; Hart, Daitue, & Iltus,1997; Fittman, Ferber, & Irby, 2000). Youth participation has been linked to greater organizational sustainability and effectiveness (Zeldin, McDaniel, Topitzes, & Calvert, 2000; Rajani, 2000) and, on a macrolevel, national democratic, social, and economic development (Rajani, 2000). Not surprisingly, then, the idea of youth participation has garnered broad support across a range of disciplines and practices. However, the frustrations experienced by the young people cited at the start of this article point to a central issue within this growing field: even adults and youth with the best intentions struggle with just what youth participation means. What does it look like? How does it happen?

Participation is a broad term, encompassing several dimensions. The CRC defines youth participation as freedom of expression on issues affecting young people (Hart, 1992). Participation can also be organized around three general themes: access to social, political, and economic spheres; decision making within organizations that influence one's life; and planning and involvement in public action (Tolman & Pittman, 2001). For the purposes of this article, we understand youth participation as a constellation of activities that empower adolescents to take part in and influence decision making that affects their lives and to take action on issues they care about.

This article provides a sketch of the state of the field of youth participation, reviewing what is known about what participation looks like, how it functions, and where it takes place (for a more complete review see Hart, 1992; Rajani, 2000; Irby, Ferber, & Pittman, 2001). As this is a developing field, a lack of empirical evidence and understanding can potentially fuel myths around youth participation. We address four of these myths here.

Youth Participation in Research and Practice

Youth development researchers have noted a shift in youth work in the past two decades from prevention (programs designed to treat and prevent the problems of "at-risk" youth) to preparation (building skills and supporting broader development for all youth) to participation and power sharing (actively engaging young people as partners in organizational and public decision making) (Pittman et al., 2000). These shifts represent a broadening of focus from looking solely at individual-level outcomes to also examining the impact of youth participation at organizational and community level.

The CRC defines youth participation as freedom of expression on issues affecting young people.

With this expanding focus, efforts to take youth participation seriously have extended beyond traditional youth development activities to embrace youth involvement in other areas. For example, researchers, policy-makers, and program evaluators are beginning to involve young people as research partners, working to understand better the lives of youth and the institutions that influence them (see also Kirshner, O'Donoghue, & McLaughlin, 2005). Internationally, young people have been central to grassroots social, environmental, and economic change movements (e.g. Brandao, 1998; Espinosa & Schwab, 1997; Hart & Schwab, 1997), a pattern that is beginning to show up in the United States as well. Moreover, many nonprofit and youth organizations have come to embrace the notion that youth voices should be part of organizational decision making (Zeldin et al., 2000), and young people have begun to be engaged in school reform efforts (Mitra, 2006; Fielding, 2001).

Most observers agree, however, that the corresponding research on youth participation—its prerequisites, organizational features, current scope, and impacts—remains in the early stages. In part, this reflects a lack of consensus on conceptual frameworks and definitions ("What Evidence," 2001), especially ones that take into account the influence of local contexts. Effective approaches to youth participation in Brazil, for example, have been shown to be less successful when implemented in the United States because of differing policy and organizational contexts (Brandao, 1998). Broad and meaningful participation seems to require a larger policy context in which the voices of youth are listened to and taken seriously, and we still have much to learn about the multiple ways in which context influences local efforts.

Similarly, little consensus exists on where youth participation most appropriately or effectively occurs. The majority of work around youth engagement has tended to focus on the experiences of young people in community-based or nongovernmental organizations (Hart, 1992; Hart et al., 1997; Ferber & Pittman, 1999; Pittman et al., 2000; Tolman & Pittman, 2001). These organizations often do not face the same sets of constraints as public institutions, and as a result, they may offer young people the type of alternative spaces that they need to reflect critically and build capacity for action. Youth organizing efforts are also typically based in community, whether in formal organizations or less-formal grassroots movements, and often work outside the system or act in opposition to public institutions. While acknowledging the strength and importance of such efforts, researchers and practitioners have begun to point to the need to bring youth participation to public institutions as well, working to create change from within. Many consider youth participation in schools, for example, critical to creating sustainable and significant change (Hart & Schwab, 1997; Rajani, 2000). Greater youth participation in public institutions can lead to substantive improvements in government effectiveness ("Youth Evaluating Programs," 2002).

Outcomes for Youth, Organizations, and Communities

Research on outcomes for youth and organizations has provided broad evidence of the benefits of youth participation. Some promising evidence about youth outcomes stems from research on student motivation in classrooms, in which participation in decision making has been correlated with greater effort, intrinsic interest, and more effective learning strategies (Ames, 1992; Eccles Wigfield, & Schiefele, 1998). Youth development practitioners also have found that participation

is an effective strategy for engaging youth, especially older high school students, who typically avoid youth organizations that do not give them a voice in decision making or planning (Ashley, Samaniego, & Chuen, 1997; McLaughlin, 2000). Such engagement has been found to have an impact on the host organizations, which report that youth participation in decision making leads to changes in the organizational climate and a deeper commitment by adults to youth development principles (Zeldin et al., 2000). Finally, meaningful participation is said to foster democratic habits in youth, such as tolerance, healthy disagreement, self-expression, and cooperation (Hart, 1992). Recent work studying community impact, although challenging to measure, has begun to document the ways in which youth participation has led to meaningful community change as well (Tolman & Pitman, 2001).

Myths of Youth Participation

Although youth participation is an international phenomenon, it is also closely linked to local context. As such, we focus our lens here on the current policy climate in the United States, which is often divided between defenders of more adult-controlled policies and practices for youth, on one hand, and adherents of youth participation, on the other. The first group tends to see youth as problems to be fixed or dependents to be taken care of. In the United States, these youth participation naysayers play a powerful role in shaping discussions of youth policy that often reinforce perceptions of young people as dangerous and disengaged. Studies showing the intractability of these negative constructions of youth in the minds of adults demonstrate the challenge of creating a broad movement of youth participation in the United States (Bales, 2000).

Participation in decision making has been correlated with greater effort, intrinsic interest, and more effective learning strategies.

In contrast, there are many who have wholeheartedly embraced the notion of youth participation, sometimes promoting an overly romantic notion of youth involvement. We refer to this often sentimental position as one held by the "true believer." Themes of voice and participation echo rich traditions in progressive education that value the autonomy of the child and the importance of appealing to his or her passions and interests. Yet in the struggle to convince others of the rights and abilities of young people to engage in organizational or public decision making and action, careful and critical understanding of youth participation is required.

As the idea of youth participation gains steam, the field is at a critical juncture. It is more important than ever before to identify and uncover the myths surrounding youth participation in order to build a convincing, evidence-rich case for its merits. We outline four such myths and discuss key issues facing supporters of youth participation.

Myth 1: Youth participation is accomplished by placing one youth on a board or committee

Many school boards, city councils, and boards of directors of nonprofit organizations have begun to create space for youth representatives. Although this marks a potentially important first step in opening the door to youth voice and participation, it also may limit the involvement of young people. Such a conception carries with it two related problems: tokenism and exclusivity.

Inserting one or a few youth into an adult-created and adult–driven process runs the risk of involving youth as tokens or "decorations," (Hart, 1992), precluding any opportunity for substantive influence. An authentic process is not one that is determined solely by adults. Rather, youth need multiple spaces for engagement. In this way, youth participation efforts can tap into the interests, passions, and skills of young people. Alternative points of entry can also open the space for youth to redesign and recreate the institutions that influence their lives.

In addition to the risk of tokenism, involving a few youth as representatives of larger groups may result in exclusivity, whereby only the most privileged or skilled youth are chosen to participate. Authentic youth involvement that creates space for broad and inclusive participation requires intentionality (Andersen, 1998; Baksh-Soodeen, 2001). This means building structures, practices, and cultures that support the participation of youth who may not come from privileged backgrounds or who may not yet have the skills to participate effectively. Creating inclusive participation also means overcoming the idea of representativeness. Although youth participation implies that youth share common interests, it is important to remember how multiple and diverse their backgrounds and experiences are. Young people engage with the public world as individuals, not as representatives of all youth, African American youth, or gay youth, for example.

Myth 2: Youth participation means that adults surrender their roles as guides and educators

Whereas Myth 1 is based on limited assumptions about the involvement of youth, the challenge with Myth 2 lies in limited assumptions about the involvement of adults. Too often, discussions of youth participation are silent about the roles that adults must play as supporters and educators, despite the fact that adults play critical roles providing guidance and connecting youth to needed information and resources.

In youth participation projects, adults socialize youth into practices and habits of the professional world. For example, Deborah Alvarez-Rodriguez points out her role as a "sympathetic critic" of the members of Youth IMPACT—a youth-led evaluation program in San Francisco. If youth made a presentation and the audience did not understand what they were saying or if young people did not take their professional obligations seriously, she gave them feedback to help them improve ("Youth Evaluating Programs," 2002). In other words, supporters of youth participation must be open to the unique voices and contributions of youth, but they also must help youth learn how to recognize the norms of the public arena or the specific practices of the field in which they hope to participate. This is not so that youth will merely adopt these norms, but so that they can be effective in shaping broader arenas.

Adults also often play roles as critical guides, especially in projects that are oriented toward civic participation or political activism. Youth wishing to make an impact on their community may need knowledge of political processes or an awareness of the multiple causes of deep-seated public problems. Without these, most would agree that such projects would be flawed efforts at youth participation.

Myth 3: Adults are ready for youth participation

An assumption of adult readiness brings some of the most intractable problems to youth participation efforts. As seen in the episode that opened this article, even the best-intentioned adults may not yet understand what youth participation means. Adults need to adapt to youth participation as much as (if not more than) youth do. This requires ongoing training and development of adults in how best to support youth and fulfill their roles as adult allies. Successful youth-adult partnerships recognize the importance of supporting adult learning and change to nurture effective youth participation.

Authentic youth engagement requires that young people be given the time and space to develop the skills they need to participate effectively.

A greater challenge, however, may come from the need for adults to change their frames, that is, their understandings of youth and how to work with them. Even in institutions created to develop and serve youth, young people often face ambivalence from adults about their ability to participate in real-world decision making and action (see for example, Costello et al., 2000). True participation, then, means changing deeply held beliefs of adults—not just about age but also constructions around race, ethnicity, class, and "at-risk" status. At its most basic level, it requires a "willingness to be changed" (see "Youth Evaluating Programs," 2002).

Myth 4: Youth are ready to participate; they just need the opportunity

Just as adults need support and training, authentic youth engagement requires that young people be given the time and space to develop the skills they need to participate effectively. This does not mean that youth need to learn now and participate later, but rather that they have ongoing training and support during the participation process. This training includes domain-specific skills. Projects that involve youth in program evaluation, for example, need to train youth in research methods, such as interviewing or data analysis, which typically are not part of a regular school curriculum. Youth preparation also includes the development of broader skills. To engage meaningfully in decision making, youth (like adults) may need workshops and practice in facilitation, public speaking, and collaborative processes. Finally, youth too may need experiences that alter their frames about what is possible for young people. Involvement with real-world issues and projects where they can see the larger community or public impact may be the best way for youth to learn what they are capable of.

Moving Forward

The myths articulated here represent key barriers to meaningful youth participation. They highlight the need for honest discussion and analysis around issues of power. Are adults prepared to involve youth in meaningful ways? Are they prepared to look critically at patterns of privilege and exclusion that cut across age, race, ethnicity, class, gender, sexual orientation, and ability? How will they build structures and processes that work to overcome these? Are they ready to change, taking on roles as allies and partners rather than just directors or instructors? Equally important, are youth prepared to take on their roles as decision makers and public actors? Do they have access to the necessary knowledge and skills? Answering these questions will be crucial to understanding and strengthening youth participation efforts.

Note

1. Anecdote taken from researcher field notes, Aug. 22, 2002.

References

Ames, C. (1992). Classrooms: Goals, structures, and student motivation. *Journal of Educational Psychology, 84* (3), 261–271.

Anderson, G. L. (1998). Toward authentic participation: Deconstructing the discourses of participatory reforms in education. *American Educational Research Journal, 35*(4), 571–603.

Ashley, J., Samaniego, D., & Chuen, L. (1997). How Oakland turns its back on teens: A youth perspective. *Social Justice, 24,* 170–177.

Baksh-Soodeen, R. (2001). Lessons from the gender movement: Building a discipline to support practice. *CYD Journal, 2*(2), 61–64.

Bales, S. (2000). *Reframing Youth Issues for Public Consideration and Support.* Washington, DC: FrameWorks Institute.

Brandao, C. (1998). The landmark achievements of Brazil's social movement for children's rights. *New Designs for Youth Development, 14*(3). Available at: www.cydjournal.org/NewDesigns/ND_98Fall.

Costello, J., Toles, M., Spielberger, J., & Wynn, J. (2000). *History, Ideology and Structure Shape the Organizations that Shape Youth, Youth Development: Issues, Challenges and Directions.* Philadelphia: Public/Private Ventures.

Eccles, J. S., Wigfield, A., & Schiefele, U. (1998). Motivation to succeed. In W. Damon (Ed.), *Handbook of Child Psychology, Vol. 3: Social, Emotional and Personality Development* (pp. 1017–1094). John Wiley & Sons.

Espinosa, M. F., & Schwab, M. (1997). Working children in Ecuador mobilize for change. *Social Justice, 24*(3), 64–70.

Ferber, T., & Pittman, K. (1999). *Finding Common Agendas: How Young People Are Being Engaged in Community Change Efforts.* Takoma Park, MD: International Youth Foundation—U.S.

Fielding, M. (2001). Students as radical agents of change. *Journal of Educational Change, 2*(2), 123–141.

Hart, R. (1992). *Children's Participation: From Tokenism to Citizenship.* Florence, Italy: UNICEF, International Child Development Centre.

Hart, R., Daiute, C., & Iltus, S. (1997). Developmental theory and children's participation in community organizations. *Social Justice, 24*(3), 33–63.

Hart, R., & Schwab, M. (1997). Children's rights and the building of democracy: A dialogue on the international movement for children's participation. *Social Justice, 24*(3), 177–191.

Irby, M., Ferber, T., & Pittman, K. (2001). *Youth action: Youth Contributing to Communities, Communities Supporting Youth.* Takoma Park, MD: Forum for Youth Investment, International Youth Foundation.

Kirshner, B., O'Donoghue, J., & McLaughlin, M.(2005). Youth-led research collaborations: Bringing youth voice to the research process. In J. L. Mahoney, R. W. Larson, and J. S. Eccles (Eds.) *Organized Activities as Contexts of Development: Extracurricular Activities, After-School and Community Programs,* (pp. 131–156). Mahwah, NJ: Erlbaum.

McLaughlin, M. W. (2000). *Community Counts: How Youth Organizations Matter for Youth Development.* Washington, D.C.: Public Education Network.

Mitra, D. (2006). Increasing Student Voice and Moving Toward Youth Leadership. *The Prevention Researcher, 13*(1), 7–9.

Pittman, K., Ferber, T., & Irby, M. (2000). *Youth as Effective Citizens.* Takoma Park, MD: International Youth Foundation—US.

Rajani, R. (2000). *The Participation Rights of Adolescents: A Strategic Approach* (Working Paper). New York: United Nations Children's Fund.

Tolman, J., & Pittman, K. (2001). *Youth Acts, Community Impacts: Stories of Youth Engagement with Real Results.* Takoma Park, MD: Forum for Youth Investment, International Youth Foundation.

What evidence do we have that youth participation actually works? (2001, Spring). *International Insights on Youth and Communities, Volume II.* Forum for Youth Investment.

Youth evaluating programs for youth: Stories of Youth IMPACT. (2002). In B. Kirshner, J. O'Donoghue, and M. McLaughlin (Eds), *Youth Participation: Improving Institutions and Communities. New Directions for Youth Development Theory Practice Research.* (pp. 101–117). San Francisco, CA, U.S.: Jossey-Bass.

Zeldin, S., McDaniel, A. K., Topitzes, D., & Calvert, M. (2000). *Youth in Decision-Making: A Study of the Impacts of Youth on Adults and Organizations.* Chevy Chase, MD: National 4-H Council.

JENNIFER L. O'DONOGHUE, MPA, is a doctoral student in educational administration and policy analysis at the Stanford University School of Education. **BENJAMIN KIRSHNER,** PhD is an assistant professor at University of Colorado, Boulder. **MILBREY McLAUGHLIN,** PhD is the David Jacks Professor of Education and Public Policy at Stanford University, executive director of the John W. Gardner for Youth and Their Communities, and co-director of the Center for Research on the Context of Teaching.

This article is condensed and adapted from O'Donoghue, J. L., Kirshner, B., & McLaughlin, M, (2002). Introdction: Moving youth participation forward, In B. Kirshner, J. O'Donoghue, and M. McLaughlin (Eds.), *Youth Participation: Improving Institutions and Communities. New Directions for Youth Development, 96*, 15–26. Copyright @ 2002, Wiley Periodicals, Inc. Reprinted with permission of John Wiley & Sons, Inc.

UNIT 2

Developmental Changes of Adolescents: Physical, Cognitive, and Social

Unit Selections

Key Points to Consider

- What are the reasons for teens making rush decisions?

- What are the challenges that mental health issues pose to college applicants?

- What is the prevalence of body dissatisfaction among teens?

- What psychological damage to girls is the result of the sexual media?

- What influence does various kinds of music have on teen behavior?

- What impact does early experience have on individual development?

- What effect does increased stressful life experiences and a person's ability to cope have on adjustment to mental health problems?

- What is the overlap between teens with ADHD and substance use?

Student Website

www.mhcls.com

Internet References

ADOL: Adolescence Directory On-Line
http://site.educ.indiana.edu/aboutus/AdolescenceDirectoryonLineADOL/tabid/4785/Default.aspx

At-Risk Children and Youth
http://www.ncrel.org/sdrs/areas/at0cont.htm

Educational Forum on Adolescent Health: Youth Bullying
http://www.ama-assn.org/ama1/pub/upload/mm/39/youthbullying.pdf

Teens Health
http://www.teenshealth.org

Teens in Distress Series: Adolescent Stress and Depression
http://www.extension.umn.edu/distribution/youthdevelopment/DA3083.html

The physical changes accompanying the onset of puberty are usually the first clear indicators that a child is entering the period of adolescence. The changes can be a source of both pride and humiliation for the developing adolescent. These physiological changes are regulated by a structure in the brain known as the hypothalamus. The hypothalamus is responsible for stimulating increased production of hormones that control development of the primary and secondary sex characteristics. Primary sex characteristics include physical changes in the reproductive system, such as growth of the ovaries and testicles. Secondary sex characteristics are physical changes not directly involved in reproduction. Examples include voice changes, height increases, growth of facial hair in males, and breast development in females.

The hypothalamus signals the pituitary gland, which in turn stimulates the gonads to produce hormones (androgens and estrogens). The hypothalamus then detects the level of sex hormones present in the bloodstream and either calls for more or less hormone production. During childhood, the hypothalamus is very sensitive to sex hormones and keeps production at a low level. For some reason that is not yet completely known, the hypothalamus changes its sensitivity to the sex hormones in adolescence. As a result, significantly greater quantities of sex hormones are needed before the hypothalamus signals the pituitary gland to shutdown production. The thyroid and adrenal glands also play a role in the development of secondary sex characteristics.

The physiological changes themselves occur over a 5 to 6 year span. Girls generally begin to undergo puberty 18 to 24 months before boys, with the typical onset at age 10 or 11. The earliest pubertal changes in girls are breast budding, height spurt, and sparse pubic hair. Experiencing a first menstrual cycle is a mid-pubertal event, with the average age of menarche in the United States currently being 12 years old. For boys, initial signs of puberty are that the testicles begin to increase in size and the height spurt begins. Facial hair, deepening voice, and first ejaculation occur later.

The sequence of pubertal change is fairly constant across individuals; however, the timing of puberty varies greatly from one person to the next. Some adolescents are out of step with their peers because they mature early, whereas others mature late. The advantages and disadvantages of early versus late maturation have been the subject of much research, so a few readings touch on this topic. One conclusion is that early maturation is correlated with earlier involvement in risk-taking behaviors like alcohol use and sexual activity. In extreme cases, biological disorders result in delayed or precocious puberty, but there are new medications for treating these conditions.

The onset of puberty is affected by diet, exercise, and genetic history. Largely due to improved nutrition and to better control of illnesses, puberty occurs 3 to 4 years earlier in the twenty-first century than it did 150 years ago. Adolescents today also grow several inches taller and weigh more. A visit to historical homes will show that the doorways and beds were much smaller in previous centuries. This trend toward earlier maturation is a worldwide phenomenon that has presumably reached a leveling off point. Adolescents experience psychological and social challenges related to puberty. For example, sexual arousal increases and the teenager must learn how to handle sexual situations. Likewise, gender-typical behavior is more expected by

© BananaStock/PunchStock

others observing the youth. The adolescent must also incorporate bodily changes into his or her self-image. Concerns about physical appearance become a major preoccupation and play a significant role in self-esteem at this time. These issues are addressed in this unit. In particular, the readings examine the body image concerns adolescents experience. This contributes to adolescents' anxiety about their bodies and how "normal" they are. On the other hand, other cultures employ rites of passage to mark entrance into manhood or womanhood. Many such rites of passage involve physical markings on the adolescent, such as circumcision or body tattooing.

Adolescence entails changes in cognitive capacities that are just as monumental as the biological changes. Whereas children tend to be more literal, more tied to reality and to the familiar—adolescents are more abstract, systematic, and logical. Adolescents can appreciate metaphors and sarcasm, they can easily think about things that do not exist, they can test abstract ideas against reality, and they can readily conceive of multiple possibilities. Many of these improvements in thinking ability contribute to conflicts with adults as adolescents become better able to argue a point or take a stand. They are better at planning out their case and anticipating counter arguments. They are also more likely to question the way things are because they now conceive of alternate possibilities.

The study of cognitive changes that occur in adolescence has largely been based on the work of the Swiss psychologist, Jean Piaget, and his colleague Barbel Inhelder. Piaget and Inhelder described the adolescent as reasoning at the formal operational stage. Children from the approximate ages of 7 to 11 years old were described as being in the "concrete operational" stage. Not all researchers agree with Piaget and Inhelder that changes in adolescent cognitive abilities represent true stage-related changes. They do, however, agree that adolescent thought is characteristically more logical, abstract, and hypothetical than that of children. Recognize, though, that having certain mental capacities does not mean that adolescents, or even adults for that matter, will always reason at their rational best!

Piaget's views on cognitive development have been very influential, particularly in the field of education. Awareness of the cognitive abilities and shortcomings of adolescents can make their behaviors more comprehensible to parents, teachers, counselors, and other professionals who work with them. Similarly, as Piaget suggested, schools need to take the developmental abilities and needs of adolescents into account in planning programs and designing curricula. In addition, Piaget's general philosophy was that learning must be active. Others in the field of education, however, caution that there are other important issues left un-addressed by Piaget. For example, the United States has an elevated school dropout rate, so we need to find alternatives for keeping the nation's youth in school.

Building on the work of Piaget and Inhelder, David Elkind has argued that the newly emerging formal operational cognitive abilities of adolescents lead to some troublesome consequences. For one thing, adolescents tend to over intellectualize. They often make things too complex and fail to see the obvious, a phenomenon that Elkind calls pseudostupidity. Teachers often bear the brunt of this phenomenon as adolescents over-analyze every word of a multiple-choice question. Elkind also maintains that much of the extreme self-consciousness of adolescents occurs because of the construct of an imaginary audience. Formal operations make it possible for adolescents to think about other people's thoughts. Adolescents lose perspective and think that others are constantly watching them and thinking about them. A related mistake is that adolescents are likely to believe that everyone shares their concerns and knows their thoughts. This belief, that one is at the center of attention, further leads to the development of what Elkind calls the personal fable. Namely, if everyone is paying so much attention to me I must be special and invulnerable. Bad things won't happen to me. I won't get in a car crash. I won't get pregnant. The phenomena—pseudostupidity, the imaginary audience, and the personal fable—diminish as adolescents' cognitive abilities mature and as they develop friendships in which intimacies are shared. Peer interaction helps adolescents see that they are not as unique as they thought, nor are they the focus of everyone else's attention.

Schools focus on individual students and on punishment. Only when schools take student concerns into account will schools become environments that stimulate attendance, interest, and harmony. School violence by disenchanted youth has peaked in the United States. Schools will need to promote a sense of belonging if disaffected and potentially violent students are to become members of the school community.

While developmentalists in the Piagetian tradition focus on the ways in which the thought processes of children and adolescents differ, other researchers have taken a different track—a psychometric approach. In this approach, the emphasis is on quantifying cognitive abilities such as verbal ability, mathematical ability, and general intelligence (IQ). The measurement of intelligence, as well as the very definition of intelligence, has been controversial for decades. A classic question is whether intelligence is best conceptualized as a general capacity that underlies many diverse abilities or as a set of specific abilities. Traditional IQ tests focus on abilities that relate to success in school and ignore abilities such as those that tap creativity, mechanical aptitude, or practical intelligence.

The role of genetic versus environmental contributions to intelligence have also been controversial. At the turn of the century, the predominant view was that intelligence was essentially inherited and was little influenced by experience. Today, the consensus is that an individual's intelligence is very much a product of both nature and nurture. An even greater controversy focuses on the role that heredity versus the environment plays in explaining racial, ethnic, and gender differences in performance on various cognitive tests such as IQ tests.

Adolescents clearly have larger vocabularies, more mathematical knowledge, better spatial ability, etc., than children. Their memories are better because they process information more efficiently and use memory strategies more effectively. Adolescents possess a greater general knowledge base than children, which enables them to link new concepts to existing ideas. Stated another way, psychometric intelligence may well increase with age. On the other hand, because of comparisons to age peers, the relative performance of adolescents on aptitude tests remains fairly stable. A 9-year-old child's outstanding performance on an IQ test, for example, is fairly predictive that the same individual's IQ score at age 15 will be better than the score of most peers.

Performance on standardized tests, IQ or otherwise (e.g. achievement tests), is often used to place junior high and high school students in ability tracts, a practice that is increasingly questioned. Similarly, standardized test results compared across schools are being used to measure a school's educational effectiveness. These types of issues are addressed in the following set of articles.

Each age period is associated with developmental tasks. A major aspect of psychosocial development for adolescents is the formation of a coherent personal identity. Erik Erikson referred to this as the adolescent identity crisis. Identity formation is a normative event, but it represents a turning point in human development that has consequences for later psychosocial skills.

Children's identities often represent an identification with parents and significant others. Adolescents reflect on their identity and come to some sense of who they are and who they are not. Identity formation involves an examination of personal likes and dislikes; political, religious, and moral values; occupational interests, as well as gender roles and sexual behaviors. Adolescents must also form an integrated sense of their own personality across the various roles they engage in (e.g., son or daughter, student, boyfriend or girlfriend, part-time worker, etc.).

The first article addresses the links between student health and academic performance. Eddy Ramirez explains the challenges that mental health issues pose to college applicants. An understanding of factors that increase the risk for body dissatisfaction can help guide preventive efforts presented by Presnell, Bearman, and Madeley. Stacy Weiner describes the troubling trend in women and girls' sexual media depiction. She explains that Pop Culture images are targeting younger girls, which often leads to eating disorders, lower self-esteem, and depression. The following article discusses the influence of various kinds of music on teen behavior. Dr. Sroufe outlines some of the arguments surrounding the impact of early experiences. Adolescent stress and coping with stress are presented by two authors. The final selection in this section is on ADHD and the overlap between ADHD and substance use disorder.

Healthier Students, Better Learners

The Health Education Assessment Project helps teachers provide the skills-based, standards-based health instruction that students need.

BETH PATEMAN

When we think back on health classes from our school days, many of us have only vague memories. We may recall some discussion of food groups, a film about puberty, or a lecture on dental hygiene conducted when the weather was too rainy to go outside for physical education. Few of us remember our K-12 health education experiences as being relevant to our lives outside the classroom.

Fortunately, that picture is changing. Asserting that "healthy students make better learners, and better learners make healthy communities," the Council of Chief State School Officers (CCSSO) and the Association of State and Territorial Health Officials (ASTHO) (2002) have summarized compelling research evidence that students' health significantly affects their school achievement. Even if their schools have the most outstanding academic curriculum and instruction, students who are ill or injured, hungry or depressed, abusing drugs or experiencing violence, are unlikely to learn as well as they should (Kolbe, 2002).

Effective health education programs have a vital role to play in enhancing students' health and thus in raising academic achievement. Kolbe's 2002 review of the research found that modern school health programs can improve students' health knowledge, attitudes, skills, and behaviors and enhance social and academic outcomes. How do these modern health programs differ from those that most of us remember from our school days? Thanks to growing knowledge about how to prevent unhealthy and unsafe behaviors among young people, today's exemplary health education combines *skills-based* and *standards-based* approaches.

Focus on Skills

The Centers for Disease Control and Prevention have identified six types of behavior that cause the most serious health problems in the United States among people over 5 years old: alcohol and other drug use, high-risk sexual behaviors, tobacco use, poor dietary choices, physical inactivity, and behaviors that result in intentional or unintentional injury. Stressing the importance of education efforts, the Centers state that

these behaviors usually are established during youth; persist into adulthood; are interrelated; and are preventable. In

addition to causing serious health problems, these behaviors contribute to many of the educational and social problems that confront the nation, including failure to complete high school, unemployment, and crime. (n.d.)

Effective health education programs have a vital role to play in enhancing students' health and thus in raising academic achievement.

In response to the Centers' focus on these major health-risk behaviors, education researchers have worked to identify educational approaches that positively affect health-related behaviors among young people. Many research studies have established the effectiveness of skills-based school health education in promoting healthy behavior and academic achievement (ASTHO & Society of State Directors of Health, Physical Education, and Recreation, 2002; Collins et al., 2002; Kirby, 2001). Lohrmann and Wooley (1998) determined that effective programs

- Focus on helping young people develop and practice personal and social skills, such as communication and decision making, to deal effectively with health-risk situations;
- Provide healthy alternatives to specific high-risk behaviors;
- Use interactive approaches that engage students;
- Are research-based and theory-driven;
- Address social and media influences on student behaviors;
- Strengthen individual and group norms that support healthy behavior;
- Are of sufficient duration to enable students to gain the knowledge and skills that they need; and
- Include teacher preparation and support.

Health Education Standards

- *Standard 1: Students will comprehend concepts related to health promotion and disease prevention.* For example, students will be able to identify what good health is, recognize health problems, and be aware of ways in which lifestyle, the environment, and public policies can promote health.
- *Standard 2: Students will demonstrate the ability to access valid health information and health-promoting products and services.* For example, students will be able to evaluate advertisements, options for health insurance and treatment, and food labels.
- *Standard 3: Students will demonstrate the ability to practice health-enhancing behaviors and reduce health risks.* For example, students will know how to identify responsible and harmful behaviors, develop strategies for good health, and manage stress.
- *Standard 4: Students will analyze the influence of culture, media, technology, and other factors on health.* For example, students will be able to describe and analyze how cultural background and messages from the media, technology, and friends influence health choices.
- *Standard 5: Students will demonstrate the ability to use interpersonal communication skills to enhance health.* For example, students will learn refusal and negotiation skills and conflict resolution strategies.
- *Standard 6: Students will demonstrate the ability to use goal-setting and decision-making skills to enhance health.* For example, students will set reasonable and attainable goals—such as losing a given amount of weight or increasing physical activity—and develop positive decision-making skills.
- *Standard 7: Students will demonstrate the ability to advocate for personal, family, and community health.* For example, students will identify community resources, accurately communicate health information and ideas, and work cooperatively to promote health.

Source: Joint Committee on National Health Education Standards. (1995).

New Standards for a Skills-Based Approach

In 1995, the American Cancer Society sponsored the development of national health education standards that use a skills-based approach to learning (Joint committee on National Health Education Standards, 1995). The standards, summarized below, advocate health literacy that enhances individuals' capacities to obtain, interpret, and understand basic health information and services and their competence to use such information and services in health-enhancing ways (Summerfield, 1995).

Together with the Centers for Disease Control and Prevention's priority health-risk behaviors, the national health education standards provide an important new framework for moving from an information-based school health curriculum to a skills-based curriculum. Skills-based health education engages students and provides a safe environment for students to practice working through health-risk situations that they are likely to encounter as adolescents.

An information-based approach to tobacco use prevention might require students to memorize facts about the health consequences of tobacco use, such as lung cancer, heart disease, and emphysema. In contrast, a skills-based approach ensures that students demonstrate the ability to locate valid information on the effects of tobacco use. Students learn and practice a variety of skills: For example, they use analysis to identify the influences of family, peers, and media on decisions about tobacco use and they use interpersonal communication skills to refuse tobacco use.

The skills-based approach outlined in the national health education standards helps students answer questions and address issues that are important in their lives. For example, young children need to learn how to make friends and deal with bullies. Older children need to practice a variety of strategies to resist pressures to engage in risky health behaviors while maintaining friendships. Early adolescents need to learn how to obtain reliable, straightforward information about the physical, emotional, and social changes of puberty. High school students need to learn to weigh their health-related decisions in terms of their life plans and goals. All students need to learn how to respond to stress, deal with strong feelings in health-enhancing ways, and build a reliable support group of peers and adults.

The Health Education Assessment Project

Standards-based health education requires a new approach to planning, assessment, and instruction. Although many educators are excited about the prospect of standards-based teaching in health education, they may lack a clear picture of what standards-based performance would look like in their classrooms. To address this need, the Council of Chief State School Officers' State Collaborative on Assessment and Student Standards initiated the Health Education Assessment Project in 1993 (see www.ccsso.org/scass).

The Health Education Assessment Project develops standards-based health resources through a collaborative process. Funding for the project comes from the Centers for Disease Control and Prevention and the membership fees of 24 state and local education agencies. During its first decade, the project has built a foundation for a health education assessment system, created an assessment framework, developed and tested a pool of assessment items, and provided professional development and supporting materials to help teachers implement the assessment system and framework.

A skills-based approach to tobacco use prevention ensures that students demonstrate the ability to locate valid information on the effects of tobacco use.

professional development opportunities to practice aligning standards, assessment, and instruction for their own classrooms (CCSSO, 2003).

Classrooms in which students are evaluated by health education standards and criteria are substantially different from classrooms in which many teachers have taught and been taught. Teachers need hands-on preparation and experience with planning, implementing, and evaluating curriculum and instruction aligned with standards and assessment. The Health Education Assessment Project can improve the health of students by providing teachers with the tools they need to meet the important health needs of today's youth.

References

Association of State and Territorial Health Officials & Society of State Directors of Health, Physical Education, and Recreation. (2002).*Making the connection: Health and student achievement* (CDROM). Washington, DC: Authors.

Centers for Disease Control and Prevention, Division of Adolescent and School Health. (n.d.). *Health topics* [Online]. Available: www.cdc.gov/nccdphp/dash/risk.htm

Collins, J., Robin, L., Wooley, S., Fenley, D., Hunt, P., Taylor, J., Haber, D., & Kolbe, L. (2002). Programs that work: CDC's guide to effective programs that reduce health risk behavior of youth. *Journal of School Health, 72*(3), 93–99.

Council of Chief State School Officers. (2003). *Improving teaching and learning through the CCSSO-SCASS Health Education Assessment Project.* Washington, DC: Author.

Council of Chief State School Officers & Association of State and Territorial Health Officials. (2002). *Why support a coordinated approach to school health?* Washington, DC: Authors.

Joint Committee on National Health Education Standards. (1995). *National health education standards: Achieving health literacy.* Reston, VA: Association for the Advancement of Health Education.

Kirby, D. (2001). *Emerging answers: Research findings on programs to reduce teen pregnancy.* Washington, DC: The National Campaign to Prevent Teen Pregnancy.

Kolbe, L. J. (2002). Education reform and the goals of modern school health programs. *The State Education Standard, 3*(4), 4–11.

Lohrmann, D. K., & Wooley, S. F. (1998). Comprehensive school health education. In E. Marx & S. F. Wooley (Eds.), *Health is academic: A guide to coordinated school health programs* (pp. 43–66). New York: Teachers College Press.

Summerfield, L. M. (1995). *National standards for health education* (ERIC Digest No. ED 387 483). Washington, DC: ERIC Clearinghouse on Teaching and Teacher Education. Available: www.ericfacility.net/databases/ERIC_Digests/ed387483.html

BETH PATEMAN is an associate professor at the Institute for Teacher Education, University of Hawaii at Manoa, Honolulu, HI 96822; (808) 956-3885; mpateman@hawaii.edu.

Sample Performance Task: Advocacy for Mental Health

Student Challenge
Your challenge is to select and examine a mental health problem, such as anxiety, depression, eating disorders, suicide ideation, bipolar disorder, or schizophrenia. Your tasks are to

- Locate and analyze valid information sources to determine the causes and symptoms of the problem.
- Explore treatment options and health-enhancing ways of managing the problem.
- Recommend helpful tips for talking with friends or family members who might be experiencing the problem.
- Provide a list of helpful community resources.
- Design a computer-generated brochure or presentation targeted to high school students that includes a summary of your information on causes, symptoms, and management/treatment; tips for talking with others; and a list of community resources.

Assessment Criteria for a Great Presentation
Your work will be assessed using the following criteria. You will be required to

- Provide accurate and in-depth information and draw conclusions about relationships between behaviors and health.
- Cite your information sources accurately and explain why your sources are appropriate.
- Provide specific recommendations for health-enhancing ways of managing stress and ways of talking with others about the problem.
- Demonstrate awareness of your target audience (high school students) and persuade others to make healthy choices.

Additional criteria may be determined by class members.

The project helps educators translate theory into practice. It provides educators with a wide range of assessment items developed in a variety of formats, including selected response, constructed response, and performance tasks (see the sample below). The project provides teacher and student rubrics for assessing performance and examples of student papers for scoring practice. Perhaps the greatest benefit to educators has been the hands-on

Mental Assessment Test

Eddy Ramirez

Colleges Scrutinize Applications from Troubled Students More Closely

Growing up in New York City, Emily Isaac studied Hebrew, performed in school musicals, and played soccer. She fantasized about going to a prestigious university like Harvard and becoming a lawyer for Hollywood celebrities. But her drive and ambition faded when she reached high school. She ignored homework assignments and argued with teachers. Her grades dropped to mostly C's and D's. She was so difficult that she was asked to leave three private schools in two years. Emily says she was angry and depressed over a family member's drug use. At age 17 last fall, she was applying to colleges and had a tough decision to make: How to present herself to admissions officers increasingly wary of troubled students?

Concerned about liability and campus safety in the wake of shootings at Northern Illinois University and Virginia Tech, more colleges and universities are scrutinizing the character of applicants. They want to know about students' past behavior, and, if there is any doubt, they will call high school counselors for answers. Admissions officers say "youthful indiscretions" like a schoolyard brawl or an unpaid traffic ticket aren't likely to result in denial letters. But a pattern of troubling behavior could cost someone an admission.

"We're not only admitting students for intellectual reasons but for community reasons," says Debra Shaver, director of admissions at Smith College, a private women's liberal arts school in Massachusetts. "We want to make sure they will be good community members." Smith and other schools acknowledge that making judgments about character is sometimes a messy process. It doesn't involve precise measures like SAT scores or grade-point average. "In some cases, you say, 'This makes me nervous,' and maybe it is an intuition and some reasonable people would disagree, but it goes with the territory," says Bruce Poch, dean of admissions at Pomona College in Claremont, Calif.

Full disclosure. It's not surprising, then, that students like Emily agonize over the decision to disclose personal and academic problems. "We finally hired an independent counselor," says Lisa Kaufman, Emily's mother.

Not all counselors agree on what advice to give families. Some discourage students from bringing up mental illnesses and emotional problems altogether. Others say full disclosure helps when a student's records show poor grades or other inconsistencies that are likely to make colleges suspicious. Shirley Bloomquist, an independent college counselor in Great Falls, Va., says she once called a liberal arts college in Massachusetts to say she was disappointed by its decision to reject an applicant who had written about overcoming a drug addiction. The student had completed a drug rehabilitation program and had been clean for a year. "Colleges are more concerned than ever about student emotional stability," Bloomquist says. "I think it is imperative that the student, the parent, and the high school counselor discuss the situation and decide what should or should not be revealed."

Sally Rubenstone, senior counselor with collegeconfidential.com and coauthor of *Panicked Parents' Guide to College Admission*, says being forthright about past behavior or mental health problems doesn't mean "The Jerry Springerization of the College Admissions Essay." "Sometimes I have to implore [students] to stay mum," she says. "There are clearly times when personal problems are too personal—or inappropriate—to include in a college essay."

Emily's problems, however, needed airing—but not all of them. For example, she didn't disclose her troubles in middle school because colleges asked only (via the Common Application) about academic and behavioral misconduct in high school. She says she was asked to leave one high school after a confrontation with another student, but the offense was never recorded in her file, so she didn't volunteer that information either. On the advice of her counselor, Emily wrote cover letters and an essay focusing instead on the reasons for her documented troubles in school and how she had grown from those experiences.

Although colleges would know from her transcripts that she had been at a boarding school for troubled teens, Emily didn't explicitly mention depression in her essay. Rubenstone, who served as Emily's counselor in the admissions process, says, "Colleges can run scared when they hear the word depression." Emily, who got treatment, hoped colleges would pay attention to her improvement instead. "I thought I was taking a risk, but I had faith that people would understand," she says. In one of her cover letters, Emily wrote: "What I am trying to say is that my past no longer dictates my future and that I am a far more capable, hard-working, mature student than depicted in my forms."

Colleges cannot legally deny admission specifically on the basis of mental illness, but it's hard to account for how that characteristic figures into the calculus of who gets in and who doesn't. Admissions officers undoubtedly are aware that the shooters at Virginia Tech and Northern Illinois had troubled histories before they applied to school: Indeed, the graduate student responsible for the NIU attack had written about his emotional struggles in adolescence in his admission application. Admissions officers, ever mindful of the diversity on campus, also are aware that reports of depressed college students are on the rise.

Not all colleges offer students a second chance. One high school senior in Tucson, Ariz., with an impressive academic record was rejected by a selective liberal arts college after his counselor says he told the school that the student had been disciplined for smoking marijuana on a field trip. The counselor says he helped the student with his essay, believing that if it struck the right tone and offered a sincere apology and a pledge from the student that he would not make the same mistake again, the essay would persuade the college to admit him. It didn't. "This particular school was trying very hard to diminish its reputation as being 'kind of tolerant of druggies'—the very words used by the college representative," the counselor says.

Barmak Nassirian of the American Association of Collegiate Registrars and Admissions Officers says too much pressure is being put on college admission officers who lack the expertise to evaluate the seriousness of an offense or an applicant's emotional well-being. In the absence of clear guidelines, Nassirian says, colleges should stop asking about past behavior altogether. "It's very tempting for colleges to say we're excluding the next Jack the Ripper from sitting next to your son or daughter," he says. "But it's really your son or daughter who is getting nabbed and getting nabbed for having done something stupid in high school."

Common Application

That may be the reason that many high schools don't disclose information about a student's disciplinary history. A recent survey of 2,306 public and private high schools found that only 23 percent of schools said they allowed for the disclosure of such information to colleges, 39 percent said they disclose sometimes, and 38 percent said they never do. The results refer to questions asked by about 340 colleges that use the Common Application, which inquires if students have ever been convicted of a crime or been severely disciplined in high school. This year, 347,837 high school students used the Common Application. Of those, only 2 percent said they had a serious discipline problem in high school, and 0.22 percent said they were convicted of a misdemeanor or felony.

It's not clear how many students refuse to answer the questions or conceal their past troubles. In what one admissions counselor sees as a separate, disturbing trend, high schools that once suspended or expelled students for offenses such as academic dishonesty now strike deals with parents and students that result in less severe consequences and no record of the student's indiscretion. One New York student who has been accepted to several competitive schools says he caught a lucky break when the private high school he attended his freshman year decided that rather than expel him, it would let him quietly transfer to another school after he was caught stealing a biology exam. The school told him it would not notify colleges about the incident. At his new high school, the student was suspended for insulting another student. And again he was able to cut a deal with the principal at that school. The student, who requested anonymity, says he was able to "work off" the suspension from his record by performing community service. He says his guidance counselor discouraged him from bringing up either incident on his college applications. "It's not that I wanted to lie," he says. "I just didn't want to lose everything that I've worked so hard for."

If an applicant's school records raise suspicion, colleges say they will make every effort to verify the information. Some, for instance, will turn to Google, Facebook, or another source on the Internet. But it's not clear how thorough most colleges are when high schools don't cooperate. It is often the case, some say, that an anonymous tipster or an upset parent of a child who was not admitted to the school will come forward. Colleges say a high school's refusal to share information could damage the school's relationship with the college, especially in the event that the applicant is admitted and later commits a crime.

Marlyn McGrath Lewis, director of admissions at Harvard, says high schools that knowingly withhold troubling information about applicants will be held responsible. "We're not a detective agency," she says. "We operate on the assumption that schools are behaving honorably." If administrators learn that an applicant has lied, colleges can rescind offers of admission. That's what happened in 1995 when Harvard administrators found out that an admitted applicant had killed her mother when she was 14. The applicant, a straight-A student, had not disclosed the incident in her Harvard application on the advice of her lawyer.

Seth Allen, dean of admissions at Grinnell College, a liberal arts school in Iowa, says colleges expect that students will answer questions about their past behavior truthfully and completely. "We want to understand if you slipped up why it happened," he says. "If we understand that there is a death in the family or a personal crisis that would help us say, 'This is not a normal pattern of behavior,' we can forgive you." Sometimes, he adds, an honest and thoughtful response can make a candidate more appealing.

Earlier this year, Emily was offered admission to six schools; she has decided to attend Simmons College in Boston. She was turned down by four other schools. "I'm grateful because I feel people are willing to take a chance on me," she says. "It just makes me hopeful that the world is moving away from fear and towards acceptance of those of us who haven't had the easiest times."

From *U.S. News & World Report*, May 12, 2008, pp. 40–41. Copyright © 2008 by U.S. News & World Report. Reprinted by permission.

Body Dissatisfaction in Adolescent Females and Males: Risk and Resilience

KATHERINE PRESNELL, PhD, SARAH KATE BEARMAN, PhD, AND MARY CLARE MADELEY, BA

One of the most remarkable and consistent research findings is the overwhelming prevalence of weight and shape-related concerns among adolescents. Estimates from community samples of adolescents suggest that as many as 46% of girls and 26% of boys report significant distress about their body size and shape, while only 12% of girls and 17% of boys indicate that they are satisfied with their body shape (Neumark-Sztainer, Story, Hannan, Perry, & Irving, 2002; Ricciardelli & McCabe, 2001). In fact, body dissatisfaction has become so commonplace in Western culture that it has been termed a "normative discontent" (Rodin, Silberstein, & Striegel-Moore, 1985). This is especially troubling because, at the upper end of the continuum, body dissatisfaction is associated with high levels of subjective distress, unhealthy weight control behaviors, and extreme methods of altering appearance, such as cosmetic surgery and steroid use (Neumark-Sztainer, Paxton, Hannan, Haines, & Story, 2006).

As many as 46% of girls and 26% of boys report significant distress about their body size and shape.

Body image is a broad term comprised of an individual's internal perceptions, thoughts, and evaluation of their outward physical appearance. Body dissatisfaction is one component of body image, and refers to the subjective negative evaluation of some aspect of one's physical appearance (Thompson, Heinberg, Altabe, & Tantleff-Dunn, 1999). Body dissatisfaction has been consistently shown to place adolescents at increased risk for the development and maintenance of disordered eating (Stice & Shaw, 2002), because strategies such as extreme dietary restriction or compensatory measures may be used in an attempt to alter weight and shape. Moreover, body image concerns are often resistant to change during treatment for eating disorders, and persistent body image disturbances are associated with relapse in anorexia and bulimia nervosa (Keel, Dorer, Franko, Jackson, & Herzog, 2005). Body dissatisfaction is also a strong predictor of depressed mood and low self-esteem among adolescents (Paxton, Neumark-Sztainer, Hannan, & Eisenberg, 2006). The negative impact of body dissatisfaction on a range of psychological problems underscores the need to explore factors that contribute to its development. Recent research also suggests that reducing body dissatisfaction may be successful in preventing the onset of depression and eating pathology (Bearman, Stice, & Chase, 2003).

Adolescence is a critical developmental period, bringing numerous physical changes, social challenges, and role transitions that increase vulnerability to body dissatisfaction. Theories of the development of body dissatisfaction highlight multiple contributing factors, including individual, familial, peer, and sociocultural influences. This article will highlight factors that influence the development of body dissatisfaction during adolescence, and consider protective factors that may decrease adolescents' risk of body image concerns. Understanding the mechanisms that link these factors to body dissatisfaction can help guide the development of effective prevention interventions.

Sociocultural Influences
Ideal-body Internalization

Beauty standards that are sanctioned by an individual's culture are hypothesized to influence how individuals perceive and evaluate their bodies. Western culture currently endorses an ultra-thin figure for women and a lean, muscular one for men. Pressure to conform to these ideals is evident in messages from the media, parents, and peers. As these ideals become increasingly difficult to attain, a sense of dissatisfaction often develops in those who place high importance on achieving them. Historically, there has been greater sociocultural emphasis on appearance and thinness for females, and research indicates consistently higher rates of body dissatisfaction among females in relation to males (Thompson et al., 1999). However, body dissatisfaction is also a substantial concern among adolescent boys. Adolescent boys are more likely than girls to engage in behaviors to increase weight and musculature, and there is evidence that boys are divided between those who desire to lose weight and those who wish to gain weight and musculature (e.g., Neumark-Sztainer et al., 1999). Thus, there may be two pathways to body dissatisfaction among boys—weight concerns and muscularity concerns—whereas girls consistently report a desire to be thinner. Regardless of gender, however, failure to attain a highly-valued ideal has been shown to lead to body dissatisfaction (Jones, 2004).

Differences in Ideals across Cultures

There is some evidence that beauty ideals and body dissatisfaction vary among cultural or ethnic groups. Ethnic groups that place greater emphasis on thinness tend to have higher levels of body dissatisfaction, particularly as obesity rates rise. For example, African American girls generally endorse a larger body ideal and report greater body satisfaction than Caucasian girls (Perez & Joiner, 2003). However, recent research indicates that this gap in body dissatisfaction may be decreasing, and that the most pronounced disparity occurs during the college-age years (Roberts, Cash, Feingold, & Johnson, 2006). Other research also suggests few differences in body dissatisfaction among African American, Asian American, and Hispanic women (Grabe & Hyde, 2006). Moreover, ethnic status failed to moderate the relation between body dissatisfaction and depression for girls, suggesting that regardless of ethnic identity, dissatisfaction with one's body increases the risk of depression (Siegel, 2002).

Media Influences

Use of media that conveys messages about body ideals is consistently associated with greater body dissatisfaction, and experimental exposure to images portraying the thin-ideal result in moderate decreases in self-esteem and increases in body dissatisfaction among females (e.g., Stice & Shaw, 1994). Some evidence suggests that media and peer influences are more influential during adolescence than parental influences for girls (Shroff & Thompson,

2006), but that the effect of media may be less pronounced among boys (McCabe & Ricciardelli, 2001).

Parent and Peer Influences

Although societal norms regarding ideal body shape and weight are transmitted in a variety of ways, messages from one's immediate subculture may be particularly salient in communicating these values. These may be transmitted through parental modeling of eating and body-related attitudes and behaviors, as well as through direct comments about weight and encouragement of weight loss. Adolescent girls perceive greater feedback from their mothers to lose weight and increase muscle tone than do boys, and this perception is greater for girls who are heavier (McCabe & Ricciardelli, 2001). Direct messages from parents encouraging their children to lose weight predict higher drive for thinness and body dissatisfaction among daughters, and appear to have a greater influence than parental modeling of dieting behaviors (Wertheim, Martin, Prior, Sanson, & Smart, 2002).

Relatedly, criticism and teasing about appearance have been associated with greater body dissatisfaction, although this may differ by gender. Boys tend to receive more messages from family and friends regarding increasing muscles and these messages decrease over time, whereas girls receive more messages regarding weight loss, and these messages increase over time (McCabe & Ricciardelli, 2005). For both adolescent boys and girls, messages from their parents and closest same-sex friend resulted in attempts to change physical size and shape.

In addition to direct pressure, lack of social support or support that is perceived as conditional on meeting appearance expectations, may promote body dissatisfaction. Indeed, deficits in social support from parents and peers predicted body dissatisfaction for both adolescent girls and boys (Bearman, Presnell, Martinez, & Stice, 2006).

Biological Factors
Body Mass and Pubertal Status

Biological factors may play a role in the development of body dissatisfaction when they deviate from culturally-sanctioned attractiveness ideals. Pubertal changes, including increased body fat, move girls farther from the thin-ideal. Increasing body mass is consistently associated with greater body dissatisfaction among girls, although dissatisfaction is not always associated with being objectively overweight, as many normal-weight females also express displeasure with their bodies (Presnell, Bearman, & Stice, 2004). Boys, however, may have a more complex relationship between body mass and body dissatisfaction. Overweight boys report lower self-esteem and greater self-consciousness than normal-weight boys, yet adolescent boys report nearly equal rates of wanting to lose versus gain weight, suggesting the optimal weight range may fall in the middle (Blyth et al., 1981). Indeed, research suggests that body dissatisfaction is greatest for boys who are over-or underweight, with those of average weight being the most satisfied with their appearance (Presnell, Bearman, & Stice, 2004). Both types of concerns have been associated with elevated body dissatisfaction among boys, although they may employ different strategies to achieve this ideal weight, including dieting to reduce body mass, or excessive exercise and steroid use to increase size and muscularity (Ricciardelli & McCabe, 2003).

Pubertal timing may also be associated with body dissatisfaction. McCabe and Ricciardelli (2004) noted that early-maturing and on-time girls reported higher levels of body dissatisfaction than girls whose pubertal development was delayed relative to peers. Again, this may be because pubertal increases in body size move girls farther from the ideal. In contrast, boys who physically matured earlier than their same-sex peers had the highest levels of body satisfaction. However, other research suggests that pubertal status may interact with other variables, such as initiating dating, to place adolescents at risk for body dissatisfaction (Cauffman & Steinberg, 1996).

Individual Risk Factors
Negative Mood
Mood disturbances have also been implicated in the development of body dissatisfaction because depressed mood induces selective attention to negative information about oneself and the world. This may result in a focus on displeasing aspects of one's body and foster negative comparisons to others. Experimental studies indicate that temporary increases in negative mood result in temporary increases in body dissatisfaction in girls, suggesting at least a short-term relation (Baker, Williamson, & Sylve, 1995). However, prospective studies have failed to demonstrate this relationship, perhaps because the experimental studies may not represent the types of mood disturbances experienced outside of the laboratory. There is some evidence that this relation may differ by gender, with boys showing a stronger relation between negative affect and body dissatisfaction than girls (Presnell et al., 2004). Additionally, negative affect also predicted body change strategies in a sample of adolescent boys (Ricciardelli & McCabe, 2003).

Dieting
Adolescents who believe that being thin will result in psychosocial benefits may turn to dieting as a means of altering their physique. Adolescent girls in particular may attempt to counter pubertal weight gain by restricting their caloric intake. However, research suggests that self-reported attempts to restrict caloric intake predict weight gain, rather than weight loss (Stice et al., 1999). Thus, dieting may increase frustration and reduce feelings of self-efficacy for producing weight change. Indeed, self-reported dieting attempts predict increases in body dissatisfaction among both girls and boys (Bearman et al., 2006). Despite the suggestion that boys may be more likely to strive to achieve bulk in the form of muscle rather than to lose weight, boys who express concern about weight loss and dieting are also more likely to express body dissatisfaction (Jones & Crawford, 2005). Additionally, boys with lower levels of body satisfaction are more likely to diet, and less likely to engage in activities that might increase muscle, such as physical activity (Neumark-Sztainer et al., 2006)

Self-reported attempts to restrict caloric intake predict weight gain, rather than weight loss.

Potential Protective Factors
Few studies have identified factors that either enhance body image or buffer the negative effects of risk factors for body dissatisfaction. To date, this work has primarily focused on positive parental relationships. Feeling supported by one's immediate social network may serve as a protective factor from the myriad pressures that are hypothesized to foster body dissatisfaction. One prospective study found that a supportive maternal relationship was associated with increased body satisfaction (Barker & Galambos, 2003). Another found that feeling close to either parent was associated with fewer concurrent weight and eating concerns among girls, but the prospective association between parental closeness and weight concerns was not significant (Swarr & Richards, 1996). Several studies have demonstrated no impact of parental relationships or acceptance on body dissatisfaction for boys (e.g. Barker & Galambos, 2003).

It will be important for future research to consider other variables that may mitigate the impact of body dissatisfaction. Theoretically, cognitive factors such as attributional style or perceived control, which have been linked to disorders such as depression and anxiety, may be associated with body dissatisfaction. Control-related beliefs play a role in the impact of life stressors on depressed mood and perceived helplessness regarding the future (Weisz, Southam-Gerow & McCarty, 2001). It is possible that individuals who have control-related beliefs regarding their weight and shape may face less risk of body dissatisfaction because they believe they are capable of changing their appearance or adapting to those displeasing aspects. Higher levels of perceived control have been shown to act as protective factors for depression among youth (Weisz, Sweeney, Proffitt, & Carr, 1993); future research should examine the role control related beliefs play in the development of body dissatisfaction, as well as other potential buffering factors that have been implicated in research of other related disorders.

Conclusions

Body dissatisfaction has been identified as one of the most potent and consistent risk factors for eating disorders, and contributes significantly to poor self-esteem and depression among adolescents. An understanding of the factors that increase the risk for body dissatisfaction can help guide prevention efforts for these outcomes. This article has highlighted internalization of socially-prescribed body ideals, body mass, media influences, and messages from parents and peers as key risk factors for the development of body dissatisfaction, whereas others have received less consistent support. Given the complexity of the development of body image concerns, interventions aimed at reducing body dissatisfaction will likely need to target multiple factors, including individual, familial, and sociocultural factors. Interventions that reduce sociocultural pressures to be thin and educate adolescents to more critically evaluate messages from the media hold promise in reducing body dissatisfaction. Unfortunately, there is relatively little research on protective factors that may aid youth in developing a positive body image. Additional research is needed to determine how best to foster greater body satisfaction or mitigate the effects of established risk factors.

References

Baker, J.D., Williamson, D.A., & Sylve, C. (1995). Body image disturbance, memory bias, and body dysphoria: Effects of negative mood induction. *Behavior Therapy, 26,* 747–759.

Barker, E.T., & Galambos, N.L. (2003). Body dissatisfaction of adolescent girls and boys: Risk and resource factors. *Journal of Early Adolescence, 23,* 141–165.

Bearman, S.K., Presnell, K., Martinez, E., & Stice, E. (2006). The skinny on body dissatisfaction: A longitudinal study of adolescent girls and boys. *Journal of Youth and Adolescence, 35,* 229–241.

Bearman, S.K., Stice, E., & Chase, A. (2003). Evaluation of an intervention targeting both depressive and bulimic pathology: A randomized prevention trial. *Behavior Therapy, 34*(3), 277–293.

Blyth, D.A., Simmons, R.G., Bulcroft, R., Felt, D., Van Cleave, E.F., & Bush, D.M. (1981). The effects of physical development in self-image and satisfaction with body image for early adolescent males. *Research in Community and Mental Health, 2,* 43–73.

Cauffman, E., & Steinberg, L. (1996). Interactive effects of menarcheal status and dating on dieting and disordered eating among adolescent girls. *Developmental Psychology, 32,* 631–635.

Grabe, S. & Hyde, J.S. (2006). Ethnicity and body dissatisfaction among women in the United States: A meta-analysis. *Psychological Bulletin, 132(4),* 622–640.

Jones, D.C. (2004). Body image among adolescent girls and boys: A longitudinal study. *Developmental Psychology, 40,* 823–835.

Jones, D.C., & Crawford, J.K. (2005). Adolescent boys and body image: Weight and muscularity concerns as dual pathways to body dissatisfaction. *Journal of Youth and Adolescence, 34(6),* 629–636.

Keel, P.K., Dorer, D.J., Franko, D.L., Jackson, S.C., & Herzog, D.B. (2005). Postremission predictors of relapse in women with eating disorders. *American Journal of Psychiatry, 162,* 2,263–2,268.

McCabe, M.P., & Ricciardelli, L.A. (2001). Parent, peer, and media influences on body image and strategies to both increase and decrease body size among adolescent boys and girls. *Adolescence, 36,* 225–240.

McCabe, M.P., & Ricciardelli, L.A. (2004). A longitudinal study of pubertal timing and extreme body change behaviors among adolescent boys and girls. Adolescence, 39, 145–166.

McCabe, M.P., & Ricciardelli, L.A., (2005). A prospective study of pressures from parents, peers, and the media on extreme weight change behaviors among adolescent boys and girls. *Behaviour Research and Therapy, 43,* 653–668.

Neumark-Sztainer, D., Paxton, S.J., Hannan, P.J., Haines, J., & Story, M. (2006). Does body satisfaction matter? Five-year longitudinal associations between body satisfaction and health behaviors in adolescent females and males. *Journal of Adolescent Health, 39,* 244–251.

Neumark-Sztainer, D., Story, M., Falkner, N.H., Beuhring, T., & Resnick, M.D. (1999). Sociodemographic and personal characteristics of adolescents engaged in weight loss and weight/muscle gain behaviors: Who is doing what? *Preventive Medicine, 28,* 40–50.

Neumark-Sztainer, D., Story, M., Hannan, P.J., Perry, C.L., & Irving, L.M. (2002). Weight-related concerns and behaviors among overweight and nonoverweight adolescents: Implications for preventing weight-related disorders. *Archives of Pediatric Adolescent Medicine, 156,* 171–178.

Paxton, S.J., Neumark-Sztainer, D., Hannan, P.J., & Eisenberg, M.E. (2006). Body dissatisfaction prospectively predicts depressive mood and low self-esteem in adolescent girls and boys. *Journal of Clinical Child and Adolescent Psychology, 35,* 539–549.

Perez, M., & Joiner, T.E. (2003). Body image dissatisfaction and disordered eating in black and white women. *International Journal of Eating Disorders, 33,* 342–350.

Presnell, K., Bearman, S.K., & Stice, E. (2004). Risk factors for body dissatisfaction in adolescent boys and girls: A prospective study. *International Journal of Eating Disorders, 36,* 389–401.

Ricciardelli, L.A., & McCabe, M.P. (2001). Dietary restraint and negative affect as mediators of body dissatisfaction and bulimic behavior in adolescent girls and boys. *Behaviour Research and Therapy, 39,* 1,317–1,328.

Ricciardelli, L.A., & McCabe, M.P. (2003). Sociocultural influences on body image and body changes among adolescent boys and girls. *Journal of Social Psychology, 143,* 5–26.

Roberts, A., Cash, T.F., Feingold, A., & Johnson, B.T. (2006). Are black-white differences in females' body dissatisfaction decreasing? A meta-analytic review. *Journal of Consulting and Clinical Psychology, 74,* 1,121–1,131.

Rodin, J., Silberstein, L., & Striegel-Moore, R. (1985). Women and Weight: A Normative Discontent. Nebraska Symposium on Motivation, Lincoln, Nebraska: University of Nebraska Press, 267–307.

Shroff, H., & Thompson, J.K. (2006). The tripartite influence model of body image and eating disturbance: A replication with adolescent girls. *Body Image, 3,* 17–23.

Siegel, J.M. (2002). Body image change and adolescent depressive symptoms. *Journal of Adolescent Research, 17,* 27–41.

Stice, E., Cameron, R.P., Killen, J.D., & Taylor, C.B. (1999). Naturalistic weight-reduction efforts prospectively predict growth in relative weight and onset of obesity among female adolescents. *Journal of Consulting & Clinical Psychology, 67,* 967–974.

Stice, E., & Shaw, H.E. (1994). Adverse effects of the media portrayed thin-ideal on women and linkages to bulimic symptomatology. *Journal of Social and Clinical Psychology, 13,* 288–308.

Stice, E., & Shaw, H.E. (2002). Role of body dissatisfaction in the onset and maintenance of eating pathology: A synthesis of research findings. *Journal of Psychosomatic Research, 53,* 985–993.

Swarr, A.E., & Richards, M.H. (1996). Longitudinal effects of adolescent girls' pubertal development, perceptions of pubertal timing, and parental relations on eating problems. *Developmental Psychology, 32,* 636–646.

Thompson, J.K., Heinberg, L.J., Altabe, M., & Tantleff-Dunn, S. (1999) *Exacting Beauty: Theory, Assessment, and Treatment of Body Image Disturbance.* Washington, D.C.: American Psychological Association.

Weisz, J.R., Sweeney, L., Proffitt, V., & Carr, T. (1993). Control-related beliefs and self-reported depressive symptoms in late childhood. *Journal of Abnormal Psychology, 102,* 411–418.

Weisz, J., Southam-Gerow, M.A., & McCarty, C.A. (2001). Control-related beliefs and depressive symptoms in clinic-referred children and adolescents: Developmental differences and model specificity. *Journal of Abnormal Psychology, 110,* 97–109.

Wertheim, E.H., Martin, G., Prior, M., Sanson, A., & Smart, D. (2002). Parent influences in the transmission of eating and weight-related values and behaviors. *Eating Disorders, 10,* 321–334.

KATHERINE RESNELL, PHD, is an Assistant Professor in the Department of Psychology at Southern Methodist University (SMU) and Director of the Weight and Eating Disorders Research Program at SMU. Her research focuses on understanding sociocultural, psychological, and behavioral risk factors that contribute to eating disorders and obesity, as well as developing effective prevention interventions for these disorders. **SARAH KATE BEARMAN, PHD,** is a postdoctoral fellow at the Judge Baker Children's Center, Harvard Medical School. Her research interests include the etiology and prevention of youth depression and body image concerns, as well as the effectiveness of evidence-based interventions for children in real-world settings. **MARY CLARE MADELEY, BA,** is a graduate student in the Department of Psychology at Southern Methodist University. Her research interests focus on risk factors for eating disorders.

From *The Prevention Researcher,* September 2007, pp. 3–6. Copyright © 2007 by Integrated Research Services, Inc. Reprinted by permission.

Goodbye to Girlhood

As pop culture targets ever younger girls, psychologists worry about a premature focus on sex and appearance.

STACY WEINER

Ten-year-old girls can slide their low-cut jeans over "eye-candy" panties. French maid costumes, garter belt included, are available in preteen sizes. Barbie now comes in a "bling-bling" style, replete with halter top and go-go boots. And it's not unusual for girls under 12 to sing, "Don't cha wish your girlfriend was hot like me?"

American girls, say experts, are increasingly being fed a cultural catnip of products and images that promote looking and acting sexy.

"Throughout U.S. culture, and particularly in mainstream media, women and girls are depicted in a sexualizing manner," declares the American Psychological Association's Task Force on the Sexualization of Girls, in a report issued Monday. The report authors, who reviewed dozens of studies, say such images are found in virtually every medium, from TV shows to magazines and from music videos to the Internet.

While little research to date has documented the effect of sexualized images specifically on *young* girls, the APA authors argue it is reasonable to infer harm similar to that shown for those 18 and older; for them, sexualization has been linked to "three of the most common mental health problems of girls and women: eating disorders, low self-esteem and depression."

Said report contributor and psychologist Sharon Lamb: "I don't think because we don't have the research yet on the younger girls that we can ignore that [sexualization is] of harm to them. Common sense would say that, and part of the reason we wrote the report is so we can get funding to prove that."

Boys, too, face sexualization, the authors acknowledge. Pubescent-looking males have posed provocatively in Calvin Klein ads, for example, and boys with impossibly sculpted abs hawk teen fashion lines. But the authors say they focused on girls because females are objectified more often. According to a 1997 study in the journal Sexual Abuse, 85 percent of ads that sexualized children depicted girls.

Even influences that are less explicitly erotic often tell girls who they are equals how they look and that beauty commands power and attention, contends Lamb, co-author of "Packaging Girlhood: Rescuing Our Daughters from Marketers' Schemes" (St. Martin's, 2006). One indicator that these influences are reaching girls earlier, she and others say: The average age for adoring the impossibly proportioned Barbie has slid from preteen to preschool.

When do little girls start wanting to look good for others? "A few years ago, it was 6 or 7," says Deborah Roffman, a Baltimore-based sex educator. "I think it begins by 4 now."

While some might argue that today's belly-baring tops are no more risque than hip huggers were in the '70s, Roffman disagrees. "Kids have always emulated adult things," she says. "But [years ago] it was, 'That's who I'm supposed to be as an adult.' It's very different today. The message to children is, 'You're already like an adult. It's okay for you to be interested in sex. It's okay for you to dress and act sexy, right now.' That's an entirely different frame of reference."

It's not just kids' exposure to sexuality that worries some experts; it's the kind of sexuality they're seeing. "The issue is that the way marketers and media present sexuality is in a very narrow way," says Lamb. "Being a sexual person isn't about being a pole dancer," she chides. "This is a sort of sex education girls are getting, and it's a misleading one."

Clothes Encounters

Liz Guay says she has trouble finding clothes she considers appropriate for her daughter Tanya, age 8. Often, they're too body-hugging. Or too low-cut. Or too short. Or too spangly.

Then there are the shoes: Guay says last time she visited six stores before finding a practical, basic flat. And don't get her started on earrings.

"Tanya would love to wear dangly earrings. She sees them on TV, she sees other girls at school wearing them, she sees them in the stores all the time. . . . I just say, 'You're too young.'"

"It's not so much a feminist thing," explains Guay, a Gaithersburg medical transcriptionist. "It's more that I want her to be comfortable with who she is and to make decisions based on what's right for her, not what everybody else is doing. I want her to develop the strength that when she gets to a point where kids are offering her alcohol or drugs, that she's got enough self-esteem to say, 'I don't want that.'"

Some stats back up Guay's sense of fashion's shrinking modesty. For example, in 2003, tweens—that highly coveted marketing segment ranging from 7 to 12—spent $1.6 million on thong underwear, Time magazine reported. But even more-innocent-seeming togs, toys and activities—like tiny "Beauty Queen" T-shirts, Hello Kitty press-on nails or preteen make-overs at Club Libby Lu—can be problematic, claim psychologists. The reason: They may lure young girls into an unhealthy focus on appearance.

Studies suggest that female college students distracted by concerns about their appearance score less well on tests than do others. Plus, some experts say, "looking good" is almost culturally inseparable for girls from looking sexy: Once a girl's bought in, she's hopped onto a consumer conveyor belt in which marketers move females from pastel tiaras to hot-pink push-up bras.

Where did this girly-girl consumerism start? Diane Levin, an education professor at Wheelock College in Boston who is writing an upcoming book, "So Sexy So Soon," traces much of it to the deregulation of children's television in the mid-1980s. With the rules loosened, kids' shows suddenly could feature characters who moonlighted as products (think Power Rangers, Care Bears, My Little Pony). "There became a real awareness," says Levin, "of how to use gender and appearance and, increasingly, sex to market to children."

Kids are more vulnerable than adults to such messages, she argues.

The APA report echoes Levin's concern. It points to a 2004 study of adolescent girls in rural Fiji, linking their budding concerns about body image and weight control to the introduction of television there.

In the United States, TV's influence is incontestable. According to the Kaiser Family Foundation, for example, nearly half of American kids age 4 to 6 have a TV in their bedroom. Nearly a quarter of teens say televised sexual content affects their own behavior.

And that content is growing: In 2005, 77 percent of prime-time shows on the major broadcast networks included sexual material, according to Kaiser, up from 67 percent in 1998. In a separate Kaiser study of shows popular with teenage girls, women and girls were twice as likely as men and boys to have their appearance discussed. They also were three times more likely to appear in sleepwear or underwear than their male counterparts.

Preteen Preening

It can be tough for a parent to stanch the flood of media influences.

Ellen Goldstein calls her daughter Maya, a Rockville fifth-grader, a teen-mag maniac. "She has a year's worth" of Girls' Life magazine, says Goldstein. "When her friends come over, they pore over this magazine." What's Maya reading? There's "Get Gorgeous Skin by Tonight," "Crush Confidential: Seal the Deal with the Guy You Dig," and one of her mom's least faves: "Get a Fierce Body Fast."

"Why do you want to tell a kid to get a fierce body fast when they're 10? They're just developing," complains Goldstein. She

also bemoans the magazines' photos, which Maya has plastered on her ceiling.

"These are very glamorous-looking teenagers. They're wearing lots of makeup. They all have very glossy lips," she says. "They're generally wearing very slinky outfits. . . . I don't think those are the best role models," Goldstein says. "When so much emphasis is placed on the outside, it minimizes the importance of the person inside."

So why not just say no?

"She loves fashion," explains Goldstein. "I don't want to take away her joy from these magazines. It enhances her creative spirit. [Fashion] comes naturally to her. I want her to feel good about that. We just have to find a balance."

Experts say her concern is warranted. Pre-adolescents' propensity to try on different identities can make them particularly susceptible to media messages, notes the APA report. And for some girls, thinking about how one's body stacks up can be a real downer.

In a 2002 study, for example, seventh-grade girls who viewed idealized magazine images of women reported a drop in body satisfaction and a rise in depression.

Such results are disturbing, say observers, since eating disorders seem to strike younger today. A decade ago, new eating disorder patients at Children's National Medical Center tended to be around age 15, says Adelaide Robb, director of inpatient psychiatry. Today kids come in as young as 5 or 6.

Mirror Images

Not everyone is convinced of the uglier side of beauty messages.

Eight-year-old Maya Williams owns four bracelets, eight necklaces, about 20 pairs of earrings and six rings, an assortment of which she sprinkles on every day. "Sometimes, she'll stand in front of the mirror and ask, "Are these pretty, Mommy?""

Her mom, Gaithersburg tutor Leah Haworth, is fine with Maya's budding interest in beauty. In fact, when Maya "wasn't sure" about getting her ears pierced, says Haworth,"I talked her into it by showing her all the pretty earrings she could wear."

What about all these sexualization allegations? "I don't equate looking good with attracting the opposite sex," Haworth says. Besides, "Maya knows her worth is based on her personality. She knows we love her for who she is."

"Looking good just shows that you care about yourself, care about how you present yourself to the world. People are judged by their appearance. People get better service and are treated better when they look better. That's just the way it is," she says. "I think discouraging children from paying attention to their appearance does them a disservice."

Magazine editor Karen Bokram also adheres to the beauty school of thought. "Research has shown that having skin issues at [her readers'] age is traumatic for girls' self-esteem," says Bokram, founder of Girls' Life. "Do we think girls need to be gorgeous in order to be worthy? No. Do we think girls' feeling good about how they look has positive effects in other areas of their lives, meaning that they make positive choices academically, socially and in romantic relationships? Absolutely."

Some skeptics of the sexualization notion also argue that kids today are hardier and savvier than critics think. Isaac Larian, whose company makes the large-eyed, pouty-lipped Bratz dolls, says, "Kids are very smart and know right from wrong." What's more, his testing indicates that girls want Bratz "because they are fun, beautiful and inspirational," he wrote in an e-mail. "Not once have we ever heard one of our consumers call Bratz 'sexy.'" Some adults "have a twisted sense of what they see in the product," Larian says.

"It is the parents' responsibility to educate their children," he adds. "If you don't like something, don't buy it."

But Genevieve McGahey, 16, isn't buying marketers' messages. The National Cathedral School junior recalls that her first real focus on appearance began in fourth grade. That's when classmates taught her: To be cool, you needed ribbons. To be cool, you needed lip gloss.

Starting around sixth grade, though, "it took on a more sinister character," she says. "People would start wearing really short skirts and lower tops and putting on more makeup. There's a strong pressure to grow up at this point."

"It's a little scary being a young girl," McGahey says. "The image of sexuality has been a lot more trumpeted in this era. . . . If you're not interested in [sexuality] in middle school, it seems a little intimidating." And unrealistic body ideals pile on extra pressure, McGahey says. At a time when their bodies and their body images are still developing, "girls are not really seeing people [in the media] who are beautiful but aren't stick-thin," she notes. "That really has an effect."

Today, though, McGahey feels good about her body and her style.

For this, she credits her mom, who is "very secure with herself and with being smart and being a woman." She also points to a wellness course at school that made her conscious of how women were depicted. "Seeing a culture of degrading women really influenced me to look at things in a new way and to think how we as high school girls react to that," she says.

"A lot of girls still hold onto that media ideal. I think I've gotten past it. As I've gotten more comfortable with myself and my body, I'm happy not to be trashy," McGahey says. "But most girls are still not completely or even semi-comfortable with themselves physically. You definitely still feel the pressure of those images."

STACY WEINER writes frequently for Health about families and relationships. Comments: health@washpost.com.

Influence of Music on Youth Behaviors

Young people who listen to hip hop and rap may be more likely to engage in substance abuse and aggression than those who listen to other types of music, such as country and western or the top 40. According to a new study funded by the National Institute of Alcohol Abuse and Alcoholism, frequent exposure to music that contains references to violence and substance use is significantly associated with illicit-drug use, problems with alcohol and aggressive behaviors in young people. A positive association was also found between listeners of reggae or techno and alcohol and illicit drug use.

The study raises questions about current marketing techniques using popular rap and hip hop artists to deliver key advertising messages that promote alcoholic beverages. According to a press release issued by the Pacific Institute for Research and Evaluation (PIRE), MengJinn Chen, Ph.D., the study's lead investigator and research scientist at PIRE, stated that "People should be concerned about rap and hip hop being used to market alcoholic beverages, given the alcohol, drug and aggression problems among listeners." This is particularly true, he says, considering the popularity of hip hop and rap with young people today.

Chen and his team suggest that the messages contained in rap and hip hop might also reflect the listening preferences of youngsters who are already predisposed to such behaviors, which reinforces their positive attitudes towards substance use and violence.

The study was carried out using self-administered questionnaires from 1,056 students, ages 15 to 25 years (mean age 18.9; 86% younger than 21 years; 57% female; 62% non-white) attending a California community college. The students received a $20 incentive for participating in the study.

Respondents were asked to indicate their frequency of involvement in (a) *music listening* based on a list of 15 categories of music; (b) *alcohol use and alcohol-use disorder* measured by the Alcohol Use Disorders Identification Test (AUDIT; Babor et al., 2001); (c) *illicit drug use* of marijuana and of club drugs (i.e., methylenedioxymethamphetine [MDMA], gamma hydroxybutyrate [GHB], ketamine; amphetamines and methamphetamines [e.g., crystal, ice, speed]; and hallucinogens (e.g., lysergic acid diethylamide [LSD], mushrooms, and phencyclidine [PCP]); (d) *aggressive behaviors* (e.g., engaging in a fist fight or gang fight, starting a fist fight or shoving match, threatening someone with a gun or knife, and attacking with intent to seriously injure); (e) *sensation seeking* using the Zuckerman-Kahlman Personality Questionnaire (e.g., degree of preference for going to wild parties, doing "crazy" things for fun, doing scary things,

watching sexy movies and acting impulsively). *Demographic variables* included respondents' age, gender, race/ethnicity, school enrollment status, employment and parents' level of education.

Nearly all of the respondents (94%) reported listening to music "daily or almost daily," with rap music the most popular type of music in this sample. The investigators found that the frequency of any alcohol use was positively and significantly associated with frequent listening to heavy metal, alternative music, punk, rap, R&B, reggae, rock and techno, but negatively and significantly associated with world music.

Compared with other music genres, rap music was consistently and positively associated with use of alcohol, malt-liquor, potential alcohol-use disorder, marijuana, club drugs, and aggressive behaviors after controlling for demographic variables, listening to other types of music and sensation seeking.

Compared with other music genres, rap music was consistently and positively associated with use of alcohol, malt-liquor, potential alcohol-use disorder, marijuana, club drugs, and aggressive behaviors.

Some genres of music were negatively associated with substance use and aggressive behavior. Listening to world music was negatively associated with less alcohol and marijuana use, country and western music associated with less club-drug use, and rock music associated with fewer aggressive behaviors. However, the investigators caution that the negative associations were less consistent than the positive associations and that the type of music consistently related to lower risk (world music) was only "often" listened to by one tenth of the study sample. It would be premature, therefore, to suggest that listening to certain types of music is related to fewer behavior problems among youth.

The lowest levels of alcohol and marijuana were reported by Asian-American students compared with the other ethnic groups, also taking into account other variables. Although Asian students were more likely to listen to techno music than whites and Latinos (42% compared with 24% white students and 36% Latinos), they were just as likely to listen to rap music (65% compared with 64% whites and 70% Latinos) but apparently were not as much at risk for substance use. The researchers suggest that "future studies should examine whether factors that are protective of

Asian Americans regarding substance use also help lessen the connections between substance use and music preference."

While levels of substance use reported by black students were similar to those of students in other non-Asian racial/ethnic groups, the black students reported significantly more aggressive behavior, taking into account other control variables. The investigators indicate that previous studies (e.g., Barongan et al., 1995; Johnson et al., 1995; Wester et al., 1997) report that "aggression expressed in gangsta rap is violence against women, particularly black women," although this was not measured in the present study.

One of the study limitations is that the respondents were not asked to report the amount of time they spent listening to different types of music, the degree of attention they paid to the lyrics, and to prioritize their music preferences. Because the respondents listened to more than one genre of music, it was not possible to make a clear estimate of the differential influences on behaviors, say the researchers. The findings are also limited by the fact that the sample may not be representative of all community-college students, and that a large proportion of the sample was nonwhite.

"While we don't fully understand the relationship between music preferences and behavioral outcomes," says MengJinn, "our study shows that young people may be influenced by frequent exposure to music lyrics that make positive references to substance use and violence."

Researchers Examine the Impact of Early Experience on Development

L. ALAN SROUFE, PHD

Theory and clinical wisdom have suggested a special place in development for early experience and for representations of self and others that derive from that experience. Yet many researchers have argued that such propositions are without scientific evidence.

Oftentimes, measures from the early years have not yielded much power in predicting later functioning, and when cross-time linkages have been reported, critics have quickly pointed to the need to rule out plausible alternative hypotheses.

Until now, definitive statements about a special role for early experience in normal and disturbed development have been difficult to make.

To demonstrate a special place for early experience numerous issues must be resolved. For example, what if early experience is simply often a harbinger of later experience? Could it not be then that early experience only indirectly leads to later problems, with the more explicit cause lying in later experience? Or perhaps some correlate of early experience, such as parental pathology or level of poverty, is responsible for any observed relationship to outcome. Or maybe characteristics of the child, such as an irritable temperament, are responsible for both the quality of care and any later negative outcome, with the link between care and outcome again being fortuitous. These are the arguments critics have made.

Clearly, what is needed, and what we have been conducting for the last 30 years, is a comprehensive, detailed study of individual development, beginning before birth and examining early experience along with all pertinent factors in the developmental landscape, age by age.

We have reported our findings in a recent book (*The Development of the Person: The Minnesota Study of Risk and Adaptation from Birth to Adulthood;* Guilford Press, 2005). Here, some key findings and implications will be briefly reviewed. I will speak not just to the question of whether early experience is significant, but also to what our data say about how and why this is so; that is, the nature of the developmental process.

Key Findings

We did indeed find that, even in competition with a host of other factors, nothing is more important than vital aspects of the child's early experience for predicting disturbance or healthy functioning.

Especially salient is the reliability and responsiveness of care provided by parent figures (including measures of the quality of attachment and child maltreatment).

Measures of responsive care, cumulated across the first 3 years, predicted dropping out of high school with 77% accuracy, a substantially better prediction than that from either child or parent IQ.

Maltreatment and disorganized attachment in the first years predicted dissociation and other psychopathological symptoms in late adolescence, with correlations in the 0.40s. These predictions were dramatically stronger than those based on measures of child temperament any time in the first 3 years. In general, a variety of disorders, from anxiety and depression, to conduct problems and ADHD were found to be developmental constructions, rooted in experience.

Security of attachment in infancy predicted social competence and quality of social relationships age by age, from pre-school to adulthood, and it did so with later quality of parental care statistically controlled.

Rather than competing with other developmental forces, early experience works with them in leading to outcomes. Predictions were improved when early and later experience was considered together. The more years of experience cumulated, the more the child became an active force in his or her own development, and the more stable was the adaptation. Moreover, not just experience with parents, but experience with peers also proved important.

For some, outcomes experience with peers proved especially important; for other outcomes experience with parents clearly dominated. But for most outcomes, both parents and peers played a role, often with parental experiences laying a foundation for successful peer relationships which then promoted later competence. Finally, predictions were strengthened even more when the surrounding context of stresses and supports also was considered.

Early history is not destiny, important as it is.

Change in functioning, as well as stability, was lawful. Early history is not destiny, important as it is. As parental stress, support or depression clearly increased or decreased, child functioning improved or worsened. Such findings preclude the tendency to simply blame parents when development goes awry. They also, in part, counter simple genetic explanations for problems, because, for example, any genetic vulnerability is held constant as parent depression waxes and wanes.

The Process of Development

Our findings on adaptation over time and on continuity and change in development lead to a new view of resiliency. Some children function well in the face of adversity, and some children show improved functioning after a sustained period of problems. Both such groups of children may be described as "resilient." However, our prospective longitudinal data show that such resilience is best characterized in terms of developmental processes.

Resilience, like psychopathology, is a developmental construction. Most notably, we found that children showing this capacity to rebound were dramatically more likely to have had an early secure attachment relationship; that is, their capacity to respond well to adversity was built upon an early positive foundation. When positive early history and current available supports were considered together, virtually all resilience was accounted for.

More generally, our body of results showed that even following change, early experience and prior adaptation are not erased. They remain part of the developmental landscape. Negative patterns may be reactivated, especially in times of stress or special vulnerability, and positive patterns may be reactivated when a period of challenge passes or new supports are available.

Just as research on deprived rhesus monkeys showed that even those who had apparently been thoroughly rehabilitated nonetheless reverted to infant stereotypic behavior when placed in test cages (Novak et al., 1992), our research showed that children may revert to maladaptive patterns or take advantage of new opportunities, following periods of apparently stable change.

Finally, we were able to confirm that representations are the carriers of experience. By measuring representations of self and relationships in multiple ways across ages (stories, play, drawings, projectives, interview procedures), we were able to show that they mediated ties between early experience and later functioning. Moreover, we demonstrated a reciprocal relation between representation and experience.

Representations, based on prior experience, framed interactions with the environment and thus impacted subsequent experience. At the same time, fundamental changes in experience altered prior representations. Complex statistical models showed that such an ongoing interaction was required to account for continuity and change in behavior.

Clinical Implications

There are numerous clinical implications of these findings that we lay out in the final chapters of our book. We list some of the key ones here.

First, our data suggest a renewed focus on the lived experience of the child, which recently has been relatively ignored during the current preoccupation with inherent biological variations.

Our data suggest a renewed focus on the lived experience of the child, which recently has been relatively ignored during the current preoccupation with inherent biological variations.

Broad-based early intervention, with an emphasis on supports for families is indicated. Repeatedly, we have found that as parental support increases and parental stress decreases, child behavior and emotional problems subside.

Work at multiple levels, including surrounding supports, social relationships, child behavior, and inner representations would seem most fruitful.

Such work often may require considerable time. It is unrealistic to think that brief interventions can alter long-established patterns of adaptation or firmly established inner models of self, other and relationships. New, vital relationship experiences likely will be required.

References

Novak M, O'Neill P, Beckley S, Suomi S: Naturalistic environments for captive primates. In E. Gibbons, E. Wyers, & E. Waters (Eds.), *Naturalistic habitats in captivity* (pp. 236–258). New York: Academic Press, 1992. Sroufe LA, Egeland B, Carlson E, Collins WA: *The development of the person: The Minnesota study of risk and adaptation from birth to adulthood.* New York: Guilford Press, 2005.

L. ALAN SROUFE is a Professor at the Institute of Child Development, University of Minnesota.

Adolescent Stress

The Relationship between Stress and Mental Health Problems

KATHRYN E. GRANT, PHD, ET AL.

Although exposure to some negative events is considered a normal part of development, stressful life experiences can threaten the well-being and healthy development of children and adolescents. Adolescents, in particular, are exposed to high rates of stressful life experiences (e.g., romantic break-ups, community violence, date rape), and there is some evidence that increases in stressors account, at least in part, for the increased rates of psychological problems adolescents experience (e.g., depression, conduct disorder, substance abuse) (Arnett, 1999).

This article will summarize recent research on the relation between stressful life experiences and mental health problems in adolescents. It will provide a definition of stress, present a conceptual model of the ways in which stressors affect adolescent mental health, and summarize research that has tested each of the basic tenets of the conceptual model. To clarify theory and research findings, illustrations based on the authors' own research with adolescents living in urban poverty will be provided.

Defining Stress

Few constructs in mental health have been as important, yet as difficult to define, as the concept of stress. The common theme across all prevailing definitions of stress is a focus on environmental events or conditions that threaten, challenge, exceed, or harm the psychological or biological capacities of the individual (Cohen, Kessler, & Gordon, 1995).

In recent decades, the most widely accepted definition of stress has been the transactional definition offered by Lazarus and Folkman (1984): "Psychological stress involves a particular relationship between the person and the environment that is *appraised* by the person as taxing or exceeding his or her resources and endangering his or her well being" (p. 19, emphasis added).

Recently, however, researchers have begun to question the appropriateness of a definition that relies on cognitive appraisals for children and adolescents. Results of research on stress during infancy indicate there are clear negative effects of maternal separation, abuse, and neglect on infants (Field, 1995). These negative effects occur, presumably, without the cognitive appraisal component that is central to the transactional definition. In addition, preliminary research indicates that cognitive appraisal processes that play a significant role later in development do not play the same role among younger children exposed to stressors (e.g., Turner & Cole, 1994). During adolescence, the brain continues to develop, and it is not clear when or to what extent cognitive appraisals influence the effects of stress.

Also, in recent years, theoretical models of the ways in which stressful experiences lead to mental health problems in adolescents have become more sophisticated, and there is greater emphasis on processes that influence or explain the relation between stressors and mental health problems (Cicchetti & Cohen, 1995). A model of stress that "lumps" potential intervening processes (i.e., processes that influence or explain the association between stressors and mental health problems), such as cognitive appraisal, in with stressors is conceptually unclear and poses problems for examining each of these factors individually (Reiss & Oliveri, 1991). To fully understand how stressful experiences and intervening processes relate to one another in the prediction of mental health problems, it is important to define and measure each of these variables, explicitly. This is particularly true in adolescent research, as the role of specific intervening processes is likely to shift across development.

Stressful life experiences can threaten the well-being and healthy development of children and adolescents.

For these reasons, we have proposed that stress be defined as *environmental events or chronic conditions that objectively threaten the physical and/or psychological health or well-being of individuals of a particular age in a particular society* (Grant,

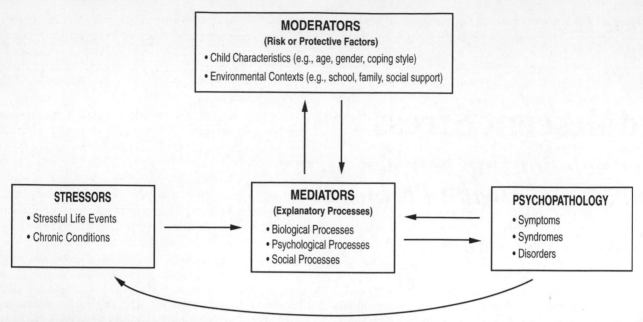

Figure 1 General conceptual model of the role of stressors in the development of mental health problems in adolescents.

Compas, Stuhlmacher, et al., 2003). Such a definition is consistent with traditional "stimulus-based" definitions of stress (Holmes & Rahe, 1967) and more recent definitions of "stressors" (Rice, 1999) and "objective stress" (Brown & Harris, 1989).

Relationship between Stress and Mental Health Problems

We (Grant et al., 2003) have proposed a general conceptual model of the role of stressors in the development of mental health problems for adolescents. This model builds on previously proposed specific models of psychopathology (e.g., Albano, Chorpita, & Barlow, 2001; Hammen & Rudolph, 2001) and includes five central hypotheses: 1) stressors lead to psychopathology; 2) moderators influence the relation between stressors and psychopathology; 3) mediators explain the relation between stressors and psychopathology; 4) there is specificity in the relations among particular stressors, moderators, mediators, and types of psychopathology; and 5) relations among stressors, moderators, mediators, and psychopathology are reciprocal and dynamic (See Figure 1). Each of these central hypotheses are described in detail below.

Stressors Lead to Psychopathology

The first hypothesis, that stressors lead to psychopathology, provides the conceptual basis for all studies of the relation between stressors and psychological problems in adolescents. Our recent review of longitudinal studies (Grant, Compas, et al., 2004) revealed consistent evidence that stressful life experiences predict psychological problems in adolescents over time. Likewise, there is growing evidence that youth who are exposed to high rates of stressful life experiences are at heightened risk for mental health problems.

For example, poverty sets the stage for an extraordinary number of stressful life experiences ranging from major life events (e.g., increased levels of child abuse), to chronic interpersonal stressors (e.g., marital conflict), to community violence, to the daily hassles associated with "trying to make ends meet" (Guerra et al., 1995). Extant research on psychological symptoms in low-income, urban youth has indicated that these youth are at heightened risk for a range of psychological problems including anxiety/depression, aggression, delinquency, social problems, withdrawal, and somatic complaints (Grant, Katz, et al., 2004). These findings provide further evidence of the most basic relation between stressors and psychopathology.

Influence of Moderators

The second tenet of the model is that moderators influence the relation between stressors and psychopathology. Moderators may be conceptualized as risk or protective factors, as they represent pre-existing characteristics (in existence prior to exposure to the stressor) that increase or decrease the likelihood that stressors will lead to psychopathology. Potential moderating variables include age, gender, social support, and coping styles. Moderating variables may be the result of genetic vulnerabilities (or protective factors), non-stressor environmental influences (e.g., parenting/peer influences), or, in some cases, stressful experiences. For example, exposure to severe and chronic stressors may lead to changes in the way adolescents view the world (e.g., they may develop a more pessimistic, less trusting perspective) and these changes in thinking may actually make adolescents more vulnerable to psychological symptoms when they are exposed to future stress (Grant et al., 2003).

Our recent review of the literature on moderators of the association between stressors and psychological problems in young people revealed few consistent findings (Grant, Compas, et al., 2005). One possible reason for the lack of consistency is that researchers have not focused on a particular risk or protective factor and examined it systematically across a number of studies. Unfortunately, this means that we know very little about factors that can break the connection between stressors and mental health problems in young people. Some individual studies have found evidence of particular protective effects and there is mounting evidence that having a cluster of protective factors is most beneficial (Beam, Gil-Rivas, Greenberger, & Chen, 2002; Meschke & Patterson, 2003). There is also some disconcerting evidence that youth exposed to the most pervasive and severe stressors (e.g., low-income urban youth of color) may be least likely to benefit from any particular protective factor (Gerard & Buehler, 2004; Luthar, 1991; Seidman, Lambert, Allen, & Aber, 2003). For example, in our own work with low-income urban youth, we have found preliminary evidence that youth who rely on particular individually-based coping strategies without broader supports may actually do more poorly over time than youth who report they don't have any protective factors at all (Grant, 2005).

Mediators

Although some factors may serve either a moderating or mediating function (e.g., cognitive attributions, coping), mediators are conceptually distinct from moderators in that they are "activated" or "caused by" the current stressful experience and serve to, conceptually and statistically, account for the relation between stressors and psychopathology (Baron & Kenny, 1986). Whereas moderators are characteristics of the child or his/her social network prior to the stressor, mediators become characteristics of the child or his/her social network in response to the stressor. Mediators may include variables such as coping styles, cognitive perceptions, and family processes (Grant et al., 2003).

Our recent review of the literature on mediators of the relation between stressors and psychological problems in young people (Grant et al., 2005) revealed that significant progress has been made in this area. The most frequently examined and empirically supported conceptual model has been one in which negative parenting mediates the relation between poverty (or economic stressors) and adolescent psychopathology (Grant et al., 2005). In particular, research suggests that, as parents experience economic pressures associated with poverty, they become less nurturant and more hostile toward their children, which leads to adolescent psychological problems (Conger, 2001). In our own work with low-income urban youth, we have seen evidence of similar patterns (Grant, McCormick, et al., in press).

Specificity

The fourth hypothesis is that there is specificity in relations among particular stressors, moderators, mediators, and psychological outcomes. According to this proposition, a particular type of stressor (e.g., urban poverty) is linked with a particular type of psychological problem (e.g., somatic complaints)

through a particular mediator (e.g., a belief that expressions of anxiety or depression will make one look weak and leave one more vulnerable to victimization by others) in the context of a particular moderator (e.g., being a female adolescent). Analysis of full specificity models such as this one have yet to be reported in the literature.

There have been a large number of studies testing for specificity between particular stressors and particular psychological outcomes in young people, but these studies have yielded inconsistent results (McMahon et al., 2003). Nonetheless, some individual studies have found interesting evidence of specificity. For example, in our own work, we have found that particular types of psychological symptoms appear to be particularly common in the context of urban poverty. Somatic complaints is the internalizing symptom most frequently reported in our sample (Grant, Katz, et al., 2004). We have speculated that somatic complaints may be especially adaptive in a hostile urban environment. More stereotypically internalizing symptoms, such as anxiety or depression, may leave adolescents more vulnerable to victimization, but somatic complaints (like a stomach ache or headache) may allow them to avoid dangerous situations while still "saving face." Somatic complaints may also allow low-income urban youth to garner the most possible support from a network that may already be taxed with stressors of its own (Grant, Katz, et al., 2004).

Relations Are Reciprocal & Dynamic

The final hypothesis that relations among stressors, moderators, mediators, and psychopathology are reciprocal and dynamic broadly encompasses the following specific hypotheses: 1) each variable in the model influences the other (with some exceptions, for example, fixed moderators such as age will not be influenced by other variables); 2) the role of specific variables within the model may vary across specific stressors and shift over time (e.g., a mediator that developed in response to a particular stressor may become a fixed pattern of responding and, thus, interact as a moderator with subsequent stressors); 3) reciprocal and dynamic relations among stressors, moderators, and mediators will predict not only the onset of psychological problems, but also the exacerbation of symptoms and the movement along a continuum from low-level symptoms to the development of a clinically diagnosable disorder.

Of the basic tenets of our proposed conceptual model, this last hypothesis has received the least research attention. That is notable given that examination of this hypothesis, in particular, is essential for understanding the ways in which stressors influence adolescents, as it addresses the shifting nature of relations among variables across development. So far, the only consistent evidence for this proposition is that a number of studies have found that stressors not only predict psychological symptoms, but symptoms, in turn, predict exposure to additional stressful experiences (Grant, Compas, et al., 2004). In our own work with urban youth, we too have found evidence that psychological symptoms place youth at greater risk for exposure to additional stressors over time (Grant, Thomas, et al., 2005). This finding suggests that some youth are caught in a vicious cycle. Exposure to heightened rates of stressors places them at heightened risk for psychological symptoms, which, in turn, place them at risk for exposure to even more stressors, which place them at heightened risk for even more psychological distress (Grant, Thomas, et al., 2005).

Summary and Implications for Prevention

Recent research in the area of stressors and mental health problems in adolescents has led to the following conclusions:

1. Stress should be defined as *environmental events or chronic conditions that objectively threaten the physical and/or psychological health or well-being of individuals of a particular age in a particular society.*
2. There is strong evidence that stressful life experiences are predictive of mental health problems in adolescents. Adolescents exposed to high rates of stressful life experiences are at increased risk for a range of mental health problems.
3. The relation between stressors and mental health problems is thought to be affected by moderating variables. However, there is little consistent evidence of particular moderating effects. Additional research on protective factors is especially needed.
4. There is strong evidence that mediators explain the relation between stressors and mental health problems in adolescents. For example, the effects of poverty on adolescent mental health appear to be mediated by poverty's effects on family processes.
5. The relations among stressful life experiences, moderating and mediating processes, and psychopathology are thought to be specific, such that particular types of stressors are linked with particular types of mental health problems through particular intervening processes. There has been little systematic investigation of this hypothesis; consequently, little consistent evidence has been found for full specificity models.
6. The relations among stressful life experiences, moderating and mediating processes, and psychopathology are thought to be reciprocal and dynamic. This hypothesis has received little research attention, but there is growing evidence that stressors not only predict psychopathology, but psychopathology also predicts additional exposure to stress.

Implications

Given the risks associated with stressors, efforts to reduce adolescents' exposure to stressful life events are needed. These might include efforts at the individual family level to reduce marital conflict and domestic violence or to prevent child abuse. They might also include development of programs at the school or neighborhood level designed to reduce the effects of stressors associated with poverty, such as programs that provide affordable child care and job training. Most important are advocacy efforts at the sociopolitical level to address the inequities of our society that contribute to high poverty rates and childhood exposure to community violence in economically disadvantaged urban settings.

In addition, more research is needed to understand what variables (if any) are actually capable of breaking the connection between stressful life events and mental health problems in young people. These protective factors could then be promoted through educational curricula, after-school programming, parent trainings, and other prevention efforts. Until stronger evidence is found for particular protective factors, it will be important to help young people develop protective contexts which facilitate development of a number of particular protective factors. For example, adolescents should be involved in at least one protective structure (e.g., family, school, church, after-school program), which facilitates the development of strong interpersonal relationships, which provide modeling, encouragement, and advice, which, in turn, facilitate the development of a positive value system or world view and healthy coping strategies (Grant, 2005). A constellation of protective factors, such as these, are likely to contribute to positive adolescent mental health.

References

Albano, A. M., Chorpita, B. F., & Barlow, D. H. (2001). Childhood anxiety disorders. In E. J. Mash & R. A. Barkley (Eds.), *Child Psychopathology. Second Edition.* New York, NY: Guilford Press.

Arnett, J. J. (1999). Adolescent storm and stress, reconsidered. *American Psychologist, 54,* 317–326.

Baron, R. M., & Kenny, D. A. (1986). The moderator-mediator variable distinction in social psychology research: Conceptual, strategic, and statistical considerations. *Journal of Personality and Social Psychology, 51,* 1,173–1,182.

Beam, M. R., Gil-Rivas, V., Greenberger, E., & Chen, C. (2002). Adolescent problem behavior and depressed mood: Risk and protection within and across social contexts. *Journal of Youth and Adolescence, 31,* 343–357.

Brown, G., & Harris, T. O. (1989). Depression. In G.W. Brown & T. O. Harris (Eds.), *Life Events and Illness* (pp. 49–93). New York: Guilford Press.

Cicchetti, D., & Cohen, D. (1995). Perspectives on developmental psychopathology. In D. Cicchetti, & D. Cohen, (Eds.), *Developmental Psychopathology Vol 1: Theory and Methods. Wiley Series on Personality Processes* (pp. 3–20). New York: John Wiley & Sons.

Cohen, S., Kessler, R. C., & Gordon, L. U. (1995). *Measuring Stress.* New York: Oxford University Press.

Conger, R. D. (2001). Understanding child and adolescent response to caregiver conflict: Some observations on context, process, and method. In A. Booth & A. C. Crouter (Eds.), *Couples in Conflict* (pp. 161–172). Mahwah, NJ: Lawrence Erlbaum Associates.

Field, T. (1995). Infants of depressed mothers. *Infant Behavior and Development, 18*(1), 1–13.

Gerard, J. M., & Buehler, C. (2004). Cumulative environmental risk and youth maladjustment: The role of youth attributes. *Child Development, 75,* 1,832–1,849.

Grant, K. E. (June, 2005). *Stressors and Adolescent Mental Health: Protective Factors in the Lives of Urban Youth.* Paper presented at the annual meeting of the William T. Grant Foundation Scholars' program, Jackson, WY.

Grant, K. E., Compas, B. E., Stuhlmacher, A., Thurm, A. E., McMahon, S., & Halpert, J. (2003). Stressors and child/ adolescent psychopathology: Moving from markers to mechanisms of risk. *Psychological Bulletin, 129,* 447–466.

Grant, K. E., Compas, B. E., Thurm, A.E., McMahon, S. D., & Gipson, P. Y. (2004). Stressors and child and adolescent psychopathology: Measurement issues and prospective effects. *Journal of Clinical Child and Adolescent Psychology, 33*(2), 412–425.

Grant, K. E., Compas, B. E., Thurm, A. E., McMahon, S. D., Gipson, P., Campbell, A. J., & Krochock, K. (2005). *Moderating and Mediating Processes in the Relation Between Stressors and Child/Adolescent Psychopathology. Manuscript submitted for publication.*

Grant, K. E., Katz, B. N., Thomas, K. J., O'Koon, J. H., Meza, C. M., DiPasquale, A. M., Rodríguez, V. O., & Bergen, C. (2004). Psychological symptoms affecting low-income urban youth. *Journal of Adolescent Research, 19*(6), 613–634.

Grant, K. E., McCormick, A., Poindexter, L., Simpkins, T., Janda, C. M., Thomas, K. J., Campbell, A., Carleton, R., & Taylor, J. (in press). Family and neighborhood processes in the relation between poverty and psychological symptoms in urban African American adolescents. *Journal of Adolescence.*

Grant, K. E., Thomas, K. J., Apling, G. C., Gipson, P. Y., Mance, G. A., Carleton, R. A., Ford, R. E., Taylor, J. J., & Sajous-Brady, D. L. (2005). *Stressors and Psychological Symptoms in Urban Youth: A Test of a Conceptual Model.* Manuscript submitted for publication.

Guerra, N. G., Huesmann, L. R., Tolan, P. H., Van Acker, R., & Eron, L. D. (1995). Stressful events and individual beliefs as correlates of economic disadvantage and aggression among urban children. Special Section: Prediction and prevention of child and adolescent antisocial behavior. *Journal of Consulting & Clinical Psychology, 63*(4), 518–528.

Hammen, C., & Rudolph, K. D. (2001). Childhood depression. In E. J. Mash & R. A. Barkley (Eds.), *Child Psychopathology. Second Edition* New York, NY: Guilford Press.

Holmes, T. H., & Raye, R. H. (1967). The Social Readjustment Rating Scale, *Journal of Psychosomatic Research, 11,* 213–218.

Lazarus, R. S., & Folkman, S. (1984). *Stress, Appraisal, and Coping.* New York: Springer.

Luthar, S. S. (1991). Vulnerability and resilience: A study of high-risk adolescents. *Child Development, 62,* 600–616.

McMahon, S. D., Grant, K. E., Compas, B. E., Thurm, A. E., & Ey, S. (2003). Stress and psychopathology in children and adolescents: Is there evidence of specificity? *Journal of Child Psychology and Psychiatry and Allied Disciplines: Annual Research Review, 44,* 107–133.

Meschke, L. L., & Patterson, J. M. (2003). Resilience as a theoretical basis for substance abuse prevention, *The Journal of Primary Prevention, 23,* 483–514.

Reiss, D., & Oliveri, M. (1991). The family's conception of accountability and competence: A new approach to the conceptualization and assessment of family stress. *Family Process, 30,* 193–214.

Rice, P. L. (1999). *Stress and Health.* New York: Brooks/Cole Publishing Company.

Seidman, E., Lambert, L. E., Allen, L., & Aber, J. L. (2003). Urban adolescents' transition to junior high school and protective family transactions. *Journal of Early Adolescence, 23,* 166–193.

Turner, Jr., J. E., & Cole, D. A. (1994). Developmental differences in cognitive diatheses for child depression. *Journal of Abnormal Child Psychology, 22,* 15–32.

KATHRYN E. GRANT, PHD, is a licensed Clinical Psychologist, Associate Professor, and Director of Clinical Training at DePaul University. She and her research team are currently conducting a longitudinal study of stress and its effects on urban adolescents. Steven Behling, BS, is a doctoral student at DePaul University. His research interests include prevention of family violence and child maltreatment. Polly Y. Gipson, MA, is a doctoral student at DePaul University. She recently completed her thesis on stress and anxiety in urban adolescents. Rebecca E. Ford, MA, is a doctoral student at DePaul University. She recently defended her dissertation on the effects of acculturation on Latino adolescent mental health.

Coping with Stress

Implications for Preventive Interventions with Adolescents.

BRUCE E. COMPAS, PhD, JENNIFER E. CHAMPION, BA, AND KRISTEN REESLUND, BS

Considerable evidence suggests that exposure to stress and the ways that individuals cope with stress are of central importance for the prevention of psychopathology and other problems of adjustment during childhood and adolescence. Careful consideration of theory and research on stress and coping during adolescence is of potentially great importance for the development of preventive interventions for young people. In this article we first summarize the relationship between stress and psychopathology in children and adolescents, then discuss current research on coping. We conclude by discussing stress and coping approaches to preventive interventions, using an example from our current research with families of depressed parents.

Stress and Psychopathology

Traumatic events, stressful life events, and chronic stressful conditions affect the lives of millions of youth. Examples of these stressful experiences include natural and human disasters, neighborhood violence, economic hardship, personal or parental chronic illness, and minor events or hassles. Moreover, there is strong evidence that stress plays a clear role in the etiology and maintenance of psychopathology (Cicchetti & Toth, 1997; Haggerty et al., 1994). Research shows that stressors can be acute incidents (i.e., natural disaster, loss of a loved one) or more stable, chronic conditions (i.e., poverty, chronic illness) and that both types of stressors are associated with an increased risk for psychopathology in children and adolescents (Grant et al., 2003). Despite frequent exposure to acute or chronic stress, the vast majority of youth navigate adolescence without developing any form of psychopathology. For those who do develop psychological disorders, however, adolescence marks a period of significant increase in psychopathology across a wide range of disorders, including, for example, eating disorders, conduct disorder, and depression (Compas, 2004).

Research on child and adolescent stress has improved considerably over the past two decades (see Grant et al., 2003, 2004; McMahon et al., 2003). However, there is still considerable inconsistency in the field in the way stress is defined and measured. There is also much more to be learned about the impact that stress has on psychological outcomes in children and adolescents, and the implications that this has for prevention and intervention. There is strong evidence, though, that exposure to stressful events at one point in time predicts increases in internalizing and externalizing symptoms in adolescents above and beyond initial symptoms. However, the specific relationship between stress and outcome, as well as the mediators and moderators that affect this relationship are not yet well understood (Grant et al., 2004).

Current evidence shows that stressors are a general non-specific risk for psychopathology; however, the exact relationship between the two is yet to be defined. In their comprehensive review, McMahon and colleagues (2003) found that there is currently little evidence to support the specificity hypothesis in the relationship between stressors and outcome. An example of specificity would occur when a specific stressor (e.g., poverty) leads to a specific outcome (e.g., conduct disorder). Instead, there is more evidence to support the hypotheses of equifinality, where multiple stressors (e.g., poverty or loss of a loved one) lead to a specific outcome (e.g., conduct disorder), and multifinality, where a specific stressor (e.g., poverty) leads to multiple outcomes (e.g., conduct disorder or depression). Thus, exposure to stress appears to function as a non-specific risk factor for psychopathology. Recent research also shows that there is a reciprocal and dynamic relationship between stressors and psychological outcomes—stress leads to psychopathology but psychopathology also leads to the generation of stressful events in the lives of affected individuals (Grant et al., 2004).

Some children and adolescents exhibit a vulnerability to developing psychopathology. That is, these individuals when exposed to risk, in this case stress, are more likely to develop a negative outcome as compared to peers who do not have such vulnerability (Wolchik et al., 2000). Therefore, even when faced with similar levels of stress some youth may have risk factors, characteristics that are related to an increased probability of developing a negative outcome (Kraemer et al., 1997), whereas other youth may have protective factors, characteristics that are related to positive outcomes in the face of risk, and show resilience (Luthar & Cicchetti, 2000).

Coping with Stress

Conclusions regarding the association between stress and symptoms are insufficient without taking into account the ways that individuals cope with stress. Coping refers to self-regulatory processes enacted when faced with stress (Compas et al., 2001). The most widely cited definition of coping is given by Lazarus and Folkman (1984) as "constantly changing cognitive and behavioral efforts to manage specific external and/or internal demands that are appraised as taxing or exceeding the resources of the person" (p. 141). More specifically, coping involves conscious volitional efforts to regulate one's own behavior, emotions, thoughts, physiology, and the environment in response to a stressor (Compas et al., 2001).

Coping is one subset of a broader domain of self-regulation. It includes only regulatory efforts that are volitional and intentional responses to a stressful event or circumstance (Compas et al., 1999, 2001). These regulatory processes are influenced by the cognitive, behavioral, and emotional capacity of the individual as well as the social environment. Ways of reacting to stress that are involuntary or automatic are grouped into a more general classification of self-regulatory processes enacted in response to stress and are not considered coping (Compas et al., 2001). Furthermore, coping is situation specific—the ways in which an individual responds to a stressor is affected by the demands of the situation.

Stress responses can be broken down along two broad dimensions: voluntary (controlled) versus involuntary (automatic), and engagement versus disengagement. It is the distinction between voluntary and involuntary responses that distinguishes coping within the broader classification of stress responses; that is, coping refers to voluntary, controlled responses to stress. Both voluntary and automatic responses to stress can be further broken down into efforts to engage or disengage from the stressor and one's responses. Engagement coping strategies are characterized by direct attempts to influence either the stressor itself or one's emotions in response to the stressor (primary control coping), or efforts to adapt to the stress by regulating one's cognitions (secondary control coping). See Table 1.

Primary control coping (also referred to as active coping in other theoretical models) includes strategies that are directed at actively changing the situation or one's emotional responses, such as problem solving (e.g., I try to think of different ways to change the problem or fix the situation), emotional expression (e.g., I let my feelings out by writing or talking with someone), and emotional regulation (e.g., I do things to calm myself down). Secondary control coping, on the other hand, involves adaptation to the stressor through acceptance (e.g., I realize I just have to live with things the way they are), distraction (e.g., I think about positive things to take my mind off the problem), cognitive restructuring (e.g., I try to see the good that will come from the situation or what I will learn from it), and positive thinking (e.g., I tell myself everything's going to be all right). Unlike engagement coping behaviors which are focused on dealing with the stressful situation or one's emotions, disengagement coping refers to efforts to distance oneself emotionally, cognitively, and physically from the stressor. Such coping includes behaviors such as avoidance (e.g., I try to stay away from things that remind me of the problem), denial (e.g., I tell myself that this isn't happening to me), and wishful thinking (e.g., I wish someone would come get me out of this problem).

Involuntary responses to stress can also be distinguished along the dimension of engagement and disengagement responses. Involuntary engagement refers to automatic responses oriented towards the stressor and is comprised of rumination, intrusive thoughts, and emotional and physiological arousal. Involuntary disengagement responses include uncontrolled behaviors

Table 1 Stress Responses

Voluntary/Controlled Responses (Coping)		Involuntary/Automatic Responses	
Voluntary Engagement Coping: Dealing with the stressful situation or one's emotions	**Voluntary Disengagement Coping:** Efforts to distance oneself emotionally, cognitively and physically from the stressor	**Involuntary Engagement:** Automatic responses oriented toward the stressor	**Involuntary Disengagement:** Uncontrolled behaviors focused away from the source of stress
Primary Control Coping: Direct attempts to influence the stressor or one's emotions in response to the stressor. Examples include: • Problem solving • Emotional expression • Emotional regulation	Examples include: • Avoidance • Denial • Wishful thinking	Examples include: • Rumination • Intrusive thoughts • Emotional & physiological arousal	Examples include: • Emotional numbing • Cognitive interference • Inaction
Secondary Control Coping: Adaptation to the stressor. Examples include: • Acceptance • Distraction • Positive thinking			

focused away from the source of stress, such as emotional numbing, cognitive interference, inaction, and escape (Connor-Smith et al., 2000).

Over 60 studies have established that coping is associated with symptoms of psychopathology in children and adolescents (Compas et al., 2001). More specifically, primary and secondary control coping efforts have both been found to be related to fewer internalizing and externalizing symptoms in various populations. Because coping is situation specific, the most effective coping behaviors are dependent on the characteristics surrounding the stressor. Primary control coping has been found to be most successful when dealing with stressors that are perceived as controllable, whereas secondary control coping efforts may be more adaptive with uncontrollable stressors (Compas et al., 2001). In contrast to the positive outcomes associated with engagement coping, disengagement coping is typically associated with increased levels of internalizing and externalizing symptoms.

The pattern of relations between coping and symptoms has been investigated across various populations. For example, in a sample of adolescents reporting on economic strain and family conflict, primary and secondary control coping were both related to fewer internalizing and externalizing symptoms (Wadsworth & Compas, 2002). Similarly, youth dealing with recurrent abdominal pain reported fewer somatic and anxiety-depression symptoms with higher levels of primary and secondary control coping (Thomsen et al., 2002).

One focus of our current research is the significant risk for adolescents associated with living with a depressed parent. When examining the relationship between coping and psychological functioning in children of depressed parents, adolescents' use of primary control coping to deal with their parent's depression was associated with fewer aggressive symptoms, while secondary control coping was found to be related to lower levels of both anxiety-depression and aggression (Langrock et al., 2002). Although primary control coping was associated with fewer symptoms, due to the context-dependent nature of coping and the uncontrollability of the stressor (as children of depressed parents can't relieve their parent's depression and thus aren't capable of changing their situations), secondary control coping behaviors appear to be most adaptive in this population. Involuntary engagement, conversely, showed significant increases in both internalizing and externalizing symptoms. These findings were further supported by a study conducted by Jaser et al. (2005), who compared adolescent reports of coping strategies in response to the stress of parental depression with parental reports of adolescent adjustment. In this research, secondary control coping was related to fewer symptoms of depression/anxiety, while involuntary engagement was associated with increased levels of these symptoms.

To fully understand the relation between coping and symptoms, however, it is important and necessary to consider the nature of the stressor and the role of coping as a mediator or moderator in the relation between a stressor and psychopathology. As a potential moderator or mediator in the link between stress and symptoms, coping may serve to influence or explain the relation between the two (e.g., Connor-Smith & Compas, 2002). A moderator may be conceptualized as a protective factor, meaning a pre-existing characteristic that increases or decreases the probability of developing symptoms of psychopathology in response to a stressor. Coping may perform in such a manner, with some individuals possessing a tendency to use more adaptive coping strategies when dealing with stress, while others cope in a less effective way that increases the likelihood of developing psychopathology regardless of the stressor. The role of coping as a moderator may also serve to explain the issue raised earlier regarding why a single stressor may lead to various symptoms or why various stressors may result in the same outcome.

Coping may also function as a mediator, which means that it is set off by the stressor and accounts for the resulting symptoms (e.g., Jaser et al., 2005). In this case, coping behaviors would serve as a direct cause of the preceding stressor and produce certain symptoms. When looking at the relationship between stress, coping, and outcome in children of depressed parents, adolescents' reports of secondary control engagement coping and involuntary engagement stress responses were found to mediate the relation between adolescents' reports of parental stress and parents' reports of adolescents' anxiety/depression symptoms (Jaser et al., 2005). This finding emphasizes the potential benefits for preventive interventions to increase adaptive coping skills by teaching secondary control coping strategies and reducing involuntary stress reaction in order to decrease symptoms and promote better adjustment.

Preventive Interventions

Given the significant role of stress as risk factor for child and adolescent psychopathology and the potential for coping to serve as a protective factor against the adverse effects of stress, it is logical that stress and coping processes are potential targets for preventive interventions. In simplest terms, prevention efforts could be designed to reduce stress and enhance adaptive coping in young people. However, this seemingly simple principle belies a much more complicated set of issues in prevention programs to reduce the adverse effects of stress.

Reducing stress. One target for preventive interventions could certainly be to reduce the burden on children by decreasing their exposure to stress. There are a number of significant sources of stress in the lives of young people that could be reduced, or exposure to these stressors could be reduced or altered. For example, stressors that arise within family environments are potentially reduced through interventions aimed at parents. These include interventions to reduce the incidence of physical and sexual abuse, family conflict, and parental psychiatric disorders. Stressors that arise in schools can also be reduced by restructuring school environments or school demands. For example, the timing of the transition from primary education to middle school can be adjusted to reduce the likelihood that this transition coincides with other developmental changes and challenges. Moreover, to the extent that dependent stressful events are associated with child characteristics, their incidence may be reduced by interventions that change relevant aspects of children's behavior or cognition.

However, the practical limits to reducing stress in young people's lives quickly become apparent because many sources of stress in children and adolescents' lives are uncontrollable. Parental divorce, parental death, neighborhood violence and other chronic stressors that emanate from poverty, and some forms of chronic illness are themselves not preventable. Thus, there will naturally be limits in the degree to which stress can be reduced.

Enhancing coping. Given the limited control that can be gained over young people's exposure to many forms of stress, a second important target for preventive interventions is to increase children's abilities to cope with stress. Improved skills in problem solving, emotion regulation, and access to adequate social support may increase children's resilience in the face of stress. The cognitive and behavioral skills that characterize effective coping with stress are malleable and there is promising evidence that these skills can reduce the adverse outcomes of stress in the lives of children. Several examples of preventive interventions that reflect a stress and coping framework can be found in the literature, including interventions for children of divorce and bereaved children (e.g., Wolchik et al., 2000). Our focus here is on a relatively new program that our research group has developed for children of depressed parents.

Preventive intervention for children exposed to parental depression: An example of stress and coping in prevention. The risk for psychopathology and other adjustment problems in children of parents who suffer from major depressive disorder is substantial. Estimates are that as many as 70% of children of depressed parents will develop a psychiatric disorder, including but certainly not limited to, depression. Several mechanisms are implicated in the transmission of risk from depressed parents to their offspring, including genes, innate disruption of biological regulatory processes, and stressful parent-child interactions. Clarke and colleagues (2001) have shown preventive effects for a group cognitive-behavioral intervention for adolescents of parents with a history of depression. Our current research builds on this research by intervening with parents and children to address both the sources of stress and ways of coping in families of depressed parents.

Sources of stress within families of depressed parents and the ways that youth cope with these stressors represent two possible targets for preventive interventions. Stressful interactions between depressed parents and their children that are the result of parental withdrawal and parental irritability/intrusiveness are associated with higher levels of both internalizing and externalizing problems in children (Jaser et al., 2005; Langrock et al., 2002). Further, the effects of these parental stressors on children's problems are mediated by the ways that children react to and cope with parent-child stress. Specifically, children who are more stress reactive (i.e., respond to stress with higher levels of emotional and physiological arousal, intrusive thoughts) are higher in internalizing and externalizing problems. In contrast, children who are able to enlist secondary control coping strategies in response to these parental stressors are lower in internalizing and externalizing difficulties.

Based on the identification of these risk and protective factors, we have developed a family-based preventive intervention to enhance the ability of depressed parents to more effectively parent their children (and as a result, reduce parental withdrawal and irritability/intrusiveness) and children's ability to use secondary control coping strategies in response to parental stressors (Compas et al., 2002). The intervention is comprised of eight weekly sessions and four monthly follow-up sessions delivered to four families at a time. Through didactic presentations and role plays during the sessions and extensive homework between sessions, the emphasis is on the development of skills that will lead to reductions in parent-child stress and the increased ability of children to cope with these stressors when they do occur.

Initial findings from an open trial with 30 families are promising. Risk factors were reduced from pre- to post-intervention, as reflected in significant reductions in parental depressive symptoms and parental withdrawal. Concomitantly, children's use of secondary control coping increased significantly from before to after the intervention. And most importantly, there were significant declines in both internalizing and externalizing problems from pre- to post-intervention. Effect sizes were generally moderate in magnitude. The intervention is now being tested in a clinical trial in which families are randomized to receive the group intervention or an information-only control condition. These preliminary data suggest that teaching parenting skills may contribute to reductions in parents' depressive symptoms, perhaps by helping parents interact with their children in ways that help them to feel competent. Enhanced parenting skills are also associated with decreased withdrawal by depressed parents, making them more physically and emotionally available to their children and thus reducing a significant source of stress for children.

Conclusion

Sources of stress in the lives of adolescents serve as a significant source of risk for psychopathology. However, the effects of stress are mediated and moderated by the ways that children and adolescents react to and cope with stress. As a consequence, interventions that aim to reduce sources of stress and enhance effective coping provide a promising avenue for preventive interventions aimed at improving the lives of children and adolescents who are at-risk for psychopathology. Interventions aimed at stress and coping processes within families may be a particularly fruitful direction for such work, as interventionists may be able to simultaneously reduce levels of stress within families and improve the coping abilities of children and adolescents.

References

Cicchetti, D., & Toth, S.L. (Eds.) (1997). *Developmental Perspectives on Trauma: Theory, Research and Intervention*. Rochester, NY: Rochester University Press.

Clarke, G.N., Hornbrook, M., Lynch, F., Polen, M., Gale, J., Beardslee, W., O'Connor, W., & Seeley, J. (2001). A randomized trial of a group cognitive intervention for preventing depression in adolescent offspring of depressed parents. *Archives of General Psychiatry, 58(12)*, 1,127–1,134.

Compas, B.E. (2004). Processes of risk and resilience during adolescence: Linking contexts and individuals. In R.M. Lerner

& L. Steinberg (Eds.), *Handbook of Adolescent Psychology* (2nd ed., pp. 263–296). New Jersey: John Wiley & Sons, Inc.

Compas, B.E., Connor, J.K., Saltzman, H., Thomsen, A.H., & Wadsworth, M. (1999). Getting specific about coping: Effortful and involuntary responses to stress in development. In M. Lewis & D. Ramsey (Eds.), *Soothing and Stress* (pp. 229–256). New York: Cambridge University Press.

Compas, B.E., Connor-Smith, J.K., Thomsen, A.H., Saltzman, H., & Wadsworth, M.E. (2001). Coping with stress during childhood and adolescence: Progress, problems, and potential in theory and research. *Psychological Bulletin, 127,* 87–127.

Compas, B.E., Langrock, A.M., Keller, G., Merchant, M.J., & Copeland, M.E. (2001). Children coping with parental depression: Processes of adaptation to family stress. In S. Goodman & I. Gotlib (Eds.), *Children of Depressed Parents: Alternative Pathways to Risk for Psychopathology.* Washington, DC: American Psychological Association.

Connor-Smith, J.K., & Compas, B.E. (2002). Vulnerability to social stress: Coping as a mediator or moderator of sociotropy and symptoms of anxiety and depression. *Cognitive Therapy and Research, 26,* 39–55.

Connor-Smith, J.K., Compas, B.E., Wadsworth, M.E., Thomsen, A.H., & Saltzman, H. (2000). Responses to stress in adolescence: Measurement of coping and involuntary responses to stress. *Journal of Consulting and Clinical Psychology, 68,* 976–992.

Grant, K.E., Compas, B.E., Thurm, A., McMahon, S., & Gipson, P. (2004). Stressors and child and adolescent psychopathology: Measurement issues and prospective effects. *Journal of Clinical Child and Adolescent Psychology, 33:2,* 412–425.

Grant, K.E., Compas, B.E., Stuhlmacher, A.F., Thurm, A.E., McMahon, S.D., & Halpert, J.A. (2003). Stressors and child and adolescent psychopathology: Moving from markers to mechanisms of risk. *Psychological Bulletin, 129(3),* 447–466.

Haggerty, R.J., Sherrod, L.R., Garmezy, N., & Rutter, M. (Eds.). (1994). *Stress, Risk and Resilience in Children and Adolescents: Processes, Mechanisms, and Interventions.* New York: Cambridge University Press.

Jaser, S.S., Langrock, A.M., Keller, G., Merchant, M.J., Benson, M.A., Reeslund, K., Champion, J.E., & Compas, B.E. (2005). Coping With the Stress of Parental Depression II: Adolescent and Parent Reports of Coping and Adjustment. *Journal of Clinical Child and Adolescent Psychology, 34(1),* 193–205.

Kraemer, H.C., Kazdin, A.E., Offord, D.R., Kessler, R.C., Jensen, P.S., & Kupfer, D.J. (1997). Coming to terms with the terms of risk. *Archives of General Psychiatry, 54,* 337–343.

Langrock, A.M., Compas, B.E., Keller, G., Merchant, M.J., & Copeland, M.E. (2002). Coping with the stress of parental depression: Parents' reports of children's coping, emotional, and behavioral problems. *Journal of Clinical Child and Adolescent Psychology, 31,* 312–324.

Lazarus, R.S., & Folkman, S. (1984). *Stress, Appraisal, and Coping.* New York: Springer.

Luthar, S.S. & Cicchetti, D. (2000). The construct of resilience: Implications for interventions and social policy. *Development and Psychopathology, 12,* 857–885.

McMahon, S.D., Grant, K.E., Compas, B.E., Thurm, A.E., & Ey, S. (2003). Stress and psychopathology in children and adolescents: Is there evidence of specificity? *Journal of Child Psychology and Psychiatry,* 44:1, 107–133.

Thomsen, A.H., Compas, B.E., Colletti, R.B., Stanger, C., Boyer, M.C., & Konik, B.S. (2002). Parents' reports of coping and stress responses in children with recurrent abdominal pain. *Journal of Pediatric Psychology, 27,* 215–226.

Wadsworth, M.E., & Compas, B.E. (2002). Coping with economic strain and family conflict: The adolescent perspective. *Journal of Research on Adolescence, 12,* 243–274.

Wolchik, S.A., West, S.G., Sandler, I.N., Tein, J.Y., Coatsworth, D., et al. (2000). An experimental evaluation of theory-based mother and mother-child programs for children of divorce. *Journal of Consulting and Clinical Psychology, 68,* 843–856.

BRUCE E. COMPAS, PhD, is the Patricia and Rodes Hart Professor of Psychology & Human Development and Pediatrics at Vanderbilt University where he also serves as Director of Clinical Psychology Training and Director of Psychological Oncology at the Vanderbilt-Ingram Cancer Center. **JENNIFER CHAMPION**, BA, is a doctoral student in clinical psychology at Vanderbilt University. **KRISTEN REESLUND**, BS, is a doctoral student in clinical psychology at Vanderbilt University.

ADHD and the SUD in Adolescents

Timothy E. Wilens, MD

Overlap Between ADHD and SUD

The overlap between Attention Deficit Hyperactivity Disorder (ADHD) and alcohol or drug abuse (referred to here as substance use disorders [SUD]) in adolescents has been an area of increasing clinical, research, and public health interest. ADHD onsets in early childhood and affects from 6 to 9 percent of children and adolescents worldwide (Anderson, et al., 1987) and up to 5 percent of adults (Kessler, in press). Substance use disorders (SUD) usually onset in adolescence or early adulthood and affect between 10 to 30 percent of U.S. adults, and a less defined, but sizable number of juveniles (Kessler, 2004). The study of comorbidity between SUD and ADHD is relevant to both research and clinical practice in developmental pediatrics, psychology, and psychiatry with implications for diagnosis, prognosis, treatment, and healthcare delivery.

In adolescent studies incorporating structured psychiatric diagnostic interviews assessing ADHD and other disorders in substance abusing groups have indicated that from one third to one-half of adolescents with SUD have ADHD (DeMilio, 1989; Milin, et al., 1991). Data largely ascertained from adult groups with SUD also show an earlier onset and more severe course of SUD associated with ADHD (Carroll & Rounsaville, 1993; Levin & Evans, 2001).

ADHD as a Risk Factor for SUD

The association of ADHD and SUD is particularly compelling from a developmental perspective as ADHD manifests itself earlier than SUD; therefore, SUD as a risk factor for ADHD is unlikely. Thus, it is important to evaluate to what extent ADHD is a precursor of SUD. Prospective studies of ADHD children have provided evidence that the groups with conduct or bipolar disorders co-occurring with ADHD have the poorest outcome with respect to developing SUD and major morbidity (Biederman, et al., 1997; Mannuzza, et al., 1993). As part of an ongoing prospective study of ADHD, differences in the risk for SUD in ADHD adolescents (mean age 15 years) compared to non-ADHD controls were found. The controls were accounted for by comorbid conduct or bipolar disorders (Biederman, et al., 1997); however, we also show that the age of risk for SUD onset in non-comorbid ADHD is approximately 17 years in girls and 19 years old for boys (Biederman, et al., 2006a; Milberger, et al., 1997b).

SUD Pathways Associated with ADHD

An increasing body of literature shows an intriguing association between ADHD and cigarette smoking. It has been previously reported that ADHD was a significant predictor for early initiation of cigarette smoking (before age 15) and that conduct and mood disorders with ADHD put youth at particularly high risk for early onset smoking (Milberger, et al., 1997a) (see Figure below). Data also suggest that one-half of ADHD smokers go on to later SUD (Biederman, et al., 2006b); not surprising given that not only does smoking lead to peer group pressures and availability of illicit substances; but that nicotine exposure may make the brain more susceptible to later behavioral disorders and SUD (Trauth, et al., 2000). Furthermore, nicotinic modulating agents are increasingly being evaluated for the treatment of ADHD (Wilens, et al., 2006). Of interest, very recent NIDA-funded prospective data suggests that stimulant treatment of

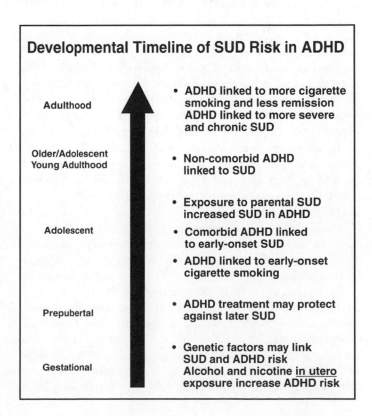

Developmental Timeline of SUD Risk in ADHD

Adulthood
- ADHD linked to more cigarette smoking and less remission ADHD linked to more severe and chronic SUD

Older/Adolescent Young Adulthood
- Non-comorbid ADHD linked to SUD

- Exposure to parental SUD increased SUD in ADHD

Adolescent
- Comorbid ADHD linked to early-onset SUD

- ADHD linked to early-onset cigarette smoking

Prepubertal
- ADHD treatment may protect against later SUD

Gestational
- Genetic factors may link SUD and ADHD risk Alcohol and nicotine in utero exposure increase ADHD risk

ADHD reduces not only the time to onset but also the incidence of cigarette smoking (Monuteaux, et al., 2004).

The precise mechanism(s) mediating the expression of SUD in ADHD remains to be seen. The self-medication hypothesis is compelling in ADHD considering that the disorder is chronic and often associated with demoralization and failure, factors frequently associated with SUD in adolescents. Moreover, we recently found that among substance abusing adolescents with and without ADHD, ADHD adolescents reported using substances more frequently to attenuate their mood and to help them sleep. No evidence of differences in types of substances has emerged between ADHD and nonADHD substance abusing teens (Biederman, et al., 1997). In addition, the potential importance of self-medication needs to be tempered against more systematic data showing the strongest relationship between ADHD and SUD being mediating by the presence of comorbidity in addition to familial contributions such as exposure to parental SUD during vulnerable developmental phases.

Diagnosis and Treatment Guidelines

Evaluation and treatment of comorbid ADHD and SUD should be part of a plan in which consideration is given to all aspects of the teen's life. Any intervention in this group should follow a careful evaluation of the adolescent including psychiatric, addiction, social, cognitive, educational, and family evaluations. A thorough history of substance use should be obtained including past and current usage and treatments. Although no specific guidelines exist for evaluating the patient with active SUD, experience has shown that at least one month of abstinence is useful in accurately and reliably assessing for ADHD symptoms. Semi-structured psychiatric interviews or validated rating scales of ADHD are invaluable aids for the systematic diagnostic assessments of this group.

The treatment needs of individuals with SUD and ADHD need to be considered simultaneously; however, the SUD needs to be addressed initially (Riggs, 1998). If the SUD is active, immediate attention needs to be paid to *stabilization of the addiction(s)*. Depending on the severity and duration of the SUD, adolescents may require inpatient treatment. Self help groups offer a helpful treatment modality for many with SUD. In tandem with addiction treatment, SUD adolescents with ADHD require intervention(s) for the ADHD (and if applicable, comorbid psychiatric disorders).

Medication serves an important role in reducing the symptoms of ADHD and other concurrent psychiatric disorders. Effective agents for adolescents with ADHD include the stimulants, noradrenergic agents, and catecholaminergic antidepressants (Wilens, et al., 2002). Recent findings from a metanalysis of 10 studies of open and controlled trials suggest that medications used in adolescents and adults with ADHD plus SUD have only a meager effect on the ADHD, but have little effect on substance use or cravings (Riggs, et al., 2004; Schubiner, et al., 2002; Wilens, et al., 2005). Of interest, no evidence exists that treating ADHD pharmacologically through an active SUD

exacerbates the SUD—consistent with work of Grabowski et al. (2004) who have used stimulants to block cocaine and amphetamine abuse. Not surprisingly, work by Volkow et al. (1998) have demonstrated important differences between binding at the dopamine transporter between methylphenidate and cocaine resulting in very different abuse liabilities.

Summary

There is a strong literature supporting a relationship between ADHD and SUD. Both family-genetic and self-medication influences may be operational in the development and continuation of SUD in ADHD. Adolescents with ADHD and SUD require multimodal intervention incorporating addiction and mental health treatment. Pharmacotherapy in ADHD and SUD individuals needs to take into consideration timing, misuse and diversion liability, potential drug interactions, and compliance concerns.

While the existing literature has provided important information on the relationship of ADHD and SUD, it also points to a number of areas in need of further study. The mechanism by which untreated ADHD leads to SUD, as well as the risk reduction of ADHD treatment on cigarette smoking and SUD needs to be better understood. Given the prevalence and major morbidity and impairment caused by SUD and ADHD, prevention and treatment strategies for these adolescents need be further developed and evaluated.

References

Anderson, J.C., Williams, S., McGee, R., & Silva, P.A. (1987). DSM III disorders in preadolescent children. Prevalence in a large sample from the general population. *Arch Gen Psychiatry* 44: 69–76.

Biederman J., Monuteaux M., Mick, E. et al. (2006a). Young Adult Outcome of Attention Deficit Hyperactivity Disorder: A Controlled 10 year Prospective Follow-Up Study. *Psychol Med* 36: 167–179.

Biederman, J., Monuteaux, M., Mick, E., et al. (2006b). Is Cigarette Smoking a Gateway Drug to Subsequent Alcohol and Illicit Drug Use Disorders? A Controlled Study of Youths with and without ADHD. *Biol Psychiatry* 59: 258–64.

Biederman, J., Wilens, T. & Mick, E. et al. (1997). Is ADHD a risk for psychoactive substance use disorder? Findings from a four year follow-up study. *J Am Acad Child Adolesc Psychiatry* 36: 21–29.

Carroll, K.M. & Rounsaville, B.J. (1993). History and significance of childhood attention deficit disorder in treatment-seeking cocaine abusers. *Comrpehensive Psychiatry* 34: 75–82.

DeMilio, L. (1989). Psychiatric syndromes in adolescent substance abusers. *Am J Psychiatry* 146: 1212–1214.

Grabowski, J., Shearer, J., Merrill, J. & Negus, S.S. (2004). Agonist-like, replacement pharmacotherapy for stimulant abuse and dependence. *Addict Behav* 29: 1439–1464.

Kessler, R.C. (in press). A recent replication of the National Comorbidity Study estimating the prevalence of adult ADHD among persons 18–44 in the US. *Psychol Med.*

Kessler, R.C. (2004). The epidemiology of dual diagnosis. *Biol Psychiatry* 56: 730–7.

Levin, F.R. & Evans, S.M. (2001). Diagnostic and treatment issues in comorbid substance abuse and adult attention-deficit hyperacity disorder. *Psychiatric Annals* 31: 303–312.

Mannuzza, S., Klein, R.G., Bessler, A., Malloy, P. & LaPadula, M. (1993). Adult outcome of hyperactive boys: Educational achievement, occupational rank, and psychiatric status. *Arch Gen Psychiatry* 50: 565–576.

Milberger, S., Biederman, J., Faraone, S., Chen, L. & Jones, J. (1997a). ADHD is associated with early initiation of cigarette smoking in children and adolescents. *J Am Acad Child Adolesc Psychiatry* 36: 37–44.

Milberger, S., Biederman, J., Faraone, S., Wilens, T. & Chu, M. (1997b). Associations between ADHD and psychoactive substance use disorders: Findings from a longitudinal study of high-risk siblings of ADHD children. *Am J Addict* 6: 318–329.

Milin, R., Halikas, J.A., Meller, J.E. & Morse, C. (1991). Psychopathology among substance abusing juvenile offenders. *J Am Acad Child Adolesc Psychiatry* 30: 569–574.

Riggs, P.D. (1998). Clinical approach to treatment of ADHD in adolescents with substance use disorders and conduct disorder. *J Am Acad Child Adolesc Psychiatry* 37: 331–332.

Riggs, P.D., Hall, S.K., Mikulich-Gilbertson, S.K., Lohman, M. & Kayser, A. (2004). A Randomized Controlled Trial of Pemoline for Attention-Deficit/Hyperactivity Disorder in Substance-Abusing Adolescents. *J Am Acad Child Adolesc Psychiatry* 43: 420–429.

Schubiner, H., Saules, K.K. & Arfken, C.L. et al. (2002). Double-blind placebo-controlled trial of methylphenidate in the treatment of adult ADHD patients with comorbid cocaine dependence. *Exp Clin Psychopharmacol* 10: 286–94.

Trauth, J.A., Seidler, F.J. & Slotkin, T.A. (2000). Persistent and delayed behavioral changes after nicotine treatment in adolescent rats. *Brain Res* 880: 167–72.

Volkow, N., Wang, G. & Fowler, J. et al. (1998). Dopamine transporter occupancies in the human brain induced by therapeutic doses of oral methylphenidate. *Am J Psychiatry* 155: 1325–1331.

Wilens T., Monuteaux M., Snyder L., Moore B.A. (2005). The clinical dilemma of using medications in substance abusing adolescents and adults with ADHD: What does the literature tell us? *J Child Adolesc Psychopharmacol* 15: 787–98.

Wilens T., Verlinden M.H., Adler L.A., Wozniak P.A. & West S.A. (2006). ABT-089, A Neuronal Nicotinic Receptor Partial Agonist, for the Treatment of Attention-Deficit/Hyperactivity Disorder in Adults: Results of a Pilot Study. *Biol Psychiatry* 59: 1065–70.

Wilens, T.E., Biederman, J. & Spencer, T.J. (2002). Attention Deficit/Hyperactivity Disorder across the Lifespan. *Ann Rev Med* 53: 113–131.

DR. TIMOTHY E. WILENS is Associate Professor of Psychiatry at Harvard Medical School in Boston, Massachusetts. In addition, he is Director of the Substance Abuse Services in the Pediatric Psychopharmacology Clinic at Massachusetts General Hospital.

Dr. Wilens earned his BS in literature, science, and arts at the University of Michigan Honors College, and his MD at the University of Michigan Medical School in Ann Arbor. His peer reviewed articles concerning the relationship of Attention Deficit Hyperactivity Disorder (ADHD), bipolar disorder, and substance abuse and related topics number more than 170. Dr. Wilens has also published more than 65 book chapters, and 225 abstracts and presentations for national and international scientific meetings. He may be contacted at Twilens@partners.org.

Acknowledgments—This research was supported by NIH BOI DA14419 and K24 DA016264 to TW.

UNIT 3

Relationships of Adolescents: Family, Peers, Intimacy, and Sexuality

Unit Selections

Key Points to Consider

- What suggestions will improve parent-teenager relationships?

- How should teenage girls maintain their relationship with their fathers?

- How much is too much time spent playing computer and video games?

- What are the warning signs for aggression in teen dating?

- Why are parents being held criminally liable for their teen's drinking parties?

- Why is the expectation of a soul mate a recipe for disaster?

- What is the abstinence curriculum being presented to teenagers?

- What are the main points in the controversy between abstinence only and comprehensive sex education?

- Why does living together before marriage lead couples to wed for the wrong reasons?

Student Website
www.mhcls.com

Internet References

American Sexual Behavior
http://www.norc.uchicago.edu/online/sex.pdf
CDC National AIDS Clearinghouse
http://www.cdcnpin.org/
CYFERNET: Cooperative Extension System's Children, Youth, and Family Information Service
http://www.cyfernet.org/
Family Violence Prevention Fund
www.endabuse.org

Girls Inc.
http://www.girlsinc.org
Help for Parents of Teenagers
http://www.bygpub.com/parents/
National Council of Juvenile and Family Court Judges
http://www.ncifci.org
Stepfamily Association of America
http://www.stepfam.org
Welcome to about Health
http://www.abouthealth.com/

The family is the most important and most intimate social context for adolescents. Families are vitally involved in providing the skills necessary for adolescents to become functioning adults in society. They pass along the attitudes, skills, and values needed in society. Families promote survival and offer comfort for adolescents. A family is indeed a complex system that responds to its members. When a teenager is included in the family system, changes occur which affect other members and their relationships. Both the functions of the family and the expectations of the family change. At times it may be less stable and predictable. Teens often expect greater autonomy, which may cause friction with parents.

American teens spend much more time with their peers than with their parents or siblings. The shift from family to peers is influenced by the trend toward smaller families, more dual-earner families, and access to an increased number of peers. Many adolescents look to their peers as a group to provide information about what is normal and expected. The peer group offers a baseline for judging his/her performance and serves as a knowledgeable audience. Teens have a need to belong, and the need is satisfied with their peer group.

Adolescents are, without a doubt, more peer-oriented than any other age group. But it is simplistic to assume that peer influence is always negative and that it outweighs parental influence. Research demonstrates that the nature of the parent-child relationship is consistently the best predictor of adolescent psychological health and well-being. Adolescents who have poor relationships with their parents are precisely the adolescents who are most susceptible to negative peer influences. Poor parent-adolescent relationships are not the norm during the pubertal years; conflicted relationships more likely represent a continuation of poor family relationships from childhood.

Research also indicates that most adolescents feel close to and respect their parents. Most adolescents share their parents' values, especially when it comes to moral, religious, political, and educational values. The school the adolescent attends, the kind of neighborhood the parents live in, whether the parents attend religious services, and what parents do for a living all influence their children. Parental choices such as these have a definite impact on their children for the network of friends they select.

Several factors have contributed to the misconception that adolescents reject their parents in favor of peers. First, peers play a greater role in the adolescent's day-to-day activities, style of dress, and musical tastes than do parents. Second, parents often confuse the adolescent's struggle for autonomy with rebellion. G. Stanley Hall's views of adolescence as a biologically necessary time of "storm and stress" contributed to this confusion as well. Similarly, Anna Freud, arguing from her father's psychoanalytic tradition and her own experience with troubled adolescents, maintained that the adolescent-parent relationship is highly laden with conflicts causing adolescents to turn to their peers. According to Anna Freud, such conflicts ensure a successful resolution of the Oedipus/Electra complex. This model of intense parent-adolescent conflict has not been empirically supported and can be detrimental if parents fail to seek

© BananaStock/PunchStock

help because they believe intense conflict is "normal" during adolescence.

Another myth about peer influence during adolescence is that it is primarily negative. As Thomas Berndt discusses in his research, peer influence is mutual and has both positive and negative effects. Peer pressure is rarely coercive, as is popularly envisaged. It is a more subtle process where adolescents influence their friends and the friends influence them. Just as adults do, adolescents choose friends who already have similar interests, attitudes, and beliefs.

Another misconception about peer relations is that teen culture is a unified culture with a single way of thinking and acting. A visit to any secondary school today will reveal the variety of teen cultures that exist. The formation of peer groups and adolescent crowds is partly a function of a school structure and school activities. As in past decades, one can find jocks, populars, brains, delinquents, and nerds. One would also encounter members of today's grunge and body-piercing crowds. Media attention is often drawn toward bizarre or antisocial groups further contributing to the myth that peer influence is primarily negative.

Music is very much a part of youth culture, although there is no universal type of music liked by all adolescents. One way adolescents have always tried to differentiate themselves from adults has been though music. On the other hand, today, adults are concerned that music, movies, and television have gone too far in the quest for ever-more shocking and explicit sexual and violent content. Widespread and easy access to the Internet has also compounded concerns about the types of material to which today's adolescents are exposed.

Like other aspects of psychological development, sexuality is not an entirely new issue that surfaces for the first time during adolescence. Children are known to be curious about their bodies at a very early age. And of course, sexual interest and development continues after adolescence. Most would argue that adolescence is a fundamentally important time for the development of sexuality.

During adolescence there is an increase in the sex drive as a result of hormonal changes. During puberty individuals become capable of sexual reproduction. Individuals also develop the secondary sex characteristics that serve as a basis for sexual attraction and as dramatic indicators that the young person is no longer physically a child.

The nature and extent of adolescent sexuality clearly have changed in recent years. Several different patterns of sexual behavior characterize contemporary adolescents. Many of the patterns include engagement in sexual behaviors that place the young person at risk of experiencing health, psychological, and social problems.

In much of American culture, the link between marriage and sexual activity has practically disappeared. This means that there is no particular age for sanctioning the initiation of sexual activity. Largely as a result of such changes, sexual activity is initiated at earlier ages than in the past, by increasing proportions of adolescents.

Attitudes toward sex became more liberal from the late 1960s through the 1970s. The changed attitude has had a major impact on several implications for youth's attitude today toward sex. First, there has been a greater openness in our society in sexual matters. Both the printed page and media openly discuss such topics as abortion, rape, and sexual abuse. Just a generation ago such topics were not discussed as openly as today. The natural consequence is that youth today, who have been brought up in this atmosphere, are much more open and often feel more comfortable discussing sexual issues openly and honestly with both peers and adults. A second attitude change is that more adults and teens (than a generation ago) consider sexual intercourse outside of marriage as acceptable. No longer do many consider legal marriage as a required sanction for sex. Many believe that sex is acceptable within a "relationship," and some youth have adopted the liberal attitude that casual sex or sex for primarily personal pleasure whether or not a relationship exists is acceptable.

Many adolescents are initiating sexual intercourse at an earlier age than in the previous generation. Gender attitudes continue to demonstrate a difference in belief systems. Young women are much more likely than men to desire a strong relationship or even marriage before engaging in sexual intercourse.

Many of the problems associated with teenage sexual activity have increased with more teens' sexual involvement. American teenagers have one of the highest rates of premarital pregnancies in the world. Although more teenagers are now using contraceptives than in the past, there is still a large number who use no method of birth control, or fail to use it properly. Legal abortion is an option that has become increasingly available even though it continues to be highly controversial. Because youth often delay making a decision to abort the baby, more complications persist. In addition, mental agony and guilt accompany making such a major decision.

Increased sexual activity also corresponds to a rise in sexually transmitted diseases. The most common among youth is gonorrhea, chlamydia, and herpes. Although some of the sexually transmitted diseases (STD) may continue in the body for the rest of their life and effect reproduction, AIDS often results in an early, painful death. In an attempt to prevent a nationwide epidemic, educational programs teaching about sex, diseases, and how to prevent the spread of disease are being presented around the country. Although not accepted by many, abstinence is the only true method to prevent sexually transmitted diseases.

Angela J. Huebner and Jay A. Mancini discuss how the recent wars in Iraq and Afghanistan have heightened our awareness of the stresses placed on military service members and their families. Many parents are wondering how much is too much time spent playing computer and video games. Jennifer Wagner attempts to answer the question and explains that many teens become addicted. In many teen romantic relationships, youth act out aggressively toward each other. The next article reviews adolescent dating aggression, focusing on warning signs and methods of prevention. In the following article, Emma Schwartz explains that parents are being held criminally liable for their teen's drinking parties.

Polly Shulman combines research and the experience of many relationship experts to explain that the expectation that a partner should be a soul mate could be a recipe for disaster and unhappiness. Bill Taverner discusses, in detail, the abstinence education curriculum being presented to teenagers today. The next article discusses the two sides: abstinence only or comprehensive sex education. The last article in this section provides evidence that living together before marriage may lead couples to wed for all the wrong reasons.

Supporting Youth during Parental Deployment

Strategies for Professionals and Families

Angela J. Huebner, PhD, and Jay A. Mancini, PhD

The Global War on Terrorism has heightened our awareness of the sacrifices of military service members and their families. Over half (55%) of active military members are married and about 43% have children (40% of whom are under the age of 5 years, 32% between the ages of 6 and 11, and 24% between the ages of 12 and 18) (Office of the Deputy Under Secretary of Defense, 2005). There are currently about 263,000 service members deployed overseas, with the vast majority located in Iraq and Afghanistan (Glod, 2008). Their service has often included multiple deployments—meaning that they have been in war zones for 12–15 months, back in the U.S. for 12 months, then deployed again (Morse, 2006). The experience of being deployed is obviously a stressful situation for both the military service member and his or her family. There are particular and significant ways youth development professionals can provide support to youth and to their families. These strategies are briefly described below. Quotes from youth who participated in our focus groups are included to highlight some of the deployment-related issues they face.

The Deployment Cycle and Families' Adjustment

Deployment is the assignment of military personnel to temporary, unaccompanied (meaning no family) tours of duty. It is usually divided into three phases: (1) Pre-Deployment/Preparation, (2) Deployment/Separation, and (3) Post-Deployment/Reunion. Each phase of the deployment cycle has unique associated family Stressors (Morse, 2006).

Pre-deployment usually includes "mobilization." During mobilization, service members prepare for war or other national emergencies by organizing their resources. Although service members are not necessarily sent overseas during mobilization, they may be required to relocate to a military installation to complete their tasks. Mobilization begins the process of family separation and the associated Stressors, including loss (Huebner, Mancini, Wilcox, Grass, & Grass, 2007). Mobilization raises family concerns about financial constraints, employment changes, increased childcare needs, and social support. Depending on the family structure, plans may be made for the military connected youth to go live with relatives or other guardians. In our investigations (e.g. Huebner & Mancini, 2005) we often find that grandparents assume a pivotal role in providing various kinds of support for youth and their families. If the relatives are not nearby, this may mean changing schools and leaving friends. These are important issues families must consider before the military member leaves.

Deployment occurs when the service member is actually assigned a tour of duty. During this phase of the cycle, the service member usually becomes geographically separated from his or her family. Regardless of whether or not the family has to relocate, the absence of the service member is stressful for the family. However, in some families, the absence relieves family tension. The service member's spouse is now acting as a single parent. He or she likely has sole responsibility for maintaining the household and raising the children. The family financial situation may necessitate the parent take on a new job or change jobs. If the deployed parent was a single parent to begin with, these problems are intensified.

If youth are unable to communicate with their deployed parent they may feel isolated. They worry about their parent's safety, particularly due to the massive media coverage of conflicts. Because of the changed family structure, youth may be experiencing inconsistent parenting, or changes in the family schedule, responsibilities, and rules. These changes may be particularly acute for National Guard and Reserve members who have traditionally had part-time commitments. They and their families may have never defined themselves as military families and thus never accessed military support systems.

> "The first day after he [dad] left, it was like no one wanted to do anything. We just wanted to sit in the house and stare at the walls. . ."
>
> —Teen Male

Post-Deployment refers to the time when the service member returns home. Although this is a potentially joyful time, it is also stressful due to struggles over family reorganization. Depending on the length of the deployment, the family may have functioned without the military member for several months or even years. Usually the family has adapted to the new structure and roles. When the military member returns, it may upset the balance that had been achieved. Roles need to be renegotiated, not just between adults in the family but also between adults and youth. Returning military members may feel like they are no longer needed in their families and youth may be hesitant to give up newly acquired responsibilities. In addition, very pragmatic issues are faced, including concerns about the service member's civilian employment status.

When the military member returns . . . roles need to be renegotiated, not just between adults in the family but also between adults and youth.

Deployment Impacts on Families

Families experience the impacts of military deployments in various ways. Although deployment is a stressful situation for all families, families vary in their degree of resilience in coping with the situation. Several factors have been shown to influence the effect of deployments on families. These include the quality of pre-deployment family relationships; the age, sex, and maturity of children; the meaning of the absence to the family; the extent of danger to which the military member is exposed; and how the remaining spouse deals with the absence, including her or his coping skills and mental health status (Huebner & Mancini, 2005; Huebner & Powell, 2007; Jensen & Shaw, 1996).

Researchers have linked parental deployment (usually defined as father deployment) to several youth outcomes. These include depression, acting out or negative behavioral adjustment, poor academic performance, and increased

irritability and impulsiveness (Hiew, 1992; Hillenbrand, 1976; Huebner & Mancini, 2005; Jensen, Martin, & Watanabe, 1996; Levai, Kaplan, Ackerman, & Hammock, 1995; Yeatman, 1981). Research conducted with military families also demonstrates that the mental health of the at-home parent (usually the mother) is very influential in determining child adjustment (Huebner & Powell, 2007; Jensen et al., 1996).

Research conducted with military families demonstrates that the mental health of the at-home parent is very influential in determining child adjustment.

> "When my dad left, I stayed separate from the family. I would really keep to myself. . . . I was taking on more and more responsibilities and I was taking charge so I tried to hide my feelings because my mom and my sister were constantly crying and stuff so I was always trying to comfort them. And I couldn't show any emotion for that because I had to he the strong one. I was hiding my emotions at certain times then always lashing out at certain people that maybe I shouldn't have been."
>
> —Teen Female

Providing Support

In the summer of 2004, early in the deployments for the Global War on Terrorism, we conducted focus groups with youth who were currently experiencing parental deployment to an active war zone (Huebner et al., 2007; see Huebner & Mancini, 2005 for the full report). For those affiliated with the National Guard or Reserve force, this marked the first time for such a separation; it also marked the first time these youth even considered themselves part of the military system. The primary purpose of this study was to explore the many dimensions of the deployment experiences of teens in military families, so that military and civilian program professionals could be more intentional and directed regarding developing support programs for young people.

Youth were identified via their attendance in one of several camps sponsored by the National Military Family Association designed for those with deployed military parents. Study participants were 107 ethnically diverse adolescent boys and girls ranging in age from 12 to 18 years. Active duty service representation included 39% Army, 3% Navy, 10% Air Force, and 4% Marines; 23% of participants had parents in the National Guard (all services), and 13% in the Reserves (all services). The vast majority of youth in this study stated that they had a father deployed.

As part of the process, youth were asked about their support networks. Youth's responses clustered around 1) informal supports, 2) formal supports, and 3) support processes.

Informal support received from family members, friends, and others not connected with a support service or program are invaluable for providing opportunities for youth to deal with concerns associated with a parent's deployment. Informal support is evidenced in talking about worries, or merely by having others to spend time with in enjoyable activities. Youth mentioned a number of sources that were supportive to them, including parents and grandparents, friends who are also in military families, as well as friends who are not. They reported that others often gave them a chance to release tensions by talking. Having others to engage with in activities diverted their attention from deployment worries.

It is important to note that some reported they did *not* seek out people with whom to talk about deployment-related worries—they spoke about times when informal support was *not* helpful. For example, some teens said they felt others almost over-reacted when hearing about their concerns on deployment, or felt that people were just being polite by listening to them.

> "I've got one friend that will actually talk about it because she has a brother being deployed soon. But all the rest of my friends don't, it sort of makes them uncomfortable for me to talk about it, and that makes me uncomfortable, too."
>
> —Teen Female

We associate formal support as that originating within agencies and organizations, including churches, civic groups, as well as military youth serving agencies (Mancini, Bowen, & Martin, 2005). Within these formal organizations, relationships among participants often develop, so that formal support and informal support become interrelated. Formal support personnel include teachers, counselors and therapists, and youth workers. Regardless of formal support source, most teens are open to formal support services if the teens feel like those services are relevant and that the adults offering those services can empathize with teens because of their own similar experiences with deployment.

> "I feel like my teachers are more understanding and you know, more apt to give me an extension on my homework because they know about my family. Because I had this one teacher whose dad was deployed and he died while he was over there. And you know, she just took me under her wing and was like my counselor throughout the rest of the year."
>
> —Teen Female

Within both formal and informal support are a set of processes, called support functions, which teens find helpful. Usually these functions are associated with what individual people say or do. These processes can be instrumental or practical, or more emotional or psychological. Youth told us about a wide variety of support processes they used. Support processes that youth say are helpful include listening, understanding, and providing assurance. They also mentioned that sometimes being "distracted" with other activities was helpful because it provided them a break from thinking about deployment. Interestingly, teens were also quick to point out displeasure with those who provided "fake" support or whose support faltered over time.

> "At first when my dad got deployed, there was a lot of support as in like people calling, people giving us, you know, food and stuff. But then as time went on, it just kind of died down and nobody really cared that he was deployed."
>
> —Teen Male

> "I don't want to talk about it 24/7. I want to go out, have fun, get together, eat, you know? I don't want to just talk about it, you know, deployment and stuff because there's other things happening in our lives, you know."
>
> —Teen Female

Implications for Program Professionals
Support for Youth

Findings from the study point to several ways youth development professionals can be supportive to youth in military families. Support for youth fall into one of three categories: (1) increasing knowledge/awareness of deployment-related issues; (2) increasing knowledge of and vigilance around depression and stress symptoms in youth; and (3) increasing opportunities for connection and support of these youth.

Increasing Knowledge and Awareness about Deployment Related Issues

Youth-serving professionals and other support personnel can support youth during parental deployment by;

- understanding the unique situation of teens with deployed parents. Because a broad array of formal support organizations come in contact with teens in military families, all could benefit from receiving information about families and deployment.

- developing public awareness campaigns to educate local communities about issues facing military families.
- learning about the significance of the deployment cycle and how teens' reactions vary depending on the specific stage, as well as on their own age.

Increasing Knowledge of and Vigilance around Depression and Stress Symptoms in Youth

This can be accomplished by:

- recognizing signs and symptoms of depression and other mental health issues in teens. Very often it is assumed that the natural resilience of youth will carry them through difficult times, yet our data show otherwise.
- recognizing that a range of emotions are experienced by teens when a parent is deployed and tailoring intervention efforts to deal with these complexities, rather than assume a narrow range of emotional responses by teens.

Increasing Opportunities for connection and Support

Increasing support and connection can be accomplished by:

- making a special effort to connect with teens that have a deployed parent. Many youth will be reluctant to express their concerns about a deployed parent, but will respond to others who show concern for them.
- helping teens to develop social networks with other teens who have deployed parents. These could occur in school, community, or religious organizational settings.
- supporting the informal networks of teens by intentionally developing networking skills among teens that include how to communicate feelings, and how to develop bonds with other military teens. This may include developing social support or mentoring programs led by young adults who have themselves experienced the deployment of a parent.
- providing ongoing, accessible social activities for teens so that they have distraction opportunities. Youth can only focus on worries connected with the welfare of a deployed parent for so long without experiencing extreme fatigue. This type of support may involve partnering with other youth serving organizations to increase the number of available program options. Try to recruit teens to participate in programs that include recreation as well as life skills development.
- ensuring appropriate support systems for the at-home parent. The at-home parent is the linchpin in the well-being of the adolescent.

Support for Parents

Our research findings also point to implications about how to support those parents experiencing spousal deployment in supporting their own children. Program professionals can help support parents by providing educational information in three areas: (1) recognizing reactions to deployment related stress; (2) becoming intentional about providing consistency in family routines and rituals; and (3) providing and accessing informal support systems.

Recognizing Reactions to Deployment Related Stress

Content areas should include:

- the importance of parents taking a developmentally appropriate and intentional approach to discussing deployment and subsequent family changes with teens. We discovered many adults were over-informing younger youth, and adding unnecessary strains in their lives. Parents need to learn how to make developmentally appropriate disclosures about family issues and war information.
- the awareness that teens often do not have adequate ways to discuss their worries about parental deployment, and that some teens are not speaking with anyone about their concerns.
- the importance of recognizing that teens' behaviors and emotions may vary with different stages of the deployment cycle and with different developmental levels, each requiring attention from parents. Deployment-related adjustment is ongoing, and it is a mistake to assume youth fears are resolved in the short-term.
- signs and symptoms of depression and other mental health issues for teens. Parents must be better equipped to monitor how well their children are dealing with ongoing deployment-related worries and changes. They should also be aware of the range of emotions teens may experience and ways to teach them to express these emotions in a healthy manner.
- how parents can model appropriate self-care and stress reduction, so that teens do not feel responsible for parental emotional well-being. Certain parents forget that their own condition has dramatic effects on the well-being of their children.

Teens often do not have adequate ways to discuss their worries about parental deployment, and . . . some teens are not speaking with anyone about their concerns.

Becoming Intentional about Providing Consistency in Family Routines and Rituals

Educational information for parents about family routines and rituals should include:

- the importance of maintaining consistent expectations about school, work, and family responsibilities. Young people need consistency and predictability in environments. This is one area in which they may feel like they have some control over their lives. Information for parents should also highlight the importance of doing pleasurable things together as a family, as a way of building family rapport and supporting family adjustment to deployment.

- the importance of maintaining family rituals and creating new ones to support family identity and continuity. Families need intentional ways of connecting with each other, and of acknowledging that their living situation and family life has changed. This may include ideas for documenting events and rituals the deployed member may miss.

Providing and Accessing Informal Support Systems

Content for parents in this area include:

- the importance of getting teens involved in social support networks and information on potential opportunities for youth involvement.

- teaching parents to encourage teens to gain new life skills in areas such as stress management, cooking, budgeting, car maintenance, and lawn care, that can prepare them to successfully take on more responsibilities at home.

Deployment-related adjustment is ongoing, and it is a mistake to assume youth fears are resolved in the short-term.

Supporting Youth, Supporting Families: Conclusions

For the most part, youth in military families are underserved by both military support systems and community support systems. In addition to the normative and usual developmental challenges, youth in military families are faced with unique challenges stemming from the deployment of one or both parents. While most military-affiliated youth have the raw materials for resilience, they require supports that enable them to mobilize their abilities while their family situations change. Support for youth can be best accomplished by supporting the adults in the family,

insuring that those adults have the necessary skills, characteristics, and personal efficacy to guide, support, and protect their children.

". . . Like when they come home is that like awkward bonding phase all over again, like you're starting from scratch. And then like they've missed out on so much stuff and it's like hard to catch them up with it. Like some of the stuff you just had to be there and they weren't. And it's not like you can be mad at them for it, like inside you're going to be a little bit mad, but you know it's not their fault."

—Teen Female

References

Glod, M. (2008, July 17), Coping with their parents' war. *The Washington Post,* pp. Al, A9,

Hiew, C.C, (1992), Separated by their work: Families with fathers living apart. *Environment and Behavior, 24,* 206–225.

Hillenbrand, E.D. (1976). Father absence in military families. *The Family Coordinator, 25,* 251–258.

Huebner, A. J., & Mancini, J.A. (June 2005). *Adjustment Among Adolescents in Military Families When a Parent is Deployed: A final report submitted to the Military Family Research Institute and the Department of Defense Quality of Life Office.* Falls Church, Virginia: Virginia Tech, Department of Human Development. Available online at http://www.cfs.purdue.edu/ mfri/pages/research/Adjustments_in_adolescents.pdf

Huebner, A., Mancini, J., Wilcox, R., Grass, S., & Grass, G. (2007). Parental deployment and youth in military families: Exploring uncertainty and ambiguous loss. *Family Relations, 56*(2), 112–122.

Huebner, A., & Powell, C. (2007, November). *Exploring Attachment and Family Adjustment During Deployment: "When Momma ain't Happy, ain't Nobody Happy".* Paper presented at the 67th National Council on Family Relations Annual Conference, Minneapolis, MN.

Jensen, P.S., Martin, D., & Watanabe, H, (1996), Children's response to separation during Operation Desert Storm. *Journal of the American Academy of Child and Adolescent Psychiatry, 35,* 433–441.

Jensen, P., & Shaw, J. (1996). The effects of war and parental deployment upon children and teens. In R. Ursano & A. Norwood (Eds.), *Emotional Aftermath of the Persian GulfWar: Veterans. Families, Communities, and Nations* (pp.83–109). Washington, DC: American Psychiatric Press.

Levai, M., Kaplan, S., Ackerman, R., & Hammock, M. (1995). The effect of father absence on the psychiatric hospitalization of Navy children. *Military Medicine, 160,* 103–106.

Mancini, J.A., Bowen, G.L., & Martin, J.A. (2005). Community social organization: A conceptual linchpin in examining families in the context of communities. *Family Relations: Interdisciplinary Journal of Applied Family Studies, 54,* 570–582.

Morse, J, (2006), *The New Emotional Cycle of Deployment.* Retrieved June 28, 2007 http://deploymenthealthlibrary.fhp.osd. mil/products/Emotional%20Cycles%20of%20Deployment%20 (241).pdf

Office of the Deputy Under Secretary of Defense (2005). *2005 Demographics Report.* Retrieved October 25, 2007, from Purdue

University, Military Family Research Institute Web site: http://www.cfs.purdue.edu/mfri/pages/military/2005_Demographics_Report.pdf

Yeatman, G.W. (1981). Parental separation and the military child. *Military Medicine, 146,* 320–322.

ANGELA J. HUEBNER, PHD, (ahuebner@vt.edu) is an Associate Professor in the Department of Human Development, in the Marriage and Family Therapy Program at Virginia Tech in Fails Church. Virginia. Her research focuses on issues of positive youth development, and adjustment and adaptation among youth. **JAY A. MANCINI, PHD,** is a Professor in the Department of Human Development, and a Senior Research Fellow with the institute for Society, Culture, and Environment at Virginia Tech, His research focuses on the lifespan, vulnerable populations, and building community capacity and resilience. He is a Fellow of the National Council on Family Relations, and a Fellow of the World Demographic Association.

When Play Turns to Trouble

Many Parents Are Now Wondering: How Much Is Too Much?

JENNIFER SETER WAGNER

Ollie Morelli, 7, logs on to the family laptop before sunup to make sure his pet lion, Cedric, is set for the day. The character in the online game Webkinz would appear to be: His house, furnished by Ollie, boasts a football-shaped refrigerator, a football-helmet coffee table, a couch, and a flat-screen TV. Cedric requires hours of after-school attention, too—and sometimes inspires an outburst when Mom and Dad say, "Enough!" Like many parents these days, Ollie's have wondered uneasily where childish pastime begins to edge toward obsession. "The issue is not the amount of time," says Brian Morelli. "We can control that. It's the fact that he gets up before everyone else and sneaks onto the computer. It's like he sets his internal clock so he can play Webkinz."

Concern is spreading among parents and mental-health professionals that the exploding popularity of computer and video games has a deeper dark side than simple couch-potatohood. Software sales jumped 28 percent last year to $9.5 billion; an average of nine games were sold every second of the year, according to the Entertainment Software Association. Studies show that 92 percent of children under age 18 play regularly. According to the Media Research Lab at Iowa State University, about 8.5 percent of 8-to-18-year-old gamers can be considered pathologically addicted, and nearly one quarter of young people—more males than females—admit they've felt addicted. Little wonder: In February, a team at Stanford University School of Medicine showed that areas of the brain responsible for generating feelings of addiction and reward are activated during game play. "We are seeing it over and over again," says Liz Woolley, founder of On-Line Gamers Anonymous (www.olganonboard.org), a virtual 12-step program for gaming addicts. "We're losing [kids] into the games, and it's turning their brains to mush."

Software sales hit $9.5 billion last year, an average of nine games sold each second.

Saying when. How can parents know when a lot is too much? Media experts are quick to point out that computer and video games are not inherently bad for kids; indeed, most players find a balance, says David Walsh, founder of the National Institute on Media and the Family in Minneapolis: "They play their video games; they do their homework; they keep up with their responsibilities and have other interests. No problem."

But when the other areas of a child's life begin to suffer, parents may have cause to take corrective action. Kimberly Young, director of the Center for Internet Addiction Recovery in Bradford, Pa., points to several common warning signs of pathological behavior: fantasizing or talking about game characters or missions when offline; lying about or hiding how much time is spent playing or disobeying parental limits; losing interest in sports and hobbies; choosing the game over time with friends; and continuing to play despite plummeting grades, loss of a scholarship, a breakup with a partner. An addicted gamer's physical appearance may also change as he loses sleep, neglects to shower, and skips meals.

Team first. The games most apt to be overplayed are what people in the industry call MMORPGs, or "massively multiplayer online role-playing games." Games of this type—World of Warcraft and Call of Duty are two popular examples—connect players in cyberspace who then form "guilds" or "clans" that participate in raids against opposing squads. Generally, each player is represented by an avatar—usually a three-dimensional character that either the game or the player creates—and has a role to play, such as defender or strategist. Guild members may be from all over the world, and the missions can go on for days. "Let's say I'm a ninth grader, with teammates in Japan and Bulgaria, and Mom says it's time to do homework," says Walsh. "I E-mail my teammates I need to stop, and their response is: 'Are you nuts?' The membership on the teams becomes very important to these kids. Dropping out of a mission is not OK." The longer you play, says Young, "the more you begin to identify with this make-believe world."

One mother and physician in the Midwest, who asked for anonymity to protect her son, is all too familiar with the siren call of the game. Her son, now 21, started playing computer games as a young child, graduated to World of Warcraft in high school, and spent so much time online as a college freshman that he got mostly F's and was forced to withdraw. His mom says that the progression from great kid and student to self-destructive abuser stupefied the family. "I didn't understand this was a whole different thing," she says of the game. "I'd call him to dinner, and he couldn't come," she says. " 'We're in the middle of a raid!' he'd say. 'They need me!"

Once he left college, he had to make a choice: either find somewhere else to live and play the game, at his expense, or quit the game, start working, and go back to school part time. He chose the latter and is now finishing up an associate's degree. "We determined there would be no computer games allowed in our house when we saw how destructive they could be," says his mother. The family even locked up the computers. "The longer he spends away from this, the more he'll realize how destructive and what a fantasy world it was," she says. "But I don't know what will happen when he goes out on his own."

Therapy wasn't an option, since the young man was an adult and refused to go. But even when age or willingness isn't an issue, finding effective professional help can be a challenge. For now, game addiction is not recognized by the American Psychiatric Association, which means that there are no national guidelines for what therapy should entail. Whether this will change in 2012, the date a new APA handbook on mental disorders is scheduled to come out, is still up for discussion. Pathological video and computer game play would now be considered one of a broad group of "behavioral addictions" that also includes compulsive shopping and addiction to online pornography, for example. The only behavioral addiction now specifically listed in the handbook is pathological gambling. To treat these disorders, cognitive behavioral therapy is often used to identify the thought processes that lead to the compulsion and to change the destructive thinking. Families seeking help may need to pay out of their own pockets, because insurance typically doesn't cover addictions that

---

Resources for Parents

A few places for worried families to look for guidance:

On-Line Gamers Anonymous (www.olganonboard .org). A virtual 12-step program aimed at helping gamers and their families battle game addiction.

Center for Internet Addiction Recovery (www.netaddiction.com). Educational information about Internet addictions, online support group, quiz for those who suspect an online gaming addiction.

Aspen Education Group (www.aspeneducationgroup. com/gameaddiction/suws.asp). Information about how wilderness therapy may help the gaming addict.

Smith & Jones Center (http://www.smithandjones.nl/ eng/index.html). Video game residential addiction treatment center in Amsterdam.

---

don't officially exist. That said, many young gamers are diagnosed with other conditions such as depression or obsessive-compulsive disorder.

Elsewhere in the world, the problem is recognized as huge. Governments in China and South Korea have helped fund treatment centers and hotlines for electronic game addicts. Keith Bakker, director of the Smith and Jones Center in Amsterdam, a residential detox center that treats video game addicts from around the world, compares their poison to crack cocaine. But "it's easier to treat a coke addict than it is a gamer," he says. "The gamer's denial is so great, and it's compounded by family and community," he says. "Who in the world thinks gaming is a problem?" At first, the center kept gamers physically apart from other addicts, but results were much better when the kids took group therapy with residents troubled by eating disorders, marijuana, or cocaine. "They began to see the similarities between themselves," Bakker says. After they stop denying they have an addiction and the damage it's causing, he notes, many young people never pick up a game again.

Outside help. In this country, some families are turning to wilderness therapy. The Aspen Education Group, a California-based organization that treats underachievers from around the country, provides young people ages 11 to 18 with a back-to-nature approach to ending their gaming obsessions. "At home when they have frustrations, they go to their video games," says therapist Aaron Shaw. "Here they have cold weather, hiking." By being away from their screens for seven to nine weeks, he says, "they learn some healthier coping mechanisms." Shaw first tries to discover kids' reasons for playing; often, he finds, it's to find freedom and fun and out of a need for greater acceptance from their parents. (If Mom is always nagging that games are a waste of time, notes Shaw, "they say: 'Screw you, my friends online love me, and I'll hang out with them.'")

To that point, Young advises parents who want to head off serious trouble to find ways to limit play without blaming or criticizing. Better to set—and enforce—time restrictions, as the Morellis do, put electronics in a well-trafficked area, and make it easy for a child to choose clubs or sports. Games should never be a child's main focus, cautions Woolley. Her wisdom is hard won. Several years ago, Woolley's son committed suicide in front of his computer with his favorite game on the screen.

From *U.S. News & World Report,* May 19, 2008, pp. 51–53. Copyright © 2008 by U.S. News & World Report. Reprinted by permission.

Aggression in Adolescent Dating Relationships: Predictors and Prevention

Jennifer Connolly, PhD, and Wendy Josephson, PhD

The emergence of romantic relationships is one of the most striking features of adolescence. By the late adolescent years, most teenagers have been in a romantic relationship at least once and roughly half of teens are dating currently. Alarmingly though, in many of these relationships adolescents act aggressively toward each other and this behavior appears almost as early as relationships emerge (Connolly, Pepler, Craig, & Taradash, 2000). Aggression in adolescent dating relationships is of high concern. There are negative psychological consequences as well as the risk of physical injury. Moreover, use of aggression in dating relationships may set in motion a pattern of interpersonal violence that continues into adulthood. On the bright side, adolescence is a period of transition and opportunity. Preventing dating aggression at this developmental stage may reap significant positive outcomes later in life. In this article, we provide a review of adolescent dating aggression, focusing on warning signs and methods of prevention.

Prevalence and Impact

Adolescence is a period of heightened risk for aggression between dating partners (see Table 1 for definitions). Recent estimates indicate that between 20% and 50% of adolescents have been in an aggressive relationship. Very few studies have focused on dating aggression in gay and lesbian relationships, but the available information suggests that the rates are similar to those reported in heterosexual relationships (Johnson, 2006). In heterosexual adolescent couples, dating aggression occurs for both genders. Both boys and girls report perpetration of aggression as well as victimization and these roles frequently occur within the same relationship. In one study, 66% of adolescent dating aggression was bi-directional (Gray & Foshee, 1997). It may, though, occur for different reasons. Boys more often

Table 1   Definitions of Dating Violence and Dating Aggression

Dating aggression is now the term researchers commonly use to refer to actual or threatened harm between adolescent dating partners. Often it is these milder forms of aggression (e.g., pushing, slapping, or shoving) that occur between young dating partners.

Dating violence is actual or threatened harm between current or former partners.

Physical violence is the intentional use of physical force that could cause harm to another person. It includes mildly **aggressive** behaviors such as scratching, pushing, and shoving, as well as more severely **violent** behaviors such as biting, choking, shaking, slapping, punching, burning, or use of a weapon.

Psychological or emotional violence involves verbally abusive and coercive tactics intended to control, embarrass, humiliate, or isolate the partner from friends and family; it often precedes physical violence.

report dating aggression because of anger and girls more often report aggression in self-defense (O'Keefe, 2005). It is also important to keep in mind that, in heterosexual relationships, girls' aggression is far less physically injurious than that of boys. While boys almost always report being unhurt by their girlfriends' aggression, very few girls reported being unhurt.

Dating aggression is not a trivial occurrence, limited to a single relationship or a single episode. Rather repeated aggression within a relationship is a risk for at least some adolescents who remain in a relationship even though there have been acts of aggression. And equally worrying, there are some adolescents who appear to be prone to aggression in their relationships as they report aggression later on in a new romantic relationship.

Although understudied in comparison to research on adult intimate violence, it is now becoming clear that adolescent dating aggression has a serious negative impact on the victims' health and well-being. In a study of high school girls, Jay Silverman and colleagues (2001) found that girls who reported being hurt by their boyfriends were more likely to report substance use, disordered eating, risky sexual behaviors, and suicidal thoughts. Although less is known about this, it does appear that the negative impact extends to boys and that both genders report fear, anxiety, and emotional disturbance in association with dating aggression as well as an increased probability of running away from home and dropping out of school.

Risk Factors and Warning Signs

So, what are the warning signs for dating violence? A complex array of factors, such as family violence, attitudes, peers, problem behavior, and couple hostility increase the risk for dating aggression. To understand how these multiple risk factors might be linked, psychologists distinguish between two types of risk factors. The first of these are **"background"** factors, so-called because they provide powerful models that can lead an adolescent to use aggression as a response to interpersonal problems generally. Particularly significant background factors are violence in the family of origin, prior use of aggression with peers, a peer group that tolerates romantic aggression, and an attitude of accepting the use of aggression to solve romantic problems. These background factors form the social context in which the adolescent grows up and learns about relationships. They predispose the adolescent to respond with aggression in future interactions with a dating partner. Then **"situation"** factors take over. These are specific features of the dating relationship that lead an adolescent to respond aggressively with that particular romantic partner. Some of the most significant of these are the quality of the relationship, the use of psychological or verbal aggression, partner aggression, and poor interpersonal skills. These factors play a pivotal role in that they are the developmental outcome of aggression-tolerant family or peer contexts and also most directly lead to aggression towards a dating partner.

Background Risk Factors
Aggression in the Family of Origin

Researchers have been very interested in the long-term effects of growing up in a home in which there is violence between the parents or from the parent to the child. It is a reasonable hypothesis that adolescents who have witnessed aggression between their parents or who have experienced very harsh parenting might carry these patterns forward into their own intimate relationships. However, the research support is mixed. As summarized recently by O'Keefe (2005), some studies identify these links, especially for boys, while other studies do not find the link. Focusing on high-risk youth though, the findings are clearer that child maltreatment is a significant risk factor for later dating violence. Wolfe and his colleagues (2004) studied dating violence among adolescents in child protection and found a significant link between child abuse and dating aggression in adolescence. Families from which a child is removed for safety experience high levels of stress and disruption, in addition to maltreatment, and these factors collectively contribute to the adolescent's increased risk for perpetrating dating aggression.

Aggression with Peers

In contrast to the mixed findings for direct family influences, there is growing evidence that peer relationships are formative for dating aggression. These influences are both direct and indirect. For example, adolescent boys who fight and are aggressive with their peers also show these same behaviors with a romantic partner. Equally though, the aggressive behavior of adolescents' friends can influence dating aggression. Adolescent boys who talk together about girls in hostile or disrespectful ways are equally at risk for dating aggression (Capaldi et al., 2001). Adolescents who believe that their friends would be aggressive to a romantic partner are also more likely to act with aggression toward their own dating partner.

Recently, bullying peers has been identified as a significant risk behavior for dating aggression (Connolly et al., 2000; Pepler et al., 2006). Bullying refers to aggressive behaviors, either physical or psychological, that youth use to exert their power over other young people who are less able to defend themselves. Over half of young people are involved in bullying at some point during their elementary or high school years and perhaps 10% of adolescents bully others frequently and persistently. While in the past bullying was often dismissed as a passing problem of childhood, there is now substantial evidence that it can set a young person on a pathway to using aggression to get his or her way in a wide range of relationships, including those with a romantic partner. During the transition to adolescence, as romantic relationships emerge and sexuality becomes a sensitive issue for young people, youngsters who bully frequently appear to transfer their power-asserting aggression to dating relationships. Both sexual harassment of peers and aggression towards a romantic partner are common behaviors of both boys and girls who bully.

Aggression-Tolerant Attitudes

Most adolescents have very disapproving attitudes toward dating aggression, especially physical or sexual aggression by boys against girls (Josephson & Proulx, in press). Some are more tolerant of dating aggression under particularly provocative circumstances, such as infidelity or the other person hitting first. The more teens think that dating aggression is justified in a variety of situations, the more likely they are to be aggressive to their own dating partners.

Situational Risk Factors
Quality of the Relationship

Dating relationships characterized by high levels of conflict and low levels of intimacy and satisfaction are at risk for dating aggression (O'Keefe, 1997). Adolescents with a history of bullying their peers are more likely to be involved in the low quality relationships that are vulnerable to dating aggression. Although their dating relationships are very important to them, adolescents who bully their peers have romantic relationships that are less affectionate, intimate, committed, and equitable than the romantic relationships experienced by their peers (Connolly et al., 2000).

Psychological Aggression to Romantic Partner

Psychological aggression typically precedes physical aggression and can be a warning sign of violence to come (O'Leary & Slep, 2003). It is also very common. Most studies of verbal aggression in dating relationships report that it occurs in at least 80% of romantic couples. Psychological and emotional aggression can seriously undermine the recipient's self-esteem. Illogically, some aspects of psychological aggression, the controlling behaviors and jealousy-related verbal rages, are sometimes interpreted by the recipient as originating from love, which may lead to a paradoxical intensifying of commitment to the relationship following aggression. However, the verbally abusive and humiliating aspects of psychological aggression are not subject to this kind of mis-attribution, and appear to have a stronger negative effect on self-esteem than being subjected to physical dating aggression. Consequently, psychological and emotional aggression may be a stronger impetus for ending a physically aggressive relationship than is the severity of the physical aggression.

Partner Aggression

Adolescent dating aggression is primarily bi-directional (Gray & Foshee, 1997). In fact, a dating partner's aggression is often the strongest predictor of an adolescent's own dating aggression. Gray and Foshee found that adolescents in mutually aggressive relationships perpetrated more aggression, and sustained more injuries, than those in relationships for which aggression was one-sided. This may be because of the tendency for aggressive adolescents to form romantic relationships with others who are similarly aggressive and so partners provoke each other and learn aggressive tactics from each other. This is one very important way in which adolescent dating aggression differs from the patterns found in long-term adult relationships. Aggression is more likely to be mutual in adolescent dating relationships than in the relationships of adults. Probably this is because control is usually distributed more evenly in adolescents' dating relationships although when there is unequal power it presents a risk factor for young women's victimization from physical aggression (Johnson, 2006).

Aggression is more likely to be mutual in adolescent dating relationships than in the relationships of adults.

Poor Interpersonal Skills

Poor conflict resolution tactics are associated with psychological and emotional aggression. One recent study (Josephson & Proulx, in press) found that failure to use reasoning and negotiation effectively to resolve conflicts was associated with an escalating pattern of resorting to psychological aggression and, ultimately, physical aggression.

Prevention of Dating Aggression

Taking this profile of risk factors into consideration, there is quite a strong consensus about the features that are necessary for effective prevention of dating aggression:

- **A comprehensive approach:** Prevention programs work better if they reach more of the levels (individual, family, peer group, couple) at which adolescents may be put at risk for dating aggression. Comprehensiveness includes taking a holistic approach to the adolescent as a whole person, providing a variety of different activities. For example, the *Healthy Relationships* curriculum (Men for Change, 1994) provides 53 activities intended to help adolescents build knowledge, change attitudes, and develop skills to positively affect the cognitive, emotional, and behavioral aspects of relationships with friends, family, dating partners, and others in their school and community.

- **Peer involvement:** Because of the critical role of peers in adolescents' lives, as role models, norm enforcers, and preferred providers of advice and support, it is especially important to engage young people themselves in prevention activities. For example, the RISE program (*Respect in Schools Everywhere*, Weiser & Moran, 2006) trains high school volunteers for 12 weeks about bullying, dating violence, and healthy relationships, then provides them with coaching and support to give two workshops on these topics to every classroom in their own schools and nearby middle schools. The "upside" of the strong role of peers in the development of dating aggression is that they are a powerful force to prevent it, if their influence is positive. For this reason, universal programs are recommended over targeted interventions with just those who are at risk, even though additional supports may need to be put in place for high risk adolescents.

- **Appropriate goals for change:** Prevention efforts that address the real pattern of mutual and less severe dating aggression in adolescent relationships will be more effective than those based on the one-sided "intimate terrorism" model that better fits intensive interventions for perpetrators of domestic violence (Johnson, 2006). For instance, the BRIGHT program (*Building Relationships in Greater Harmony Together,* Cascardi & Avery-Leaf, 1998) was designed to take a gender-neutral focus on dating aggression. Program developers believe that this will avoid having prevention efforts undermined by the resistance that they anticipated if they appeared to be unfairly stereotyping men and presenting a version of dating aggression that did not correspond to the experiences of adolescents. Because many young people will receive a prevention program before they even begin dating, and many dating relationships have no physical dating aggression at all, prevention programs should focus on changing those factors that put young people at risk for physical dating aggression: psychological and emotional aggression, tolerant attitudes toward dating aggression, and poor interpersonal skills.

- **Emphasis on building skills:** In their focus group study on dating aggression, Heather Sears and colleagues (2006) found that high school students wanted assistance to develop skills for maintaining healthy relationships and dealing with relationship conflict. Prevention programs should provide a chance for adolescents to build strong skills for promoting healthy relationships. For example, the *Fourth R* program (Townsley et al., 2005) provides role play activities and scenarios to help young people learn general communication and conflict management skills, problem solving, social perspective taking, assertiveness, and frustration tolerance. Skill-building activities are best begun as early as possible, with opportunities for practice, such as role playing activities, and taking on more challenging situations as skills develop.

Conclusion

Adolescent dating aggression is a serious problem for many teenagers. Yet like other forms of aggression, warning signs are often present that a young couple may be at risk. By understanding these precursors we can help adolescents avoid problematic situations and instead develop healthy dating relationships that will set in place a solid foundation for satisfying relationships throughout life.

References

Capaldi, D.M., Dishion, T.J., Stoolmiller, M., & Yoerger, K. (2001). Aggression toward female partners by at-risk young men: The contribution of male adolescent friendships. *Developmental Psychology, 37,* 61–73.

Cascardi, M., & Avery-Leaf, S. (1998). *Building Relationships in Greater Harmony Together (BRIGHT) Program.* Glen Ridge, NJ: DVPP, Inc.

Connolly, J., Pepler, D., Craig, W., & Taradash, A. (2000). Dating experiences of bullies in early adolescence. *Child Maltreatment, 5,* 299–310.

Gray, H.M., & Foshee, V. (1997). Adolescent dating violence: Differences between one-sided and mutually violent profiles. *Journal of Interpersonal Violence, 12,* 126–141.

Johnson, M.P. (2006). Violence and abuse in personal relationships: Conflict, terror and resistance in intimate relationships. In A.L. Vangelisti & D. Perlman (Eds.), *The Cambridge Handbook of Personal Relationships* (pp. 557–576). New York: Cambridge University Press.

Josephson, W.L., & Proulx, J.B. (in press). Violence in young adolescents' relationships: A path model. *Journal of Interpersonal Violence.*

Men for Change (1994). *Healthy Relationships: A violence-prevention curriculum* (Second ed.). Halifax, NS: Author.

O'Keefe, M. (1997). Predictors of dating violence among high school students. *Journal of Interpersonal Violence, 12,* 546–568.

O'Keefe, M. (2005). Teen dating violence: A review of risk factors and prevention efforts. *Applied Research Forum,* 1–13.

O'Leary, K.D., & Slep, A.M.S. (2003). A dyadic longitudinal model of adolescent dating aggression. *Journal of Clinical Child and Adolescent Psychology, 32,* 314–327.

Pepler, D., Craig, W., Connolly, J., Yuile, A., McMaster, L., & Jiang, D. (2006). A developmental perspective on bullying. *Aggressive Behaviour, 32,* 376–384.

Sears, H.A., Byers, E.S., Whelan, J.J., Saint-Pierre, M., & the Dating Violence Research Team (2006). "If it hurts you, then it is not a joke": Adolescents' ideas about girls' and boys' use and experience of abusive behavior in dating relationships. *Journal of Interpersonal Violence, 21,* 1,191–1,207.

Silverman, J.G., Raj, A., Mucci, L.A., & Hathaway, J.E. (2001). Dating violence against adolescent girls and associated substance use, unhealthy weight control, sexual risk behavior, pregnancy, and suicidality. *Journal of the American Medical Association, 286,* 572–579.

Townsley, D., Crooks, C., Hughes, R., & Wolfe, D.A. (2005). *The Fourth R: Relationship-Based Violence Prevention.* London, ON: CAMH Centre for Prevention Science.

Weiser, J., & Moran, M. (2006). *RISE Manual: How to Engage Youth in Violence Prevention Strategies.* Toronto, ON: East Metro Youth Services.

Wolfe, D., Wekerle, C., Scott, K., Straatman, A., & Grasley, C. (2004). Predicting abuse in adolescent dating relationships over one year: The role of child maltreatment and trauma. *Journal of Abnormal Psychology, 113,* 406–415.

DR. JENNIFER CONNOLLY is a Professor of Clinical-Developmental Psychology at York University in Toronto, Canada and is the Director of the LaMarsh Centre for Research on Violence and Conflict Resolution. With Dr. Josephson, she is currently examining the use of peer-led interventions to prevent dating aggression in middle/high schools. **DR. WENDY JOSEPHSON** is a Professor of Social Psychology at the University of Winnipeg, in Winnipeg, Canada. Her research is primarily in the areas of aggression and violence reduction, including media effects on aggression, prevention of dating violence, and the effects of youth engagement in violence prevention.

From *The Prevention Researcher*, December 2007, pp. 3–5. Copyright © 2007 by Integrated Research Services, Inc. Reprinted by permission.

A Host of Trouble

More Parents are Being Held Criminally Liable for Their Teens' Drinking Parties.

EMMA SCHWARTZ

The day had gone just as Les Foster had planned. More than 100 friends had gathered at his private dirt track for an annual day of car racing in Gardner, Kan., where Foster's team won the prized traveling trophy. By sunset, he had retired happily to his house down the road. The peace did not last. A few hours later, Foster, who runs an auto repair shop, was jolted awake by a knock on the door. It was the police, and they wanted to know what Foster could tell them about a 17-year-old boy who had been killed on the racetrack when his intoxicated teenage friend ran over him.

With that tragic episode began a two-year legal nightmare. Foster, 43, was convicted in 2006 of allowing underage drinking on his property, even though he says he did not know that the teens had returned to the track. He was sentenced to a year's probation and ordered to deliver six speeches about underage drinking to high school students. Then the victim's family filed a civil suit against him, demanding he pay them $2.5 million. His insurance company settled for $452,000.

Foster's is an experience that more and more adults—especially parents—may encounter as a growing number of states pass laws increasing parental liability for teenage drinking. Twenty-three states have now passed "social host" laws targeting adults who allow underage drinking in their homes. And 33 states have some form of civil liability laws. "Homeowners and parents are at risk now because they don't appreciate what their kids are doing in the backyard," says Suzanne Bass, a Florida attorney who has handled these suits.

Binge drinking

Although teen drinking rates have declined significantly over the past few decades, they remain disturbingly high: More than 40 percent of college students say they binge drink. And at more than 5,000 a year, alcohol-related fatalities remain the leading cause of death among teens.

The key statistic behind the new laws, however, is that two thirds of teens get their booze from adults. Some parents provide it deliberately, believing that if they condone it in moderation, their children will be less likely to abuse it. Stanton Peele, a psychologist and addiction expert, says research bears that theory out. "It's accurate to say that *not* drinking at home with parents is a significant risk factor," says Peele.

But advocates of the new laws take just the opposite view. Stricter parental liability, they say, can reverse society's tacit acceptance of underage drinking just as tougher laws have changed the public's attitude toward drunk driving. "We have to get adults to understand the ways in which [they] contribute to this problem," says Richard Bonnie, a law professor at the University of Virginia and coeditor of a 2003 study by the National Academy of Sciences that called for increased enforcement against parents. "We're not going to change social norms among kids if we don't change social norms among parents."

Heightened parental liability raises thorny questions about where the balance of responsibility and punishment should lie. Should parents be jailed for allowing teens to drink? Can the law hold adults liable if they're not even aware of the drinking? Does a zero-tolerance policy encourage worse drinking habits among teens?

Critics say this prohibitionist tack will never eliminate teen drinking and is likely to push thoughtful discussion out of the public arena. "How much more do we need to spend in order to achieve enforcement that constitutes success?" asks John McCardell, the former president of Middlebury College who is leading a national campaign to lower the drinking age to 18.

Jail sentence

There is no research on whether social host laws are effective, and most adults arrested under them are siblings or friends in their 20s. Still, it is clear the penalties are falling harder on parents. In June, Elisa Kelly of Charlottesville, Va., was sentenced to 27 months in jail for hosting a drinking party for her teenage son. She bought the alcohol and thought she was protecting the kids by taking their car keys for the night. And an Illinois couple, Jeffrey and Sara Hutsell, were convicted for allowing their son to host a drinking party after which two teens died in a car crash. A judge last week sentenced Sara to probation and her husband to 14 days in jail, with time off to go to work.

How You Can Protect Yourself

If you have a teen and own your home, you are at risk

The good news for parents is that so-called social host cases can be difficult to litigate, and they are likely only in the event of a catastrophic injury or death resulting from underage drinking. But that doesn't mean you're free from risk.

Homeowners face the greatest threat from these types of lawsuits since a home is insured and it's a financial asset that a plaintiff can try to tap. Liability laws differ from state to state. Minnesota, for instance, says a liable host knowingly provides a minor with alcohol, while in California, a host is liable only if he provides alcohol to "an obviously intoxicated person."

Regardless of the law, homeowners who are sued may face resistance from their insurers. "The insurance company's first reaction will be to try to find a way to disprove coverage," says Richard Campbell, an attorney who handles social host liability cases in Massachusetts.

The insurance company's first reaction may be to deny coverage.

Lawyers suggest parents check their homeowners policies to see what is covered. Most policies will cover some form of legal liability, but some may have exceptions for underage drinking and may not protect against a steep judgment. Homeowners insurance may or may not cover legal fees, which can mount quickly.

In short, there is only one sure way to avoid legal trouble, lawyers say. Make sure there is never underage drinking on your property—period.

—E.S.

Barrington, R.I., is an affluent seaside community where two teens died in drunk-driving accidents in 2005. Police there observed that more parents were allowing their children to drink at home. But they had trouble charging parents because they couldn't always prove that the parents had bought the alcohol for the teens.

It was a dilemma faced by other Rhode Island towns. So in 2006, the General Assembly passed a law allowing police to charge parents criminally for permitting underage drinking even if they didn't provide the booze. It allows for religious exemptions (such as drinking wine on the Jewish Sabbath) but is otherwise among the nation's stiffest. The penalty is a minimum $350 fine and up to six months behind bars.

The college town of Salisbury, Md., doesn't have a social host law. But single mother Janet Lane found herself in legal trouble last year when the police broke up a party thrown by her two sons while she was at a business conference. Responding to a tip from another parent, police found music blaring, beer bottles strewn on the lawn, and one teen gagging on his own vomit. Breathalyzer tests showed that 11 of the 24 teens—although not Lane's sons—had been drinking. Lane, a paralegal, says she knew nothing of the ruckus, but police slapped her with more than a dozen charges of allowing minors to drink.

The evidence—largely based on partygoers who were themselves intoxicated—was shaky, and a neighbor was eventually convicted of buying the booze. Eventually, though, Lane pleaded guilty to having a disorderly house, and the police dropped the other charges. But the experience left Lane with $3,000 in legal bills and a bitter taste. "They had a good reason for trying to understand who did it," she says. "But how they went about it was wrong."

In California, meanwhile, officials have taken a different approach to teen drinking: steep fines. The state does not have a criminal social host ordinance, but individual counties have targeted parents with civil laws that allow police to fine them—in some cases up to $2,500—for allowing underage drinking. Officials in Marin County, a liberal enclave north of San Francisco, worried that criminalizing parental involvement would send the wrong message; the goal wasn't to punish people but to deter bad behavior. So the county passed a civil fine ordinance under which police have cited four people, including one 19-year-old who called the police herself when a party got out of hand.

A Threat to Teen Brains

Alcohol's harms are worse for young people

Everyone knows the deleterious effects of heavy drinking. But the effects are far more pronounced for young people. That's because research shows that the brain doesn't fully develop until the mid-20s.

The areas that show the most change between the teens and mid-20s are the brain's frontal lobes, which are central to planning, decision making, impulse control, and language. This physiological transformation helps explain why even level-headed teens are prone to riskier behavior, a tendency only aggravated by alcohol.

The consequences are both short- and long-term. Young drinkers are more likely to drive drunk, get into fights, or engage in unprotected or unwanted sex. And alcohol-related incidents remain the leading cause of death among teens, from car accidents (38 percent), homicides (32 percent), and suicides (6 percent).

Over the long haul, early alcohol consumption can hurt brain development. And the earlier youths begin drinking, the more likely they are to have chronic alcohol and other health problems.

Teenagers who start drinking before age 15 are four times as likely to become alcoholics as those who wait until they are 21. And those who drink at a young age are more likely to have other substance abuse problems as well.

—E.S.

One of the two parents fined under the ordinance was Mill Valley businesswoman Deborah Walters. She had allowed her 17-year-old son to host some friends for a barbecue and explicitly forbade drinking. She was in the house when the police came (in answer to a neighbor's complaint) and found the boys drinking beer outside. Walters was fined $750, a penalty she is making her son pay back at $100 a month. "He knows that if he does it again," she says, "he doesn't have a place to live."

In some jurisdictions, proposed liability laws have encountered challenges. Davette Baker, director of a substance abuse project in Harrodsburg, Ky., successfully pushed through a social host ordinance in her town. But when she took the proposal to nearby Burgin, she struck out. The police chief argued that state laws already on the books, such as one concerning an unlawful transaction with a minor, gave him the ability to charge adults.

Fatal crash

In other cases, prosecutions have failed. Rebekah Perrin of Warren, Mass., lost her 19-year-old daughter, Abbigayle, in a drunk-driving accident just after Christmas in 2005. Abbigayle, a vivacious athlete and recent high school graduate, hadn't been drinking. But she had left a house party after midnight in a car with a friend who had. The friend crashed into a guardrail, and Abbigayle was killed almost instantly.

Prosecutors charged the friend, then went after Marc Holly, the father of the teen who held the party, alleging that he not only allowed the drinking party but joined the youths in a game of beer pong. During his trial on a misdemeanor charge, Holly denied condoning the drinking and said he found out only when he returned from an evening out. (Jurors also didn't know he had been incarcerated for coming to court high on cocaine.)

Although some party-goers testified against him, Holly was acquitted. Says an angry Perrin: "It should have been this man who paid the price." Trying to make him do just that, Perrin has filed a civil suit against Holly's wife, who owns their home. Holly's lawyer, Michael Erlich, says his client is not responsible. "It can get to a point where [the law is] not reasonable anymore," he says. "We have to hold teens to some standard that *they* can take responsibility."

Few would disagree with that sentiment, but the pressure is on public officials to fight teen drinking on all fronts. That's why Tucson, Ariz., which has also passed a social host ordinance, is focusing on landlords. In 2001, Tucson alerted landlords that they could be in legal trouble if they didn't take action against underage revelers. So Ricardo Fernandez, who manages a 300-unit apartment complex near the University of Arizona, declared that renters would be evicted if they violated the city's underage drinking laws. Other landlords followed suit. The result: Citywide arrest rates for minors caught with alcohol have dropped almost 20 percent since 2004.

Likewise, the city of Long Beach, N.Y., has taken a broader approach by extending the limits of its ban on outdoor drinking. "Social host is not a silver bullet," says Lt. John Radin of the Long Beach Police Department. "It's got to be part of a systematic strategy."

Great Expectations

Has the quest to find the perfect soul mate done more harm than good? Psychologists provide insight into how the never-ending search for ideal love can keep you from enjoying a marriage or a healthy relationship that you already have.

POLLY SHULMAN

Q: How do you turn a good relationship sour?
A: Pursue your inalienable right to happiness, hot sex, true love and that soul mate who must be out there somewhere.

Marriage is dead! The twin vises of church and law have relaxed their grip on matrimony. We've been liberated from the grim obligation to stay in a poisonous or abusive marriage for the sake of the kids or for appearances. The divorce rate has stayed constant at nearly 50 percent for the last two decades. The ease with which we enter and dissolve unions makes marriage seem like a prime-time spectator sport, whether it's Britney Spears in Vegas or bimbos chasing after the Bachelor.

Long live the new marriage! We once prized the institution for the practical pairing of a cash-producing father and a home-building mother. Now we want it all—a partner who reflects our taste and status, who sees us for who we are, who loves us for all the "right" reasons, who helps us become the person we want to be. We've done away with a rigid social order, adopting instead an even more onerous obligation: the mandate to find a perfect match. Anything short of this ideal prompts us to ask: Is this all there is? Am I as happy as I should be? Could there be somebody out there who's better for me? As often as not, we answer yes to that last question and fall victim to our own great expectations.

Nothing has produced more unhappiness than the concept of the soul mate.

That somebody is, of course, our soul mate, the man or woman who will counter our weaknesses, amplify our strengths and provide the unflagging support and respect that is the essence of a contemporary relationship. The reality is that few marriages or partnerships consistently live up to this ideal. The result is a commitment limbo, in which we care deeply for our partner but keep one stealthy foot out the door of our hearts. In so doing, we subject the relationship to constant review: Would I be happier, smarter, a better person with someone else? It's a painful modern quandary. "Nothing has produced more unhappiness than the concept of the soul mate," says Atlanta psychiatrist Frank Pittman.

Consider Jeremy, a social worker who married a business-woman in his early twenties. He met another woman, a psychologist, at age 29, and after two agonizing years, left his wife for her. But it didn't work out—after four years of cohabitation, and her escalating pleas to marry, he walked out on her, as well. Jeremy now realizes that the relationship with his wife was solid and workable but thinks he couldn't have seen that 10 years ago, when he left her. "There was always someone better around the corner—and the safety and security of marriage morphed into boredom and stasis. The allure of willing and exciting females was too hard to resist," he admits. Now 42 and still single, Jeremy acknowledges, "I hurt others, and I hurt myself."

Like Jeremy, many of us either dodge the decision to commit or commit without fully relinquishing the right to keep looking—opting for an arrangement psychotherapist Terrence Real terms "stable ambiguity." "You park on the border of the relationship, so you're in it but not of it," he says. There are a million ways to do that: You can be in a relationship but not be sure it's really the right one, have an eye open for a better deal or something on the side, choose someone impossible or far away.

Yet commitment and marriage offer real physical and financial rewards. Touting the benefits of marriage may sound like conservative policy rhetoric, but nonpartisan sociological research backs it up: Committed partners have it all over singles, at least on average. Married people are more financially stable, according to Linda Waite, a sociologist at the University of Chicago and a coauthor of *The Case for Marriage: Why Married People are Happier, Healthier and Better Off*. Both married men and married women have more assets on average than singles; for women, the differential is huge.

We're in commitment limbo: We care deeply for our partner but keep one stealthy foot out the door of our heart.

The benefits go beyond the piggy bank. Married people, particularly men, tend to live longer than people who aren't married. Couples also live better: When people expect to stay together, says Waite, they pool their resources, increasing their individual standard of living. They also pool their expertise—in cooking, say, or financial management. In general, women improve men's health by putting a stop to stupid bachelor tricks and bugging their husbands to exercise and eat their vegetables. Plus, people who aren't comparing their partners to someone else in bed have less trouble performing and are more emotionally satisfied with sex. The relationship doesn't have to be wonderful for life to get better, says Waite: The statistics hold true for mediocre marriages as well as for passionate ones.

The pragmatic benefits of partnership used to be foremost in our minds. The idea of marriage as a vehicle for self-fulfillment and happiness is relatively new, says Paul Amato, professor of sociology, demography and family studies at Penn State University. Surveys of high school and college students 50 or 60 years ago found that most wanted to get married in order to have children or own a home. Now, most report that they plan to get married for love. This increased emphasis on emotional fulfillment within marriage leaves couples ill-prepared for the realities they will probably face.

Because the early phase of a relationship is marked by excitement and idealization, "many romantic, passionate couples expect to have that excitement forever," says Barry McCarthy, a clinical psychologist and coauthor—with his wife, Emily McCarthy—of *Getting It Right the First Time: How to Build a Healthy Marriage.* Longing for the charged energy of the early days, people look elsewhere or split up.

Flagging passion is often interpreted as the death knell of a relationship. You begin to wonder whether you're really right for each other after all. You're comfortable together, but you don't really connect the way you used to. Wouldn't it be more honest—and braver—to just admit that it's not working and call it off? "People are made to feel that remaining in a marriage that doesn't make you blissfully happy is an act of existential cowardice," says Joshua Coleman, a San Francisco psychologist.

Coleman says that the constant cultural pressure to have it all—a great sex life, a wonderful family—has made people ashamed of their less-than-perfect relationships and question whether such unions are worth hanging on to. Feelings of dissatisfaction or disappointment are natural, but they can seem intolerable when standards are sky-high. "It's a recent historical event that people expect to get so much from individual partners," says Coleman, author of *Imperfect Harmony,* in which he advises couples in lackluster marriages to stick it out—especially

if they have kids. "There's an enormous amount of pressure on marriages to live up to an unrealistic ideal."

Michaela, 28, was drawn to Bernardo, 30, in part because of their differences: She'd grown up in European boarding schools, he fought his way out of a New York City ghetto. "Our backgrounds made us more interesting to each other," says Michaela. "I was a spoiled brat, and he'd been supporting himself from the age of 14, which I admired." Their first two years of marriage were rewarding, but their fights took a toll. "I felt that because he hadn't grown up in a normal family, he didn't grasp basic issues of courtesy and accountability," says Michaela. They were temperamental opposites: He was a screamer, and she was a sulker. She recalls, "After we fought, I needed to be drawn out of my corner, but he took that to mean that I was a cold bitch." Michaela reluctantly concluded that the two were incompatible.

In a society hell-bent on individual achievement and autonomy, working on a difficult relationship may get short shrift.

In fact, argue psychologists and marital advocates, there's no such thing as true compatibility.

"Marriage is a disagreement machine," says Diane Sollee, founder of the Coalition for Marriage, Family and Couples Education. "All couples disagree about all the same things. We have a highly romanticized notion that if we were with the right person, we wouldn't fight." Discord springs eternal over money, kids, sex and leisure time, but psychologist John Gottman has shown that long-term, happily married couples disagree about these things just as much as couples who divorce.

"There is a mythology of 'the wrong person,'" agrees Pittman. "All marriages are incompatible. All marriages are between people from different families, people who have a different view of things. The magic is to develop binocular vision, to see life through your partner's eyes as well as through your own."

The realization that we're not going to get everything we want from a partner is not just sobering, it's downright miserable. But it is also a necessary step in building a mature relationship, according to Real, who has written about the subject in *How Can I Get Through to You: Closing the Intimacy Gap Between Men and Women.* "The paradox of intimacy is that our ability to stay close rests on our ability to tolerate solitude inside a relationship," he says. "A central aspect of grown-up love is grief. All of us long for—and think we deserve—perfection." We can hardly be blamed for striving for bliss and self-fulfillment in our romantic lives—our inalienable right to the pursuit of happiness is guaranteed in the first blueprint of American society.

This same respect for our own needs spurred the divorce-law reforms of the 1960s and 1970s. During that era, "The culture shifted to emphasize individual satisfaction, and marriage was part of that," explains Paul Amato, who has followed more than 2,000 families for 20 years in a long-term study of marriage and divorce. Amato says that this shift did some good by freeing people from abusive and intolerable marriages. But it had an unintended side effect: encouraging people to abandon relationships that may be worth salvaging. In a society hell-bent on individual achievement and autonomy, working on a difficult relationship may get short shrift, says psychiatrist Peter Kramer, author of *Should You Leave*?

We get the divorce rate that we deserve as a culture, says Peter Kramer.

"So much of what we learn has to do with the self, the ego, rather than giving over the self to things like a relationship," Kramer says. In our competitive world, we're rewarded for our individual achievements rather than for how we help others. We value independence over cooperation, and sacrifices for values like loyalty and continuity seem foolish. "I think we get the divorce rate that we deserve as a culture."

The steadfast focus on our own potential may turn a partner into an accessory in the quest for self-actualization, says Maggie Robbins, a therapist in New York City. "We think that this person should reflect the beauty and perfection that is the inner me—or, more often, that this person should compensate for the yuckiness and mess that is the inner me," says Robbins. "This is what makes you tell your wife, 'Lose some weight—you're making me look bad,' not 'Lose some weight, you're at risk for diabetes.'"

Michaela was consistently embarrassed by Bernardo's behavior when they were among friends. "He'd become sullen and withdrawn—he had a shifty way of looking off to the side when he didn't want to talk. I felt like it reflected badly on me," she admits. Michaela left him and is now dating a wealthy entrepreneur. "I just thought there had to be someone else out there for me."

The urge to find a soul mate is not fueled just by notions of romantic manifest destiny. Trends in the workforce and in the media create a sense of limitless romantic possibility. According to Scott South, a demographer at SUNY-Albany, proximity to potential partners has a powerful effect on relationships. South and his colleagues found higher divorce rates among people living in communities or working in professions where they encounter lots of potential partners—people who match them in age, race and education level. "These results hold true not just for unhappy marriages but also for happy ones," says South.

The temptations aren't always living, breathing people. According to research by psychologists Sara Gutierres and Douglas Kenrick, both of Arizona State University, we find reasonably attractive people less appealing when we've just seen a hunk or a hottie—and we're bombarded daily by images of gorgeous models and actors. When we watch Lord of the Rings, Viggo Mortensen's kingly mien and Liv Tyler's elfin charm can make our husbands and wives look all too schlumpy.

Kramer sees a similar pull in the narratives that surround us. "The number of stories that tell us about other lives we could lead—in magazine articles, television shows, books—has increased enormously. We have an enormous reservoir of possibilities," says Kramer.

And these possibilities can drive us to despair. Too many choices have been shown to stymie consumers, and an array of alternative mates is no exception. In an era when marriages were difficult to dissolve, couples rated their marriages as more satisfying than do today's couples, for whom divorce is a clear option, according to the National Opinion Research Center at the University of Chicago.

While we expect marriage to be "happily ever after," the truth is that for most people, neither marriage nor divorce seem to have a decisive impact on happiness. Although Waite's research shows that married people are happier than their single counterparts, other studies have found that after a couple years of marriage, people are just about as happy (or unhappy) as they were before settling down. And assuming that marriage will automatically provide contentment is itself a surefire recipe for misery.

"Marriage is not supposed to make you happy. It is supposed to make you married," says Pittman. "When you are all the way in your marriage, you are free to do useful things, become a better person." A committed relationship allows you to drop pretenses and seductions, expose your weaknesses, be yourself—and know that you will be loved, warts and all. "A real relationship is the collision of my humanity and yours, in all its joy and limitations," says Real. "How partners handle that collision is what determines the quality of their relationship."

Such a down-to-earth view of marriage is hardly romantic, but that doesn't mean it's not profound: An authentic relationship with another person, says Pittman, is "one of the first steps toward connecting with the human condition—which is necessary if you're going to become fulfilled as a human being." If we accept these humble terms, the quest for a soul mate might just be a noble pursuit after all.

POLLY SHULMAN is a freelance writer in New York City.

Reclaiming 'Abstinence' in Comprehensive Sex Education

BILL TAVERNER, MA

My first real understanding of the dis-taste some sexologists have for the word "abstinence" came to light in 2006 as I proudly stood by my poster presentation at a conference given by the American Association of Sexuality Educators, Counselors, and Therapists (AASECT). The poster described a new, positive, and comprehensive model to replace the problematic abstinence-only-until-marriage programs of old. As colleagues walked by the four-panel poster that my intern, Laura Minnichelli, had created, many veered off their paths suddenly, as if the word "abstinence," would jump off the poster and bite them. Some looked briefly at the poster and gave a look of disgust, perhaps wondering how an "abstinence" poster infiltrated a sexology conference. Those who stopped to ask about it seemed puzzled initially. They saw the poster's worksheets on personal definitions of abstinence; on masturbation and outercourse; on the lack of efficacy of virginity pledge programs; and they gradually came to recognize that this was a call for a different type of abstinence education program. As these thoughtful individuals left, they offered words of thanks and encouragement that there was finally a sex ed program out there that was reframing abstinence education.

There is no doubt that any self-respecting sex educator has good reason to be skeptical of a new abstinence paradigm. I can understand and even appreciate the sideways looks that some sexologists give after ten years of federal funding for abstinence-only-until-marriage programs, and 25 years since the first "chastity education" federal funds were issued. Over $1 billion has produced curricula that are ineffective, directive, simplistic and insulting to teens—programs that want to tell teens what to think, not how to think for themselves.

Over $1 billion has produced curricula that are ineffective, directive, simplistic and insulting to teens—programs that want to tell teens what to think, not how to think for themselves.

Abstinence-only-until-marriage programs virtually ignore the nearly 50 percent of teens who are having intercourse (Centers for Disease Control, 2006). They tell these teens to get with the program, but have no advice, otherwise, for teens that don't get with the program. At worst, they give misleading or inaccurate information about condom and contraceptive efficacy. These programs ignore lesbian and gay teens (and their families) who are told to abstain until marriage, but who don't have a legal right to marry, unless they are residents of Massachusetts. These programs produce virginity pledge programs, where 88 percent of teens who pledge virginity fail to keep that pledge, and are one-third less likely to use condoms at first intercourse (Brückner & Bearman, 2005), elevating their risk for sexually transmitted infections and unplanned pregnancy.

There are many reasons to bemoan the current state of abstinence education. Just read Congressman Henry Waxman's report (U.S. House of Representatives, 2004), which tells us that 80 percent of federally-funded abstinence-only-until-marriage education programs contain false, misleading, or distorted information about reproductive health. Consider the wisdom of Dr. Michael Carrera, who reminds us that expecting outcomes when we tell kids to "Just say no" is no different than expecting success in the treatment of clinical depression by saying, "Have a nice day!" Or listen to teacher/columnist Deborah Roffman, who compares abstinence-only education to the sex-hungry media. Both, Roffman explains, tell teens exactly what to do. The media scream, "Always say yes," abstinence-only programs admonish, "Just say no," but neither encourage teens to think for themselves. That is, of course, the whole point of learning.

Two e-mails I received illustrate the contentious nature of the debate, and the negative reactions some people have to the word "abstinence." Both came from separate ends of the ideological universe, and the subject of this electronic wrath was the new theoretical and pedagogical concepts introduced in a sex education manual I co-authored with Sue Montfort, Making Sense of Abstinence: Lessons for Comprehensive Sex Education (Taverner & Montfort, 2005).

The first e-mail followed a very short editorial in the *Wall Street Journal* that commented on one of the themes of the manual—that it was necessary to discuss with youth the way they define abstinence, so as to better help them be successful with this decision. The e-mail began as follows:

Dear Mr. Taverner:
Abstinence means NO SEX. Only a pointy head liberal could think there was some other definition, and it is pointy headed liberals that give liberalism a bad name. It takes the cake that you would . . . write some papers on trying to define abstinence. I have done that in four words above.

More later on this writer's comments about defining abstinence—and on my seemingly pointy head, too! The more recent e-mail followed the announcement of the annual sex ed conference of The Center for Family Life Education (CFLE) that went to thousands of sex educators by e-mail. Themed on the manual, the announcement was titled "The Abstinence Experience: Teaching about Abstinence in the Context of Comprehensive Sex Education." The conference featured sex education leaders from prominent organizations —Answer (Formerly the Network for Family Life Education), the California Family Health Council, Montclair State University, the Sexuality Information and Education Council of the United States (SIECUS), and trainers from the CFLE. This e-mail read, simply:

Please REMOVE my email address from this mailing list. I am 100 percent against ABSTINENCE!

This is not the first time someone has asked to be taken off the e-mail list, though usually such requests are polite. But beyond the rude tone of this request, the last sentence stopped me in my tracks:

I am 100 percent against ABSTINENCE!

The capitalized ABSTINENCE was the writer's doing, not mine. Did I read this right? Or did he mean he was against abstinence education? Maybe he meant abstinence-only-until-marriage-education? But I did read it correctly; in fact, I cut and pasted the writer's remarks to this article! He was against ABSTINENCE. How could that be? If a person chooses to abstain from sexual intercourse, or any other sexual behaviors, or drugs, alcohol, chocolate, or what-ever, how could anyone be against that? And yet this is a common theme I have experienced since we began exploring the subject of abstinence more thoughtfully. It seems some comprehensive sex educators and advocates are turned off by the word "abstinence." The atmosphere among some might best be described as anti-abstinence. The anecdotal evidence:

Upon reviewing the final manuscript for our new abstinence manual, one well-respected reviewer asked not to be identified in the acknowledgments. She explained that while she thought the manual was great, she also thought it would be a bad career move to become too closely associated with the "world of abstinence."

Upon reviewing the final manuscript for our new abstinence manual, one well-respected reviewer asked not to be identified in the acknowledgments. She explained that while she thought the manual was great, she also thought it would be a bad career move to become too closely associated with the "world of abstinence."

One prominent sex education leader urged us to reconsider the title of both our manual and our conference. He did not think we should be promoting abstinence, instead favoring the term "delaying intercourse." (Imagine a title such as Making Sense of Delaying Intercourse—what could more clearly illustrate the disconnect between adults and teens who never think of themselves as "delaying intercourse," but who do sometimes choose abstinence?)

An educator on my staff asked a colleague if he would be coming to our annual conference. The colleague said he had not yet received our flyer. The educator was surprised, since we had sent the flyers out over a month ago, and this individual had been on our mailing list for many years. Upon hearing the title of the conference, he replied, "That was you? I threw that out when I saw the word 'abstinence'!"

What was going on here? Making Sense of Abstinence had been nominated for four sex ed awards, to date, winning two. It had been show-cased by SIECUS at a Congressional Briefing in Washington, D.C. And yet while most colleagues were embracing this new model for abstinence education, some were clearly shunning the idea of any abstinence education.

Certainly there are many reasons that justify the distaste of some of our colleagues for the current abstinence education paradigm among sex educators. The state of abstinence-only education is manipulative-to-insulting, from the moralizing, shame, and fear-based tactics to the sideshow industry that markets ineffective abstinence slogans on billboards, t-shirts, mugs, and even chewing gum. ("Abstinence gum—for chewzing an abstinent lifestyle.")

But all complaints about abstinence-only-until-marriage education aside, what is wrong with educating about the choice of abstinence? Doesn't the polling research say that American parents want their children to learn about abstinence? When comprehensive sex educators trumpet the latest polling data from groups like the Kaiser Family Foundation that says parents support comprehensive sex education, how do we miss the fact that the same polling data also reveals parental desire for their kids to learn about abstinence? What are we doing about this, and how can we react to the word "abstinence" so negatively when we are supposedly teaching it as a part of comprehensive sex education?

A New Model

The pedagogical concepts introduced in Making Sense of Abstinence make it unlike other abstinence education manuals. There are four key themes that are woven throughout the manual's sixteen lessons: (1) abstinence education needs to help young people define abstinence in ways that help them understand and apply their decisions in real life; (2) abstinence education needs to include decision-making, skills-building opportunities; (3) abstinence education is not just talking about which behaviors to avoid, but also the behaviors that are permitted in a person's decision; (4) abstinence education needs to help young people protect their sexual health, and transition safely when they decide to no longer abstain.

Defining Abstinence

Remember the guy who called me a "pointy headed liberal"? Define abstinence? Well, DUH! Abstinence means "no sex," right? Next time you are with a group of professionals, or a group of students, ask them to take out their cell phones and call three friends, colleagues, coworkers, children, parents, etc. and ask them to define the terms "sex" and "abstinence." You will be amazed, as I always am, with the discordant results you get. Do the definitions address only vaginal intercourse? Oral or anal intercourse? Other touching behaviors? Masturbation? What reasons or motivations emerge? Religious? Parental? Pregnancy prevention? Prevention of sexually transmitted infections? Assessing one's readiness? Marriage? Protecting one's mental or emotional health? When one person defines "sex," as "a loving, intimate, physical, connection between two people," does that mean that kissing or holding hands is sex? And, thus, abstinence is no kissing? When one says, simply, that "abstinence means no sex," does this mean one must also avoid the aforementioned feelings of intimacy and love?

If this seems like a trivial exercise, consider the following definitions of abstinence printed or posted by a variety of health-promoting organizations:

"Abstinence is . . . not having sex with a partner. This will keep the sperm from joining the egg." (www.coolnurse.com)

> **Next time you are with a group of professionals, or a group of students, ask them to take out their cell phones and call three friends, colleagues, co-workers, children, parents, etc. and ask them to define the terms "sex" and "abstinence." You will be amazed, as I always am, with the discordant results you get.**

"Abstinence is . . . no intercourse. Not even any semen on the vulva. Pretty straightforward." (Kinsey Institute's Sexuality Information Service for Students)

Hmmm. So abstinence means no vaginal intercourse. But wait. . .

"For protection against infection . . . abstinence means avoiding vaginal, anal, and oral-genital intercourse, or participating in any other activity in which body fluids are exchanged." (www.managingcontraception.com)

So, the motivation here is avoiding infections that may be transmitted via body fluid exchange. This could include oral, anal, or vaginal inter-course. It also seems to refer tacitly to another fluid through which HIV could be transmitted: breast milk. So, does one practice abstinence by not breastfeeding her child? From the Dictionary of Sexology (Francoeur, 1997):

"A definition of abstinence may include not engaging in masturbation."

and

"The practices of tantric yoga recommend short periods of abstinence to concentrate one's sexual energy and prepare for more intense responses when sexual intercourse is resumed."

Ah, so abstinence is periodic, for the purpose of making sex better! How about some input from abstinence-only programs:

"Abstinence is . . . voluntarily refraining from all sexual relationships before marriage in order to uplift your own self-worth and provide the freedom to build character, develop career potentials and practice true love." (As cited by Kempner, 2001)

Abstinence for career potential? Never came up in my job interviews, but who knows today? Back to reality, Thoraya Obaid, executive director of the United Nations Populations Fund, reminds us that abstinence is not always a choice:

"Abstinence . . . is meaningless to women who are coerced into sex."

As I collected all these definitions, I was surprised when glossaries on websites for lesbian, gay, bisexual, and transgender teens repeatedly came up empty on definitions for abstinence. I asked my friend and colleague, Lis Maurer, about this. Lis is the director of Ithaca College's Center for LGBT Education and Outreach Services, and she explained:

"I remember a high school class where we were taught about abstinence. Afterward, several of us non-straight students got together and reacted. Some said, "OK—we're totally in the clear!" Others said, "No, we were ignored—they really don't know we exist!" and yet others were just completely confused, as if the lecture was in some other language."

Finally, the website *well-net.com* sums up all this confusion quite nicely:

"Abstinence is. . .avoiding sex. Sex, of course, means different things to different people."

Indeed. What might abstinence mean to a teen?

"I'm proud that my boyfriend and I have decided to be abstinent. We have oral sex, but definitely not real sex, you know?"

The importance of helping teens define abstinence cannot be underscored enough. A recent evaluation of one abstinence-only program found that teens developed more positive attitudes toward abstinence following the program. That seems like good news, but the study went on to explain that "abstinence" meant "abstaining from sexual intercourse," which meant, "the male's penis is in the female's vagina. Some slang names for sexual intercourse are 'having sex,' 'making love,' or 'going all the way.'" (Laflin, et al, 2005, p. 110). So while these teens were developing their positive feelings toward abstinence, they were learning nothing about how abstinence might also mean avoiding other sexual behaviors, including anal and oral intercourse that could transmit a sexually transmitted infection. The teen who said earlier that oral sex is not real sex could easily have been a participant in this abstinence-only education program.

The evidence is clear that teens need opportunities to discuss what abstinence means to them. They need worksheets, activities, and discussion opportunities to reflect on their reasons for choosing abstinence, and specifically what behaviors they will avoid while abstaining. If they ultimately decide not to avoid oral sex, anal sex, etc., then they need further information about protection from sexually transmitted infections. They need opportunities to learn to become effective with the choice of abstinence.

Decision-Making, Skills-Building Lessons

Maybe you've seen a billboard sign that says, "VIRGIN: Teach Your Kid It's Not a Dirty Word!" Or maybe you're familiar with the slogan, "Quit your urgin', be a virgin!"

One of the abstinence slogans that always gets a chuckle is "Good cowgirls keep their calves together." The list goes on and on, and many of them are cute, catchy, and memorable. But none of them speaks to the complex decision-making skills that really need to be developed in young people to help them make decisions that are meaningful and responsible in their lives.

Young people need opportunities to develop concrete steps for "using" abstinence effectively. Abstinence is not just a state of being; it is a method to be used. This is an important distinction. The former implies passivity; i.e., no need to think about anything when abstinence is the foregone conclusion. The latter encourages young people to think about how they are going to be effective with their decisions, to develop the skills to be successful with their decisions, and to re-evaluate their decisions as need be.

Abstinence skills include learning to plan for sexual abstinence, and practicing assertive communication, so that one can better stand up for one's decisions. It involves learning about sexual response, so that one can understand and manage their sexual feelings in ways that are consistent with their values and decisions. It involves enforcing boundaries with one's partner. It involves so much more than "Just say no!" or other simplistic, "educational" approaches that are far more directive than they are educational.

> Abstinence skills include learning to plan for sexual abstinence, and practicing assertive communication, so that one can better stand up for one's decisions. It involves so much more than "Just say no!" or other simplistic, "educational" approaches that are far more directive than they are educational.

A relatively new model, supported by the federal government seeks to improve upon abstinence-only programs by teaching an "ABC" model. ABC stands for "Abstinence," "Be faithful," and "Use Condoms," and unfortunately it does not engage young people in thoughtful decision-making any more than its abstinence-only cousin. The United States exported its ABC's to Uganda for the purposes of HIV prevention. In Uganda, this hierarchical model stressed Abstinence first; with Be faithful reserved for those who couldn't seem to practice Abstinence; and Condoms reserved strictly for the sex workers.

This model has been championed by President George W. Bush, and new federal monies have been made available for ABC programming in the United States, despite questionable results (and different meanings of "A," "B," and "C") abroad (Cohen, 2003; Sindling, 2005). But a closer look at this simplistic approach exposes a model that is devoid of critical thinking and skills building. For example, what if a person is using "B" but their partner isn't? That person is likely to learn about three new letters, "S," "T," and "I," (sexually transmitted infections). Further, what if a person ditches "A," in favor of "B" without using C? Does anyone in these programs ever mention the possibility of an unplanned or unwanted "P" (for pregnancy)? Simplistic models like this continue to reveal the importance of helping young people think through their abstinence decisions and become effective abstinence users.

It's Not What You Avoid

Why is it that we are not talking about masturbation when we are teaching about abstinence? Twelve years ago U.S. Surgeon General Joycelyn Elders was fired for suggesting this might be a good idea. Masturbation is one of the safest sexual behaviors around, perhaps the safest. There is no risk of getting pregnant, no risk of getting a sexually transmitted infection, no risk of getting anything, except pleasure. As Woody Allen said, "Don't knock masturbation. It's having sex with someone you love!"

So why does masturbation have such a stigma in America. I have a clue that maybe it has some-thing to do with the things that have been written about it. Sylvester Graham, a New York preacher, wrote in 1834 that a masturbator grows up:

> "with a body full of disease, and with a mind in ruins, the loathsome habit still tyrannizing over him, with the inexorable imperiousness of a fiend of darkness."
> —(Graham, 1834)

And, in 1892, a prominent nutritionist, John Harvey Kellogg, wrote this:

> "As a sin against nature, [masturbation] has no parallel except in sodomy. The habit is by no means confined to boys; girls also indulge in it, though it is to be hoped, to a less fearful extent than boys, at least in this country. Of all the vices to which human beings are addicted, no other so rapidly undermines the constitution, and so certainly makes a complete wreck of an individual as this, especially when the habit is begun at an early age. It wastes the most precious part of the blood, uses up the vital forces, and finally leaves the poor victim a most utterly ruined and loathsome object.
>
> Suspicious signs are: bashfulness, unnatural boldness, round shoulders and a stooping position, lack of development of the breasts in females, eating chalk, acne, and the use of tobacco."
> —(Kellogg, 1892)

No wonder the anxiety! It didn't matter that none of these statements were true. People still flocked to buy the recommended antidotes, Sylvester's Graham crackers and Kellogg's Corn Flakes, both of which were supposed to suppress the urge to masturbate (and neither of which contained sugar or cinnamon in those days!)

More than a century later, as Americans continue to eat Graham crackers and Corn Flakes, we still retain myths and misinformation about masturbation. Perhaps if we can make young people feel a little less anxious about a behavior in which so many already engage, we can help them recognize masturbation as an important, safe alternative to intercourse.

Abstinence education needs to discuss other safer sexual behaviors, including outercourse, that get young people thinking about non-genital activities that are safe, and will keep them free of sexually transmitted infections and pregnancy. These behaviors—masturbation and outercourse—have inexplicably been omitted from abstinence-only curricula. It is as if we really think that if we don't mention these topics, teens won't think of it either! Have we really become that dis-connected with our nation's youth? We really need to examine why information about masturbation and outercourse is omitted in abstinence education. Is it to keep information about sexual pleasure from young people? What gives anyone the right to withhold any information from young people, especially information that might help keep them safe, while feeling positively about themselves? One of the most frustrating aspects of being a teacher must be school policies—written or unspoken—that prevent teachers from being able to engage their students in an open, honest dialogue about sexual pleasure while they are also teaching about sexual safety. But the two go together when it comes to masturbation and outercourse.

Abstinence education needs to discuss other safer sexual behaviors, including outer-course, that get young people thinking about non-genital activities that are safe, and will keep them free of sexually transmitted infections and pregnancy. These behaviors—masturbation and outercourse—have inexplicably been omitted from abstinence-only curricula.

Susie Wilson, who used to run the Network for Family Life Education (now called Answer), gave a review of Making Sense of Abstinence, and she put it better than I could have:

"[Students] will learn that there is a long continuum of behaviors between "saying no" and "doing it" that will keep them safe, not sorry. Educators will feel more secure about teaching tough topics such as oral sex, masturbation and outercourse, when they see they are allied with discussion about personal values, decision-making and communication."

Help Young People Protect Themselves If/When Their Decisions Change

A final, critical part of abstinence education is the need to help young people protect themselves if and when their abstinence decisions change. It is no longer enough for us to bury our heads in the sand and just hope that teens remain abstinent through high school, college, and into young adulthood (or up until age 29, as the new federal abstinence-only guidelines suggest). We need to equip them with the skills to make that transition safely.

One way is to help them identify signs of "sexual readiness." Students might read stories about other teens who are making sexual decisions, and assess and discuss how ready (or not) these teens are against any number of sexual readiness checklists. Consider these two teen quotes:

> "At times I get all hot with my partner and I feel like I really want to have sex. At other times, I know that I shouldn't have sex until I am ready. The problem is that sometimes I feel like I am ready and other times I feel like I am not ready. What should I do?"

and

> "I've been going out with this guy—he's 18. Everything was romantic at first, but now he's gotten real pushy. Last time we were alone, he gave me a beer. I didn't feel like drinking, but he kept pushing it on me, so I drank it just to shut him up. Now he's pushing the sex thing on me. It's like we don't talk about anything but sex. I know he's tired of waiting for me, but I think things are getting out of hand, and I'm not sure I'm ready."

Both teens deserve much more than a catchy slogan. They need tools and discussion to help them identify how one knows when one is ready, and how to identify coercion in a relationship, and how to leave coercive relationships. We need to help young people actively think of their decisions in their sexual lives. Sexual intercourse is not something that people are just supposed to stumble into, without thinking of their decisions and their potential consequences. By contrast, the current culture of abstinence-only education supports teens making virginity pledges, which simply do not work. Eighty-eight percent of teens who make such a pledge break it! (Brückner & Bearman, 2005). And those teens are less likely to use protection, because they've never learned about condoms or contraceptives, or they've been taught only about failure rates.

[Teens] need tools and discussion to help them identify how one knows when one is ready, and how to identify coercion in a relationship, and how to leave coercive relationships.

In training teachers, I often say, "Sex education today is not necessarily for tonight." This is very applicable when it comes to abstinence education. We need to think about sex education in the context of a lifetime of sexual decision-making, and abstinence as a conscious decision that is one's right to assert at anytime in their life. At the same time, we need to help teens gain knowledge and develop skills to protect their sexual health (i.e., learn about condoms and contraception) if and when they decide to no longer abstain, whether it is tonight, or in college, or when they celebrate a commitment ceremony, or after they walk down the aisle.

Young people need more from sex education. They need education that includes the choice to abstain. They need accurate information, not evasive, undefined terms, or misleading, or false information. Young people need and deserve respect, not to be subjected to scare tactics. They need to develop skills to be successful with abstinence; not to hear catchy slogans. They need to be met where they are, and recognized for their ability to make responsible decisions about their sexual lives. They need abstinence education, but they deserve better than what they've been getting so far.

References

Brückner, H. & Bearman, P. (2005). "After the promise: the STD consequences of adolescent virginity pledges," *Journal of Adolescent Health,* No. 36: 271–278.

Centers for Disease Control and Prevention. (2006). Youth risk behavior surveillance—United States, 2005. Atlanta, GA: Centers for Disease Control.

Cohen, S.A. (2003). "Beyond slogans: Lessons learned from Uganda's Experience with ABC and HIV/AIDS," The Guttmacher Report on Public Policy, 6(5).1–3.

Francoeur, R.T. (1997). *The Complete Dictionary of Sexology,* New York: Continuum.

Graham, S. (1834). A Lecture to Young Men on Chastity. Boston, MA: Pierce.

Kellogg, J.H. (1892). Plain Facts for Old and Young. Burlington, IA: I.F. Segner.

Kempner, M.E. (2001). Toward a Sexually Healthy America: Abstinence-Only-Until-Marriage Programs that Try to Keep Our Youth 'Scared Chaste.' New York: Sexuality Information & Education Council of the United States.

Laflin, M.T., Sommers, J.M., & Chibucos, T.R. (2006). "Initial Findings in a Longitudinal Study of the Effectiveness of the Sex Can Wait Sexual Abstinence Curriculum for Grades 5–8," *American Journal of Sexuality Education,* l(l):103–118.

Sindling, S. (2005). "Does 'CNN' (condoms, needles, negotiation) work better than 'ABC' (abstinence, being faithful and condom use) in attacking the AIDS epidemic?" *International Family Planning Perspectives,* 31(1):38–40.

Taverner, B. & Montfort, S. (2005). Making Sense of Abstinence: Lessons for Comprehensive Sex Education. Morristown, NJ: The Center for Family Life Education, Planned Parenthood of Greater Northern New Jersey.

U.S. House of Representatives, Committee on Government Reform (2004). The Content of Federally Funded Abstinence-Only Education Programs, prepared for Rep. Henry A. Waxman. Washington, DC: The House, December 2004.

BILL TAVERNER, MA, is the director of The Center for Family Life Education at Planned Parenthood of Greater Northern New Jersey, and is the coeditor of the American Journal of Sexuality Education.

Give Students the Knowledge to Make Wise Choices about Sex

Three out of four respondents to November's Your Turn believe schools should teach a comprehensive sex education curriculum. Abstinence-only education, they say, is unrealistic for media-savvy teens who may already be having sex.

As a Minnesota reader put it, "If public schools don't teach a comprehensive sex education curriculum, Madonna will."

This Your Turn marks the debut of the ASBJ Reader Panel, a group of readers who are joining an e-mail conversation with us to supplement the printed Your Turn question. (Interested? Sign on at www.asbj.com/readerpanel.)

At this early stage, the Reader Panel is a resounding success. We've received hundreds of responses and many thoughtful comments. We can't print them all, but we can offer a representative sample of your views.

In addition to the 75 percent who supported a comprehensive sex-ed curriculum, 16 percent favored abstinence-only education, 8 percent offered various other responses, and 1 percent said, "Don't teach sex education at all."

Like the reader who cautioned against ceding sex education to Madonna, many of you said it was unrealistic, dangerous, and even dishonest to teach abstinence only when many teens are having sex and will continue to do so regardless of what their teachers tell them.

"The program should stress the importance of abstinence but must be comprehensive," said Lee Doebler, a board member from Alabama. "We cannot ignore the fact that many teens are sexually active and that sexual activity is beginning earlier and earlier as children reach puberty at an earlier age."

"Teaching abstinence-only sex education is like teaching nutrition without covering sugars and fats," added another reader. "Abstinence should certainly be emphasized in the curriculum; however, students should be given all the information so they could make that determination for themselves."

William Higgins, a board member from Washington state, said he favors a strong abstinence message along with other information. "It is urgent that we get a handle on the number-one addictive drug of choice among our youth—sex," he said.

"I advocate a comprehensive program of graduated information, based on age and grade level, that has a strong emphasis on abstinence. The idea is to keep kids smart—and safe!"

While we want students to abstain, there are other things we need to teach them along with abstaining that will strengthen their resolve, said Kim S. Rogers, a board member from North Carolina. "We cannot force our children to abstain. And if we don't educate them on the emotional and physical stress of teen sex, that has the effect of diluting the importance of abstaining—which, in my opinion, is the ultimate goal of sex education. Not talking about it doesn't make it go away."

Many of those favoring the abstinence-only approach said sex education should be handled by parents, not schools.

"Parents have the right and duty to decide how to present this information to their children," said an Indiana board member.

Added Texas Superintendent Paul Vranish: "It seems that 'how-to' instruction should best be left to parents."

Such "how to" instruction can give teens a false sense of confidence, several readers said. As one Missouri board member put it, "There is too much false information being taught about the safety of the use of condoms as it relates to 'safe sex.'"

Ann Johnson, a registered nurse and Indiana board member, said she favors abstinence-only education as the best way to deter students from making choices that could harm them physically and psychologically.

"I believe students need to understand the anatomy and physiology of human reproduction," Johnson said. "It is also important to have some discussion on the emotional and hormonal changes that occur in developing from preteen to adolescent to young adult and on the financial, emotional, and physical demands that result from unplanned and too early pregnancies."

Among those favoring no sex education in school was Perry Shumway, a board member in Idaho. "If sex education weren't taught at all in public schools, private institutions, such as families, churches, and youth groups, would step up to the plate and fill in the void," Shumway said.

However, most respondents agreed with Linda Smith Kortemeyer, an Iowa board secretary/treasurer who said abstinence only isn't enough.

"If we adopt a curriculum limiting what children are allowed to learn because of our restrictive beliefs, we basically are telling children we don't believe in their ability to work through life's difficult problems," Kortemeyer said. "When we encourage them to learn all they can, we tell them we have faith in their abilities to make the right choices. . . . Children may not make the same choices as we did, but they will have the opportunity to make decisions based on the knowledge we provided them. Hopefully, these choices are made with wisdom and courage."

From *American School Board Journal,* January 2006, pp. 10–11. Copyright © 2006 by National School Board Association. Reprinted by permission.

The Perils of Playing House

Living together before marriage seems like a smart way to road test the relationship. But cohabitation may lead you to wed for all the wrong reasons—or turn into a one-way trip to splitsville.

NANCY WARTIK

Forget undying love or shared hopes and dreams—my boyfriend and I moved in together, a year after meeting, because of a potential subway strike. He lived in Manhattan, and I across the river in Brooklyn. Given New York City taxi rates, we'd have been separated for who knows how long. And so, the day before the threatened strike, he picked me up along with two yowling cats and drove us home. Six years, one wedding and one daughter later, we still haven't left.

Actually, if the strike threat hadn't spurred us to set up housekeeping, something else would have. By then, we were 99 percent sure we'd marry some day—just not without living together first. I couldn't imagine getting hitched to anyone I hadn't taken on a test-spin as a roommate. Conjoin with someone before sharing a bathroom? Not likely!

With our decision to cohabit, we joined the mushrooming ranks of Americans who choose at some point in their lives to inhabit a gray zone—more than dating, less than marriage, largely without legal protections. Thirty or 40 years ago, cohabitation was relatively rare, mainly the province of artists and other questionable types, and still thought of as "living in sin." In 1970 only about 500,000 couples lived together in unwedded bliss.

Now, nearly 5 million opposite-sex couples in the United States live together outside of marriage; millions more have done it at some point. Some couples do choose to live together as a permanent alternative to marriage, but their numbers are only a tiny fraction: More than 50 percent of couples who marry today have lived together beforehand. (At least 600,000 same-sex couples also cohabit, but their situation is different, since most don't have the choice to marry.)

"It's not this bad little thing only a few people are doing," says University of Michigan sociologist Pamela Smock. "It's not going away. It's going to become part of our normal, typical life course—it already is for younger people. They think it would be idiotic not to live with someone before marriage. They don't want to end up the way their parents or older relatives did, which is divorced."

In my and my husband's case, the pre-matrimonial experiment seems to have worked out well. But according to recent research, our year of shacking up could have doomed our relationship. Couples who move in together before marriage have up to two times the odds of divorce, as compared with couples who marry before living together. Moreover, married couples who have lived together before exchanging vows tend to have poorer-quality marriages than couples who moved in after the wedding. Those who cohabited first report less satisfaction, more arguing, poorer communication and lower levels of commitment.

Many researchers now argue that our penchant for combining households before taking vows is undermining our ability to commit. Meaning, the precautions we take to ensure marriage is right for us may wind up working against us.

From Toothbrush to Registry

Why would something that seems so sensible potentially be so damaging? Probably the reigning explanation is the inertia hypothesis, the idea that many of us slide into marriage without ever making an explicit decision to commit. We move in together, we get comfortable, and pretty soon marriage starts to seem like the path of least resistance. Even if the relationship is only tolerable, the next stage starts to seem inevitable.

Because we have different standards for living partners than for life partners, we may end up married to someone we never would have originally considered for the long haul. "People are much fussier about whom they marry than whom they cohabitate with," explains Paul Amato, a sociologist at Penn State University and one of the theory's originators. "A lot of people cohabit because it seems like a good idea to share expenses and have some security and companionship, without a lot of commitment."

Couples may wind up living together almost by accident. "People move in their toothbrush, their underwear, pretty soon a whole dresser," says Marshall Miller, coauthor with his partner,

Dorian Solot, of *Unmarried to Each Other: The Essential Guide to Living Together as an Unmarried Couple.* "Then someone's lease is up and since they're spending all their time together anyhow . . ."

Or, two people may move in together without a firm future plan because one partner isn't sure the other is good marriage material: He drinks too much; she gets really nasty during fights. Rather than commit, they take a trial run. Once they've shacked up, relatives start noodging: "So when are you going to get married already?" At friends' weddings, people ask, "When will it be your turn?"

"There's an inevitable pressure that creates momentum toward marriage," says Amato. "I've talked to so many cohabiting couples, and they'll say, 'My mother was so unhappy until I told her we were getting married—then she was so relieved.'" On top of the social pressure, Amato points out, couples naturally start making investments together: a couch, a pet—even a kid. Accidental pregnancies are more common among cohabiting couples than among couples who don't live together.

Once their lives are thoroughly entangled, some couples may decide to wed more out of guilt or fear than love. "I know a lot of men who've been living with women for a couple of years, and they're very ambivalent about marrying them," says John Jacobs, a New York City psychiatrist and author of *All You Need Is Love and Other Lies About Marriage.* "What sways them is a feeling they owe it to her. She'll be back on the market and she's older. He's taken up a lot of her time." Women in particular may be afraid to leave an unhappy cohabiting relationship and confront the dating game at an older age. "If you're 36, it's hard to take the risk of going back into the single world to look for another relationship," says Jacobs.

Younger people think it would be idiotic not to live with someone before marriage. They don't want to end up the way their parents did—divorced.

Charles, a 44-year-old New Yorker (who asked that his name be changed), admits that in his 30s, he almost married a live-in girlfriend of three years for reasons having little to do with love. The two moved in together six months after meeting when his sublet came to an end. "I thought it probably wasn't the best idea, but it was so much easier than looking for an apartment," Charles says. "I told myself: 'Keep trying, and maybe it will work.'"

Eventually his girlfriend insisted they either marry or break up, and he couldn't find the strength to leave. The two got engaged. Weeks before the date, Charles realized he couldn't go through with it and broke off the engagement. "Her father told me, 'I'm sorry horsewhips are a thing of the past,'" Charles recalls, still pained by the memory. Even now, he regrets moving in with her. "It was a terrible idea," he says. "You get entwined in each other's lives. If you're not sure you want to be entwined,

Would You Be My . . . Roommate?

EVERYONE WHO'S MARRIED remembers how, when and where the momentous question was popped. But when two people move in together, they're often much more cavalier about it. "It's a bigger decision than a lot of couples realize," says Galena Kline, a research assistant at the Center for Marital and Family Studies at the University of Denver. "It's really going to change their life and relationship more than they might think. But a lot of couples don't necessarily communicate about it."

• **TALK, TALK, TALK:** Sitting down to discuss the feelings and expectations about living together before making a move is the best way for couples to ensure a good experience. It's helpful for partners to talk about topics ranging from the sublime to the mundane: marriage, kids, life goals—and who will take out the garbage or feed the cat.

• **FINANCIAL FIRST STEP:** Decide how you'll deal with money matters. "We don't recommend immediately combining your accounts," cautions Marshall Miller, coauthor with Dorian Solot of *Unmarried to Each Other.* Keeping money and credit separate initially, he says, removes an area of potential conflict during a time of adjustment and lets partners see how compatible their financial styles really are.

• **THE SHAKEDOWN:** If you want to test the waters before hiring a moving van, do a "trial cohabitation." Solot and Miller suggest living with your potential partner for a week or two, but caution, "Don't be enticed by fantasies of spending long, lazy days in bed followed by heartfelt conversations while you prepare dinner elbow to elbow, looking adorable . . . Give yourselves a real feel for the pressure of the morning dash, the low energy I-just-want-to-crash-in-front-of-the-TV evening and the negotiation over who will do the dishes."

—NW

you shouldn't put yourself in a position where it's definitely going to happen."

Some evidence indicates that women have less control over the progress of the cohabiting relationship. She may assume they're on the road to marriage, but he may think they're just saving on rent and enjoying each other's company. Research by sociologist Susan Brown at Bowling Green State University in Ohio has shown there's a greater chance cohabiting couples will marry if the man wants to do so. The woman's feelings don't have as much influence, she found: "The guy has got to be on board. What the woman wants seems to be less pivotal."

Cohabiting men may carry their uncertainty forward into marriage, with destructive consequences. A 2004 study by psychologist Scott Stanley, based on a national phone survey of nearly 1,000 people, found that men who had lived with their spouse premaritally were on average less committed to their marriages than those who hadn't. By contrast, cohabitation didn't seem to change how women felt about their partners.

Based on this finding and others, Stanley, director of the Center for Marital and Family Studies at the University of Denver and another originator of the inertia theory, believes women should be especially wary of moving in before getting engaged. "There are plenty of young men who will say, 'I'm living with a woman but I'm still looking for my soul mate,'" he says. "But how many women know the guy is thinking that way? How many women are living with a guy thinking he's off the market, and he's not?" Men also get trapped in troubled relationships, admits Stanley, but women are more likely to bear the brunt of ill-considered cohabitation decisions for the simplest reason—they are the ones who have the babies.

Charles almost married a live-in girlfriend for reasons having little to do with love. "It was so much easier than looking for an apartment. I told myself: 'Keep trying, and it will work.'"

The Cohabiting Type

The inertia theory is not the only way to explain why couples who move in before marriage are less likely to stick it out for the long haul. There may also be something specific about the experience that actually changes people's minds about marriage, making it seem less sacrosanct. "A couple of studies show that when couples cohabit, they tend to adopt less conventional beliefs about marriage and divorce, and it tends to make them less religious," says Amato. That could translate, once married, to a greater willingness to consider options that are traditionally frowned upon—like saying "so long" to an ailing marriage.

Nonetheless, there's a heated debate among social scientists about whether the research to date has been interpreted properly or overplayed to some extent. Having a family income below $25,000, for example, is a stronger predictor of divorce in the first 15 years of marriage than having shared a premarital address. "Having money, a sense of an economically stable future, good communication skills, living in a safe community—all of those things are more important," says Smock.

Because it's impossible to directly compare the effects of marriage and cohabitation, there's just no way to prove cohabiters' higher divorce rates aren't a side effect of their other characteristics, says psychologist William Pinsof, president of the Family Institute at Northwestern University. They may just be less traditional people—less likely to stay in an unhappy marriage in observance of religious beliefs or for the sake of appearances. "Those who choose to live together before getting married have a different attitude about marriage to begin with. I think cohabiting is a reflection of that, not a cause of higher divorce rates," he says. One population of cohabiters also tends to have less money and lower levels of education, which in itself can strain a relationship.

In short, not everyone buys the idea that cohabitation itself is hazardous to your relationship. For some couples, it may serve a useful purpose—even when it lacks a happy ending. About half of all cohabiters split up rather than marry, and many of those splits save the parties involved from rocky marriages, miserable divorces or both.

That's the attitude Amy Muscoplat, 34, a children's librarian who lives in Santa Monica, California, now has about the man she lived with several years ago. She and Mr. X had dated for nine months when they got engaged; a few months later she gave up her rent-controlled apartment by the beach, sold most of her furniture, and the two moved in together. "We moved in in August, and by early September he flipped out," she says. "We were supposed to get married in early November. The invitations had gone out, and then he changed his mind. Living together was the reality check for him, the mirror that made him go, 'Gosh, this might not really work for me.'"

Though she and her family lost thousands of dollars when the wedding was called off, Muscoplat is grateful things fell apart when they did. If they hadn't moved in together, she says, "I think he might have been pushed to the same place at some later point, maybe some day down the road when I was pregnant. I have a religious take on it—God was really watching out for me and I dodged a bullet."

The debate over cohabitation is partly a rehash of the values and morals conflicts that tend to become political footballs in America today. But on one point, virtually all researchers agree: We need to understand the effects of cohabitation on children. Some 40 percent of all cohabiting households include kids—that's somewhere close to 3.5 million children living in homes with two unmarried opposite-sex grown-ups.

Cohabiting relationships, by their nature, appear to be less fulfilling than marital relationships. People who cohabit say they are less satisfied and more likely to feel depressed, Susan Brown has found. While the precarious finances of many cohabiters has something to do with it, Brown also points to the inherent lack of stability. Long-term cohabitation is rare: most couples either break up or marry within five years. "Cohabiters are uncertain about the future of their relationship and that's distressing to them," she says.

People who cohabit say they are less satisfied and more likely to feel depressed.

As a result, cohabitation is not an ideal living arrangement for children. Emotionally or academically, the children of cohabiters just don't do as well, on average, as those with two married parents, and money doesn't fully explain the difference. The stress of parenting in a shakier living situation may be part of the problem, says Brown. "Stability matters. It matters for the well-being of children and adults alike," she adds. "We're better off with commitment, a sense that we're in it for the long haul."

The Must-have Discussion

Cohabitation rates may be skyrocketing, but Americans are still entirely enchanted with marriage. That's a sharp contrast with some Western societies—Sweden, France or the

Canadian province of Quebec, for example—where cohabitation is beginning to replace marriage. In the United States, 90 percent of young people are still expected to tie the knot at some point.

Since most Americans are destined for marriage—and a majority will live together beforehand—how can we protect against the potentially undermining effects of cohabitation? Follow the lead of one subgroup of cohabiters: Those who make a permanent commitment to each other first. One study that tracked 136 couples through the initial months of marriage found that early intentions seem to make a big difference. About 60 of the couples in the study lived together before getting engaged, while the rest waited either until after they were engaged or after they were married to set up housekeeping. Ten months after the wedding, the group that had cohabited before being engaged had more negative interactions, less confidence about the relationship and weaker feelings of commitment than the other two groups. But the marriages of couples who had moved in together after getting engaged seemed just as strong as those who had moved in together after marrying.

Among other things, couples who get engaged before cohabiting probably have a clearer understanding of each other's expectations before they combine households. On that point, Mia Dunleavey, a 39-year-old online financial columnist living in Brooklyn, New York, can speak with the sadder-but-wiser voice of experience. In her late 20s, Dunleavey was involved with a man she hoped to marry. He reluctantly agreed to move in with her, spurred by the fact that his lease was running out, but he vacillated for so long about setting a wedding date that she finally ended the relationship. Soon after, she relocated across the country to move in with a new man she'd fallen in love with, only to find their living styles were utterly incompatible.

"When you leave the door open for quasi-commitment, quasi-commitment is what you get."

Back in New York again, she took stock. "I was terribly disappointed," Dunleavey says. "You have this faith that you're moving in with someone in order to deepen the commitment, and it doesn't necessarily happen at all. Those two things are not correlated.

"At that point, I said, 'Never ever, ever again,'" she continues. "Living together is a waste of time and energy. The piece of china you'd gotten from your mother gets broken in the move. My living-together experience was a catalog of lost and broken things, never mind my heart."

When she fell in love again, she did things differently. She moved in with her intended just two weeks before the wedding—because by that point, there was no question about their future together. "There was no take-it or leave-it," she says. "The commitment was the foundation of the marriage. Alas, my only experience of living with someone is that when you leave the door open for quasi-commitment, quasi-commitment is what you get."

Miller and Solot don't advise against cohabitation for couples without immediate plans to marry. But they do believe each partner needs to understand clearly what the other is thinking. "The most important thing is for people to treat moving in together as a serious decision, a major life choice," Miller says. "What does it mean to you both for the long and short term? If one person thinks living together means a quick path towards marriage and the other thinks it's just saving on rent and having a friend with benefits, there could be trouble. The important thing is to be on the same page."

As for my husband and me, we had this much going for us when we moved in together: We'd already discussed a lot of the important issues. We knew we wanted similar things: a family; a "for better or worse" kind of commitment; a partner who knew life had to stop on Sundays, when *Six Feet Under* or *The Sopranos* was on. Even before the ring, it was clear to me I'd found someone who'd be willing to work things through. And he has been.

Perhaps there's hope for us after all.

NANCY WARTIK is a freelance writer living in New York City.

From *Psychology Today,* vol. 38, no. 4, July/August 2005, pp. 44, 46, 48, 50, 52. Copyright © 2005 by Sussex Publishers, LLC. Reprinted by permission.

UNIT 4

The Contexts of Adolescents in Society: School, Work, and Diversity

Unit Selections

Key Points to Consider

- Why is the dropout rate rising and which programs convince students to stay in school?

- Why did a 9th grade physics teacher enroll in a 9th grade Biology class?

- How do strict rules help students who are in trouble?

- Are lockdowns necessary to keep order in some schools?

- What is the effect of part-time work on adolescents?

- What struggles do immigrant youth have in the school environment?

- What is the difference between school-based curricular programs and the efforts to change school climate to reduce school violence?

- How is taking the "cultural plunge" helpful to becoming a teacher?

- What character traits should be taught?

- Why is small size and the college context extremely important?

Student Website
www.mhcls.com

Internet References

Afterschool Alliance
http://www.afterschoolalliance.org

National Institute on Out-Of-School Time
www.niost.org

Public Education Network
www.publiceducation.org

Public/Private Ventures
www.ppv.org

School Stress
http://www.kqed.org/w/ymc/stress/index.html

What Kids Can Do
www.whatkidscando.org

Adolescence entails changes in cognitive capacities that are just as monumental as the biological changes. Whereas children tend to be more literal, more tied to reality and to the familiar—adolescents are more abstract, systematic, and logical. Adolescents can appreciate metaphors and sarcasm, they can easily think about things that do not exist, they can test abstract ideas against reality, and they can readily conceive of multiple possibilities. Many of these improvements in thinking ability contribute to conflicts with adults as adolescents become better able to argue a point or take a stand. They are better at planning out their case and anticipating counter arguments. They are also more likely to question the way things are because they now conceive of alternate possibilities.

The study of cognitive changes that occur in adolescence has largely been based on the work of the Swiss psychologist, Jean Piaget, and his colleague Barbel Inhelder. Piaget and Inhelder described the adolescent as reasoning at the formal operational stage. Children from the approximate ages of 7 to 11 years old were described as being in the "concrete operational" stage. Not all researchers agree with Piaget and Inhelder that changes in adolescent cognitive abilities represent true stage-related changes. They do, however, agree that adolescent thought is characteristically more logical, abstract, and hypothetical than that of children. Recognize, though, that having certain mental capacities does not mean that adolescents, or even adults for that matter, will always reason at their rational best!

Piaget's views on cognitive development have been very influential, particularly in the field of education. Awareness of the cognitive abilities and shortcomings of adolescents can make their behaviors more comprehensible to parents, teachers, counselors, and other professionals who work with them. Similarly, as Piaget suggested, schools need to take the developmental abilities and needs of adolescents into account in planning programs and designing curricula. In addition, Piaget's general philosophy was that learning must be active. Others in the field of education, however, caution that there are other important issues left un-addressed by Piaget. For example, the United States has an elevated school dropout rate, so we need to find alternatives for keeping the nation's youth in school.

Building on the work of Piaget and Inhelder, David Elkind has argued that the newly emerging formal operational cognitive abilities of adolescents lead to some troublesome consequences. For one thing, adolescents tend to over intellectualize. They often make things too complex and fail to see the obvious, a phenomenon that Elkind calls pseudostupidity. Teachers often bear the brunt of this phenomenon as adolescents overanalyze every word of a multiple-choice question. Elkind also maintains that much of the extreme self-consciousness of adolescents occurs because of the construct of an imaginary audience. Formal operations make it possible for adolescents to think about other people's thoughts. Adolescents lose perspective and think that others are constantly watching them and thinking about them. A related mistake is that adolescents are likely to believe that everyone shares their concerns and knows their thoughts. This belief, that one is at the center of attention, further leads to the development of what Elkind calls the personal fable.

Namely, if everyone is paying so much attention to me I must be special and invulnerable. Bad things won't happen to me. I won't get in a car crash. I won't get pregnant. The phenomena—pseudostupidity, the imaginary audience, and the personal fable—diminish as adolescents' cognitive abilities mature and as they develop friendships in which intimacies are shared. Peer interaction helps adolescents see that they are not as unique as they thought, nor are they the focus of everyone else's attention.

Schools focus on individual students and on punishment. Only when schools take student concerns into account will schools become environments that stimulate attendance, interest, and harmony. School violence by disenchanted youth has peaked in the United States. Schools will need to promote a sense of belonging if disaffected and potentially violent students are to become members of the school community.

While developmentalists in the Piagetian tradition focus on the ways in which the thought processes of children and adolescents differ, other researchers have taken a different track—a psychometric approach. In this approach, the emphasis is on quantifying cognitive abilities such as verbal ability, mathematical ability, and general intelligence (IQ). The measurement of intelligence, as well as the very definition of intelligence, has been controversial for decades. A classic question is whether intelligence is best conceptualized as a general capacity that underlies many diverse abilities or as a set of specific abilities. Traditional IQ tests focus on abilities that relate to success in school and ignore abilities such as those that tap creativity, mechanical aptitude, or practical intelligence.

The role of genetic versus environmental contributions to intelligence have also been controversial. At the turn of the century the predominant view was that intelligence was essentially inherited and was little influenced by experience. Today, the consensus is that an individual's intelligence is very much a product of both nature and nurture. An even greater controversy focuses on the role that heredity versus the environment plays in explaining racial, ethnic, and gender differences in performance on various cognitive tests such as IQ tests.

Adolescents clearly have larger vocabularies, more mathematical knowledge, better spatial ability, etc., than children. Their memories are better because they process information more efficiently and use memory strategies more effectively. Adolescents possess a greater general knowledge base than children, which enables adolescents to link new concepts to existing ideas. Stated another way, psychometric intelligence may well increase with age. On the other hand, because of comparisons to age peers, the relative performance of adolescents on aptitude tests remains fairly stable. A 9-year-old child's outstanding performance on an IQ test, for example, is fairly predictive that the same individual's IQ score at age 15 will be better than the score of most peers.

School is the place where teens spend much of their time. Their cognitive abilities are encouraged and supported. But schools offer much more than just education experience. A teen acquires new skills and comes to grips with the concerns and experiences of adult society. Educational issues of today are many and include racial integration, diversity, greater school choice, and students with exceptional abilities and needs.

In addition to attending school, a majority of American teens work. Younger teens mostly do occasional babysitting or yard work. Those 15 and over are likely to work on a steady basis in offices, restaurants, and stores. Over half of those with jobs work 15 or more hours per week during the school year and more during the summer. A large majority are paid at or close to minimum wage.

The first article in this unit explains why the dropout rate is steadily rising and which programs convince students to stay in school. Deborah Waldron reports on a high school teacher who enrolled in a 9th grade Biology class. An army-drill-instructor approach to education is discussed. Tina Kelley reports on lockdowns as a new drill in some schools. The next article reveals positive correlation between part-time work and high school success. The struggles of immigrant youth are examined next. Michael B. Greene explains how some schools attempt to change school climate. The number of students from culturally and linguistically diverse backgrounds is continuing to grow and Jesús Nieto proposes a model to help new teachers. The authors of the next article present a strong case that well-defined and implemented character education programs should exist alongside traditional academic programs. The last article explains how the two factors of small size and the college context are important in schools today.

The Dropout Problem: Losing Ground

As we strive to improve high school achievement, we must not forget the increasing number of students who fail to graduate.

PAUL E. BARTON

A recent upsurge of interest in the student dropout problem seems to have come as a surprise to U.S. school officials and policymakers. During the last two decades, complacency had set in as reports from the U.S. Census Bureau's household survey suggested that high school completion among young adults was approaching 90 percent, the goal set by the first National Education Summit in Charlottesville, Virginia, in 1989. The long-dormant concern about dropouts revived several years ago, however, when half a dozen independent researchers in universities and think tanks began publishing estimates of high school completion rates that contradicted the official rates. As a result, the issue of high school dropouts has returned to the front burner.

Many Estimates, Similar Results

The recent independent estimates of high school completion rates are almost always lower than the official estimates—including those that states have reported to the U.S. Department of Education under the requirements of No Child Left Behind and the state estimates from the National Center for Education Statistics. These independent estimates—derived through different methods and not always pertaining to the same year—vary somewhat, but they are all in the same ballpark. Jay Greene at the Manhattan Institute estimated a high school completion rate of 71 percent for 1998; Christopher Swanson and Duncan Chaplin at the Urban Institute estimated 66.6 percent for 2000; Thomas Mortenson of *Postsecondary Education Opportunity* estimated 66.1 percent for 2000; Andrew Sum and colleagues at Northeastern University estimated 68.7 percent for 1998; and Walter Haney and colleagues at Boston College estimated 74.4 percent for 2001. I describe these studies and their methodologies in detail in *Unfinished Business: More Measured Approaches in Standards-Based Reform* (Barton, 2005a).

The well-publicized contradictions of official estimates led to a minor political explosion, particularly after the Education Trust (2003) attacked the accuracy of the states' reports to the Department of Education. Then-Secretary of Education Rod Paige appointed a task force to look into the matter. Later, the National Governors Association convened a Task Force on State High School Graduation Data to propose a plan for how states could develop a high-quality, comparable high school graduation measure. All of this is being weighed in Washington and in state capitals.

A Closer Look at the Statistics

My own analysis (Barton, 2005a) confirmed the estimates of other researchers. I relied on two numbers I knew to be actual counts. One was the census count of the population cohort that would be of graduation age (17 or 18) in spring 2000; the other was the number of regular public and private high school diplomas awarded that year as reported by the National Center for Education Statistics. My final analysis estimated that 69.6 percent of youth who were of graduating age had received diplomas in 2000.

To measure change over time, I made estimates for 1990 using the same approach and found a completion rate of 72 percent for that year. For both 1990 and 2000, I also estimated individual state completion rates, which varied broadly. For 1990, the spread was from 90.6 percent in Iowa down to 61.7 percent in Florida (and 59.9 percent in Washington, D.C.). In 2000, the percentage ranged from 88.2 percent in Vermont down to 55 percent in Arizona (and 48 percent in Washington, D.C.). Only seven states showed an increase in high school completion rates during the decade; rates in the remaining states declined (Barton, 2005b).

Other researchers have found that minorities have lower completion rates than white students. For example, Elaine Allensworth (2005) carried out an excellent study of Chicago schools, which had individual student records available to track students. Among boys, only 39 percent of black students graduated by age 19, compared with 51 percent of Latino students and 58 percent of white students. Girls fared better: Comparable rates were 57 percent for black students, 65 percent for Latino students, and 71 percent for white students.

Research on the path that students travel through the grades may also shed light on the dropout problem. For example, one study identified an important trend that has developed over the last decade: the "9th grade bulge." Compared with past years, an increasing number of 9th graders are failing to be promoted to the 10th grade. Haney and colleagues (2004) found that in 2001, 440,000 more students were enrolled in grade 9 than in grade 8 the previous year. By 2001, seven states had at least 20 percent more students enrolled in the 9th grade than had been enrolled in that grade in the prior year, and one-half had at least 10 percent more. We know that there is an association between failing a grade and dropping out. And we know that more students are dropping out at younger ages.

The research conducted in the last couple of years raises many questions. One issue is why the U.S. Census Bureau household survey estimates differ from the lower completion rates found by independent researchers. We can explain this difference in part by the fact that the census lumped regular diplomas and GEDs together. The GED is a well-respected substitute, but it is not a regular diploma earned after completing four years of high school. Numerous research studies show that GED recipients tend to fare better than dropouts, but not as well as graduates with diplomas (Boesel, Alsalam, & Smith, 1998). Although the number of GEDs has become a growing proportion of total graduates, inclusion of GED recipients does not entirely account for the gaps among the estimates. Further analysis is needed to reconcile the remaining discrepancies.

Low achievement and grade retention are precursors to leaving school.

Another question raised by the research is why completion rates, in terms of regular diplomas, fell during the last decade in so many states. Some of the likely suspects include the decrease in two-parent families, the previously mentioned 9th grade bulge, and higher standards for graduation. However, my analysis did not produce evidence conclusively linking high school completion rates to any of these factors.

A Deteriorating Economic Position

At the same time that high school completion rates have fallen, labor market prospects for dropouts are becoming increasingly dire. In 2003, 1.1 million 16- to 19-year-olds did not have a high school diploma and were not enrolled in school. In the landscape of the economy, these dropouts are often lost travelers without a map. Only 4 in 10 of the 16- to 19-year-olds are employed, as are fewer than 6 in 10 of 20- to 24-year-old dropouts. Black and Latino youth are doing considerably less well than others (T. Morisi, U.S. Bureau of Labor Statistics, personal communication, July 14, 2004).

What about the earning power of those dropouts who do have jobs? Do they make enough money to support a household? For 25- to 34-year-old dropouts who manage to work full-time, the average annual salary of males dropped from $35,087 (in 2002

constant dollars) in 1971 to $22,903 in 2002, a decline of 35 percent. The comparable annual earnings for females without a diploma were $19,888 in 1971, declining to $17,114 in 2002. Even when they work full-time, the average earnings of this age group of dropouts are not far above the poverty line for a family with children—and most dropouts do not even reach this level of earnings. The earnings of high school graduates also have declined since 1971, but not as steeply as those of dropouts (National Center for Education Statistics [NCES], 2004, Tables 14–1, 14–2, and 14–3).

Factors That Affect the Dropout Rate

Which student conditions and life experiences are correlated with failure to complete high school? A 2002 report from the U.S. General Accounting Office (GAO)[1] summarized the research. Factors that correlated with low completion rates included coming from low-income or single-parent families, getting low grades in school, being absent frequently and changing schools. These factors vary considerably by state, as do high school completion rates.

These predictive factors do not determine completion rates, but they do show the conditions that schools need to overcome in their effort to maximize completions. Some schools rise above expectations, some schools meet them, and some schools do less well than expected.

To find out how the individual states performed in 2000 compared with what we might expect on the basis of conditions in each state, I computed the correlation of completion rates with expectations based on three factors: state average socioeconomic characteristics (family income, education, and occupation); the percentage of two-parent families; and the rate at which students change schools. I found that these factors accounted for almost 60 percent of the variation in state completion rates.

This comparison of the *expected* completion rates with the *actual* completion rates disclosed that the actual rate fell within 4 percentage points of the expected rate in 24 states. Except for Rhode Island and Hawaii, actual rates in the remaining states were within 10 points of the expected rates. The states doing the best in exceeding their expected completion rates were Hawaii, Maryland, Vermont, Connecticut, and West Virginia. The states doing the worst were Rhode Island, Indiana, South Carolina, and Arizona (Barton, 2005a). To learn more about increasing school completion rates, we should study both those states that greatly exceed the expected high school completion rate and those that fall far below it for clues about what these states are doing differently.

Increasing School Retention

The factors identified in the GAO report—that low-income students and high-mobility students are high-risk, that low achievement and grade retention are precursors to leaving school—provide a guide for what we need to do to improve high school completion rates. In my research, the factor *most* predictive was coming from a single-parent family (even after controlling for socioeconomic status). The extra effort that schools make to support students in all these circumstances will likely determine whether schools achieve higher or lower high school completion rates than expected.

In the landscape of the economy, dropouts are often lost travelers without a map.

Evaluations have established the effectiveness of a number of programs and models designed to increase school retention. The following models, described in more detail in *One-Third of a Nation: Rising Dropout Rates and Declining Opportunities* (Barton, 2005b), merit a close look by any state, district, or school wishing to embark on efforts to retain students in school.

- *The Talent Development High School* was developed by the Center for Research on the Education of Students Placed At Risk (CRESPAR), a collaboration between Johns Hopkins University and Howard University. This model emphasizes small learning communities, curriculum reforms, professional development, interdisciplinary teams of teachers, longer class periods, and employer advisory boards. There are now 33 such high schools in 12 states.
- *Communities in Schools* is designed specifically to keep students in school. Schools and community agencies form partnerships to deliver services and provide resources to students, such as individual case management, counseling, volunteers and mentors, remedial education, tutoring, classes teaching life skills and employment-related topics, and a variety of after-school programs.
- *Maryland Tomorrow* is a large-scale statewide dropout prevention effort operating in 75 high schools and is directed at students considered at risk of dropping out. Among other components, the program includes counseling, intensive academic instruction during the summer and the school year, career guidance and exploration, a variety of summer activities, and adult mentors.
- *The Quantum Opportunities Program* was launched in 1989 with funding from the Ford Foundation and the U.S. Department of Labor. Although the funding ended in 1999, the program's features offer a roadmap for providing supplemental services to students in schools that have large proportions of low-income and minority families. The program targeted randomly selected at-risk 9th graders entering inner-city high schools with high dropout rates. Using a comprehensive case management approach, the program provided year-round services to the participants throughout their four years of high

school. Components included tutoring and homework assistance, computer-assisted instruction, life and family skills training, supplemental after-school education, developmental activities, mentoring, community service activities, and financial planning.

The documented results of these programs, together with the growing research on public alternative schools (Kleiner, Porch, & Farris, 2002), provide a knowledge base about comprehensive approaches to increasing both academic achievement and high school completion rates—which generally go hand in hand.

Any reform initiatives that do not make inroads on the dropout situation can hardly be considered successful.

When it comes to working with individual students to avert a decision to drop out, however, there is a serious impediment. Guidance counselors, working with teachers, are the logical people to identify, track, and help students who show the well-known predropout behaviors: frequent absenteeism, course failure, and negative attitudes. But these professionals can hardly perform such work given the current ratio of 1 counselor to almost 300 high school students—a ratio that is even worse in high-minority schools (NCES, 2004, Table 27–1). In addition, almost all of a counselor's time goes to scheduling courses, helping students with college choice and admissions, performing hall and lunchroom duty, and, increasingly, dealing with test administration (NCES, 2001).

Somehow, schools must recruit individuals who have the time to interact with students one-on-one: more counselors, more volunteers, and more paid and unpaid mentors and tutors. How schools achieve this aim will vary, but any viable approach will require additional effort and resources at the school, school district, or state level (or all three).

Schools attempting to tackle the dropout problem face strikingly different circumstances. At one end of the spectrum are the schools in suburban neighborhoods where most students graduate and go on to college. Here, the relatively few students who appear dropout-prone can be identified, and resources are likely to be available to help them. At the other end are the schools in poor inner-city neighborhoods where families may have less time to supervise after-school activities or interact with the schools to address student absenteeism, misbehavior, or concerns about homework. Here, efforts to increase high school completion will require considerable additional resources, including the help of the larger community. All sorts of school situations lie in between, and no handy formula will apply across the board. But policymakers, administrators, and legislators have a base of knowledge to draw on, as well as information about good practices that work at the school and classroom levels.

A Battle on Two Fronts

The growing demands for high school reform have emphasized the need for higher achievement levels for students who graduate from high school so that they are prepared to either succeed in college or go directly into academically demanding jobs.

Although such efforts are important, any reform initiatives that do not also make inroads on the dropout situation can hardly be considered successful. We face a hard battle on two fronts—one to make high school more rigorous, and the other to keep more students in high school through graduation.

Note

1. Effective July 7, 2004, the GAO's legal name became the U.S. Government Accountability Office.

References

Allensworth, E. (2005). *Graduation and dropout trends in Chicago: A look at cohorts of students from 1991 through 2004.* Chicago: Consortium on Chicago School Research.

Barton, P. (2005a, January). *Unfinished business: More measured approaches in standards-based reform.* (Policy Information Report). Princeton, NJ: Educational Testing Service, Policy Information Center. Available: www.ets.org/Media/Education_Topics/pdf/unfinbusiness.pdf

Barton, P. (2005b). *One-third of a nation: Rising dropout rates and declining opportunities.* Princeton, NJ: Educational Testing Service, Policy Information Center. Available: www.ets.org/Media/Education_Topics/pdf/onethird.pdf

Boesel, D., Alsalam, N., & Smith, T. M. (1998). *Educational and labor market performance of GED recipients.* Washington, DC: U.S. Department of Education, National Education Library.

Education Trust. (2003, December). *Telling the whole truth (or not) about high school graduation.* Washington, DC: Author.

Haney, W., Madaus, G., Abrams, L., Wheelock, A., Miao, J., & Gruia, I. (2004). *The education pipeline in the United States, 1970–2004.* Chestnut Hill, MA: National Board on Educational Testing and Public Policy.

Kleiner, B., Porch, R., & Farris, E. (2002, September). *Public alternative schools and programs for students at risk of education failure, 2000–01.* Washington, DC: National Center for Education Statistics.

National Center for Education Statistics [NCES]. (2001). *Survey on high school guidance counseling.* Washington, DC: Author.

NCES. (2004). *The condition of education 2004.* Washington, DC: Author.

U.S. General Accounting Office. (2002). *School dropouts: Education could play a stronger role in identifying and disseminating promising prevention strategies.* (GAO–02–240). Washington, DC: Author.

PAUL E. BARTON is a Senior Associate at Educational Testing Service's Policy Information Center and an independent education writer and consultant; paulebarton@aol.com

From *Educational Leadership*, February 2006, pp. 14–18. Copyright © 2006 by ASCD. Reprinted by permission. The Association for Supervision and Curriculum Development is a worldwide community of educators advocating sound policies and sharing best practices to achieve the success of each learner. To learn more, visit ASCD at www.ascd.org

My Year as a High School Student

A stint in students' shoes helped a science teacher examine her own practice.

DEBORAH WALDRON

Like countless other teachers, I decided to take a class last fall. Unlike most teachers, though, I chose to take a biology class at the school where I teach physics, Yorktown High School in Arlington, Virginia.

I had begun pursuing National Board Certification in Adolescence and Young Adulthood/Science, and I faced the hurdle of showing breadth of knowledge across the four major areas of biology, chemistry, earth and space science, and physics. My biology knowledge was woefully inadequate. Rather than enrolling in a class at the local community college, I decided to sit in on Allyson McKowen's 9th grade Intensified Biology class.

I attended class every day, took notes, did my homework, read the textbook, worked in a lab group, wrote up labs, and took the tests and quizzes. Except for my age and the fact that I came and went from class without a hall pass, I was a typical student. The amount of time I spent on after-school activities probably paralleled the time commitments of a typical high school student. I had family responsibilities as well as a fairly time-consuming "extracurricular activity"—I taught an evening physics class at the local community college. My stint in students' shoes gave me insight into the challenges that high school students face and led me to make changes in my own teaching. The following are my observations from the other side of the desk about practices that I believe help create the best conditions for learning.

What Looks Good from the Student Side

Give students more time for creative projects. Although I have fairly well-honed time management skills, I found myself starting a lot of creative assignments for class late at night. No matter how hard I tried, my daily responsibilities and workload kept me from getting a head start on a pending long-term assignment.

For example, one assignment involved creating an analogy for how a cell functions. I chose to compare a cell to a restaurant, reasoning that just as the various parts of a cell perform the functions necessary to maintain cell health, each staff member at a restaurant performs certain jobs to ensure the restaurant's continued success. Not only did I have to write a paper explaining the logic of my analogy, but I also had to create a physical model of the analogy. This was an incredible learning experience that truly taught me the structure of a cell and the functions of its parts—but it was one of several assignments I finished at 1:00 a.m.

I used to give my physics students a hard time when they complained about late-night study sessions. Now I realize that students' extracurricular and academic commitments often make it hard to work ahead. In teaching future classes, I plan to break long-term assignments into smaller chunks so that students have multiple deadlines along the way and to cut back on homework during weeks when longer assignments are due.

Occasionally use short, straightforward assessments. Although I believe all assessments should require students to demonstrate deep, authentic understanding, at times it is preferable to accomplish this with simple, straightforward assessments. These more traditional assessments can be structured in a way that gauges student learning and probes for true understanding. I remember one lab assignment in which Allyson told us that all we needed to do was analyze the data and complete six questions at the end of the lab. My lab partner and I looked at each other and almost simultaneously declared, "Thank goodness!" We had recently completed a formal lab write-up on a separate experiment, and neither of us had the energy or time to tackle another. The questions were enough for Allyson to make sure we understood the material and had completed the lab without drowning us in work.

Reinforce ethics and clarify plagiarism. In early October, our first formal paper was due. We had been studying water properties and had recently completed a lab on surface tension. This assessment required us to write the introductory section of a formal lab write-up as well as answer several in-depth questions about our data. My schedule that week was quite busy, and I didn't get a chance to sit down and start writing until 11:00 p.m. the night before the paper was due. Around 11:15 p.m., I thought to myself, "Hey, if I don't go to class tomorrow, I won't have to turn the paper in yet." The thought was extremely tempting, and

I went to bed. Somewhere around 3:00 a.m. I woke up, thought better about my choice, and finished my paper.

My year as a 9th grade student was enjoyable and stressful, and it provided a dose of reality that strengthened my teaching practice.

When I talked with Allyson about my dilemma, she mentioned that she always calls home to talk with the parents of a student who is absent the day a big assignment is due. I suspect that this kind of outside pressure helps students make wiser choices. Without such pressure, even as a teacher and a supposed role model, I made a poor choice for about four hours.

Later in the year, we had to create a brochure about a particular genetic disorder, explaining when the disorder was discovered, its symptoms, the genetic cause of the disorder, how common the condition is, and what treatments are available. I was assigned clubfoot and spent a significant amount of time researching it over the weekend. Although I had done the research and processed the information, I didn't get a chance to actually create the brochure until the following Thursday evening, after I had taught my night class.

That evening, as I drove home from the community college, I continued to plan my brochure in my head. I was tired and wanted to do it as quickly as possible while still doing a good job. At home, I started lining up Web sites from which I could cut and paste the information. After a few minutes, it dawned on me that I was about to plagiarize the entire assignment. When I thought about the situation later, I realized that as a teacher I simply expect my students to know what plagiarism is. Teachers need to be more specific with students and provide concrete examples throughout the year that will help them realize what is and is not academically acceptable.

Change student seats often. Simple as it sounds, shaking up student seating every six weeks or so makes a huge difference in the dynamics of the classroom. I initially knew none of the students in the class. At first, my lab partners were leery of me, but over time they warmed up to me and treated me as normally as possible, even teasing me about getting a low quiz grade. However, had we stayed in the same seats for the entire year, I would have only gotten to know these 3 students in a class of 22.

My experience as the "new kid" made me realize the importance of creating an environment in which students can meet many other students. Because Allyson switched the student seats eight times over the course of the year, I got to know almost the entire class. The regular rearrangement of seats and reassignment of lab groups created a supportive classroom environment in which students felt comfortable asking any other student, not just a friend, for assistance. I now periodically rearrange student seats in my physics classes; I also assign lab groups rather than let students choose them.

How I Learned to Love the "Squishy Stuff"

The most enjoyable thing that I discovered in my year studying 9th grade biology was that it's the teacher, not the content, that makes the class. As a physics teacher, I had no expectation of enjoying biology. I called it the "squishy stuff." Allyson McKowen made me fall in love with biology. Her way of presenting the material and interacting with students made class enjoyable. Allyson's classroom was student-focused, and her leadership helped every student feel comfortable and courageous. Students asked and answered questions without fear. I looked forward to class and found myself doing outside reading in a college text so I could understand the material on a deeper level. I used to think that British physicist Ernest Rutherford was right when he said, "All science is either physics or stamp collecting." After a year of biology with Allyson, I know Rutherford was wrong.

My year as a 9th grade student was enjoyable and stressful, and it provided a dose of reality that strengthened my teaching practice. Although I learned an incredible amount of biology, I was more impressed with what I learned about teaching. A year from now, when I'm teaching physics to some of my former biology classmates, I'll draw on my experiences with them that have made me a better teacher.

DEBORAH WALDRON teaches physics at Yorktown High School, 5201 N. 28th St., Arlington, VA 22207; 703–228–5378; Deborah_Waldron@apsva.us.

From *Educational Leadership,* March 2006, pp. 63–65. Copyright © 2006 by ASCD. Reprinted by permission. The Association for Supervision and Curriculum Development is a worldwide community of educators advocating sound policies and sharing best practices to achieve the success of each learner. To learn more, visit ASCD at www.ascd.org

School's New Rule for Pupils in Trouble: No Fun

WINNIE HU

Like a bouncer at a nightclub, Melissa Gladwell was parked at the main entrance of Cheektowaga Central Middle School on Friday night, with a list of 150 names highlighted in yellow marker, the names of students barred from the after-hours games, crafts and ice cream because of poor grades or bad attitudes.

"You're ineligible," Ms. Gladwell, a sixth-grade teacher, told one boy, who turned around without protest. "That happens. I think they think we're going to forget."

In a far-reaching experiment with disciplinary measures reminiscent of old-style Catholic schools or military academies, the Cheektowaga district this year began essentially grounding middle school students whose grade in any class falls below 65, or who show what educators describe as a lack of effort.

Such students—more than a quarter of the 580 at the school as of last week—are excluded from all aspects of extracurricular life, including athletic contests, academic clubs, dances and plays, unless they demonstrate improvement on weekly progress reports filled out by their teachers.

The policy is far stricter than those at most high schools, which generally have eligibility requirements only for varsity sports teams. It is part of a larger campaign to instill more responsibility in young adolescents in this town of 80,000 on the outskirts of Buffalo. Starting this week, the students also automatically get detention on any day they fail to wear their identification cards; 13 were punished on the first day of the new policy and 14 the second, including several repeaters.

And there are social rules that govern nearly every minute of the day, from riding the bus to using the bathroom, as part of a program known as "positive behavioral interventions and supports." Students are required to keep to the right of the dotted yellow line down the middle of hallways. They are assigned seats in the cafeteria and must wait for a teacher to call them up to get food. If enough students act up or even litter, they all risk a declaration of "silent lunch" in the cafeteria.

"I'd like to go to a normal school," said Anthony Pachetti, 12, a seventh grader who has been barred from activities for failing math, science and social studies. "It's not doing anything for me except taking everything away."

Such harsh regimens are rare, and generally have been found in tough urban schools like Eastside High in Paterson, N.J., where Joe Clark, an Army-drill-instructor-turned-principal, famously expelled dozens of students in a single day in the early 1980s, and inspired the movie "Lean on Me." Now tough policies are spreading to outlying areas like Cheektowaga at a time when they are facing increased pressure to improve academic achievement. Middle schools, in particular, have long struggled with performance slumps and competing theories on how to strike the right balance between structure and independence for students at a transitional, volatile age. But few have gone as far as Cheektowaga has in clamping down on the natural disorder of early adolescence.

Even Joe Clark's Paterson district backed away from requiring that 10th, 11th and 12th graders maintain a 2.5 grade-point average to participate in extracurricular activities in 2006. Instead, it adopted a lower standard—a 2.0 average only for athletes—after community opposition.

Critics of the tough-love approach cite studies showing that students active in extracurricular activities tend to perform better in class, and they worry that without structured activities after school, troubled youngsters will be more apt to find trouble.

"A child who only has detention to look forward to at the end of the day is less likely to come to school," said Laura Rogers, a school psychologist in Harvard, Mass. and the co-author of "Fires in the Middle School Bathroom."

Deborah Meier, a senior scholar at New York University's Steinhardt School of Education and a former New York City principal, said that such "law and order" approaches are counterproductive.

"Sounds like prison," she said of Cheektowaga. "It's such a sad, sad commentary because, in my opinion, the improvements that it can make in behavior are marginal, and it does not begin to touch upon what engages the students in school."

Some similar tactics have been tried recently in places as varied as rural Twin Falls, Idaho, where high school students with grade-point-averages below 2.0 were barred from competing in extracurricular activities and required to attend tutoring starting this year, and in the Pittsburgh suburbs, where the Penn Hills school district set a 1.5 minimum average in 2006 to qualify for activities, raised that to 1.75 this school year, and has bumped it up again, to 2.0, for next fall.

Here in Cheektowaga, the new policy arrived with a new principal, Brian Bridges, who said that over four years as an assistant principal at the school, he saw less and less respect—and more and more attitude—from students growing up in a society that he believes is too permissive.

At the same time, many teachers were not prepared for the new students brought by the demographic changes sweeping the school, he said; its enrollment has gone from overwhelmingly white and working class to 35 percent black and Hispanic in recent years as minority families have moved in from Buffalo. And nearly half the students are poor enough to qualify for free and reduced-price lunches.

Mr. Bridges, 39, is a former social worker who said that he was raised by a strict single mother who smacked him when he so much as gave her a disrespectful look. Teachers here nicknamed him "Joe Clark" and gave him a bullhorn, which he gladly accepted and sometimes uses in the hallways and to direct students to buses. He said that bringing more structure and discipline to the school creates a safer environment and teaches students to be members of a community.

So along with barring failing students from after-school activities, he has added things like pep rallies and hat and pajama days during school hours, and rewarded those who succeed under the new rules with raffle prizes.

On Friday afternoon, Mr. Bridges straddled the yellow line in a hallway to force students passing in both directions to stay on the right side.

"Go back!" he roared at an eighth grader bounding by him.

The boy stopped, protested, went back, then made the trip down the hallway again—at a fast walk.

"I'm the first one in the hallways wanting to have fun with my kids," Mr. Bridges said. "But I know I have to have a stronger hand."

It is too soon to see whether the policies will have an effect on state test scores, since this year's results will not be released until late spring. Last year, 53.8 percent of eighth graders passed the state's standardized math tests and 51 percent language arts, compared with 58.8 percent and 57 percent statewide.

Ms. Gladwell and other teachers said that there has not been an overall improvement in classroom grades, but that they had seen more homework turned in, more class participation, and fewer fights in the hallways and cafeteria. Attendance has stayed steady at about 95 percent.

The new eligibility policy for extracurricular activities drew complaints from more than two dozen parents last October after the school barred 75 students from attending the first dance, Mr. Bridges said.

But Sondra LaMacchia, a stay-at-home mother of five, said that after years of telling her 14-year-old daughter, Cortney, to study harder, the message came through much clearer when Cortney had to watch her friends and younger sister attend school dances from which she was barred.

"It's nobody's fault but hers," said Ms. LaMacchia, 35.

Some teachers have complained that enforcing the policy takes time away from academic instruction and burdens them with paperwork. There have also been concerns that the eligibility policy was keeping students from pursuing academic interests like the math and science clubs.

Ms. Gladwell, who is also the school's volleyball coach, benched one of her top players in October because she forgot to bring her progress report. Afterward, she said, the player's mother came up and thanked her.

"She never forgot again," Ms. Gladwell said. "It's about teaching them responsibility."

Ellen Pieroni, 13, an eighth grader who is co-president of the student council, had considered boycotting a dance in December because her friends could not go, but now says that she supports the policy. "I think they get lazy and don't do the work," she said. But other students said that the school had too many rules.

Having forgotten his identification card for the seventh time this year, Cameron Kaeding, a sixth grader, had to wear a temporary sticker and wait to get his lunch because students without their ID cards are served last. He has also been kept from a pep rally and two dances because of his struggles in math and social studies. "It's horrible," he said. "I think it's going a little too far because kids aren't perfect, and this school thinks that they are."

In an Era of School Shootings, Lockdowns Are the New Drill

Tina Kelley

Tim Matheney stalked the silent hallways of South Brunswick High School one recent Wednesday at 1:07 p.m., peering into dark, seemingly empty classrooms and jotting down room numbers whenever he heard giggles behind locked doors. Students were supposed to remain silent and out of sight.

Mr. Matheney, the school's principal, was roaming the suburban campus as if he were an "active shooter," à la **Virginia Tech** or Columbine, as part of a "lockdown drill" now required twice a year here and in many schools around the country.

Gone are the days of the traditional fire drill, where students dutifully line up in hallways and proceed to the playground, then return a few minutes later. Now, in a ritual reminiscent of the 1950s, when students ducked under desks and covered their heads in anticipation of nuclear blasts, many schools are preparing for, among other emergencies, bomb threats, hazardous material spills, shelter-in-place preparation (in which students would use schools as shelters if a dirty bomb's plume were to spread dangerously close) and armed, roaming sociopaths.

"I think it's really pretty necessary," said Natalie Wright, a junior honors student at South Brunswick High. "In my old school, we did have an intruder, and we didn't practice," she added, recalling how a disgruntled parent had sent her Bronx elementary school into a panic, although no one was hurt.

In the aftermath of recent school shootings, including the one on Feb. 14 at **Northern Illinois University** in which a gunman killed five people and himself, school administrators and police officers are stepping up emergency preparedness efforts, with many states encouraging schools to practice for the most dire situations.

In **New Jersey**, considered by school safety experts to be in the top tier when it comes to emergency preparedness, a task force recommended last year that districts conduct emergency drills monthly. The State Office of Homeland Security and Preparedness is working on legislation to require such drills statewide as early as next fall.

New York State requires districts and schools to have emergency response plans and to conduct emergency drills at least once a year, along with 12 fire drills annually.

Kathy Christie, a researcher at the Education Commission of the States, which advises governors and state legislators,

described the requirements that some states have developed about drills. For example, she said, Rhode Island mandates two evacuation drills and two lockdown drills a year, and Michigan requires two lockdown drills.

So far in New Jersey, the new drills have been tried in towns and cities including Newark, Teaneck and Franklin Township in Gloucester County. **Seton Hall University** is scheduled to conduct a drill with an "active shooter scenario" on Wednesday afternoon.

In Franklin Township, administrators were startled to learn four years ago that information about one of their schools was found on a laptop carried by an Iraqi in Baghdad, though the **F.B.I.** said there was no terrorism threat to the school. The Delsea Regional High School District, which educates students from Franklin Township, has had regular drills in the past four years; it also had two evacuations for bomb scares in the 2006–7 school year. But school administrators discovered they were unable to keep children from using their cellphones, which could have caused the parents to panic and descend on the scene en masse, a school official said.

"There were a couple police officers with kids who would text them, and we had officers responding before we had a chance to call the Police Department," said Superintendent Frank D. Borelli of the Delsea Regional High School District. "You have to figure out how to adjust and accommodate your plans."

Kenneth S. Trump, president of National School Safety and Security Services, a private company in Cleveland that counsels campuses on how to prepare for emergencies, praised New Jersey for energetically trying to improve school security. But he said he sees a "tremendous lack of training" nationally, particularly for school secretaries, bus drivers and other support staff.

"Who's going to take a bomb threat call? The secretary," he said. "And the first and last person a child sees many days is the bus driver. Who knows if there's a suspicious person or object on campus? A custodian. Not only are teachers and administrators not trained, the support staff needs training as well."

He said that schools should have, and should practice, plans for getting students bused home in the middle of the day, for managing parents who flock to the school in an emergency, and for talking to reporters as well.

But plans are not enough, he said. "Many schools had plans on paper, but didn't want to do something as simple as a lockdown drill for fear that it would create fear and panic among students and staff members and create undue parent attention," Mr. Trump said.

Next month, the Middlesex County Freeholders, who govern here, plan to ask their Congressional delegation to include schools among the critical infrastructures protected by the United States **Department of Homeland Security,** in hopes of getting money to pay for the drills.

"Currently, there's no funding source from the federal government, nor any direct funding from the state, that provides money to schools, public or parochial, for safety improvements," said H. James Polos, who works in real estate and is one of seven freeholders. "Since Sept. 11, more people have been killed in school buildings than in terrorist attacks in this country. We need to improve the security level."

Mr. Polos said there should be statewide standards so that drills were the same in every school district. "Procedurally, a lockdown in Camden shouldn't be any different than in Newark," he said. "For the most part, we now have schools in the same district using different protocols, and it's confusing to staff and responders."

Richard L. Cañas, director of the State Office of Homeland Security and Preparedness, said a priority was to train teachers on what to do in the 10 to 15 minutes it might take emergency workers to respond. Simply calling 911 is not sufficient, he said.

"I'm saying that's unacceptable," Mr. Cañas said. "Before the police arrive and you see someone with a gun outside your room, we rely on what the teacher does. They can't freeze like a deer in the headlights."

Mr. Cañas said that most of the state's county governments had emergency preparedness plans, but that many districts were deficient.

"There are some schools that have no locks, and it's hard to practice lockdowns if you have no locks," he said. "We're going to fix it very fast. This is not a poor state. That's inexcusable. If we can't protect our children, what good are we?"

Effects of After-School Employment on Academic Performance

ZIEROLD KM, GARMAN S, AND ANDERSON HA

Results from a new study, carried out with over 7,500 Wisconsin high school students, revealed that part-time work was not associated with less time spent doing homework, lower grades, higher absenteeism or tardiness. In fact, the study revealed less than a 3% difference for each of these characteristics between working and non-working high school students.

Although working students were "slightly more likely" to have higher grade point averages (GPAs) than their non-working peers, this difference was not statistically significant (p = 0.0669). Working students, however, were significantly more likely to cut classes at least 3 times during the school year (p < 0.0001) and were less likely to participate in school-sponsored extracurricular activities than non-working students (p < 010001).

According to the authors, Kristina M. Zierold, Ph.D. (Department of Environmental Health Services, Arnold School of Public Health, University of South Carolina, Columbia, SC) and colleagues, for many high school students, after-school employment is a major activity in their lives. Some estimates suggest that as many as 80% of youths are employed before they leave high school, and that 46% of employed youth work over 20 hours a week. There have been mixed reports on the effects of part-time work on high school students, with some researchers

concluding that work is good (or bad) for students, that it makes no difference, or has complex effects on academic performance and behavior.

Some studies, according to Zierold and colleagues, suggest that students who work part time have significantly higher rates of alcohol use and heavy drinking compared with non-working peers that could be attributed, in part, to working teens being exposed to adults and peers who drink in their job environment. Other studies have shown that students involved in school-sponsored extracurricular activities are more apt to stay in school and are less likely to be charged with criminal offenses compared with students not participating in school-sponsored activities.

Zierold and her team used a cross-sectional, anonymous, questionnaire administered by teachers to 8,071 high school students, aged 14 to 19 years, in 5 Wisconsin school districts. The response rate was 93% (N = 7,506).

Survey questions administered to all students on their school performance included their GPA, number of hours per week spent in extracurricular activities, number of days per year they skipped classes, were absent from or late for school, and the amount of time spent on homework in and out of school. They were also asked whether or not they expected to graduate. All

Table 1 Comparison of School Performance between Working and Non-Working Students

Variable	% of Working Students	% of Non-Working Students	p Value
GPA 0–2.0	12.9	14.6	0.07
Extracurricular activities ≥4 hours weekly	30.7	37.7	<0.0001
School absence ≥3 times per year	33.8	32.3	0.40*
Late for school ≥3 times per year	39.7	41.0	0.18*
Cut classes ≥3 times per year	33.0	28.0	0.0001
<60 minutes homework in school	80.0	80.0	0.79*
<60 minutes homework out of school	67.0	66.0	0.44*

* Not significant
Table adapted from Zierold et al., 2005.

data were self-reported and not independently corroborated, as the questionnaires were strictly anonymous.

Overall, for working and non-working students, the majority (87%) had a GPA of 2.1–4.0, and 91% believed they would graduate from high school. Males (17%) were more likely to have 0–2.0 GPAs than females (10%) ($p < 0.0001$).

For students who worked, 42% reported working 10 hours or less a week; 36% worked over 17 hours a week. The majority of working students (60%) worked between 7 pm and 11 pm during the school week, with females (65%) more likely to work those hours than males (54%) ($p < 0.0001$). Male students (7%) were more likely to work later than 11 pm than females (3%) ($p < 0.0001$).

Ten percent of the working students had been asked to carry out work they considered dangerous, and 16% reported having had a near-miss accident at work. Males were significantly more likely to have work-related injuries ($p < 0.0001$), to have near-miss incidents ($p < 0.0001$), and to be asked to perform dangerous tasks ($p < 0.0001$) than females.

While the consequences of balancing the demands between work and school may contribute to some negative effects, Zierold and her team say that part-time work for students can provide positive experiences. Paid employment may contribute to well-being and enhanced self-esteem. It may also help to teach responsibility, ease the transition from school to full-time employment, and provide an opportunity for students to form positive relationships with employers who may provide guidance as mentors.

ZIEROLD KM, GARMAN S, AND ANDERSON HA: A comparison of school performance and behaviors among working and nonworking high school students. *Fam Comm Health* 2005; 28(3):214–224. E-mail: zierold@gwm.sc.edu.

Immigrant Youth in U.S. Schools: Opportunities for Prevention

Dina Birman, PhD, et al.

Today 10.6% of children enrolled in kindergarten through 12th grade in the U.S. are foreign born (NCES, 2007), and 1 in 5 are children of immigrants (de Cohen, Deterding, & Clewell, 2005). Historically, immigrants have greatly contributed to the U.S. society and adapted with time. Yet immigrants also face a number of challenges during the initial period of resettlement, adjusting psychologically, socially, and economically to the realities of their new cultural context (Beiser, 2006).

For school-aged children, the most important settings are the family and the school, with the parent-child-school triangle comprising a critical mesosystem within which socialization and development take place (Bronfenbrenner, 1979). Public schools represent the setting where many of the acculturative struggles of immigrant children unfold, having traditionally served as a vehicle of socialization and "assimilation" of immigrants in the U.S. (c.f. Dewey, 1916). Thus school interventions that focus on restructuring educational programming to accommodate immigrants can provide an opportunity to intervene directly with the primary environment that shapes the youth's experience (Trickett & Birman, 1989), providing a more lasting and far-reaching solution than individual interventions. Further, because U.S. schools expect parental involvement, schools can provide an avenue to engage parents in interventions and create a bridge between the worlds of family and school in ways that do not stigmatize the family or the child.

Immigrant students bring a range of diverse experiences, which can be viewed as resources to enrich the school setting. In today's climate of increased accountability, however, schools face many political challenges to addressing the needs of new immigrants who are often perceived as a drain on limited resources. Yet there are a number of possible avenues for intervention that can enhance the success of our immigrant students by engaging existing resources. The remainder of this article first describes today's immigrants, then the stressors and challenges they face, and ends by offering suggestions for prevention and intervention strategies to promote the mental health and positive adjustment of immigrant children.

The Diversity of Today's Immigrants

One of the main features of the current migration wave is its diversity, which presents both challenges and opportunities to school teachers and administrators. While the majority of immigrants enter the U.S. voluntarily to pursue employment opportunities or to join relatives, refugees and asylum seekers are forced to flee from their homelands because of war or political violence, often coming to the U.S. after extended stays in refugee camps. Many immigrants are well educated (Frey, 2005), however some arrive with little or no prior education, or even literacy in their native language. Further, the migration flow is continually changing, making it difficult to anticipate the needs and characteristics of new arrivals. This places schools in the position of constantly confronting new languages, cultures, and circumstances, and being creative and flexible to meet the needs of such diverse students. In this context, "cultural competence" is not enough, and today's schools need to develop "multicultural competence" to serve the ever-changing student body. Such flexibility and creativity in attention to diversity can benefit all students.

Issues in Adaptation

Immigration is accompanied by dramatic changes in cultural milieu, separation from loved ones, and the need to adapt in the new society. For immigrants who are refugees there is additional stress from traumatic events prior to or during flight from their homeland. Sources of stress for immigrants can be summarized into three inter-related categories: (a) migration stress; (b) acculturative stress; and (c) traumatic stress (Birman, 2002).

Migration Stress

Migration stress involves the difficulties resulting from disruptions in children's everyday lives when removed from a familiar environment. Moving can be very stressful for children (Raviv, Keinan, Abazon, & Raviv, 1990), and moving away from one's native country can additionally be associated with "cultural bereavement" (Eisenbruch, 1992), described as feelings of loss of their past lives, cultural context, surroundings, and friends and family left behind. These feelings of loss may be more acute in children than adults because they were not in control of the decision to immigrate. The disruptions in social networks resulting from migration may also be particularly salient during the early stages of resettlement, and schools can help ensure that immigrant youth have opportunities for social support from ethnic and mainstream adults and peers who can help them cope emotionally and provide orientation to the new culture.

Acculturative Stress

Acculturative stress refers to the challenges that children and their families face in adjusting to the new culture in resettlement. In addition to learning the new language and culture, children and youth must integrate aspects of the two cultures into their own cultural identity. On one hand, acquiring competence in the new culture is instrumentally useful, and has been found to help immigrants succeed at school (Vedder, Boekaerts, & Seegers, 2005). At the same time, developing a positive ethnic identity is important psychologically (Phinney, 1990).

"Acculturation gaps" emerge in immigrant families when children acculturate to the American culture and language faster than their parents. Because parents are more connected to their native culture, whereas children are often eager to immerse themselves in the new culture, immigrant families may experience conflict and misunderstanding. Additional stress can result from children translating or "culture brokering" for their parents, as such responsibilities may be too difficult to handle at a young age. This stress, however, can be reduced for children who are able to maintain ties to their native culture because this lessens the acculturation gaps and family conflict (Birman, 2006). Schools can help by supporting students' connections to their native cultures and reaching out to their parents.

Traumatic Stress

Many immigrants, particularly refugees, have suffered trauma both before and during migration, in refugee camps, during war, or while crossing borders and hiding from authorities. Symptoms of traumatic stress reactions may manifest themselves at school as academic and behavioral problems, yet are often not recognized or addressed as a mental health concern. Without valid, culturally sensitive assessments available in the immigrant student's native language, it is impossible to determine whether the child's difficulties are due to cultural adjustment or disabilities and to arrive at a definitive diagnosis. At the same time, there is a danger that important problems will go unaddressed for several years before it is possible to rule out cultural adjustment as the main cause. What is needed is a range of strategies that teachers can use to enhance the child's academic and behavioral functioning regardless of diagnosis.

Opportunities for Prevention and Intervention

From an ecological perspective, developing interventions to alleviate the stress of migration, acculturation, and trauma requires identifying existing resources that can be brought to bear on these issues (Trickett & Birman, 1989). With respect to school interventions, potential resources include parents of immigrant children, programs for English Language Learners (ELL), and Special Education services. Suggestions presented below can reduce culture shock, support parents, create bridges between cultures of home and school, lessen the stress for newly arrived immigrant youth, and enrich the school through the talents and diversity of its immigrant students.

Parents as a Resource

When schools form relationships with immigrant parents, they can help reduce acculturative stress for immigrant students. Becoming involved in the school lives of their children can lessen the family acculturation gap. Therefore, it is important to dispel the impression sometimes held by school personnel that immigrant parents are too busy, preoccupied, or disinterested in their child's schooling to get involved (Huss-Keeler, 1997; Crozier & Davies, 2006). Rather, parents may be unaware of the extent to which they are expected to advocate for their children in American public schools and to be able to navigate among a variety of choices about programs their children

can enroll in (Birman & RyersonEspino, in press). Many immigrant parents come from societies where such decisions were made solely by schools and they may stay away from contact with schools out of respect and deference to school authorities that is the norm in many immigrant-sending countries (Delgato-Gaitan & Trueba, 1991), or due to lack of knowledge about how and when it is appropriate to contact the school (Birman & Ryerson-Espino, in press).

When schools form relationships with immigrant parents, they can help reduce acculturative stress for immigrant students.

An important component in any strategy to reach out to immigrant parents is the use of bicultural and bilingual liaisons (Huss-Keeler, 1997; Birman & Ryerson-Espino, in press), which can also be an additional way to engage immigrant parents directly in the school. Engaging immigrant parents in this way removes children from culture brokering and helps bridge the worlds of home and school. Other examples of interventions designed to involve immigrant parents in school, such as special after-school events, are presented in Table 1.

ELL Programs as a Resource

English Language Learners (ELL's) in U.S. schools participate in a variety of transitional programs that can be an excellent resource not only for English language instruction but also for providing emotional and social support and cultural orientation to new immigrant students. On one end of the continuum, full-day bilingual programs are designed to educate children in their native language in various subject areas with English as one of their subjects. A more integrative model pulls students out of mainstream classes for two to three periods a day into English as a Second Language (ESL) program. In addition, some school districts have "newcomer" programs (Boyson & Short, 2003) that pull out students with disrupted or no prior education for extensive orientation and academic support (Birman, 2005). Finally, some school districts integrate ELL students into mainstream classrooms by employing "Sheltered Instruction Observational Protocol" (SIOP) programs that are designed to provide "scaffolding" or supportive educational techniques to enable ELL students to catch up (Boyson & Short, 2003).

There are a number of ways that pull-out and newcomer ELL programs can reduce migration and acculturative stress. ELL classes tend to be smaller and often last for several class periods, allowing greater contact with the teacher. ELL teachers tend to have particular interests in helping immigrant students with their cultural adaptation, as many have experienced living abroad or are immigrants themselves. Further, these smaller and longer classes provide opportunities to get to know other students from different countries, which can help normalize students' experience of being different and can help them feel more comfortable about their own blended identity. ELL teachers can also utilize lesson plans and techniques that can simultaneously teach English and also enhance the mental health of the students by providing them with opportunities to share their experiences and receive support from peers (Birman, 2002, 2005).

However, ELL programs can also separate and marginalize both students and teachers from the mainstream of the school. Many teachers of pull-out ELL programs may not have a permanent classroom, and are the first laid off with budget cuts or as the demographics of the school shift. They may have been recruited during a sudden

Table 1 Activities/Interventions to Involve Immigrant Parents in School

Activities/Interventions	Rationale
Designate a bicultural/bilingual liaison between school and parents	A bicultural/bilingual liaison can become a trusted person for immigrant parents who don't know how to communicate with the school. Because many immigrants are used to relying on informal supports of family and friends to get information about schools and their community (Huss-Keeler, 1997), ideally such a liaison would be a member of the immigrant community, perhaps an English-speaking immigrant parent.
Conduct home visits by school teachers and/or administrators	Traditional home visits are rarely used, but visiting immigrant homes can dispel a lot of myths and help the teacher better understand the family situation (Crozier & Davies, 2006). Home visits may not be possible in many cases, but if possible they can facilitate positive teacher-parent communication.
Make interpreters available for parent-teacher conferences	Providing interpreters not only allows parents to communicate with teachers, but also takes children out of the role of "culture broker" and supports parent authority.
Offer special after-school events that incorporate immigrant culture and involve parents. Examples include: • International dinners held at school with parents of all students bringing dishes representing their heritage • School festivals that incorporate displays or activities representing immigrant cultures	Attending or participating in after-school events can help parents become more comfortable with the school and ultimately communicating with the teachers. Activities do not have to involve having parents talk with teachers. For example, watching a performance at a school festival can be less threatening and more comfortable for immigrant parents than more traditional PTA meetings or parent-teacher conferences (Hull-Keeler, 1997).
Provide school orientations for immigrant parents at the school with the help of bicultural liaisons and/or interpreters	Immigrant parents need orientation to the U.S. school system and information about how and when to contact the school. Special events organized for parents at the school reflect an interest in involving immigrant families in the education of their children. Packets of information that the schools send home, even if printed in immigrant languages, are not sufficient to educate immigrant parents about the schools.

immigrant influx and hired provisionally without adequate certification. There are a number of interventions that schools can put into place to make these teachers feel that they are a valued resource in the school and reduce their marginalization (see Table 2).

Most importantly, schools can work to create climates that support the expression of immigrant cultures as they adapt to the school. While acculturation to both the new and the native culture can bring advantages to immigrant youth, some communities and schools believe that an "assimilationist press" to adapt quickly to the host culture is best, yet this results in discrimination experienced by those immigrant students who maintain their native ethnic identity. In a recent multi-national study of immigrant youth, Berry and colleagues (2006) found that adolescents who experienced more discrimination were less likely to be bicultural. Such discrimination forces immigrant adolescents to choose between either assimilating and distancing themselves from their native culture or rejecting the culture of the new society, rather than integrating the two (Birman et al., 2005). Therefore, schools that support immigrant students in exploring their cultural identity, as they are also learning about the new culture, are more likely to endorse a diversity of different acculturative styles and create greater opportunities for successful adaptation. Table 2 provides some examples of how schools can do this.

Special Education as a Resource

Given how much attention is paid in the literature to the mental health needs of immigrant children, it is startling how little discussion there is about Special Education as a potential resource.

Special Education services are designed to provide remedial and/or developmental instruction, while also balancing grade level preparation across multiple curriculum areas. There is some concern that referral to Special Education services can impede the adaptation and integration into U.S. schools by stigmatizing and separating immigrant students; but the reality is that immigrant students may require additional supports. For example, refugee students who experience post-traumatic stress and related disorders as a result of trauma may be eligible for and can benefit from Special Education services. Without proper intervention, such mental health needs may manifest in disabilities that are likely to impair their functioning in school. Yet because of the strict laws governing Special Education, assessment and referral of immigrants from diverse countries is extremely challenging because we lack the culturally valid assessments necessary to identify true disabilities.

However, even when arriving at a "definitive" diagnosis is not possible, ELL and mainstream staff can learn from Special Education specialists about useful techniques that can help immigrant students learn, regardless of whether student's learning challenges stem from cultural adjustment, lack of prior exposure to schools and literacy, or mental disorders that are interfering with academic functioning. By utilizing the tools that Special Education specialists have developed through years of working with students with various learning challenges, needs, and strengths, school staff who work with immigrant students can help them benefit from the lessons learned in Special Education. For

Table 2 Creating a Hospitable Climate and Reducing Marginalization of Immigrant Students and ELL Teachers

Activities/Interventions	Rationale
Prioritize diversity among school teachers and staff when hiring	Having diverse ethnic and immigrant groups represented among school teachers and staff, particularly in positions of authority, communicates respect for diverse cultures and can serve as a natural bridge/liaison between home and school.
Support ELL teachers by providing avenues to certification when necessary and dedicating physical and human resources	Certification, permanent classrooms, and administrative supports can raise the status of ELL teachers and reduce their marginalization.
Place immigrant students in mainstream classrooms and provide sheltered instruction and scaffolding to the entire classroom	Sheltered Instruction Observational Protocol (SIOP) is an empirically validated program that has been used to allow immigrant students to participate in mainstream lessons rather than pull-out classes while all students benefit from enhanced instruction, group work, and multisensory lesson plans (http://www.siopinstitute.net/about.shtml)
Create art or information displays around the school about immigrant cultures and languages	Schools can display posters or pictures of immigrant countries or signs, such as a "welcome" sign, in different languages around the halls. One program in Chicago, "Changing Worlds" (www.changingworlds. org), photographed immigrant families and collected their stories. Posters were then created telling the story of migration of each family (with translations into multiple languages), a map of the country of origin, and the family picture. Such displays can help create a climate of hospitality, interest in different cultures, and inclusion of immigrant students in the life of the school.
Hold special school-wide events during the school day that incorporate immigrant cultures (such as school assemblies)	School events and assemblies can incorporate information about the history and culture of the immigrants, inviting the children and parents to contribute (Trickett & Birman, 1989). Topics can include seasonal celebrations from immigrant cultures, or anniversaries of important historical events.
Incorporate immigrant cultures into the curriculum	History and social studies classes can study immigrant cultures, and immigrant parents and students can be invited to classes to talk about their background and experiences.
Peer mentoring programs	Pairing newly arrived students with those who came earlier or were born in the country can help them become more integrated into the peer group and receive support.

Table 3 Adaptation of Special Education Techniques for Immigrant Students

Activities/Interventions	Rationale
Incorporate information specific to individual student backgrounds, including opportunities for students to explore their cultural background, when delivering the general curriculum content to all students.	Because of the diverse learning needs of Special Education students, staff do a great deal of adapting the general education curriculum to the specific learning needs and interests of the students they serve. Therefore, staff working with immigrant students can learn from Special Education staff, who have experience viewing the general curriculum as flexible to make it meaningful for individual students, but delivered to and beneficial for the rest of the students in the class.
Develop multisensory classroom activities that deliver a diversity of curricula.	Multisensory classroom activities may be geared to address the learning styles of a particular student, but can make the lessons more interesting for all students. For example, high school curricula that rely extensively on lectures and written reports can be modified to include hands-on activities, such as art and other media or oral reports, to make the work more accessible for ELL students.
Create individualized plans to enhance the learning needs for individual students. Allow students to be actively involved in the development of these plans.	Because immigrant students have a diversity of learning needs, this approach can ensure that the greatest challenges are identified and progress toward the identified goals can be monitored.
Daily check-in periods with newly immigrated students or immigrant students in the mainstream environment with school staff of their choice.	These strategies can help students feel that they are cared about as a member of the school community, provide continuous feedback about progress, and provide opportunities to make necessary adjustments to facilitate academic progress.

example, a number of regularly used tools in Special Education could be adapted as preventive activities for use with immigrant students in ELL and mainstream classrooms. Some sample accommodations are listed in Table 3. Therefore, schools need to move past their hesitancy to foster collaborations between Special Education and ELL services and personnel.

Collaboration between ELL and Special Education is especially important, because both are dealing with similar challenges regarding student learning and may be therefore providing similar supports and services for students. As a result of the separate laws and norms governing these two programs, partnership between them is rare. Yet because both of these programs struggle with limited resources, they can only benefit from working together, which could help to streamline the services schools are providing to students with unique learning challenges. This is an important policy direction to pursue because through such collaboration, schools can improve their provision of a range of mental health and educational services to immigrant children.

Conclusions

Immigrant students and their families bring a richness of experience and knowledge that can enrich schooling for all students. Given the large numbers of arrivals and diverse cultures represented among them, schools have a tremendous opportunity to create a climate that views these newcomers as resources and does not constrain the multiple ways in which they can adapt to our society. Immigrant children and parents have much that they need to learn from caring teachers and administrators. At the same time they also have much to offer as we educate our children to function in an increasingly global community.

References

Beiser, M. (2006). Longitudinal research to promote effective refugee resettlement. *Transcultural Psychiatry, 43,* 56–71.

Berry, J., Phinney, J., Sam, D., & Vedder, P. (Eds.) (2006). *Immigrant Youth in Cultural Transition: Acculturation, Identity, and Adaptation Across National Contexts.* Mahwah, NJ: Lawrence Erlbaum Associates Publishers.

Birman, D. (2002) *Refugee Mental Health in the Classroom: A Guide for the ESL Teacher.* Denver, CO: Spring Institute for Intercultural Learning, http://www.spring-institute.org.

Birman, D. (2005). *Refugee Children With Low Literacy Skills or Interrupted Education: Identifying Challenges and Strategies.* Denver, CO: Spring Institute for Intercultural Learning, 24 pp.

Birman, D. (2006). Acculturation gap and family adjustment: Findings with Soviet Jewish refugees in the U.S. and implications for measurement. *Journal of Cross-Cultural Psychology, 37*(5), 1–22.

Birman, D., & Ryerson-Espino, S. (in press). The relationship of parental practices and knowledge to school adaptation for immigrant and non-immigrant high school students. *Canadian Journal of School Psychology.*

Birman, D., Trickett, E., & Buchanan, R. (2005). A tale of two cities: Replication of a study on the acculturation and adaptation of immigrant adolescents from the former Soviet Union in a different community context. *American Journal of Community Psychology, 35*(1–2), 83–101.

Boyson, B.A., & Short, D.J. (2003). *Secondary School Newcomer Programs in the United States* (Research Report No. 12). Santa Cruz, CA and Washington, D.C.: Center for Research on Education, Diversity & Excellence.

Bronfenbrenner, U. (1979). *The Ecology of Human Development.* Cambridge, MA: Harvard University Press.

Crozier, G., & Davies, J. (2006). Family matters: A discussion of the Bangladeshi and Pakistani extended family and community in supporting the children's education. *Sociological Review, 54,* 678–695.

de Cohen, C., Deterding, N., & Clewell, B. (2005) *Who's Left Behind? Immigrant Children in High and Low LEP Schools.* Urban Institute. Available online at http://www.urban.org/url.cfm?ID=411231

Delgado-Gaitan, C., & Trueba, H. (1991). *Crossing Cultural Borders: Education for Immigrant Families in America.* Oxford, England: Falmer Press/Taylor & Francis, Inc.

Dewey, J. (1916). *Democracy and Education.* New York, NY: The Free Press.

Eisenbruch, M. (1992). Toward a culturally sensitive DSM: Cultural bereavement in Cambodian refugees and the traditional healer as taxonomist. *Journal of Nervous & Mental Disease, 180,* 8–10.

Frey, W.H. (2005). Second generation rising. *Milken Institute Review,* Second Quarter, 6–9.

Huss-Keeler, R.L. (1997). Teacher perception of ethnic and linguistic minority parental involvement and its relationships to children's language and literacy learning: A case study. *Teaching and Teacher Education, 13,* 171–182

NCES (2007). *Student Effort and Educational Progress.* Retrieved August 4, 2007 from National Center for Education Statistics website: http://nces.ed.gov/programs/coe/2007/section3/table.asp?tableID=700

Phinney, J.S. (1990). Ethnic identity in adolescents and adults: review of research. *Psychological Bulletin, 109,* 499–514.

Raviv, A., Keinan, G., Abazon, Y., & Raviv, A. (1990). Moving as a stressful life event for adolescents. *Journal of Community Psychology, 18,* 130–140.

Trickett, E.J., & Birman, D. (1989). Taking ecology seriously: A community development approach to individually based preventive intervention in schools. In B. Compas & L. Bond (Eds.), *Primary Prevention in the Schools* (pp. 361–390). Newbury Park, CA: Sage.

Vedder, P., Boekaerts, M., & Seegers, G. (2005). Perceived social support and well being in school: The role of students' ethnicity. *Journal of Youth and Adolescence, 34,* 269–278.

DINA BIRMAN is an Assistant Professor of Psychology in the Community and Prevention Research Division at the University of Illinois at Chicago. She is currently partnering with several community-based mental health agencies to study and refine school-based mental health interventions for immigrant and refugee children and youth. **TRACI WEINSTEIN** is in the Community & Prevention Research doctoral program at the University of Illinois at Chicago. From her experience working as a Special Education teacher with inner-city high school students, her research interests include investigating ways to promote academic achievement for immigrant and minority youth. **WING YI CHAN** is in the Community & Prevention Research doctoral program at UIC. She is interested in the contextual and cultural factors that are related to the resilience of refugees and immigrants. **SARAH BEEHLER** is in the Community & Prevention Research doctoral program at UIC. Her research interests include studying the effects of culturally sensitive mental health interventions for refugee and immigrant groups.

From *The Prevention Researcher*, November 2007, pp. 14–17. Copyright © 2007 by Integrated Research Services, Inc. Reprinted by permission.

Reducing School Violence

School-Based Curricular Programs and School Climate

MICHAEL B. GREENE, PhD

In this brief review, two different, though interrelated approaches to the reduction of school violence are described and critiqued. The first, and more traditional approach, involves the establishment of classroom-based educational and therapeutic programs that focus on the interpersonal skills, attitudes, emotional literacy, and risk and protective factors that are associated with aggressive behavior and attitudes. These school-based curricular[1] programs (SBCPs) promote prosoical behavior and endeavor to help students maintain peer relationships and conflicts without resorting to aggressive or violent behavior. The second approach endeavors to improve components of a school's social and interpersonal climate that are associated with aggressive and violent behavior. These components include the quality of relationships among students, staff, and administrators; norms, attitudes, and beliefs among students, staff, and administrators; perceptions and enforcement of disciplinary rules and policies; the organizational structure of schools and their capacity to address school violence; and school connectedness or bonding (Cook, Murphy, &Hunt, 2000; McEvoy & Welker, 2000; Welsh, 2000).

What Is Meant by School Violence?

In terms of a school's jurisdiction and liability, school violence is violence that occurs on school grounds, on school-supported transportation, and at school-sponsored activities. Nevertheless, violence committed on school grounds often derives from conflicts that emerge in the community (as well as vice versa). This phenomenon blurs the distinction between school and community violence and suggests that school personnel need to possess knowledge of the community in which a school is situated and that members of the community should become involved in school-based violence prevention initiatives.

Violence committed on school grounds often derives from conflicts that emerge in the community.

The "what" of school violence is more complicated and multidimensional (Furlong & Morrison, 2000). Violence is generally defined as an intentional form of behavior in which one person threatens, attempts to harm, or does harm another person. Aggression is generally defined as a form of low-level violence that includes verbal, physical, or gestural behavior that is intended to cause minor physical harm, psychological distress, intimidation, or to induce fear in another (Greene, 2005). Aggression can also be indirect or relational, as in instances in which a student is ostracized, isolated, or is the object of nasty rumors. Moreover, students are increasingly disseminating negative, compromising, or humiliating messages through electronic means (cyberbullying, the newest form of adolescent aggression).

Some researchers argue that the disproportionate imposition of negative sanctions upon certain classes of students for the same conduct, as has been found with zero-tolerance policies, is also a form of school violence in that such practices unjustly penalize some students more than others (Skiba, Michael, Nardo, & Peterson, 2002). Similarly, some have argued that institutional forms of racism and sexual oppression (as reflected in behavior, attitudes, curricula, and textbooks), an unwelcoming school atmosphere (often conceptualized as an aspect of school climate), as well as the consequences of unequal distribution of school funding, are structural or systemic forms of school-related violence (Greene, 2006). These forms of violence, however, are rarely tracked, monitored, or addressed by school violence programs.

> **Some have argued that institutional forms of racism and sexual oppression, an unwelcoming school atmosphere, as well as the consequences of unequal distribution of school funding, are structural or systemic forms of school-related violence.**

The "who" of school violence is most frequently conceptualized as student-on-student aggression or violence; ignoring the many other permutations of violence among teachers, staff, administrators, and students; for example, teacher-to-student bullying or coercion (Twemlow & Fonagy, 2005). Most SBCPs are focused on direct forms of aggression among students (fighting, hitting, pushing, verbal intimidation, and threats); excluding the indirect forms of aggression noted above. Correspondingly, as detailed below, these programs are nearly always assessed in terms of the extent to which direct aggressive behavior or known predictors of aggressive behavior (risk factors) are lessened or reduced.

School-Based Curricular Programs

Hundreds of school-based curricular programs are available on the market and described in the professional literature. Programs vary in terms of theoretical foundation, target audience, duration, and intensity, and by the training required to implement them (Fagan & Mihalic, 2003; Greene, 2005). Some programs focus on the ways in which students frame, perceive, or conceptualize the nature and appropriateness of aggressive and violent behavior (cognitive behavioral approaches), some focus on how students learn and unlearn such behaviors (social learning or coaching approaches), some utilize traditional pedagogical methods to teach social skills, some focus on rewarding positive behavior (behavioral programs), some focus on helping students better understand feelings and emotions (social-emotional literacy approaches), and some adopt more traditional therapeutic or counseling approaches.

The vast majority of SBCPs target elementary and middle school students and are designed as universal programs in which all students in a school or grade level participate. One such program is Promoting Alternative Thinking Strategies (PATHS) (Greenberg, Kusche, & Mihalic, 1998). This elementary school program focuses on the promotion of social and emotional competencies. It covers five basic conceptual domains: self-control, emotional understanding, positive self-esteem, relationships, and interpersonal problem solving. One hundred thirty-one sequenced and integrated lesson plans covering each of the five domains are taught during a five-year period. Like many SBCPs, PATHS utilizes a variety of pedagogical approaches including role plays, modeling behavior, student projects, rehearsal strategies, lectures, and classroom discussion and reflection.

Like all classroom curricula, SBCPs require teacher training. Sometimes training is limited to a manual but increasingly programs are requiring face-to-face training and telephone consultation to ensure that the program is implemented as intended and designed. However, this form of teacher training is not generally oriented to helping teachers communicate and build trust and credibility with their students, which are aspects of a school's climate that are clearly associated with peer aggression.

Some programs have additional components such as parent coaching and counseling, home visitation, and individual case management. These programs are targeted to students who exhibit known risk factors (selected programs) or students who have engaged in aggressive or violent behavior (indicated programs). FAST Track is an example of a selected program that includes, in addition to classroom activities, parent training, home visitation, case management, and academic tutoring (Conduct Problems Prevention Research Group, 1999). While FAST Track and other selected and indicated SBCPs generally do not address the quality of teacher-student relationships, they are designed to improve the quality of relationships among students and their parents or guardians.

Evaluations of SBCPs

Over the past two decades, a large body of research has demonstrated that many school-based curricular programs, if implemented properly, significantly reduce aggressive and disruptive behavior among students in the school setting (Hahn et al., 2007; Mytton et al., 2002; Wilson & Lipsey, 2007). Hahn and his colleagues (Hahn et al., 2007), in their review of the evaluation research literature on universal SBCPs, found that 15% fewer students who participate in such programs engage in aggressive behavior in comparison to similar groups of students who do not participate in such programs (an 18% reduction in elementary school programs, a 7% reduction in middle schools, and a 29% reduction in high schools). Wilson and Lipsey's (2007) analysis of the SBCP evaluation literature revealed reductions in aggressive behavior in the 25% range.

No single type of universal SBCP appears to be more effective than others (e.g., cognitive behavioral programs, social skills programs, behavioral, and counseling programs) and generally the programs were equally effective in different types of communities and with different types of populations. However, Wilson and Lipsey (2007) found that SBCPs generally had greater impact in reducing aggressive behavior among low- versus middle-income students.

Wilson and Lipsey (2007) also included selected and indicated programs in their review of the research literature on school-based violence prevention programs. They found that indicated programs were more effective in reducing aggressive behavior than selected programs, in other words, the more aggressive the students the higher the impact of the program. In addition, they found that behavioral learning strategies were significantly more effective than other types of programs for selected and indicated programs, though all types of programs that were subject to rigorous evaluation significantly reduced levels of aggression and disruptive behavior. Mytton and colleagues (2002) reviewed the research literature for SBCPs that were exclusively focused on students at high risk for violent or aggressive behavior. They also found an overall significant positive impact of these programs in reducing aggressive behavior. Their analysis, however, yielded a slightly lower level of aggression and violence reduction than did Wilson and Lipsey's review (2007).

Need for Further Study

Wilson and Lipsey (2007) found that programs that were implemented without the direct involvement of the research team that developed the program were as effective in reducing aggressive behavior as programs that did have direct program developer involvement. While the number of studies without program developer involvement was relatively small, this finding suggests that, with proper training and instruction, school administrators can implement these programs with fidelity and can achieve positive outcomes (see also Fagan & Mihalic, 2003). Nevertheless, Wilson and Lipsey's sample, as indicated above, was confined to programs that were subject to a relatively rigorous program evaluation (in other words, the sample of programs was far from representative of typical situations in which a school implements a program without direct involvement of the program developers).

Indeed, D. Gottfredson and G. Gottfredson (2002), in their examination of implementation fidelity within a national probability sample of schools (without corresponding experimental outcome evaluations), discovered that implementation quality was generally quite low. Given the research literature showing that outcomes of SBCPs are compromised when implemented with poor fidelity, the question of whether schools can routinely achieve the excellent results revealed in the research literature remains open (D. Gottfredson, 2001).

Another important factor in examining the impact of SBCPs is whether the obtained positive outcomes are sustainable over time. Generally, the follow-up period assessed in published studies is relatively short: the vast majority of studies have used a follow-up period of less than one school year. Consequently, there is no systemic data on the long-term impact of such programs (D. Gottfredson, 2007). This represents a serious gap in our understanding of SBCPs.

In addition, very few of the SBCP evaluations have utilized measures of more serious forms of violence or crimes against persons, such as shootings, aggravated assaults, or robberies (D. Gottfredson, 2007). This is due in part to the relative rarity of such behaviors and thus the requirement of very large sample sizes to detect a program impact on these behaviors. We have long known that early and chronic expression of aggressive behavior, particularly when expressed in multiple domains, predicts subsequent violent behavior. Whether short-term reductions in aggressive behavior lead to long-term reductions in more serious forms of violence remains a compelling theory but lacks direct empirical support.

The Impact of School Climate on School Violence

A robust research literature suggests that many of the components that comprise school climate—cultural norms in the schools, quality of interpersonal relationships, school policies, and student, staff, and administrator feelings and beliefs about their schools—are significantly related to levels of victimization and offending in schools (Furlong & Morrison, 2000). Moreover, because classroom climate often varies within a school, it is important to examine the impact of interpersonal climate at the classroom as well as schoolwide level (Sprott, 2004).

Several researchers have demonstrated that "school connectedness" (feelings of positive attachment to one's school, peers, teachers) is a protective factor for reducing youth violence in general, school violence in particular, and externalizing behavior (Payne, Gottfredson, & Gottfredson, 2003). Furthermore, data from the National Longitudinal Study of Adolescent Health reveal that four aspects of school climate predict school connectedness: positive classroom management, participation in extracurricular activities, tolerant discipline policies, and school size (McNeely, Nonnemaker, & Blum, 2002). These findings suggest that altering these elements will enhance school connectedness. Whether such changes will also result in reductions in peer-to-peer and other forms of school-based aggression and violence remains untested.

With regard to discipline policies, several researchers have found significant associations between the clarity, consistency, and fairness of school rules and violence perpetration and victimization. In schools in which students believe that their school's rules and discipline structure are clear, fair and consistently applied, levels of violence and aggression are generally low (Payne et al., 2003; Welsh, 2000). Similarly, G. Gottfredson and colleagues, in their large scale study of school violence in American schools, found that school climate and discipline practices were the primary distinguishing factors between low and high disorder schools (G. Gottfredson et al., 2000). High disorder schools in which students frequently disrupt classroom activities were characterized by inconsistent use of discipline practices, unclear or low expectations for students, use of zero-tolerance policies, and communication problems among students and staff.

> **In schools in which students believe that their school's rules and discipline structure are clear, fair, and consistently applied, levels of violence and aggression are generally low.**

Battistich and Hom (1997) found that "school belonging," comprised of a combined measure of interpersonal relationships and student autonomy and influence, predicted delinquency and victimization among fifth and sixth grade students. Similarly, Welsh (2000) found that respect for students was associated with lower levels of student aggression for both perpetration and victimization.

Relationships between SBCPs and School Climate

A modest research literature suggests that SBCPs are better implemented in schools that have a relatively positive school climate (Ozer, 2006). That school climate affects the implementation quality of school-based programs is suggested by studies revealing that the implementation of such programs is affected by school organization, key-stakeholder buy-in, expertise implementing programs generally, and staff turnover (Greene, 2005; Hunter, Elias, & Norris, 2001). Given that the quality of SBCP implementation is significantly associated with greater reductions in aggressive behavior, school climate appears to moderate the effectiveness of SBCPs (G. Gottfredson et al., 2000; Wilson & Lipsey, 2007).

School Climate Change Programs

In contrast to the burgeoning experimental literature of SBCPs, few experimental studies have been conducted that directly evaluate the impact of school climate change efforts on aggressive behavior and the few studies that have been conducted reveal modest to moderate effects (Cook et al., 2000; Greene, 2005). The evaluation of Coiner's School Development Program represents the truest experimental test of a climate change program (Cook et al., 2000). This program focuses specifically on changing a school's interpersonal climate through the work of three teams: a School Planning and Management Team, a Social Support Team, and a Parent Team. Each team supports the basic goals of implementing cooperative learning and problem solving and building trust among adults and students in the school. Given the focus on the social environment of the school, climate change from the perspective of staff and students, as well as resultant academic and social outcomes, are assessed. The evaluation of the Comer School Development Program by Cook and colleagues revealed a positive impact on some measures of school climate as well as reductions in acting out behavior (Cook et al., 2000).

Similarly, The Child Development Program is designed to promote caring and supporting relationships among students, staff, and parents. It focuses on the norms of social justice and responsibility, emphasizes a strengths-based approach to students, and engages students with adults in program decision-making (Battistich, Schaps, & Wilson, 2004). The evaluation of this program revealed reductions in student victimization and student misconduct as well as improvements in two aspects of school climate: students' bonding to school and improvements in teacher-student relationships.

Additional programs target multiple domains of the social ecology (teachers, administrators, school policies, family, and community members) but most of these programs focus on unidirectional influences on the child, without significantly addressing bi-directional relationships among students and the adult authorities in the school. For example the Olweus' Bullying Prevention Program (Olweus & Limber, 1999) is often cited as an evidence-based program that adopts a school climate approach. Nevertheless, key components of school climate—including coercive and aggressive behaviors by adults, student connectedness to school, and the inconsistent or unfair administration of discipline policies (though shaming as a discipline policy is discouraged)—are not addressed in this program. Consequently, this program cannot be considered a true school climate change program.

Discussion

Tremendous progress has been made over the past two decades in establishing effective school-based violence prevention programs. Nevertheless, programs designed to stem violence in schools have largely focused on reducing student-to-student aggressive behavior through curricular programs (SBCPs), essentially ignoring interpersonal relationships between students and adults in schools, student bonding to schools, disproportionalities in the application of student discipline, and related organizational factors that comprise school climate. And while selected and indicated school-based curricular programs also include family interventions, their focus has remained on reductions in student-to-student aggression.

In addition, SBCPs implicitly or explicitly adopt a "deficit" model, in that the programs are designed to provide social skills training or related skills because students lack such skills. In contrast, the predominant orientation in neighborhood-based youth programming (and incorporated in The Child Development Project described above) is "positive youth development," in which a student's interests and strengths are pursued and through such pursuits fundamental capacities and skills are developed (Wilson-Simmons, 2007). In these programs, youth are given an active role in the program operations and in some cases even in governance. While SBCPs often include exercises and student projects that rely on the use and discovery of interpersonal skills, an overall enhanced focus on positive skills and interests may yield better results and also may improve the quality of relationships between students and the teachers who oversee such activities. Indeed, the promising results from positive behavioral supports initiatives, supports this shift to an enhanced positive youth development approach (Sprague& Horner, 2006).

We know, as summarized above, that SBCPs must be implemented with fidelity in order to achieve the results attained in efficacy studies. We also know through numerous large scale studies and qualitative case studies that a number of key climate-related factors affect a school's capacity to implement programs effectively. These include strong leadership, political will, prior success in implementing programs, trust among teachers and students, emotional support of students, commitment to the program, participation in training, and ongoing assessment (G. Gottfredson et al., 2000; Greene, 2005; Sprott, 2004). A positive climate improves not only the implementation of SBCPs but such factors should act in a synergistic fashion with SBCPs so that the impact of such programs are more robust. Still, this statement requires experimental verification.

School climate approaches to school violence, in contrast to SBCPs, focus on the quality of interpersonal relationships among multiple stakeholders in the school, including teachers, staff, administrators, parents, sometimes community members, and, of course, students. The focus is on the phenomenological interpersonal world of each stakeholder as well as the organizational structure and policies of the schools. Climate change programs focus on aggressive and respectful behavior among all parties, not just the students. As such, climate approaches have the potential to effect more substantial changes not only in aggressive behavior among students but in reducing direct and indirect forms of aggression and in promoting respectful interpersonal relationships among all key stakeholders, improving the organizational structure of schools, and improving the policies and the enforcement of policies as they affect all stakeholders.

Climate change programs focus on aggressive and respectful behavior among all parties, not just the students.

Increasingly, advocates and academics are signaling the need to focus on broad spectrum climate analyses and actions. SBCPs have their place, but they are only one part of the puzzle. A growing body of research has consistently shown that schools in which students feel welcome, schools to which students feel positively connected and engaged, and schools in which students perceive their school's rules and policies are fair and consistently enforced, are likely to have lower levels of aggression and violence and higher rates of respectful behavior among all key stakeholders. Furthermore, in such schools, SBCPs may well be more effective.

The problem, of course, is that effective strategies have not been developed to change the school climate in ways that are robust and replicable. The task of changing school environments is difficult and daunting (Osher et al., 2004). With respect to strategies to change school climate, we are where we were 20 years ago with respect to SBCPs. Some programs have been developed, but we are really at an early stage in our understanding of how these programs work and in determining how effective they are. A number of ideas have been suggested as frameworks for changing school climates (e.g., a human rights orientation, schoolwide strategic planning processes, positive behavior supports, restorative justice, and reconciliation and nonviolence principles), but these ideas need to be operationalized into testable and replicable programs (Greene, 2006; Skiba, Ritter, Simmons, Peterson, & Miller, 2006).

As Osher and colleagues (2004) have stated: "A focus on individual students alone will not produce safe and successful schools" (p. 22). In short, a significantly enhanced body of research is needed on climate change that will help schools navigate the complex terrain of school climate change as a means to reduce aggressive behavior, increase prosocial and respectful behavior in our schools, and improve the implementation and effectiveness of school-based curricular programs.

Note

1. The term "curricular" is adopted to include instructional guidelines, training manuals, as well as formal curricular guides that proscribe the components of the program and how these components should be implemented.

References

Battistich, V., & Hom, A. (1997). The relationship between students' sense of their school as a community and their involvement in problem behaviors. *American Journal of Public Health, 87*(12), 1997–2,001.

Battistich, V., Schaps, E., & Wilson, N. (2004). Effects of an elementary school intervention on students' "Connectedness" to school and social adjustment during Middle School. *The Journal of Primary Prevention, 24*(3), 243–262.

Conduct Problems Prevention Research Group. (2002). The implementation of the Fast Track Program: An example of a large-scale prevention science efficacy trial. *Journal of Abnormal Child Psychology, 30*(1), 1–17.

Cook, T.D., Murphy, R.F., & Hunt, H.D. (2000). Corner's school development program in Chicago. *American Educational Research Journal, 37*(2), 535–597.

Fagan, A. A., & Mihalic, S. (2003). Strategies for enhancing the adoption of school-based prevention programs: Lessons learned from the blueprints for violence prevention replications of the Life Skills Training program. *Journal of Community Psychology, 31*(3), 235–253.

Furlong, M., & Morrison, G. (2000). The school in school violence: Definitions and facts. *Journal of Emotional and Behavioral Disorders, 8*(2), 71–82.

Gottfredson, D.C. (2001), Schools and Delinquency. New York: Cambridge University Press.

Gottfredson, D.C. (2007). Some thoughts about research on youth violence prevention. *American Journal of Preventive Medicine, 33*(2, Supplement 1), S104–S106.

Gottfredson, D.C., & Gottfredson, G.D. (2002). Quality of school based prevention programs: Results from a national survey. *Journal of Research in Crime and Delinquency, 39*(1), 3–35.

Gottfredson, G.D., Gottfredson, D.C., Czeh, E.R., Cantor, D., Crosse, S.B., & Hantman, 1. (2000). *National Study of Delinquency Prevention in Schools*. Final Report. Ellicott City, MD: Gottfredson Associates, Inc.

Greenberg, M.T., Kusche, C., & Mihalic, S.F. (1998). *Promoting Alternative Thinking Strategies (PATHS)*. Boulder, CO: University of Colorado.

Greene, M.B. (2005). Reducing violence and aggression in schools. *Trauma, Violence, & Abuse, 6*(3), 236–253.

Greene, M.B. (2006). Bullying in schools: A plea for a measure of human rights. *Journal of Social Issues, 62*(1), 63–79.

Hahn, R., Fuqua-Whitley, D., Wethington, H., Lowy, I, Crosby, A., Fullilove, M., et al. (2007). Effectiveness of universal school-based programs to prevent violent and aggressive behavior: A systematic review. *American Journal of Preventive Medicine, 33*(2, Supplement 1) S114–S129.

Hunter, L., Elias, M.J., & Norris, J. (2001). School-based violence prevention: Challenges and lessons learned from an action research project. *Journal of School Psychology, 39*(2), 161–175.

McEvoy, A., & Welker, R. (2000). Antisocial behavior, academic failure, and school climate: A critical review. *Journal of Emotional & Behavioral Disorders, 8*(3), 130.

McNeely, C.A., Nonnemaker, J.M., & Blum, R.W. (2002). Promoting school connectedness: Evidence from the National Longitudinal Study of Adolescent Health. *Journal of School Health, 72*(4), 138–146.

Mytton, J.A., DiGuiseppi, C., Gough, D.A., Taylor, R.S., & Logan, S. (2002). School-based violence prevention programs: Systematic review of secondary prevention trials. *Archives of Pediatric Adolescent Medicine, 752*–762.

Olweus, D., & Limber, S. (1999). *Bullying Prevention Program*. Boulder, CO: Center for the Study and Prevention of Violence.

Osher, D., VanAcker, R., Morrison, G.M., Gable, R., Dwyer, K., & Quinn, M. (2004). Warning signs of problems in schools: Ecological perspectives and effective practices for combating school aggression and violence. *Journal of School Violence, 3*, 13–37.

Ozer, E. (2006). Contextual effects in school-based violence prevention programs: A conceptual framework and empirical review. *The Journal of Primary Prevention, 27*(3), 315–340.

Payne, A.A., Gottfredson, D.C., & Gottfredson, G.D. (2003). Schools as communities: The relationships among communal school organization, student bonding, and school disorder. *Criminology, 41*(3), 749–777.

Skiba, R.J., Michael, R.S., Nardo, A.C., & Peterson, R.L. (2002). The Color of discipline: Sources of racial and gender disproportionality in school punishment. *Urban Review, 34*(4), 317–342.

Skiba, R., Ritter, S., Simmons, A., Peterson, R., & Miller, C. (2006). The Safe and Responsive Schools Project: A school reform model for implementing best practices in violence prevention. In S.R. Jimerson & M. Furlong (Eds.), *Handbook of School Violence and School Safety* (pp. 631–650). Mahwah, NJ: Lawrence Erlbaum.

Sprague, J.R., & Homer, R.H. (2006). School wide positive behavioral supports. In S.R. Jimerson & M. Furlong (Eds.), *Handbook of School Violence and School Safety* (pp. 413–427). Mahwah, NJ: Lawrence Erlbaum.

Sprott, J.B. (2004). The Development of Early Delinquency: Can Classroom and School Climates Make a Difference? *Canadian Journal of Criminology & Criminal Justice, 46*(5), 553–572.

Twemlow, S.W., & Fonagy, P. (2005). The prevalence of teachers who bully students in schools with differing levels of behavioral problems. *American Journal of Psychiatry, 162*(12), 2,387–2,389.

Welsh, W.N. (2000). The effects of school climate on school disorder. *The ANNALS of the American Academy of Political and Social Science, 567*(1), 88–107.

Wilson, S.J., & Lipsey, M.W. (2007). School-based interventions for aggressive and disruptive behavior: Update of a Meta-Analysis. *American Journal of Preventive Medicine, 33*(2), 130–143.

Wilson-Simmons, R. (2007). *Positive Youth Development: An Examination of the Field.* Princeton, NJ: Robert Wood Johnson Foundation.

MICHAEL B. GREENE directs the evaluation of New Jersey's Strategic Planning Framework for alcohol and substance abuse prevention initiatives at Rutgers University, Center for Applied Psychology. He is the director of violence prevention at The Nicholson Foundation, and the sole proprietor of Greene Consulting. Dr. Greene received his doctorate in developmental psychology at Columbia University. He previously established two centers for the study and prevention of violence: the Center for the Prevention of Violence at Youth Consultation Service and the Violence Institute of New Jersey at the University of Medicine and Dentistry of New Jersey. He has published numerous articles and chapters on school and youth violence, including "Bullying in Schools: A Plea for a Measure of Human Rights" and has served as Principal Investigator on federal and state grants. In the mid-1990s he was asked to serve on the American Psychological Association's Cadre of Experts in Youth Violence. Dr. Greene's research interests include bullying and harassment in schools, interventions for high-risk youth, domestic violence, and social justice.

The Cultural Plunge

Cultural Immersion as a Means of Promoting Self-Awareness and Cultural Sensitivity among Student Teachers.

JESÚS NIETO

Introduction

"The depth of this class to me has been the cultural plunges. I learned so much in those plunges that no other course at (this university) could even remotely compete with. What I learned in the plunges about myself and accepting others is something that I will carry through life . . . after I forget the statistics and psychological tests in my other classes."

The number of K–12 students from culturally and linguistically diverse backgrounds continues to increase exponentially (Major & Brock, 2003). Much attention has been focused on the ever-increasing disparity between the diverse student population and the predominantly white teaching force (Steeley, 2003). Most students entering the field of teaching continue to be white, monolingual, middle-class women (Glazier, 2003). Female European-American teachers will thus continue to comprise the great majority of educators for some time to come, but will be teaching students increasingly different from themselves in terms of ethnicity and social class. Latinos are the fastest growing segment of the nation's population, but just over 10% have a college education, compared to over 25% for all Americans (Brown, Santiago, & Lopez, 2003). It has been noted that students from the lower end of the socioeconomic spectrum face the greatest educational challenges (Prince, 2002), have much less access to quality education (Lin, 2001), and perform more poorly in school (Davis, 1989; Ornstein & Levine, 1989).

Linguistic diversity is receiving an increasing amount of attention from educators, and it has been noted that students who speak a language other than English and have limited proficiency in English are the fastest-growing population in U.S. public schools. From 1991 to 1999, the number of language-minority schoolaged children in the U.S. increased from 8 million to 15 million and the number of K–12 students who are classified as being limited-English-proficient (LEP) rose from 5.3 million to 10 million students (Smith-Davis, 2004).

Disability continues to be equated with inferiority and to lead to exclusion (Fitch, 2002). Disability issues are becoming increasingly important to "regular" teachers, as children with disabilities are being increasingly mainstreamed. According to a recent report from the U.S. Department of Education, more than 95% of students with disabilities are now served in regular schools, with 52% spending most of the school day in general education classrooms (Klotz, 2004).

Although many have voiced concern about the need for teacher education to sensitize future teachers to cultural and social concerns, few have offered concrete strategies for doing so. There has been a lack of effective teacher preparation for working with diverse, high-need students (Shinew & Sodorff, 2003); and although most teacher education programs report that they have thoroughly incorporated multicultural content and perspectives in their curriculum, this is not borne out by external examinations (Cochran-Smith, 2003).

Experiential Learning in Teacher Education

Several authors have urged the utilization of experiential learning in teacher education, often as a means of increasing cultural sensitivity. Baker (1989) believes that experiential learning is beneficial because students learn best when thinking, feeling and doing are all combined. Bergen (1989) has stated that no student teacher should be considered fully qualified for teaching until she or he has spent the equivalent of one semester involved in a "foreign" culture, and posits that Americans are very ethnocentric and thus in great need of becoming more culturally aware. Wilson (1982) believes that "Cross-cultural experiential learning should be a component of every teacher education program" (p. 184), and she outlines cultural immersion activities which are used to train members of the Peace Corps and other organizations.

Mio (1989) describes a program at a Southern California university where graduate students were matched with immigrant and refugee students in a cultural exchange. Socializing on campus, exploring ethnic restaurants in the area together, and visiting one another's homes were among the program's activities, after which participants wrote a paper about their experience. Such approaches are congruent with calls to reach unmotivated students by using educational strategies which are interesting, meaningful and at a level of difficulty that is challenging but attainable and which elicit expression of students' opinions, experiences and feelings (Berlin, 2004). These innovations in teacher training are made all the more important because many teachers have had little if any contact with students from different racial or cultural backgrounds (Milner, 2003).

The Cultural Plunge

For some years several professors at San Diego State University have been using a cultural immersion activity called a *cultural plunge*. They have used this activity in a sociology program (Gillette, 1990), in counselor education (Cook, 1990; Malcolm, 1990) and most recently, as described here, in teacher education. The author has been using the cultural plunge in teacher education since 1989, at which time he incorporated it in classes in that department, and several other teacher education faculty now use it as well. While faculty who utilize the cultural plunge tend to do so in a similar manner, there are some differences among the approaches. This article describes the way in which he approaches this activity.

Simply put, a cultural plunge is individual exposure to persons or groups markedly different in culture (ethnicity, language, socioeconomic status, sexual orientation, and/or physical exceptionality) from that of the "plunger." Most plunges last about one hour and there are a total of four required in my course. Important criteria for cultural plunges as described in my course syllabus are: (1) the majority of people there are from the focal group; (2) you are on the turf of the focal group (not in a school or restaurant); (3) this must be a type of experience you've never done before; (4) the plunge takes place after this course begins (credit cannot be given for past experiences); (5) you do not take notes; and (6) the plunge lasts at least one hour.

While the number and type of plunges I require have varied over the years, the most recently required are: (1) Attend a service at the largest African American church in the city; (2) Attend a religious ceremony in a language which you do not understand (Spanish and Vietnamese are recommended, as they constitute the two most widely spoken languages among English Learners); (3) Interact with homeless people; and (4) Interact with people with disabilities.

Cultural plunges have four major objectives which are stated in the course syllabus: (a) to have direct contact with people who are culturally different from oneself in a real-life setting which represents the target group's "turf"; (b) to gain insights into circumstances and characteristics of the focal community; (c) to experience what it is to be very different from most of the people one is around, and (d) to gain insight into one's values, biases, and affective responses.

Cultural Plunge Papers

Because people who engage in cultural immersion activities heighten their learning when they reflect upon their experience (Barrett, 1993), students write a 3-page reaction paper for each plunge. On page one, students list 10 popular stereotypes about the focal group and indicate what prior contact they've had with it. On page two, students describe their emotional response to the experience and any insights on why they reacted emotionally the way they did. Page three begins with discussion of whether the plunge experience reinforced or challenged the popular stereotypes of the focal group. The cultural plunge paper is concluded with exploration of "implications for my career." This last section is particularly significant because students often overlook the implications of the plunge experience for the classroom or other career setting. Upon further reflection, they often realize such things as the importance of greeting students warmly, learning to speak a few words of diverse languages as a sign of respect and interest in various cultures, and, most importantly, the crucial nature of not prejudging others.

Students' Reactions to the Cultural Plunge

Students' reactions to the plunges are described in detail in their cultural plunge reaction papers and tend to follow a progression of fear, excitement, and finally, appreciation. While most participants are generally afraid initially to go on cultural plunges, they almost invariably are glad they did after completion of the assignment, and tend to rate them as among the most important learning experiences they have ever had. The author surveyed 93 students enrolled in his spring and summer 2004 multicultural education classes. They were asked a variety of questions about their reaction to the course, including items about cultural plunges. They were asked to rate specific types of cultural plunges as well as the cultural plunge in general. Table 1 reports results from those surveys.

As all ratings reported on Table 1 range from 4.2 to 4.9, it is evident that cultural plunges had a "great" or "very great" impact on most respondents. These findings are similar to those of prior surveys done by the author with hundreds of students from 1989 to 1993, wherein cultural plunges received ratings ranging from 4.5 to 4.9 on a 5-point scale. In addition, cultural plunge papers have also been rated highly (4.2 to 4.5) in numerous surveys over the years.

Excerpts from Student Reaction Papers

Going beyond quantitative data, perhaps the following excerpts from students' plunge papers can best illustrate the impact that

Table 1 Impact of Cultural Plunges on Students

	Mean*	N
African American cultural plunge	4.4	93
Other Language cultural plunge	4.5	93
Homeless plunge	4.5	93
Disabled plunge	4.5	93
Gay/lesbian plunge	4.4	93
Cultural Plunge overall	4.6	93

*Ratings Code 1 = None 2 = Some 3 = Moderate 4 = Great 5 = Very Great

such experiences have on participants. The excerpts are organized around stated plunge objectives:

To Learn about the Target Community

[Farrakhan discussed] . . . some of the 'lies' that the whites use to keep African Americans down, and aren't they clever at making the blame all fall upon these people. The media portrays mainly blacks as gang members and drug dealers and this perpetuates the 'lie' and grinds away at all African Americans' sense of respect and self-esteem.

Many of my friends view Hispanics as lazy people. Nothing could be further from the truth. I saw many people, men and women, young and old, working their hearts out. Their community . . . was . . . a place of pride. As for family, when Pam told us about his family, I could see the pride and respect in his eyes.

Students are often quite surprised, even shocked, to learn that communities they visit are very different than what they had anticipated. They become intensely aware of how little they know about people unlike themselves, and often feel very ashamed about their ignorance. They often report a new desire to learn more about different cultural groups. Given the fact that gay students are among the most vulnerable students in middle school and high school (Weller, 2004), experiences which help future teachers to develop an awareness about the gay community are of particular significance.

To Experience Being an Outsider

Arriving at the church, . . . I immediately felt out of place and almost apologetic for being there. It was a strange feeling to he the minority in the group, something I have never experienced before to such a degree.

I realize much clearer now how it really must feel to be a minority. I've just taken my color for granted. It's not something I have to deal with everyday.

I can now understand more thoroughly what it is like to be in the minority, rather than the majority. The sense of isolation and loneliness is horrible, and it makes me sick to think some people live with that feeling everyday.

The underlying theme in these quotes is clearly fear. Most students who embark on cultural plunges are very anxious and occasionally even express concern for their lives. When I telephoned a student who dropped my summer, 1993 class after the first day, she told me that a big reason was because she was afraid to do the required plunge in an African American community, and both she and her husband were afraid that she might be physically harmed. Another student verbally expressed similar fears on the first day of that same class, but she decided to stay in the class and in fact had a great time on that plunge, as do almost all students.

The sad fact is that many European American students in my classes have usually managed to avoid ever going into a setting where the predominant ethnicity is different from their own, and many students of color have socialized primarily with members of their own ethnic group. Due to the influence of parents, peers, and mass media images, many White students have a profound fear of people of color and particularly of African-Americans, as these quotes reflect. Students of color are not exempt from such fears either, and they often are very anxious about visiting a community of a different ethnic group. The reality is that we all learn the same lies, and students tend to have the same biases about people different from themselves.

As these quotes indicate, cultural plunges are often the first experiences that many European American students have had of not being in the majority. Intense discomfort and a desire to leave immediately are common responses. The value of this particular lesson is profound. Students often write in their plunge reaction papers that they are now keenly aware of the importance of reaching out to their students who are ethnic outsiders. This realization is usually deepened when someone from the community reaches out to them on their plunges, which is usually the case. They thus learn firsthand what a positive impact a friendly gesture can make to a student who is culturally different from most others in a new setting, and they determine to be especially welcoming to ethnically diverse children in their future classes.

To Become More Aware of One's Values and Biases

I sat quietly in my chair listening to the conversation of the [African American] ladies around me. I really don't know what I was expecting, but these women did the same things in their lives that I did and they talked about the same things I do. It's amazing how because someone else may look different than you do you think that they act differently, too.

Throughout the (funeral) service, I was angry because I didn't see anyone cry, not even relatives. Then I learned that Buddhists believe in reincarnation; their spirit comes back to life in a form of human or animal, depending on your karma. Well, this helped me understand. I had already judged them, thinking they were morbid and insensitive people. This is where the danger lies; one starts to judge and stereotype out of ignorance or lack of understanding, which in turn, can lead to prejudice.

It caused me to reexamine how I interact with people of different cultures and how I unconsciously favor or respond better to those that relate better to my values. I also realize that while I try not to be "colonial" in mentality, I do want to be acknowledged and appreciated. Since visiting the conference and discovering this about myself, I have tried harder in communicating and listening and I have found I get far less defensive, I work far better with non-middle class students, I no longer expect acknowledgement, and I am far happier in my relations across cultural lines.

Students have many different types of insights about their values and biases as a result of cultural plunges. Whether discovering basic differences in world view, custom, or belief, or becoming more aware of similarities that exist across ethnic lines, students learn firsthand that their ideas about others are very often erroneous. They are able to discover some of their own fundamental assumptions, and are often very surprised that they were so unaware of their own values and biases.

Further Impact of Cultural Plunges: Effects on Motivation and Behavior

While the foregoing quotes from student cultural plunge reaction papers speak to three of the objectives of the plunge activity, there is another type of quote which warrants inclusion. This kind of quote speaks to the effects of cultural plunges on students' motivation and on their future behavior with people different from themselves:

That Saturday evening will stay with me for a long time. Both in my mind and in my heart. It's so easy to be oblivious and unaffected, when we don't think about things that don't concern ourselves. The thing is . . . that they do concern us, and I don't think I can forget that, or better yet, I don't want to forget!

I don't think I will ever be able to not think about what I saw on this day. No, as a matter of fact, I believe I will think about it often and I'm glad, because that means I will have to <u>do</u> something about it to be able to live with the images.

This cultural plunge really made me experience how the so called "minority" groups feel in our society. And hopefully this experience will stay with me forever so that I'm more sensitive when I'm teaching my students about the many different cultures in our society who all have an equal place here.

In all, I thought this experience was definitely worth it. I felt what it was like to be in the "minority." If this is what people of different races feel like when they are in the presence of a majority of whites, then something ought to be done to change attitudes. If this is a realistic goal, I don't know. All I know is what I have in my hands to control and I am definitely going to try.

These reactions indicate the lasting impression which cultural plunges leave on many students, and the degree of resolve which students feel to act on their newfound sensitivity. Unforgettable images, exposure to previously unknown crucial issues, and the experience of having been an outsider for the first time provide intense motivation to behave in new ways. The most commonly expressed new goals are to reach out to all students, attempt to promote increased communication and understanding between different ethnic groups, and become involved in social change efforts. All of these behaviors can significantly improve teachers' effectiveness with culturally diverse students and those students' communities.

Discussion

Cultural plunges engender a level of learning that is not possible with standard teaching methods such as lecture, texts, or discussion. Although plunge papers varied in terms of student reactions and emotional intensity, the overwhelming majority reported positive learning resulted from the experiences. This was true for students of varying ethnicity, color, gender, sexual orientation, socioeconomic status, physical attributes, religion and political views. Student enthusiasm for cultural plunges was very high, and a number of students recommended that more cultural plunges be required in the author's classes. One student stated in a reaction paper that "cultural plunges . . . should be a requirement for all future teachers," and this sentiment was quite widespread.

Perhaps the most compelling validation of cultural plunges comes from the words of students themselves. The author's students write a course reaction paper in lieu of a final examination in which they have total freedom to state their reactions to any aspects of the class which they care to comment upon. They are encouraged to be as frank as possible and to offer criticism and suggestions for improvement. Almost all students write about their cultural plunges and what they got out of them. The following excerpts are taken from course reaction papers:

> The cultural plunges are the best type of homework that one can do in order to truly learn about other cultures, customs and creeds. The benefit one obtains after such an experience is very great; more than if one had simply read an article or a book. All these plunges create that direct highway to the human heart.

> The plunges that we were sent on helped me face my fears, biases, and most of all the truth. It is amazing what first hand experience can do to a person . . . The plunges that I experienced have changed the way I think and look at things forever.

> The plunges give you that crucial first-hand experience that reading a textbook will never give you. I began to think about what kind of implications these plunges have for my career, and I became excited about how I would address these issues in my own classroom.

The learning which takes place from cultural plunges can be greatly enhanced via lectures, texts and videos. The author uses a number of powerful videos which address homelessness, discrimination against African Americans, violence against women, war, CIA experiments with drugs and diseases on Americans (including soldiers) without their knowledge or consent, and conditions in Third World sweatshops. These shocking depictions of the realities of diverse populations help to open minds and hearts and to create more empathy and compassion in future teachers. Many students have stated that the combination of lecture, video and cultural plunge has had a profound effect of their views towards homeless people and other populations.

Limitations

In the face of these results it is important to remember that there are limits to any teaching method, and the cultural plunge is no exception. One ought not overgeneralize from what one experiences on a single outing in any community, and cultural plunges certainly do not make cultural experts of anyone. Some students do not get as much out of these experiences as others, and are not very impressed with them. A few students view their plunges as negative experiences which they wish they had not been through. They might not have felt welcome, might disagree with a sermon in a church service or might strongly dislike church services in general. Such reactions are quite infrequent, however, and limited to a very small number of students (probably less than 5%). I make every effort to accommodate student concerns and requests for alternative plunges. For example, some students who are atheists have attended African America cultural events rather than go to the Baptist church service. In these types of situations, I brainstorm with the students for options which will be meaningful as well as acceptable, and leave the final decision in the hands of the student.

Conclusion

Plunges represent a type of education that is experiential, meaningful, interesting, challenging, confidence-building, growth-inducing and rewarding for most students. They represent a significant means towards students' greater understanding and acceptance of others, as well as of enhancing self-awareness; they thus have great potential as a viable educational approach in a full range of academic, business and government training programs. The fact that most plunges are one or two hours long makes their use very practical, and numerous students have said that they have gotten more out of plunges than out of service work requiring much more of a time commitment. Given the myriad challenges that confront teacher education in terms of preparing future teachers for the increasingly diverse students they will serve, the cultural plunge provides one means of helping to sensitize student teachers to social and cultural realities, to their own values and biases, and to the students of today's and tomorrow's classrooms.

References

Baker, F. (1989). How can you have experiential learning without experiential teaching? *Teacher Education Quarterly, 16*(3), 35–43.

Barrett, M. (1993). Preparation for cultural diversity: Experiential strategies for educators. *Equity & Excellence, 26*(1), 19–26.

Bergen, Jr., T. J. (1989). Needed: A radical design for teacher education. *Teacher Education Quarterly, 16*(1), 73–79.

Berlin, B. A. (2004). Reaching unmotivated students. *The Education Digest, 69*(5), 46–47.

Brown, S., Santiago, D., & Lopez, E. (2003). Latinos in higher education. *Change, 35*(2), 40–46.

Cochran-Smith, M. (2003). The multiple meanings of multicultural teacher education: A conceptual framework. *Teacher Education Quarterly, 30*(2), 7–26.

Cook, V. (1990). Personal interview. San Diego, June.

Davis, A. (1989). Teaching the disenfranchised child: The limitations of positivist research on instruction. *Teacher Education Quarterly, 16*(1), 5–14.

Fitch, E. F. (2002). Disability and inclusion: From labeling deviance to social valuing. *Educational Theory, 52*(4), 463–477.

Gillette, T. (1990). Telephone Interview. San Diego, May.

Glazier, J. (2003). Moving closer to speaking the unspeakable: White teachers talking about race. *Teacher Education Quarterly, 30*(1), 73–93.

Klotz, M. B. (2004). Help kids welcome disabled students. *The Education Digest, 69*(6), 41–42.

Lin, Q. (2001). Towards a caring-centered multicultural education within the social justice context. *Education, 122*(1), 107–114.

Major, E. & Brock, C. (2003). Fostering positive dispositions toward diversity: Dialogical explorations of a moral dilemma. *Teacher Education Quarterly, 30*(4), 7–27.

Malcolm, D. (1990). Personal interview. San Diego, April.

Milner, R. (2003). This issue. *Theory into Practice, 42*(3), 170–172.

Mio, J. S. (1989). Experiential involvement as an adjunct to teaching cultural sensitivity. *Journal of Multicultural Counseling and Development, 17*(1), 39–45.

Ornstein, A. C. & Levine, D. U. (1989). Social class, race, and school achievement: Problems and prospects. *Journal of Teacher Education, 40*(5), 17–23.

Prince, C. (2002). Attracting well-qualified teachers to struggling schools. *American Educator, 25*(4), 16–21.

Shinew, D. & Sodorff, C. (2003). Partnerships at a distance: Redesigning a teacher education program to prepare educators for diverse, high-need classrooms. *Action in Teacher Education, 25*(3), 24–29.

Smith-Davis, J. (2004). The new immigrant students need more than ESL. *The Education Digest, 69*(8), 21–26.

Steeley, S. (2003). Language minority teacher preparation: A review of alternative programs. *Action in Teacher Education, 25*(3), 59–68.

Weller, E. M. (2004). Legally and morally, what our gay students must be given. *The Education Digest, 69*(5), 38–43.

Wilson, A. (1982). Cross-cultural experiential learning for teachers. *Theory Into Practice, 21*(3), 184–192.

JESÚS NIETO is an associate professor in the School of Teacher Education at San Diego State University, San Diego, California.

From *Teacher Education Quarterly,* Winter 2006, pp. 75–84. Copyright © 2006 by Caddo Gap Press. Reprinted by permission.

Character and Academics

What Good Schools Do

Though there has been increasing interest in character education among policy makers and education professionals, many schools hesitate to do anything that might detract from their focus on increasing academic performance. The authors present evidence indicating that this may be misguided.

JACQUES S. BENNINGA ET AL.

The growth of character education programs in the United States has coincided with the rise in high-stakes testing of student achievement. The No Child Left Behind Act asks schools to contribute not to students' academic performance but also to their character. Both the federal government and the National Education Association (NEA) agree that schools have this dual responsibility. In a statement introducing a new U.S. Department of Education character education website, then Secretary of Education Rod Paige outlined the need for such programs:

> Sadly, we live in a culture without role models, where millions of students are taught the wrong values—or no values at all. This culture of callousness has led to a staggering achievement gap, poor health status, overweight students, crime, violence, teenage pregnancy, and tobacco and alcohol abuse. . . . Good character is the product of good judgments made every day.[1]

And Bob Chase, the former president of the NEA, issued his own forceful call to action:

> We must make an explicit commitment to formal character education. We must integrate character education into the fabric of the curriculum and into extracurricular activities. We must train teachers in character education—both preservice and inservice. And we must consciously set about creating a moral climate within our schools.[2]

Despite the clear national interest in character education, many schools are leery of engaging in supplementary initiatives that, although worthy, might detract from what they see as their primary focus: increasing academic achievement. Moreover, many schools lack the resources to create new curricular initiatives. Yet the enhancement of student character is a bipartisan mandate that derives from the very core of public education.

The purpose of public schooling requires that schools seek to improve both academic and character education.

If it could be demonstrated that implementing character education programs is compatible with efforts to improve school achievement, then perhaps more schools would accept the challenge of doing both. But until now there has been little solid evidence of such successful coexistence.

Definitions and Research

Character education is the responsibility of adults. While the term *character education* has historically referred to the duty of the older generation to form the character of the young through experiences affecting their attitudes, knowledge, and behaviors, more recent definitions include such developmental outcomes as a positive perception of school, emotional literacy, and social justice activism.[3]

There are sweeping definitions of character education (e.g., Character Counts' six pillars, Community of Caring's five values, or the Character Education Partnership's 11 principles) and more narrow ones. Character education can be defined in terms of relationship virtues (e.g., respect, fairness, civility, tolerance), self-oriented virtues (e.g., fortitude, self-discipline, effort, perseverance) or a combination of the two. The state of California has incorporated character education criteria into the application process for its statewide distinguished school recognition program and, in the process, has created its own definition of character education. Each definition directs the practice of character education somewhat differently, so that programs calling themselves "character education" vary in purpose and scope.

There is some research evidence that character education programs enhance academic achievement. For example, an evaluation of the Peaceful Schools Project and research on the Responsive Classroom found that students in schools that implemented these programs had greater gains on standardized test scores than did students in comparison schools.[4] The Child Development Project (CDP) conducted follow-up studies of middle school students (through eighth grade) who had attended CDP elementary schools and found that they had higher course grades and higher achievement test scores than comparison middle school students.[5] Longitudinal studies have reported similar effects for middle school and high school students who had participated as elementary school students in the Seattle Social Development Project.[6]

A growing body of research supports the notion that high-quality character education can promote academic achievement. For example, Marvin Berkowitz and Melinda Bier have identified character education programs for elementary, middle, and high school students that enhance academic achievement.[7] These findings, however, are based on prepackaged curricular programs, and most schools do not rely on such programs. Instead, they create their own customized character education initiatives. It remains to be seen whether such initiatives also lead to academic gains.

Toward an Operational Definition of Character Education

We decided to see if we could determine a relationship between character education and academic achievement across a range of elementary schools. For our sample we used the elementary schools that applied in 2000 to the California Department of Education for recognition as distinguished elementary schools, California's highest level of school attainment. Eligibility to submit an application for the California School Recognition Program (CSRP) in 2000 was based on the previous year's academic performance index (API) results.

However, 1999 was the first year for California's Public School Accountability Act (PSAA), which created the API. Thus, while the state department stated that growth on the API was the central focus of the PSAA, schools applying for the CSRP in 1999–2000 did not receive their 1999 API scores until January 2000, after they had already written and submitted their award applications. Approximately 12.7% of California elementary schools (681 of 5,368 schools) submitted a full application for the award in 2000. The average API of these schools was higher than the average for the schools that did not apply, but both were below the state expectancy score of 800. The mean API for applicant schools was 751; for non-applicant schools, 612. The API range for applicant schools was 365–957; for non-applicant schools, 302–958. Hence the sample for this study is not representative of all California elementary schools. It is a sample of more academically successful schools, but it does represent a broad range of achievement from quite low to very high.

Specific wording related to character education was included for the first time in the CSRP application in 2000. Schools were asked to describe what they were doing to meet a set of nine standards. Of these, the one that most clearly pertained to character education was Standard 1 (Vision and Standards). For this standard, schools were required to include "specific examples and other evidence" of "expectations that promote positive character traits in students."[8] Other standards could also be seen as related to character education. For these, schools were asked to document activities and programs that ensured opportunities for students to contribute to the school, to others, and to the community.

We chose for our study a stratified random sample of 120 elementary schools that submitted applications. These 120 schools were not significantly different from the other 561 applicant schools on a variety of academic and demographic indicators. For the schools in our sample, we correlated the extent of their character education implementation with their API and SAT-9 scores—the academic scale and test used by California at that time.[9]

The first problem we needed to grapple with was how to define a character education program. We spent considerable time discussing an operational definition to use for this project. After conferring with experts, we chose our final set of character education criteria, drawn from both the standards used by the California Department of Education and the *Character Education Quality Standards* developed by the Character Education Partnership.[10] Six criteria emerged from this process:

- This school promotes core ethical values as the basis of good character.
- In this school, parents and other community members are active participants in the character education initiative.
- In this school, character education entails intentional promotion of core values in all phases of school life.
- Staff members share responsibility for and attempt to model character education.
- This school fosters an overall caring community.
- This school provides opportunities for most students to practice moral action.

Each of the six criteria addresses one important component of character education. We created a rubric encompassing these six criteria and listing indicators for each, along with a scoring scale.

Character Education and Academic Achievement

Our study of these high-performing California schools added further evidence of a relationship between academic achievement and the implementation of specific character education programs. In our sample, elementary schools with solid character education programs showed positive relationships between the extent of character education implementation and academic achievement not in a single year but also across the next two academic years. Over a multi-year period from 1999 to 2002, higher rankings on the API and higher scores on the SAT-9 were significantly and positively correlated with four of our character education indicators: a school's ability to ensure a clean and safe physical environment; evidence that a school's parents and teachers modeled and promoted good character; high-quality opportunities at the school for students to contribute in meaningful ways to the school and its community; and promoting a caring community and positive social relationships.

These are promising results, particularly because the *total character education score* for the year of the school's application was significantly correlated with every language and mathematics achievement score on the SAT-9 for a period of three years. In two of those years, the same was true for reading achievement scores. In other words, good-quality character education was positively associated with academic achievement, both across academic domains and over time.

What Good Schools Do

From our research we derived principles—the four indicators mentioned above—that are common across schools with both thoughtful character education programs and high levels of academic achievement.

- *Good schools ensure a clean and secure physical environment.* Although all schools in our sample fit this description, the higher-scoring character education schools expressed great pride in keeping their buildings and grounds in good shape. This is consistent with what is reported about the virtues of clean and safe learning environments. For example, the Center for Prevention of School Violence notes that "the physical appearance of a school and its campus communicates a lot about the school and its people. Paying attention to appearance so that the facilities are inviting can create a sense of security."[11]
- One school in our sample reported that its buildings "are maintained well above district standards. . . . The custodial crew prides themselves in achieving a monthly cleaning score that has exceeded standards in 9 out of 12 months." And another noted, "A daily grounds check is performed to ensure continual safety and cleanliness." Each of the higher-scoring schools in our sample explicitly noted its success in keeping its campus in top shape and mentioned that parents were satisfied that their children were attending school in a physically and psychologically safe environment.
- All schools in California are required to have on file a written Safe School Plan, but the emphases in these plans vary. While some schools limited their safety plans to regulations controlling access to the building and defined procedures for violations and intrusions, the schools with better character education programs defined "safety" more broadly and deeply. For example, one school scoring high on our character education rubric explained that the mission of its Safe School Plan was "to provide all students with educational and personal opportunities in a positive and nurturing environment which will enable them to achieve current and future goals, and for all students to be accepted at their own social, emotional, and academic level of development." Another high-scoring school addressed three concerns in its Safe School Plan: identification of visitors on campus, cultural/ethnic harmony, and safe

ingress and egress from school. To support these areas of focus, this school's teachers were all trained to conduct classroom meetings, to implement the Community of Caring core values, and to handle issues related to cultural diversity and communication.

- *Good schools promote and model fairness, equity, caring, and respect.* In schools with good character education programs and high academic achievement, adults model and promote the values and attitudes they wish the students to embrace, and they infuse character education throughout the school and across the curriculum. Rick Weissbourd drove home this point in a recent essay: "The moral development of students does not depend primarily on explicit character education efforts but on the maturity and ethical capacities of the adults with whom they interact. . . . Educators influence students' moral development not simply by being good role models—important as that is—but also by what they bring to their relationships with students day to day."[12] The staff of excellent character education schools in our sample tended to see themselves as involved, concerned professional educators, and others see them that way as well.
- Thus one school described its teachers as "pivotal in the [curriculum] development process; there is a high level of [teacher] ownership in the curriculum. . . . Fifty percent of our staff currently serves on district curriculum committees." Another school stated that it "fosters the belief that it takes an entire community pulling together to provide the best education for every child; that is best accomplished through communication, trust, and collaboration on ideas that reflect the needs of our school and the community. . . . Teachers are continually empowered and given opportunities to voice their convictions and shape the outcome of what the school represents." A third school described its teachers as "continually encouraged" to grow professionally and to use best practices based on research. In the best character education schools, teachers are recognized by their peers, by district personnel, and by professional organizations for their instructional prowess and their professionalism. They model the academic and prosocial characteristics that show their deep concern for the well-being of children.
- *In good schools students contribute in meaningful ways.* We found that academically excellent character education schools provided opportunities for students to contribute to their school and their community. These schools encouraged students to participate in volunteer activities, such as cross-age tutoring, recycling, fundraising for charities, community clean-up programs, food drives, visitations to local senior centers, and so on.
- One elementary school required 20 hours of community service, a program coordinated entirely by parent volunteers. Students in that school volunteered in community gardens and at convalescent hospitals, and they took part in community clean-up days. Such

activities, while not directly connected to students' academic programs, were viewed as mechanisms to promote the development of healthy moral character. According to William Damon, a crucial component of moral education is engaging children in positive activities—community service, sports, music, theater, or anything else that inspires them and gives them a sense of purpose.[13]

- *Good schools promote a caring community and positive social relationships.* One school in our sample that exemplified this principle was a school of choice in its community. The district had opened enrollment to students outside district boundaries, and this school not provided an excellent academic program for its multilingual student population but also worked hard to include parents and community members in significant ways. Its Family Math Night attracted 250 family members, and its Family Literacy Night educated parents about read-aloud methods. Parents, grandparents, and friends were recruited to become classroom volunteers and donated thousands of hours.

- This particular school also rented its classrooms to an after-school Chinese educational program. The two sets of teachers have become professional colleagues, and insights from such cultural interaction have led both groups to a better understanding of the Chinese and American systems of education. One result has been that more English-speaking students are enrolling in the Chinese after-school program. And teachers in both programs now engage in dialogue about the specific needs of children. One parent wrote a letter to the principal that said in part, "It seems you are anxious to build up our young generation more healthy and successful. . . . I am so proud you are not our children's principal, but also parents' principal."

- Other schools with strong social relationship programs provide meaningful opportunities for parent involvement and establish significant partnerships with local businesses. They encourage parents and teachers to work alongside students in service projects, to incorporate diverse communities into the school curriculum, and to partner with high school students who serve as physical education and academic mentors. As one such school put it, all stakeholders "must play an important and active role in the education of the child to ensure the future success of that child."

Conclusion

It is clear that well-conceived programs of character education can and should exist side by side with strong academic programs. It is no surprise that students need physically secure and psychologically safe schools, staffed by teachers who model professionalism and caring behaviors and who ask students to demonstrate caring for others. That students who attend such schools achieve academically makes intuitive sense as well. It is in schools with this dual emphasis that adults understand their role in preparing students for future citizenship in a democratic and diverse society. The behaviors and attitudes they model communicate important messages to the young people in their charge. Future research on the relationship between character education and academic achievement should include a greater representation of schools in the average and below-average achievement categories. In particular, a study of the extent of the implementation of character education in schools that may have test scores at the low end of the spectrum—but are nevertheless performing higher than their socioeconomic characteristics would predict—would be an important contribution to our understanding of the relationship between character education and academic achievement.

While this was our initial attempt to explore the relationship between these two important school purposes, we learned a good deal about what makes up a good character education curriculum in academically strong schools. We know that such a curriculum in such schools is positively related to academic outcomes over time and across content areas. We also know that, to be effective, character education requires adults to act like adults in an environment where children are respected and feel physically and psychologically safe to engage in the academic and social activities that prepare them best for later adult decision making.

At a time when resources are scarce, we see schools cutting programs and narrowing curricula to concentrate on skills measured by standardized tests. Our research suggests that school goals and activities that are associated with good character education programs are also associated with academic achievement. Thus our results argue for maintaining a rich curriculum with support for all aspects of student development and growth.

Notes

1. U.S. Department of Education, "ED Launches Character Education Web Site," www.thechallenge.org/15-v12no4/v12n4-communitiesandschools.htm.

2. Bob Chase, quoted in "Is Character Education the Answer?," *Education World,* 1999, www.education-world.com/a_admin/admin097.shtml.

3. Marvin W. Berkowitz, "The Science of Character Education," in William Damon, ed., *Bringing in a New Era in Character Education* (Stanford, Calif.: Hoover Institution Press, 2002), pp. 43–63.

4. Stuart W. Twemlow et al., "Creating a Peaceful School Learning Environment: A Controlled Study of an Elementary School Intervention to Reduce Violence," *American Journal of Psychiatry,* vol. 158, 2001, pp. 808–10; and Stephen N. Elliott, "Does a Classroom Promoting Social Skills Development Enable Higher Academic Functioning Among Its Students Over Time?," Northeast Foundation for Children, Greenfield, Mass., 1998.

5. Victor Battistich and Sehee Hong, "Enduring Effects of the Child Development Project: Second-Order Latent Linear Growth Modeling of Students' 'Connectedness' to School, Academic Performance, and Social Adjustment During Middle School," unpublished manuscript, Developmental Studies Center, Oakland, Calif., 2003.

6. J. David Hawkins et al., "Long-Term Effects of the Seattle Social Development Intervention on School Bonding Trajectories," *Applied Developmental Science,* vol. 5, 2001, pp. 225–36.

7. Marvin W. Berkowitz and Melinda C. Bier, *What Works in Character Education?* (Washington, D.C.: Character Education Partnership, 2005).

8. "California School Recognition Program, 2000 Elementary Schools Program, Elementary School Rubric," California Department of Education, 2001. (Data are available from Jacques Benninga.)

9. For more detail on the design of the study, see Jacques S. Benninga, Marvin W. Berkowitz, Phyllis Kuehn, and Karen Smith, "The Relationship of Character Education Implementation and Academic Achievement in Elementary Schools," *Journal of Research in Character Education,* vol. 1, 2003, pp. 17–30.

10. *Character Education Quality Standards: A Self-Assessment Tool for Schools and Districts* (Washington, D.C.: Character Education Partnership, 2001).

11. "What Is Character Education?," Center for the Fourth and Fifth Rs, 2003, www.cortland.edu/c4n5rs/ce_iv.asp.

12. Rick Weissbourd, "Moral Teachers, Moral Students," *Educational Leadership,* March 2003, pp. 6–7.

13. Damon is quoted in Susan Gilbert, "Scientists Explore the Molding of Children's Morals," *New York Times,* 18 March 2003.

JACQUES S. BENNINGA is a professor of education and director of the Bonner Center for Character Education, California State University, Fresno. **MARVIN W. BERKOWITZ** is Sanford N. McDonnell Professor of Character Education, University of Missouri, St. Louis. **PHYLLIS KUEHN** is a professor of educational research, California State University, Fresno. **KAREN SMITH** is principal of Mark Twain Elementary School, Brentwood, Mo. The research described in this article was funded by a grant from the John Templeton Foundation, but the opinions expressed are those of the authors.

From *Phi Delta Kappan,* February 2006, pp. 448–452. Copyright © 2006 by Phi Delta Kappan. Reprinted by permission.

High School with a College Twist

Terry B. Grier and Kent D. Peterson

Some students just don't fit. They don't like school, dress differently, have no interest in school activities, and are fed up with high school in general. Many are extremely bright and have high potential but do not see the relationship between high school and the real world. Others are behind academically and experience daily failure and rejection at school. Unfortunately, most high schools do not have meaningful strategies to deal with such disengaged students and many of them drop out of school.

That certainly was the case in the Guilford County Schools (GCS) in Greensboro, NC: in 2000, 6% of the district's students dropped out, and the school board demanded action. After considering a variety of options, the district turned to a small-school concept called the "middle college high school" to help reconnect those students and keep them in school. A middle college high school is an alternative school that is housed on a college campus. Students enroll in college classes and take their high school courses in the alternative setting. Eventually, the district created six middle college high schools, each with a different schedule, culture, curriculum, and college context.

Key Factors

Although many unique features of middle college high schools contribute to their success, two factors—small size and the college context—are extremely important.

School Size

Although the number of students enrolled in middle college programs differs site-by-site, keeping enrollments small (100–145 students in each middle college program) is key. In GCS, most middle college high school classes do not exceed 15 students. These small group settings allow the schools to accomplish things that larger, traditional high schools cannot, such as:

- Fostering personal relationships between teacher and student. Teachers get to interact one-on-one with students, picking up on personal issues that might escalate into serious problems.
- Rekindling student academic interest. A low student-teacher ratio encourages direct assistance and immediate feedback.
- Reducing the social drama that exists in larger school settings. Social drama derives from the complex mix of students' social status, cliques, and search for acceptance.
- Reducing the student-counselor ratio. Each middle college high school has its own counselor who, because he or she serves fewer students, can address more issues, which results in more student time in school, fewer problems, and more academic focus.

In sum, small size makes it possible for a dedicated staff to give students more personalized attention to promote their academic success and improve their opportunities for long-term social and career success.

College Context

Everyone remotely connected to adolescents understands the power of peer pressure. The college campus exerts a similar, positive pressure on middle college students. Enjoying the same freedom as college students and coupling that freedom with self-responsibility is a new experience for students. Almost immediately, they feel pressure to begin acting like, studying like, and looking like college students. Most students welcome the sense that they are being treated like adults with adult rules and responsibilities. For example, they are allowed to take sodas and snacks to class, wear hats in buildings, hang out in the student center, leave the campus for lunch, and enjoy an expanded sense of freedom. In return, they follow the rules and regulations of the colleges they attend.

Although middle college students can attend classes and use the facilities of the higher education institution, they do not participate in evening or social activities. Nonetheless, students report that they feel a part of the greater mission of the school they are in. All of these aspects of the college context have a positive, and often significant, influence on these students, many of whom only returned to school because of the middle college opportunities.

Getting Started

A middle college high school can work almost anywhere in the United States where a need exists. But before any new project is implemented, the community must understand both the concept and the need for it. Data that focus on the negative impact that dropouts have on the local economy and economic development opportunities can help communities understand the need to create alternative placements. Communities will also want to see evidence that the cost of operating a middle college high school over time is no more expensive than a traditional high school—despite the small class size. Existing middle colleges can serve as models and become part of the coalition that navigates the political mine fields of change. They also can offer examples for school officials, elected officials, and community leaders to visit.

Another key element is support and approval from a local postsecondary institution. Middle colleges are located on various types of college campuses, including technical colleges, small liberal arts colleges, and large state universities. Colleges may be interested in hosting a middle college because it generates revenue, builds visibility among potential students, or supports its mission to serve students. Still, colleges view themselves as postsecondary institutions, and seeing the benefit of hosting high school students takes some convincing.

Success can build on success, however. For example, to ensure that GCS's first middle college high school was a success and that the host college understood the concept, Don Cameron, the president of Guilford Technical Community College (GTCC), agreed to fly to Nashville, TN, and tour the middle college Terry Grier helped establish there. The day after GCS's press conference announcing the establishment of a middle college high school on the GTCC campus, Craven Williams, the president of Greensboro College, called the district office and declared that Greensboro College also wanted to host a middle college high school. Both schools opened in fall 2000.

The district and the college must negotiate the use of space, access to labs and classrooms, use of the cafeteria, tuition costs when students take college level courses, and so forth. Formal agreements are necessary regarding the partnership. However, none of the colleges or universities that house GCS middle colleges charge the district fees for facility use, utilities, or maintenance costs.

Convincing college faculty members and administrators to bring in a group of high school students who will work, eat, and interact with their students and staff members also takes considerable negotiation and persuasion. One important thing to remember is that colleges do not mind referring to students as disengaged, but such descriptors as *at risk, troubled, malcontent,* and *discipline problems* should not be used. Not only are these inappropriate descriptions, college and university presidents also have boards of directors and must be politically sensitive to the image of the campus.

Implementation Challenges and Considerations
Design Concept and Proper Fit

Designing a variety of middle colleges that serve different student needs and interests was essential in a district as large as GCS. The district's six middle college high schools have unique focuses, a variety of grade spans, and different schedules. Some are single-sex programs. The programs are housed on large university, small college, and community college campuses.

It is important to consider the history, facilities, and student body of a college or a university before deciding what type of middle college to place on that campus. Every college has a different culture, and districts must give careful thought to the ethos of the host college or university before establishing a middle college.

Staff Selection

Most middle college programs provide a principal, a counselor, and seven or eight high school teachers to serve 125 students. The principal must be the first middle college employee hired and, like a symphony conductor, must understand every player's part. Principals must have the managerial skills to organize school policies and procedures; the political skills to handle the complex interactions of higher education institutions; the interpersonal abilities to work with students with complex needs; the social skills to support teachers working under flexible teaching and relational conditions; and the values and the desire to help students who have faced difficulties in high school, dropped out, and elected to return. Because middle college high school students can take college courses for dual high school and college credit, the principal must be able to communicate and work closely with the college's staff members.

Like good middle college principals, middle college teachers must have high expectations for their students and develop close and supportive relationships with them. They must exhibit unconditional positive regard for others and believe that students possess infinite worth. Successful middle college teachers combine keen insights about their students with creative strategies that help students meet academic expectations. They must be empathetic listeners, have a clear purpose as a facilitator of student learning, and be willing to give students a second chance.

Student Selection

The middle college high school program is not for everyone. It is designed to serve a small percentage of students who do not fit in traditional high schools. Students who have good grades, good school attendance, and a record of good behavior and who like school and participate in school cocurricular activities are not good candidates for the middle college high school. Usually, GCS students who participate in cocurricular activities in their home schools or who simply want to begin college early do not qualify for the program.

The recruitment and selection process should have several components that increase the likelihood of a good fit between the students and the school. Although students can show initiative and apply on their own, staff members and administrators should not passively hope that students will apply. Initially, staff members and administrators should look for students who were once successful but have either dropped out of high school or have been in significant academic trouble. They should actively seek out students by using traditional and nontraditional recruiting techniques. Over time, middle college high school students will nominate and recruit similarly disconnected students to attend their school.

GCS Middle College High Schools

Middle College at Guilford Technical Community College (GTCC)

Established 2001 on the main GTCC campus
Enrollment: 140 students in grades 9–12
Schedule: 11:30 AM–5:20 PM
Twenty-five percent of its students enrolled in 66 college courses; 95% of its seniors graduated, and 94% of those graduates began postsecondary education in 2006.

Greensboro Middle College High School

Established 2001 on the campus of Greensboro College
Enrollment: 110 students in grades 11–12
Schedule: 8:10 AM–3:10 PM
One-hundred percent graduation rate in 2006; made AYP for the last three years.

The Middle College at A&T

Established 2003 on the campus of North Carolina Agricultural & Technical State University
Enrollment: 110 students
Schedule: 9:45 AM–4:15 PM
Only serves male students; 76% of seniors graduated in 2006; the district replaced large percentage of teachers and the principal during the 2006–07 school year.

The Middle College at Bennett College

Established 2003 on the campus of Bennett College
Enrollment: 115 students
Schedule: 11:00 AM–4:30 PM
Only serves female students; 95% of seniors graduated in 2006.

Middle College of Entertainment Technology at GTCC

Established 2005 on a branch campus of GTCC
Enrollment: 120 students
Schedule: 12:00 PM–5:20 PM
School made AYP in 2006.

The GTCC Middle College East

Established 2005 on a branch campus of GTCC
Enrollment: 125 students
Schedule: 12:05 PM–5:30 PM
School made AYP in 2006.

Acceptance is not automatic. Schools may want to use an admissions project team—consisting of the middle college principal, a counselor, and a teacher—to review all applications. The GCS middle colleges have an intensive selection process that requires a formal application in addition to a written statement of interest in returning to school. In-depth interviews are held with each student and his or her parent or guardian. During the interview, students must answer questions that help determine what factors created the largest amount of stress in the student's academic and personal life.

Costs

Although core high school courses are taught by a carefully selected high school faculty, all middle college students have access to the college's facilities. Eligible students can take college courses for both high school and college credit, and most sponsoring school districts are responsible for their tuition payments. Other expenses in the North Carolina middle college high schools include:

- Computers, telephones, and office equipment
- Lower than average student-teacher ratios
- A full-time counselor who serves fewer than 140 students
- Regular school equipment as well as special equipment for special theme middle colleges

- Transportation—door-to-door transportation that is similar to those associated with regular magnet schools
- Access to Plato, a computer-based, self-paced learning program.

Eligible students can take college courses for both high school and college credit, and most sponsoring school districts are responsible for their tuition payments.

A school district must address these and other cost issues when developing and sustaining middle college high schools. Increased state revenues and negotiated cost savings from college faculty use can offset some costs. More important, the social cost of serving and returning disconnected students to school well outweigh these expenses.

Savings and Income

Although there are expenses associated with establishing a middle college high school, the schools do not have many of the high-cost programs that traditional high schools have, such as athletics. Classroom space, laboratories, media centers, cafeteria, auditoriums, athletic weight rooms, and art facilities are also provided by the colleges at no cost to the district.

GCS's middle college high schools serve more than 700 students, the equivalent of a small high school. A new, small high school that could serve these students would cost more than $38 million to build and $455,000 a year to operate. In addition, many of these students had dropped out of school, and returning them to the district's enrollment generated significant revenue to the district. Plus, earning high school diplomas will have a tremendously positive impact on them, their families, and the community.

Lessons Learned

GCS has learned a number of valuable lessons over the years:

- No plan survives initial contact. Expect bumps in the road and be flexible enough to work them out.
- Don't expect immediate support for the establishment of middle college high schools from all quarters. Critics will carefully watch and wait. Be willing to admit mistakes, but move quickly to make corrections.
- Don't underestimate the importance of early success to the survival of a middle college high school. Create and celebrate early victories, such as improved attendance, grades, and student behavior. Invite the press, elected officials, and board members to visit the schools.
- The selection of the principal and the teachers is key to the success of the school.
- A middle college high school must be located on a college campus to benefit from the power of that campus.

Conclusion

Every college and university in the country should partner with school districts and host a middle college high school. Small districts can join together to form middle college consortiums, like the one using Mott Community College in Flint, MI.

In GCS, the grades 9–12 drop-out rate has decreased from 6.34% in 1999–2000 to 3.04% in 2005–06—one of the lowest rates in the nation among metropolitan school systems. The GCS middle college high schools played a major role in that reduction, and their success has not gone unnoticed. North Carolina Governor Mike Easley and his staff members have visited GCS middle colleges on numerous occasions during the past several years. Two years ago, building on what he observed in GCS, Governor Easley developed a "Learn and Earn" Early College model that emulates many of the components of a middle college high school. The governor is partnering with the Gates Foundation to expand his concept across North Carolina.

Middle college high schools help students who were disconnected and disengaged return to school and succeed. Consider visiting a middle college. Although reading this article will better inform you about middle colleges, hearing directly from middle college teachers and students will change your views and beliefs about what can be done to save and serve disengaged high school students.

TERRY B. GRIER [griert@gcsnc.com] is the superintendent of Guilford County [NC] Schools. **KENT D. PETERSON** is a professor in the School of Education at the University of Wisconsin—Madison.GCS Middle College High Schools

UNIT 5

Problem Behaviors and Challenges of Adolescents

Unit Selections

Key Points to Consider

- When do video and computer games become obsessive and addictive for teenagers?
- How are violent video games harmful to teenagers?
- How does heavy use of computers rob teens of important social and physical experiences?
- What are the two sides to the underage drinking debate?
- What are the dangers in teen gambling?
- What are possible preventions for teen self-injurious behavior?
- What questions should be considered in displaying violence on the Internet?
- What are the emerging prevention efforts for domestic violence during adolescence?
- What can be done to help with the problem of teens abusing prescription drugs?
- What factors contribute to youths' reaction to disasters?

Student Website

www.mhcls.com

Internet References

Anorexia Nervosa and Related Eating Disorders (ANRED)
http://www.anred.com

Center for Change
http://www.centerforchange.com

Focus Adolescent Services: Alcohol and Teen Drinking
http://www.focusas.com/Alcohol.html

Higher Education Center for Alcohol and Other Drug Prevention
http://www.edc.org/hec/

Justice Information Center (NCJRS): Drug Policy Information
http://www.ncjrs.org/drgswww.html

MentalHelp.Net
http://eatingdisorders.mentalhelp.net/

National Center on Addiction and Substance Abuse at Columbia University
http://www.casacolumbia.org

National Center for Missing and Exploited Children
www.ncmec.org

National Clearinghouse for Alcohol and Drug Information
http://www.health.org/

National Institute of Mental Health
http://www.nimh.nih.gov/

National Sexual Violence Resource Center
www.nsvrc.org

National Youth Violence Prevention Resource Center
http://www.safeyouth.org

RAINN
www.rainn.org

Suicide Awareness: Voices of Education
http://www.save.org/

Youth Suicide League
http://www.unicef.org/pon96/insuicid.htm

That adolescents can and do engage in high-risk behaviors is not subject to much debate. The statistics on adolescent fatalities demonstrate their risk-taking behavior. The leading causes of death in adolescents are tragic: accidents, suicide, and homicide. Alcohol use is frequently involved, particularly in motor vehicle accidents. About half of the fatal motor vehicle accidents involving an adolescent also involves a drunk peer driver.

Why adolescents engage in high-risk behaviors is much debated. Some researchers believe that adolescent risk taking is related to cognitive development. They propose that adolescents possess a sense of invulnerability. Adolescents believe they are special and unique; things that could happen to others could not possibly happen to them. Other researchers believe (at best) this may apply only to young adolescents. By their mid-teens a majority of adolescents are too sophisticated to consider themselves invulnerable. Despite this, however, adolescents still take more risks than do adults.

If older adolescents do not perceive themselves as invulnerable, than why do they take risks? There are several possible explanations. One proposal is that adolescents may not perceive the risk. For example, adults may have a better sense of how fast they can safely drive given differing road conditions. Adolescents, simply because they are inexperienced drivers, may not recognize when road conditions are dangerous and so may not adjust their speed. Adolescents may engage in riskier behaviors than adults simply because they have the time and energy. Many adolescents have free time, money, and a car. Access to these things may allow adolescents to put themselves in dangerous situations. Adults may work, do more household chores, and take care of their children. These adults may not have time to drink, take drugs, or joy ride.

Adolescents may also be less adept than adults at extricating themselves from high-risk behavior. For example, adults who attend a party where drugs are consumed may be more comfortable declining offered drugs than adolescents, or they may be able to leave the party without depending on transportation from others. Some researchers indicate that society may be somewhat to blame for adolescents' risk taking. If impoverished adolescents have no chance of obtaining meaningful work, have limited access to recreational activities, and have little encouragement to go to school, then participation in drug-related or violent behavior may be the only options open to them. It may be up to society to provide these adolescents with an increased number of safe choices.

Adolescent risk-taking activities can take many forms. The U.S. Public Health Service identifies several categories of behavior related to health risks for adolescents. Included are behaviors that may cause injuries, such as suicide and violence, use of tobacco or illicit drugs (including alcohol), and risky behaviors related to sexuality or eating disorders. All these can clearly threaten adolescents. Moreover, alcohol use seems to exacerbate many of the other risks, as indicated by the statistics on alcohol use and violent death. And drug use can be related to accidents, health problems, and violence. Violent behaviors

© BananaStock/PunchStock

are an increasing concern to society. Murder is the second leading cause of death in adolescence; it is the leading cause of death for African American male teenagers. Suicide rates in young people have tripled since the 1950s. Eating disorders are another threat to adolescents. Millions of adolescents suffer from anorexia nervosa or bulimia in the United States.

In this unit, problem behaviors and challenges of adolescents are presented. The first article discusses the popularity of video and computer games, raising the issues of obsession and addiction among teens. Emily Sohn reports on the extensive research on violent video games and the harmful effect on teens. Lowell Monke explains how heavy use of computers may rob teens of important social and physical experiences.

Sandra Harris explains that high school students most often use forms of emotional abuse when bullying, and that only a small percentage of victims tell faculty when they are bullied. According to the author, adults can play a key role in reducing bullying by helping adolescents deal with stressful situations.

The next article discusses the two sides of the underage drinking debate. Some believe we should fight for zero tolerance while others think we should teach responsible drinking. As gambling becomes a more acceptable form of entertainment for adults, teens are becoming more involved as explained by Keith Whyte. Author Jennifer Dyl describes cutting as the most prevalent form of non-suicidal self-injurious behavior. She explores the possible prevention and intervention techniques.

Jill Smalowe wrote an article focusing on the beating of a Lakeland, Florida cheerleader that was captured on video and shown on the Internet. The video has raised questions about violence displayed on the Internet and girls exhibiting physical aggression. For the most part, the response to domestic violence has been one of crisis management. While crisis management is important, Drs. Wolfe and Jaffe examine emerging prevention efforts which focus on teens.

The abuse of prescription drugs often results in addiction and sometimes death. Bob Smithouser provides suggestions as to what can be done to help.

The last article focuses on teens' reaction to disasters. The author describes both outcomes and predictors in order to prepare professionals who may work with youth in post-disaster situations.

Video Game Violence

E MILY S OHN

W e read every message that readers submit to *Science News for Kids*, and we learn a lot from what you say. Two articles that really got you talking looked at video games. One story argued that video games can be good for you (see*"What Video Games Can Teach Us"*). The other argued that video games are bad for you (see *"The Violent Side of Video Games"*).

These stories ran 3 years ago, and we're still hearing about them, almost weekly. In particular, those of you who enjoy killing people on screen disagree with research suggesting that your game-playing habits inspire you to act out.

"I have played the most violent games available on the market today," writes Matteo, 15. "I don't go killing people or stealing cars because I see it in a game. My parents say that, as long as I remember it's a game, I can play whatever I want."

Dylan, 14, agrees. "I love violent games," he writes. "And I haven't been in a fight since I was 12 years old."

Akemi, now 22, says that he's experienced no long-term effects in 14 years of gaming. "I have been playing the games since I was at least 7," he writes. "I have no criminal record. I have good grades and have often been caught playing well into the night (that is, 4 hours or more)."

Despite what these readers say, many scientific studies clearly show that violent video games make kids more likely to yell, push, and punch, says Brad Bushman. He's a psychologist at the University of Michigan in Ann Arbor.

Bushman and his colleagues recently reviewed more than 300 studies of video media effects. Across the board, he says, the message is clear.

"We included every single study we could find on the topic," Bushman says. "Regardless of what kids say, violent video games are harmful."

TV Watching

TV has been around a lot longer than video games, so researchers have more data on the long-term effects of violent TV shows on people than they do on the effects of violent video games.

In one study, scientists at the University of Michigan recorded the TV-watching habits of hundreds of first and third graders in 1977. Fifteen years later, the researchers looked at what kind of adults these kids had become.

By the time they were in their early twenties, women who had watched violent shows as kids were four times as likely to have punched, choked, or beaten other people as were women who didn't watch such programs as kids. Boys who watched violent TV grew up to be three times as likely to commit crimes as boys who didn't watch such programs.

But that doesn't mean that *everyone* who watched violent programs ended up being violent themselves. It was just more likely to happen for some people.

In Action

Violent playing is even more powerful than violent watching, Bushman says. Maneuvering through a game requires kids to take action, identify with a character, and respond to rewards for rough behavior. Engaging in such activities reinforces effective learning, researchers say.

In the game *Carmageddon,* for example, players get extra points for plowing over elderly or pregnant pedestrians in creative ways. Players hear screams and squishing sounds.

"In a video game, you naturally identify with the violent character, and identification with violent characters increases aggression," Bushman says. "You're the person who pulls the trigger, who stabs, who shoots, who kicks. You must identify with the aggressor because you *are* the aggressor."

Now, I know what some of you are thinking: Maybe people who are already violent to begin with are the ones who seek out violent media.

"Video games may have an influence on human behavior or mentality, but I believe that whoever plays the game already has . . . a violent intent or nature within," writes Jason, 16. "I strongly doubt a nun whom you could somehow get to play *Mortal Kombat* for a while would eventually gain a violent personality or behave as such."

Jake, 15, says, "I think it depends on how the kids were raised more than anything, and if people try to play life like a game then they are IDIOTS."

But the University of Michigan study of TV watching found that people who were more aggressive as kids didn't necessarily watch more violent shows as adults. This finding suggests that watching violence leads to acting violently, not the other way around.

Inflicting Punishment

In some of Bushman's studies, kids are randomly assigned to play either a violent video game, such as *Killzone* or *Doom 3,* or an exciting, but nonviolent, game, such as *MarioKart* or a *Tony Hawk* skateboarding game, for about 20 minutes.

Then, each participant competes with a kid in another room on a task that challenges both players to press a button as quickly as possible. The winner gets to punish the loser with a blast of noise through a pair of headphones. The winner decides how long the noise will last and how loud it will be on a scale from 1 to 10.

In one of these studies, players were told that blasting their partners at level 8 or above would cause permanent hearing damage. (For safety reasons, the invisible competitor in this study was imaginary, but the setup made participants believe that they actually had the power to make another person suffer a hearing loss.)

The results showed that kids who played violent games first, then went to the task, delivered louder noises to their competitors than did kids who played nonviolent games first. Kids who played violent games *and* felt strongly connected to their on-screen characters sometimes delivered enough noise to make their invisible partners go deaf.

Because kids in these studies don't get to choose which games they play, it seems clear that playing violent games directly causes aggressive behavior, Bushman concludes.

And that aggressive behavior may appear not as criminal activity or physical violence but in more subtle ways in the ways people react to or interact with other people in everyday life.

Brain Studies

Some scientists are looking at kids' brains to see how video games might affect their behavior. In one recent study, researchers from the Indiana University (IU) School of Medicine in Indianapolis assigned 22 teenagers to play a violent game for 30 minutes. Another 22 kids played a nonviolent, exciting game.

> Brains scans show that the brains of teens playing nonviolent games and those of teens playing violent games have different patterns of activity. Those who played violent games showed greater activity in a region of the brain associated with strong emotions and less activity in a region associated with planning, focus, and self-control.
>
> Indiana University School of Medicine

Then, participants entered a special scanner that measured activity in their brains. For the next hour or so, the teens had to react to mind-bending tasks, such as pressing the "3" button when presented with three pictures of the number "1," or pressing the "blue" button when presented with the word "red" written in blue letters.

The results showed that a part of the brain called the amygdala was especially active in players in the violent-game group, especially when follow-up tasks required them to respond to loaded words, such as "hit" and "kill." The amygdala prepares the body to fight or flee in high-stress situations.

Moreover, among players in the violent-game group, a part of the brain called the frontal lobe was less active. The frontal lobe helps us stop ourselves from hitting, kicking, and performing other aggressive acts.

Frame of Mind

Findings such as these don't mean that every kid who plays *Grand Theft Auto* will end up in jail, researchers say. Nor do they suggest that video games are the single cause of violence in our society. From the brain's point of view, however, playing a violent game puts a kid in a fighting frame of mind.

"Maybe [kids have] figured out ways to control this but maybe they haven't," says IU radiologist Vincent Matthews, who led the brain-scan study.

"If they look at their behavior more closely, they may be more impulsive after they play these games," he adds. "There's a lot of denial in people about what their behavior is like."

Matthews now wants to see how long these brain changes last and whether it's possible to change the brain to its original state.

> Brain-scan studies at Michigan State University showed that playing violent video games leads to brain activity associated with aggressive thoughts.
>
> Courtesy of Michigan State University

Danger Zone

It's important that kids understand the risks of violent media, Bushman says. Studies show that virtual fighting is just as likely to make a kid act aggressively as is drug abuse, a troubled home life, or poverty.

"The link between violent media and aggression is stronger than the link between doing homework and getting good grades," Bushman says. "These games are not good for society."

Government agencies and medical organizations have been warning parents and kids about the dangers of violent media for decades. Like smoking and fast food, Bushman says, violent games are a danger we would all be better off without.

The Overdominance of Computers

Our students need inner resources and real-life experiences to balance their high-tech lives.

Lowell W. Monke

The debate chums on over the effectiveness of computers as learning tools. Although there is a growing disillusionment with the promise of computers to revolutionize education, their position in schools is protected by the fear that without them students will not be prepared for the demands of a high-tech 21st century. This fallback argument ultimately trumps every criticism of educational computing, but it is rarely examined closely.

Lets start by accepting the premise of the argument: Schools need to prepare young people for a high-tech society. Does it automatically follow that children of all ages should use high-tech tools? Most people assume that it does, and that's the end of the argument. But we don't prepare children for an automobile-dependent society by finding ways for 10-year-olds to drive cars, or prepare people to use alcohol responsibly by teaching them how to drink when they are 6. My point is that preparation does not necessarily warrant early participation. Indeed, preparing young people quite often involves strengthening their inner resources—like self-discipline, moral judgment, and empathy—before giving them the opportunity to participate.

Great Power and Poor Preparation

The more powerful the tools—and computers are powerful—the more life experience and inner strength students must have to handle that power wisely. On the day my Advanced Computer Technology classroom got wired to the Internet, it struck me that I was about to give my high school students great power to harm a lot of people, and all at a safe distance. They could inflict emotional pain with a few keystrokes and never have to witness the tears shed. They could destroy hours of work accomplished by others who were not their enemies—just poorly protected network users whose files provided convenient bull's-eyes for youth flexing newfound technical muscles.

I also realized that it would take years to instill the ethical discipline needed to say *no* to flexing that technical power. Young people entering my course needed more firsthand experiences guided by adults. They needed more chances to directly connect their own actions with the consequences of those actions, and to reflect on the outcomes, before they started using tools that could trigger serious consequences on the other side of the world.

Students need more than just moral preparation. They also need authentic experiences. As more students grow up spending much of their time in environments dominated by computers, TV, and video games, their diminished experience with real, concrete things prevents them from developing a rich understanding of what they study on computers. The computer is a purely symbolic environment; users are always working with abstract representations of things, never with the things themselves. In a few months my students could learn to build complex relational databases and slick multimedia presentations. But unless they also had a deep knowledge of the physical world and community relationships, they would be unable to infuse depth and meaning into the information they were depicting and discussing.

Do Computers Help Achievement?

Educational technology researchers, who tend to suffer from a severe inability to see the forest for the trees, typically ignore the impact that saturating society with computers and other screen environments is having on children. University of Munich economists Thomas Fuchs and Ludger Woessmann recently examined data from a study of 174,000 15-year-olds in 31 nations who took the Programme for International Student Assessment tests. They found, after controlling for other possible influences, that the more access students had to computers in school and at home, the *lower* their overall test scores were (2004). The authors suggest that rather than inherently motivating young people or helping them learn, computers more likely distract them from their studies. But there may be other problems behind this phenomenon that point to inherent contradictions in the use of educational technology.

For example, although we know that computer programs can help small children learn to read, we also know that face-to-face interaction is one of the most important ingredients in reading readiness (Dodici, Draper, & Peterson, 2003). As a result of increased time spent with computers, video games, and TV the current generation of elementary students will experience an estimated 30 percent fewer face-to-face encounters than the previous generation (Hammel, 1999). Thus, teachers may be employing the very devices for remediating reading problems that helped cause the problems in the first place.

Nearly everything children do today involves technologies that distance them from direct contact with the living world.

The issue is not just balancing computer time with other activities in schools. Both inside and outside school, children's lives are dominated by technology. Nearly everything a child does today—from chatting with friends to listening to music to playing games—tends to involve the use of technologies that distance children from direct contact with the living world. If the task of schools is to produce men and women who live responsible, fulfilling lives—not just human cogs for the high-tech machinery of commerce—then we should not be intensifying children's high-tech existence but compensating for it. Indeed, as advanced technology increasingly draws us toward a mechanical way of thinking and acting, it becomes crucial that schools help students develop their distinctly human capacities. What we need from schools is not balance in using high technology, but an effort to balance children's machine-dominated lives.

To prepare children to challenge the cold logic of the spreadsheet-generated bottom line, we need to teach them to value what that spreadsheet cannot factor in: commitment, loyalty, and tradition. To prepare them to find meaning in the abstract text and images encountered through screens, we need to first engage them in physical realities that screen images can only symbolize. To fit students to live in an environment filled with human-made products, we need to first help them know and respect what cannot be manufactured: the natural, the living, the wild. To prepare students to live well-grounded lives in a world of constant technological change, we need to concentrate their early education on things that endure.

The Cost of Failing to Compensate

Anyone who has spent time in schools knows that what is keeping today's youth from succeeding academically has nothing to do with a lack of technical skills or access to computers. Rather, it is the lack of qualities like hope, compassion, trust, respect, a sense of belonging, moral judgment, stability, community support, parental care, and teacher competence and enthusiasm that keeps so many students imprisoned in ignorance.

Ironically, what students will most need to meet the serious demands of the 21st century is the wisdom that grows out of these inner human capacities and that is developed by community involvement. If the 20th century taught us anything at all, it should have been that technology can be a very mixed blessing. Children entering elementary schools today will eventually have to wrestle with the mess that their elders have left them because of our own lack of wisdom about technology's downside: global warming, increasingly lethal weapons, nuclear waste, overdependence on automobiles, overuse of pesticides and antibiotics, and the general despoiling of our planet. They will also have to take on ethical conundrums posed by advanced technology, such as what to do about cloning, which decisions are off-limits to artificial intelligence devices, and whether or not parents should be allowed to "enhance" the genetic makeup of their offspring (only the wealthy need apply).

Those decisions should not be left to technicians in labs, CEOs in boardrooms, or politicians in debt to those who stand to profit from the technology. Our children should be at the decision tables as adults, and we want them to be able to stand apart from high technology and soberly judge its benefits and detriments to the entire human race.

How can young people develop the wisdom to judge high technology if they are told from the moment they enter school, implicitly if not explicitly, that they need high-tech tools to learn, to communicate, to think? Having been indoctrinated early with the message that their capacity to deal with the world depends not on their own internal resources but on their use of powerful external machines, how can students even imagine a world in which human beings impose limits on technological development or use?

Where to Go from Here
Keep to Essentials in the Early Years

So how, specifically, should educators make decisions and policies about the appropriateness of digital technologies for students of different ages?

One approach to tackling this dilemma comes from the Alliance for Childhood. During the last eight years, the Alliance (whose board of directors I serve on) has engaged educators, children's health professionals, researchers, and technology experts in developing guidelines for structuring a healthy learning environment for children, and has developed a list of essential conditions. Educators should ask themselves to what extent heavy use of computers and the Internet provides children in the lower grades with these essential school experiences:

- Close, lining relationships with responsible adults.
- Outdoor activity, nature exploration, gardening, and other encounters with nature.
- Time for unstructured play as part of the core curriculum.
- Music, drama, puppetry, dance, painting, and the other arts, both as separate classes and as a catalyst to bring other academic subjects to life.

- Hands-on lessons, handicrafts, and other physically engaging activities that provide effective first lessons for young children in the sciences, mathematics, and technology.
- Conversation with important adults, as well as poetry, storytelling, and hearing books read aloud.

This vision places a high priority on a child's direct encounters with the world and with other living beings, but it does not reject technology. On the contrary, tools are an important part of the vision. But at the elementary level, the tools should be simple, putting less distance between the student and the world and calling forth the students own internal resources.

Schools must also be patient with children's development. It would strike anyone as silly to give the smallest student in a 2nd grade class a scooter so that the child could get around the track as fast as the other kids his or her age. But our society shows decreasing willingness to wait for the natural emergence of students' varying mental and emotional capacities. We label students quickly and display an almost pathological eagerness to apply external technical fixes (including medications) to students who often simply aren't ready for the abstract, academic, and sedentary environment of today's early elementary classrooms. Our tendency to turn to external tools to help children cope with demands that are out of line with their tactile and physically energetic nature reflects the impact that decades of placing faith in technical solutions has had on how we treat children.

Study Technology in Depth After Elementary School

After children have had years to engage in direct, firsthand experiences, and as their abstract thinking capacities emerge more fully, it makes sense to gradually introduce computers and other complex, symbolic environments. Computer hardware and software should also become the focus of classroom investigation. A student in a technological society surrounded by black boxes whose fundamental principles he or she does not understand is as functionally illiterate as a student in a world filled with books that he or she can't read. The only thing worse would be to make technology "invisible," preventing children from even being aware of their ignorance.

By high school, digital technologies should take a prominent place in students' studies, both as tools of learning and as tools to learn about. During the last two years of high school, teachers should spend considerable time outfitting students with the high-tech skills they will need when they graduate. This "just-in-time" approach to teaching technical skills is far more efficient—instructionally and financially—than continually retraining younger students in technical skills soon to be obsolete. In addition, students at all education levels should consciously examine technology's role in human affairs.

Techno-Byte

Percentage of U.S. students who used computers in school in 2003:

- 97 percent of high school students.
- 95 percent of middle school students.
- 91 percent of students in grades 1–5.
- 80 percent of kindergarten students.
- 67 percent of nursery school students.

—National Center for Education Statistics, 2005

I am not suggesting that we indiscriminately throw computers out of classrooms. But I do believe it's time to rethink the past decision to indiscriminately throw them in. The result of that rethinking would be, I hope, some much-needed technological modesty, both in school and eventually in society in general. By compensating for the dominance of technology in students' everyday lives, schools might help restore the balance we need to create a more humane society

The irony of postmodern education is that preparing children for a high-tech future requires us to focus our attention more than ever before on the task of understanding what it means to be human, to be alive, to be part of both social and biological communities—a quest for which technology is increasingly becoming not the solution but the problem.

References

Dodici, B. J., Draper, D. C., & Peterson, C. A. (2003). Early parent-child interactions and early literacy development. *Topics in Early Childhood Special Education, 23*(3), 124–136.

Fuchs, T., & Woessmann, L. (2004, November). *Computers and student learning: Bivariate and multivariate evidence on the availability and use of computers at home and at school.* CESifo Working Paper Series (#1321). Available: www.cesifo.de/~DocCIDL/1321.pdf

Hammel, S. (1999, Nov. 29). Generation of loners? Living their lives online. *US. News and World Report,* p. 79.

LOWELL W. MONKE is Assistant Professor at Wittenberg University in Springfield, Ohio; 937-342-8648; lmonke@wittenberg.edu.

Author's note—The Alliance for Childhood has produced two publications to help parents and educators guide children toward a healthier relationship with technology: *Fool's Gold: A Critical Look at Computers in Childhood,* and *Tech Tonic: Towards a New Literacy of Technology* (both available online at www.allianceforchildhood.org).

Bullying at School among Older Adolescents

SANDRA HARRIS, PhD

The Justice Department's Bureau of Justice Statistics and the Department of Education's National Center for Education Statistics (2001) reported that overall juvenile crime rates have dropped since 1992 from 48 crimes per 1,000 students ages 12 through 18 to 33 per 1,000 students. At the same time, data indicated that students who said they were victims of any crime of violence or theft at school decreased from 10% to 8%. However, before the 2003–04 school year had even completed the first quarter, there had been school shootings in and around Chicago and Minnesota, gang feuds in Arizona, stabbings in Texas and Florida, apparent murder-suicides in California and Kentucky; and armed students in standoffs in Washington and California (Toppo, 2003).

Many argue that school violence is a product of a sense of escalating alienation and rage that seems to exist in many of today's young people. The fuel for this violence is often considered to be school bullying. In fact, a 2002 report by the Families and Work Institute interviewed 2,000 students and found that small things, such as teasing, often trigger serious episodes of violence. On school campuses, studies have found anywhere from 20% to 30% of students are frequently involved in bullying incidents either as the victim or the bully (Juvonen, Graham, & Schuster, 2003). Consequently, high school students report that bullying has seriously affected their physical, social, and academic well-being.

Bullying is intentionally harmful, aggressive behavior of a more powerful person or group of people directed repeatedly toward a less powerful person, usually without provocation. The most common form of bullying among adolescents is verbal—name calling and hurtful teasing. Bullying also includes threatening gestures, hitting, stealing, spreading rumors, intentionally excluding others, and using weapons to threaten or harm. Sexual harassment is another harmful form of bullying that increases in adolescence. In fact, Stein (1995) has noted that even as early as kindergarten there appears to be bullying conduct with sexual overtones.

High school bullies tend to pick on students who don't fit in. Boys tend to select victims who are physically weak, who are short tempered, based on who their friends are, or by their clothing. Girls, on the other hand, choose victims based on looks, emotionalism, being overweight, or who get good grades.

Being a victim of school bullying causes students to feel less connected with the high school, which often leads to poor physical health, lowered participation in extra-curricular events, violence, substance use, and suicide (Resnick et al., 1997). The ability to form natural relationships is often impaired and this rejection by peers often leads to emotional disturbances in adulthood (Ross, 1996). In high school, victims of bullying are more anxious than their high school peers, are likely to be targeted for racism or actions that cross traditionally accepted gender behaviors (such as sexual orientation), and have poorer relationships with classmates and feel lonelier than bullies, especially boys (Nansel et al., 2001).

High school students are more likely to bully with ridicule, rejection, and other forms of emotional abuse, rather than using physical bullying.

While bullies demonstrate some of the same characteristics as their victims, they are more likely to be depressed than their victims; hold higher social status than victims; use alcohol and smoke; have poorer academic achievement and perceive a poorer school climate. They are more likely to manifest defiant behavior (Nansel et al., 2001) and are more likely to have racist attitudes (Ross, 1996). The students that seem to be the most seriously affected by bullying are the bully/victims. Bully/victims are more likely to smoke, drink and have poorer academic achievement than victims; and have poorer relationships with classmates and are lonelier than bullies (Nansel et al., 2001). They also need to retaliate following acts of aggression against them (Glover et al., 2000).

Table 1 What Kind of Bullying Do Students Observe at School?

	Never	Sometimes	Often
Being Called Names	485 (26%)	880 (47%)	503 (27%)
Being Left out of Activities	607 (33%)	792 (43%)	441 (24%)
Teasing	697 (37%)	846 (45%)	320 (17%)
Hit/Kicked	999 (53%)	665 (35%)	211 (11%)
Threatened	1,082 (58%)	619 (33%)	178 (9%)

Note. n = 1,893

Because stealing and sexual harassment were not included in earlier surveys, those categories are not reported here.

Table 2 Where Do Students Observe Bullying at School?

	Never	Sometimes	Often
Classroom	315 (17%)	1,162 (62%)	398 (21%)
Lunchroom	473 (25%)	1,051 (56%)	348 (19%)
At Break	556 (32%)	879 (50%)	319 (18%)
Extracurricular Events	676 (36%)	977 (52%)	215 (12%)
Initiations of Clubs/Athletics	924 (50%)	786 (42%)	147 (8%)
On the Way Home from School	1,137 (61%)	602 (32%)	123 (7%)
On the Way to School	1,279 (70%)	465 (25%)	83 (5%)

Note. n = 1,893

Because students frequently wrote in "restrooms" and "hallways" these locations were added to later surveys, but those categories are not reported here.

Study Design

It has only been within the last few years that bully studies have been done in the United States and many of these studies have concentrated on children and young adolescents. Since 2000, my colleagues and I have conducted several studies on bullying. For this article, I used data from students in grades 8–12 to gain an understanding of bullying among older adolescents.

Participants in the study included 1,893 students in grades 8–12. Ethnic breakdown of participating students was 11% African American, 22% Hispanic, and 77% Anglo. Fifty-one percent were boys and 49% girls. Twenty-two percent of the participants were in the 8th grade, 53% were in the 9th grade, 14% were in the 10th grade, 8% were in the 11th grade, and 3% were in the 12th grade.

A diverse group of schools were represented. They were located in rural and suburban areas in Texas, Georgia, and Nebraska, and sizes varied from a small school of 250 students to a large high school of 1,500 students. Schools were selected based on convenience to the researchers and willingness of administrators to permit the studies. None of the school leaders thought that they had a problem with bullying.

The survey sought to gather data regarding the types of bullying that occurred, where bullying took place, how safe students felt at school, how bullying made them feel, who they told when they were bullied, and how interested they felt their teachers and administrators were in stopping bullying. Surveys were administered in English classes or in physical education classes by the regular classroom teacher from 1999–2004. Since the survey was revised several times during this time frame, only selected questions on each survey were used. The survey has a reliability alpha of. 69, which is appropriate.

Findings

What kind of bullying do students observe at school? As can be seen from Table 1, the most common form of bullying at school was being called names, followed by being left out of activities and teasing. Other studies have reported similar findings, noting that high school students are more likely to bully with ridicule, rejection, and other forms of emotional abuse, rather than using physical bullying (Juvonen etal., 2003).

Where do students observe bullying at school? When students were asked how often they observed bullying in certain school locations, surprisingly, 83% identified the classroom as a place where bullying occurred at least sometimes. Seventy-four percent of the students reported that the lunchroom was a place where bullying occurred at least sometimes. (See Table 2).

Student Experiences Being Bullied. While 60% of students indicated that they were never bullied at school, an alarming 16% reported that they were bullied at least once a week, while 24% reported being bullied less than once a week. When students were asked how it made them feel when they were bullied at school, 15% admitted that it made them feel angry, and 16% said they felt sad and miserable. Thirty-four percent of students indicted that it did not bother them when they were bullied.

We asked students who they would tell if they were bullied or if they became aware of someone being bullied. Forty-six percent said they would tell a friend, 27% would tell their mother, and 14% would tell their father. However, only 13% of students would tell a teacher or an administrator.

Only half of the students responded to the next question which asked if students had told someone about being bullied and, if so, what happened. Nearly 37% reported that when they told, things got better. However, 17% said they never told anyone that they had been bullied, 37% reported that nothing changed even though they told, and 9% admitted that when they told the bullying only became worse.

A critical element in reducing bullying is the leadership of adults.

How safe do students feel at school? Despite the high reported occurrences of bullying, 39% of students reported that they always felt safe at school, and 45% indicated that they usually felt safe. However, 16% of students admitted that they did not feel very safe when they were at school. Consequently, 9% of students reported that they had even stayed home from school at least once because of bullying and 14% said they had considered staying home.

How interested is the faculty? When asked if administrators were interested in stopping bullying at school, 24% of students did not think that they were; while 34% admitted that they were not sure how administrators felt about this. Only 42% of students believed that administrators were interested in stopping bullying. Students felt nearly the same way about their teachers, with 22% admitting that they did not think teachers were interested in stopping bullying and 33% were not sure how their teachers felt. Only 45% felt that teachers were interested in stopping bullying.

The Dismal Conclusions

This study looked at 1,893 self-reports of older adolescents about bullying and findings suggested the following conclusions:

- Three out of four students are aware of name-calling, students being left out of activities, and teasing at least sometimes at school
- Bullying happens at many places on the campus, even locations where there is teacher supervision, such as the classroom

Bullying at School among Older Adolescents

- Nearly one-third of students admit that being bullied causes them to feel sad and miserable, or angry
- A small percentage of students tell school faculty about being bullied; and when they do tell, for more than one-third, nothing changes, and for a small but significant number of students, things get worse
- Over one-half of students are not convinced that administrators or teachers are interested in stopping bullying

What Can We Do about Bullying at School?

A critical element in reducing bullying is the leadership of adults. Lazarus (1996) identified the importance of adults in helping young people cope with stressful situations. Likewise in the early 1970s, Daniel Olweus led Sweden and Norway to implement an anti-bullying campaign characterized by adult involvement as a critical component. Two years later, incidents of bullying had been reduced by 50% (Olweus, 1993). Yet, too often, teachers cannot identify bullies or victims at school (Leff, Kupersmidt, Patterson & Power, 1999). Due in part to a lack of trust in adults, students very rarely break the "code of silence" to "rat" on bullies. Furthermore, studies indicate

that adults are not viewed by students as being committed to reducing bullying at school (Rigby, 1996). In fact, teachers are not even sure if other teachers are committed to reducing bullying, nor, they admit, do they know how to help when they do become aware of bullying (Harris & Willoughby, 2003).

Building on the importance of adult involvement, the following model for reducing bullying at school is recommended (Harris & Willoughby, 2003)

- **Be Aware.** Adults must first recognize bullying as harmful and a precursor to more severe forms of school violence.
  Strategies: Participate in training to recognize bullies and victims; survey students, teachers, and parents regularly to identify kinds of bullying and locations on campus that are high risk; increase supervision; and develop school policies that define bullying.
- **Build Trusting Relationships.** Adults must develop a culture of trust and respect on the campus.
  Strategies: Talk with students in class discussions about bullying; encourage students to share how bullying makes them feel; be responsive to bullies' needs, as well as victims' needs; and show students that adults care about student achievement and about personal achievements.
- **Accept the Challenge to Provide Support.** Adults must be willing to accept the challenge to provide support for all students.
  Strategies: Accept the responsibility to advocate for students in need; present a united front that establishes behavior guidelines that emphasize bullying is not acceptable behavior; encourage students to tell when bullying occurs; involve parents; and be encouraged to support one another in preventing and intervening in bully situations.
- **Know How to Help.** Adults must have the skills to be able to respond appropriately to bullying situations.
  Strategies: Work collaboratively with school and community personnel to adopt school policies with anti-bully guidelines; create policies that address appropriate consequences that include counseling for the bully, as well as the victim; participate in training that provides strategies for supporting students.

Conclusion

Bullying breeds violence. It teases, torments, and taunts. While many young people ignore bullying or overcome it, some succumb to the pain it inflicts. Most suffer in silence, but a few turn to horrible acts of school violence, such as 15 year old Charles "Andy" Williams. He brought a revolver to school, fired 30 bullets, and killed two schoolmates and wounded 13 others. His father later said, "[they] accused him of being gay . . . they made fun of him for being a country boy, for his big ears. It didn't matter what he did, they made fun of him" (Booth & Snyder, 2001, A1, A6). When adults are aware, when they build trusting relationships, when they accept the challenge to provide support, and when they have the skills to know how to help hurting students, schools will be safer for everyone.

References

Booth, W., & Snyder, D. (2001). No remorse, no motive from shooting suspect. *San Antonio Express-News,* March 7, A1, A6.

Bureau of Justice Statistics and DOE National Center for Education Statistics. (2001). *Indicators of School Crime and Safety.* Washington, D.C.: Author.

Glover, D., Gough, G., Johnson, M., & Cartwight, N. (2000). Bullying in 25 secondary schools: Incidence, impact and intervention. *Educational Research, 42,* 141–156.

Harris, S., & Petrie, G. (2002). *Bullying: The Bullies, the Victims, the Bystanders.* Lanham, MD.: The Scarecrow Press, Inc.

Harris, S., & Willoughby, W. (2003). Teacher perceptions of student bullying behaviors. *ERS Spectrum, 21*(3), 11–18.

Juvonen, J., Graham, S., & Schuster, M. (2003). Bullying among young adolescents: The strong, the weak, and the troubled. *Pediatrics, 112*(6), 1,231–1,237.

Lazarus, R. (1966). *Psychological Stress and the Coping Process.* New York: McGraw-Hill.

Leff, S., Kupersmidt, J., Patterson, C., & Power, T. (1991). Factors influencing teacher identification of peer bullies and victims. *The School Psychology Review, 28*(3), 505–517.

Nansel, T., Overpeck, M., Pilla, R., Ruan, W., Simons-Morton, B., & Scheidt, P. (2001). Bullying behaviors among U.S. youth: Prevalence and association with psychosocial adjustment. *Journal of American Medical Association, 285*(16), 2,094–2,100.

Olweus, D. (1993). *Bullying at School.* Cambridge, MA: Blackwell Publishers, Inc.

Resnick, M., Bearman, P., Blum, R., Bauman, K., Harris, K., Jones, J. et al. (1997). Protecting adolescents from harm: Findings from the National Longitudinal Study on Adolescent Health. *Journal of the American Medical Association, 278,* 823–832.

Rigby, K. (1996). *Bullying in Schools: And What To Do About It.* London: Jessica Kingsley Publishers.

Ross, D. (1996). *Childhood Bullying and Teasing: What School Personnel, Other Professionals, and Parents Can Do.* Alexandria, VA.: American Counseling Association.

Stein, N. (1995). Sexual harassment in school: The public performance of gender violence. *Harvard Educational Review, 65,* 145–162.

Toppo, G. (2003, October 21). Troubling days at U.S. schools. *USA Today,* 1A, 2A

Sandra Harris received her PhD, in Educational Leadership from the University of Texas, Austin. She has more than 30 years of experience as a teacher and administrator and is currently an associate professor of educational leadership at Lamar University in Beaumont, Texas. She is the co-author of the book: *Bullying: The Bullies, the Victims, the Bystanders* (Scarecrow Press, 2003).

Underage Drinking Debate: Zero Tolerance vs. Teaching Responsibility

The federal government is in the early stages of an all-out effort to stop young people from consuming alcohol before they're 21—something that is illegal in every state. Citing evidence that someone who drinks before the age of 15 is 5 times more likely to develop alcohol problems later on than someone who waits until the age of 21, the federal government is spearheading an underage drinking prevention campaign. At the same time, however, concern is being raised that the campaign could backfire by driving underage drinking into hiding, particularly if parents are told not to allow their "children" (under age 21) to drink and schools are not allowed to teach responsible drinking.

The groundswell for the campaign started last fall with the unveiling of a public service ad campaign and the announcement by Surgeon General Richard H. Carmona, M.D., M.P.H., that he would issue a Call to Action on underage drinking. It was followed by the creation of the Interagency Coordinating Committee on the Prevention of Underage Drinking (ICCPUD), chaired by (SAMHSA) Administrator Charles G. Curie, M.A., A.C.S.W., and comprised of representatives from different federal agencies (see box).

The ICCPUD has three main goals: "strengthening the nation's commitment to fighting underage drinking, reducing the demand for and availability of alcohol among youth, and using research to improve the effectiveness of prevention." The call to action on underage drinking is still under development, mainly at the National Institute on Alcohol Abuse and Alcoholism (NIAAA), but Vice Admiral Carmona said at the time that it would ensure that "every single person in this country understands the negative health, social, and family consequences of underage drinking."

Harm Reduction

There's a challenge for prevention in the zero-tolerance message, said G. Alan Marlatt, Ph.D., professor of psychology and director of the Addictive Behavior Research Center at the University of Washington. "This just drives the drinking underground, which can have vast unintended consequences," Marlatt told CABL. These consequences include driving to remote places (and driving back drunk), and not getting help for someone who passed out because of fear of getting in trouble.

Marlatt recalls that when he was a college student, the drinking age was 18. "Students drank beer in the student union, and if someone was impaired, there was always someone there to help," he said. Now, that same college is one of the schools concerned about off-campus drinking. "The students are in the dark about how to handle it," Marlatt said.

But others, such as MADD (Mothers Against Drunk Driving), strongly believe in the zero-tolerance message. "Underage drinking is the number one drug problem, it's killing more kids than all other illicit drugs combined," Misty Moyse, spokesperson for MADD National. "When kids turn 21 they can drink, as long as they don't get behind the wheel of a car." Until then, however, they—and their parents, need a "clear and consistent" message.

'Overmoralizing'

James Mosher, director of the Center for the Study of Law and Enforcement Policy at the Pacific Institute for Research and Evaluation (PIRE), agrees. But "moralism" should not be a part of the campaign, said Mosher, who has developed a model civil ordinance regarding underage drinking. The focus should not be on the child, but on the situations that adults allow to take place—and shouldn't —he said. "The debate between the zero tolerance folks and the harm reduction folks takes the focus away from the context of situations for young people and puts it all on individual responsibility," he said. "There's way too much overmoralizing on both sides." Instead, what is needed is a "non-moralistic message" that is similar to the one Surgeon General Everett Koop had for AIDS, said Mosher. In this message, Koop focused on preventing HIV transmission by encouraging safe sex, rather than abstinence. "It's a really important message, one directed at risk."

Members of Interagency Coordinating Committee on the Prevention of Underage Drinking

U.S. Department of Defense

Office of the Assistant Secretary of Defense (Health Affairs)

U.S. Department of Education

Office of Safe and Drug-Free Schools

U.S. Department of Health and Human Services

Administration for Children and Families

Centers for Disease Control and Prevention

National Institute on Alcohol Abuse and Alcoholism

Office of the Surgeon General

Substance Abuse and Mental Health Services Administration

U.S. Department of Justice

Office of Juvenile Justice and Delinquency Prevention

U.S. Department of Transportation

National Highway Traffic Safety Administration

U.S. Department of Treasury

Alcohol and Tobacco Tax and Trade Bureau

Office of National Drug Control Policy

Federal Trade Commission (ex officio)

Bureau of Consumer Protection

Reach Out Now Teach-Ins

Reach Out Now is a collaboration by SAMHSA, HHS, and Scholastic to provide school-based, underage alcohol use prevention materials in time for Alcohol Awareness Month each April. It is designed for use by 5th and 6th grade students, families, and teachers.

At the end of the lesson, students should be able to:

- Describe some of the effects of alcohol on the brain and body
- Identify effective alternatives to using alcohol
- Work in groups to develop an effective alcohol prevention message

Teach-Ins will be conducted nationwide during the week of April 3-7, 2006, the first week of Alcohol Awareness Month.

For more information, go to **www.teachin.samhsa.gov**

From a policy standpoint, the focus should be on situations that put young people at risk, he says. "The research is getting increasingly clear that the highest risk events are at teen parties," he said. "We want to reduce the likelihood of these parties, and if they do happen, we want there to be more responsibility for them." The person responsible should be the property owner—the parent, or the landlord, he said.

Parenting

The main issue is that drinking under the age of 21 is illegal, noted Vivian B. Faden, Ph.D., deputy director of NIAAA's division of epidemiology and prevention research. Whether parents can serve alcohol to their own children is largely dependent on state laws, but there are still "unanswered questions" about the effects of scenarios such as parents serving a glass of wine at a family dinner to their child. "We don't know if that leads to better or worse outcomes," said Faden.

"Certainly giving alcohol to children other than your own or hosting a party in your home is to be discouraged,"

Faden told *CABL*. "But we don't have the research on drinking with your children at home in the states where it's legal." And Faden notes that parenting includes teaching responsibility. "Kids need to learn to be responsible about a lot of things—school, work, sexual behavior," she said. "Part of teaching children responsibility is having them understand what's legal and what's not legal. And illegal drinking is not responsible drinking."

Mosher strongly agrees that parents should not "teach" children how to drink. "If it's not the norm, you shouldn't make it be the norm," he said. "I'm not going to say kids can't have a glass of wine with their parents at Christmas. Parents giving wine at the dinner table isn't a public health concern. But I'm also not going to tell children how to drink."

The situation might be different if a drinking norm is already under way, according to Marlatt. He gave a seminar with seniors at a private high school in Seattle, where students were planning to go on to college the next year. Most were drinking already, so a harm reduction rather than abstinence approach was used, with the focus on the risks and benefits of drinking. "A principal at a private school in Seattle said he knew kids were drinking, and also one had died the previous year on prom night," Marlatt told *CABL*. "His feeling was, let's be realistic."

Marlatt said he wouldn't be able to give this course in public school. "Public schools aren't allowed to teach harm reduction because of alcohol- and drug-free requirements," he said.

And Mosher of PIRE said that's a good thing. "A responsible drinking message has not ever been shown to have responsible drinking results," he said. "And the fact is that the majority of college students don't drink at all.

The message should be: drinking causes terrible problems, and it's perfectly appropriate at your age not to drink, or to drink very, very little."

More will be heard from the federal government on the underage drinking initiative, particularly when the Surgeon General's Call to Action is released some time this spring. Around the same time, communities around the nation will hold town hall meetings on underage drinking around the country—1,500 communities can each get $1,000 stipends from SAMHSA for these meetings. All Drug-Free Communities Support Program grantees will be offered stipends, and remaining funds will go to communities identified by ICCPUD teams.

These town hall meetings are expected to bring together different groups concerned about underage drinking, with light shed on the problem by the ICCPUD and NIAAA. Communities who receive the stipends are expected to use SAMHSA "Teach In" materials in their schools.

Problem Gambling in Youth— A Hidden Addiction

KEITH WHYTE

Pathological gambling (PG) is commonly referred to as a "hidden" addiction. While in recent years, PG in adults has been recognized as an addiction that can be diagnosed and treated, PG among youth remains relatively unrecognized. Yet, a national survey indicates that the rate of pathological gambling in youth is higher than that in adults (Welte, 2002), possibly as distinct as 5% versus 1%, respectively (NCPG). And as in adults, gambling in children and adolescents has been linked to higher rates of problem behaviors, including substance abuse, violence, stealing and risky sexual behaviors (NCPG).

"Gambling in kids could very well be the gateway behavior that we used to believe marijuana was," Keith Whyte recently told *CABL*. "Scattered studies and emerging evidence suggest that early onset of gambling should be a big indicator for people to look for additional problems."

What's Changed?

"It's always been easy to gamble," Whyte admitted, "just find a deck of cards." So, what's changed? Is gambling on the rise among youth? And if so, why?

Surveys show that an increasing majority of youth gamble; while in the year 2000 roughly 80% of kids between the ages of 12 and 17 reported gambling in the past year, an increase from about 65% ten years ago (Turchi, 2005). The most popular gambling activities among youth include poker playing, betting on sports and online card playing. Rewards are sometimes monetary, but often kids are playing for coveted items like a pair of sneakers or an item of clothing, which makes the stakes seem less severe.

Rick Zehr, the Vice President of Addiction and Behavioral Services at Proctor Hospital in Peoria, Illinois, told *CABL* that today, gambling is widely considered an acceptable form of youth recreation, commonly endorsed by parents and largely overlooked by school administrators.

"You have to realize that for most of these kids, gambling has been legal for their entire lives," said Zehr. "This is the first generation for which it's really a part of the culture. It's a very acceptable activity and it has become more and more popular."

When Is Gambling a Problem?

The NCPG describes the array of gambling behaviors as ranging from "no gambling" or "social gambling" on one end of the spectrum, to "problem" and then "pathological" gambling at the other extreme.

Most clinicians distinguish between pathological gambling (PG) and problem gambling.

Problem gamblers are those individuals with gambling-related problems, including mildly affected individuals who do not meet clinical diagnostic criteria. (Hollander, 2000)

Pathological gambling is classified in the DSM-IV-TR under Impulse Control Disorders Not Elsewhere Classified. One theory holds that PG is a non-chemical addictive disorder.

In a paper calling for "an improved understanding of the biological processes underlying PG" Potenza and colleagues write, "PG is shares many similarities with the diagnostic criteria for substance dependence, e.g., tolerance, withdrawal, repeated attempts to quit or cut back, and interference in major areas of life function due to engagement in the problematic activity." (Potenza et al., 2001a).

Although gambling activities are harmless in the majority of children, it is estimated that 10 to 15% of gambling adolescents are at risk of developing problem gambling, while 1–6% become pathological gamblers (NCPG).

Studies suggest that the earlier the age of onset of gambling habits, the greater the risk for developing pathological behavior. Many adult pathological gamblers in treatment report they began gambling around the age of 11. Seventy percent of these adults are concurrently being treated for depression, and 50% for substance abuse problems (NCPG).

Screening for Gambling Problems

Rick Zehr told *CABL* that he's run into difficulty convincing his clinician colleagues to pay adequate attention to PG in kids. "The first step is for them to become aware that this problem exists, that kids are running into problems," he explained. He suggested that clinicians should add a gambling screen to their

National Gambling Awareness Week

March 6–12, 2006 is National Gambling Awareness Week, sponsored by the National Council of Problem Gambling (NCPG) and the Association of Problem Gambling Service Administrators (APGSA). The goal of this multi-level public awareness and outreach campaign is to "educate the general public and medical professionals about the warning signs of problem gambling and raise awareness about the help that is available both locally and nationally." For more information, visit www.npgaw.org.

visits with teens, particularly those who show signs of other addictive behaviors. Those that show signs of problem gambling would probably benefit from an early intervention program or private counseling. Those who meet the DSM-IV-TR criteria for PG can be referred to a comprehensive recovery program.

Zehr cited a few screening devices that are brief and relatively effective in diagnosing gambling problems, such as the SOGS-RA (Lesieur, 1987), the Gamblers Anonymous 10-Question screen, or the two-question Lie-Bet Questionnaire (Johnson, 1988).

While pharmacotherapy trials of drugs like naltrexone (Grant, 2002) and nefazodone (Palanti, 2002) have shown relatively good results in adults, pharmacotherapy is not currently recommended to treat PG in youth.

Mixed Messages

According to the NCPG, adult gambling is now legal in 48 states, compared to less than a dozen in 1976. Although gambling is illegal for anyone under 18 to 21, depending on state law, television shows depict poker playing as an exciting and legitimate form of recreation where people can get rich quickly. The National Annenberg Risk Survey of Youth (NARSY) conducted in 2003 and again in 2004 found that card playing is on the rise among male youth ages 14 to 22; in 2004, 10.8% male youth attending high school reported betting on cards at least once a week, up from 5.7% in 2003.

The Internet is believed to have contributed significantly to the growing popularity of gambling, although use is difficult to measure. The NARSY showed that in 2004, 11.4% of young weekly card players also gambled weekly on the Internet. Whyte explained that technology has made gambling a faster more exciting game, exactly the kind of activity that appeals to a teenager.

With states pouring money into promoting lotteries and an estimated fifty percent of youth gambling with their own family members (NCPG), said Whyte, "I don't think we've done a good job of considering the message we're sending to kids."

"Don't Gamble Away Our Future"

Rick Zehr believes that the Illinois Institute for Addiction Recovery (IIAR), located at Proctor Hospital in Peoria, is one of the very few in the country that has made gambling screens a regular practice, and possibly the only one that goes out of its way to educate youth about problem gambling. "I can count on one hand the number of programs that address this problem," he said. "It saddens me."

The IIAR Early Intervention program works with teenagers (12-18 yrs) who may be engaging in at-risk behaviors such as compulsive use of food or the Internet, gambling problems, or process addictions. IIAR clinicians screen for gambling as part of a comprehensive addiction screen, and based upon these results, might refer for a complete assessment.

The most common co-morbid condition in adult pathological gamblers is past or present substance use disorder, which affects from 30% to 50% (Turchi, 2005). Bob Stenander, who works with youth in the IIAR, told *CABL* that among the children that visit their clinic, depression is the most common co-morbidity. And of all the addictions they treat, pathological gamblers have the highest rate of suicidal ideation, a clear indication, he said, of the need for a regular screen. Just a few questions, he insisted, will indicate if further screening is appropriate.

IIAR has recently expanded its work to include gambling education outreach in the schools. Zehr told *CABL* that a fortuitous meeting with the Office of Juvenile Justice led to the formation of this ambitious program, which has aspirations to go national. The program, titled "Don't Gamble Away Our Future," is implementing its pilot phase in Peoria and has a ten-year goal of reaching every school-age child in the U.S. with education, interactive CD-ROMs, and teacher and parent training.

Stenander is one of the trainers who visit schools to educate 4th through 12th graders about the risks associated with gambling. His approach with all ages is to keep things fun and interactive, and he's been pleased with the results. Stenander suggested that schools should address addiction, both process and chemical, as part of their health curriculum. "I have found that if the program is presented to the groups in a positive manner, with some humor, you will have a good response."

Looking Ahead

Stenander told *CABL* that the toughest part of his work is getting kids to understand that gambling can have the same adverse consequences that they know can come with using drugs and alcohol. "Our approach," said Stenander, "is to convey information that may not be important to the adolescent today but may be for future reference . . . when they may [be at risk for] developing an addiction."

Each student goes home with a packet of information to share with their parents. Stenander and his colleagues hope that the information will put parents on the alert for problem behavior in their children. Once gambling becomes pathological, treatment

Resources

- **The National Council on Problem Gambling:** www.ncpgambling.org
- **NCPG Helpline:** 1-800-522-4700.
- **The North American Training Institute (NATI)** is a Minnesota-based, not-for-profit organization that was created in 1988 to provide information, to facilitate research and conduct professional training about gambling addiction. www.nati.org; 218-722-1503 or 1-888989-9234.
- **The Illinois Institute for Addiction Recovery:** 1-800-522-3784.

"We (NCPG) know that prevention is what we need. But what little resources we have go toward crisis efforts, such as help lines."

—Keith Whyte, National Council of Problem Gambling

This could take years of outreach efforts such as those at Proctor Hospital. "It may take another generation for the impact of this problem to reach the public conscience," Whyte said. "We're watching some enormous societal shifts and our public policy response has not even begun to catch up."

is difficult. For trainers like Stenander, education and prevention are the keys to a long-term solution.

Keith Whyte is on the same page. He told *CABL,* "We (NCPG) know that prevention is what we need. But what little resources we have go toward crisis efforts, such as help lines. We think that just to get existing substance abuse programs to incorporate screening would greatly reduce the problem."

KEITH WHYTE is the executive director of the National Council on Problem Gambling (NCPG), the national advocate for programs and services to assist problem gamblers and their families. He emphasized that NCPG is not against gambling. Rather, they are concerned about gambling as a disease. Regarding gambling problems in youth, he said, "Nobody is paying attention, really looking at some of the societal indications. It hasn't received the attention it deserves."

Understanding Cutting in Adolescents: Prevalence, Prevention, and Intervention

JENNIFER DYL, PhD

Case: Amanda is a 14 year-old girl who just began her first year of high school at a large public school. Prior to starting school, she was excited, but also anxious about making new friends. Now, a couple of months into the school year, even though she says she has made some new friends, she doesn't bring them home to meet her parents. While she previously had been an A/B middle school student, she has difficulty focusing on her schoolwork, is distracted by trying to figure out her new school, and worries about fitting in. Her parents notice she spends a lot more time in her room by herself, and they are not sure what she is doing in there. Her parents are concerned because her mother has struggled with depression and worries Amanda could be too. Amanda recently left her My Space screen open and her parents saw a message she wrote to one of her friends about cutting herself. When they confronted her, she said "It's not a big deal," and she doesn't know why her parents are so upset about it.

Amanda's presentation is an increasingly common one in inpatient, community, and school settings. Cutting is the most prevalent form of the nonsuicidal self-injurious behaviors (NSSI), defined as purposely damaging bodily tissue without the intent to die. Other NSSI behaviors include burning, sniffing, head banging, bruising. Cutting may involve razors, knives, scissors, glass, paper clips, sharp fingernails, or any other sharp object.

Prevalence

Anecdotally, middle and high school educators are reporting increasing problems with students cutting and seek guidance on how to best address this troubling behavior, while clinicians also observe that cutting has risen in adolescent psychiatric settings in the last decade. Prevalence studies report rates of 5–47% in community adolescent samples, 12–35% among college students, and 4% in general adult populations, underscoring the vulnerability of the adolescent developmental period to this problem. Among adolescent psychiatric inpatients, rates of 39–61% have been reported. Empirical evidence also supports that the prevalence has increased in recent years.

Precipitating Factors
Sociocultural and developmental influences

Hypothesized influences contributing to the prevalence of cutting are multifactorial and include sociocultural factors such as the media and peer group influences, coupled with internal psychological factors and comorbid psychiatric conditions. Identified family factors have included difficulty tolerating the expression of strong or negative emotions, viewing parents as unavailable or disinterested, and parental substance abuse and psychological problems.

With regard to media influences, trends in music and media highlighting violent and self-injurious behaviors have been identified as possible influences. Disturbingly, there are internet web sites and chat rooms dedicated to self-injury, some of which glorify cutting as chic or a source of strength. Some schools have peer subgroups in which cutting is a requirement for becoming a member. There is additional speculation that adolescents are desensitized to self-injury because of the popularity of body piercings and tattoos, with some teens rationalizing that self-injury is an extension of these forms of body art.

Developmentally, adolescence is a time to hone a sense of identity through "trying on" various behaviors, beliefs, and roles through identification with peer groups, music, fashion, etc. While it may be normative for some adolescents to experiment with peer groups with alternative dress or musical interests (i.e., the "Goth" or "Emo" groups), it is not normative when the values of a peer group involve self-injurious behaviors. In psychologically vulnerable individuals (i.e., those with depression, anxiety, or difficulty managing emotions), cutting may begin to take on a life of its own, beyond efforts to fit in. There is also a sizable proportion of adolescents who begin to cut themselves secretively and/or in the absence of direct peer influences.

Psychological functions and vulnerability

Due to increased biological, emotional, social and academic changes, adolescents experience a range of strong emotions and interpersonal challenges and many have not yet learned mature coping skills to manage them. Cutting as a way to regulate emotions or as an attempt to solve interpersonal problems may impede normative socio-emotional problem-solving and the development of healthy coping and self-soothing skills.

Nock and Prinstein (2004) conceptualized contingencies for cutting as either *internal* or *social,* and reinforcement as either *positive* or *negative*. Adolescents most often report cutting for internal negative reinforcement (i.e., "to stop bad feelings" to "relieve feeling numb or empty"), internal positive reinforcement (i.e., "to feel something, even if it is pain," "to punish yourself," "to feel relaxed"), social negative reinforcement (i.e., "to avoid doing something unpleasant you do not want to do," "to avoid being with people") and social positive reinforcement (i.e., "to get attention" to "let others know how desperate you are," to "feel more part of a group"). There is some suggestion that internal factors may be more strongly related to a greater degree of psychiatric impairment, as these reasons for cutting are reported more frequently in inpatient adolescents, while internal and social factors are reported equally in community samples.

Clinically and empirically, cutters frequently report feeling temporary relief from or "blocking out" unpleasant emotional states (i.e., tension, anger, sadness, emptiness). Some report that cutting promotes a "release" of feelings, followed by a rapid reduction in tension and increased perception of psychological equilibrium. Particularly in individuals with comorbid dissociative symptoms or chronic feelings of numbness, cutting may also function to feel in touch with one's body or to "feel pain." Others report feeling temporary "control," followed by a sense of loss of control, shame, alienation, or helplessness. Cutting may also relate to low self-worth and a desire to punish oneself or may function as an inadequately channeled self-care ritual. Cutting may be seen as an alternative form of expression for those with difficulty verbalizing feelings.

Many also describe cutting as "addictive" and there has been some exploration of differences at the neurotransmitter level in self-injurers. Over time, cutting also becomes psychologically and behaviorally habit-forming, and one hypothesis is that with greater exposure to the behavior over time, fears of injury or other negative outcomes decline and the internal reward function increases. Many report needing to cut deeper over time and increasingly employ a wider variety of methods at greater frequency. Severity of cutting (frequency, degree of injury, variety of methods) also correlates with degree of psychopathology and with risk for more serious, life-threatening injuries. Research has found a subset of cutters who do attempt suicide and in those groups the cutting tends to be more frequent and varied in methodology.

In terms of comorbidity, depression and anxiety are consistently found to be related to cutting, while other associated conditions include conduct problems, substance abuse, suicidality, eating disorders, PTSD/dissociative disorders, and a history of abuse or trauma.

Prevention/Intervention

Given the strong association between cutting and psychiatric impairment, along with the possibility that cutting will increase, rather than decrease over time in the absence of treatment, it is imperative that the problem be taken seriously and addressed as early as possible.

It is important to address the problem without reinforcing the behavior. There should be a focus on the underlying feelings and function of the cutting, not on the physical effects of cutting itself. The idea is to help the teen find healthier ways to meet their interpersonal needs (i.e., the need to communicate, the need for attention) and better ways to regulate challenging emotions.

While a variety of treatment models may successfully address cutting, Cognitive Behavioral Therapy (CBT) and Dialectical Behavioral Therapy (DBT) may be particularly effective. Adolescents may be taught DBT skills such as mindfulness, emotional regulation, distress tolerance, and interpersonal effectiveness skills. These include normalizing emotions and helping adolescents "sit with" uncomfortable feelings, emphasizing that feelings are not the problem, but "how you deal with them." Other interventions may involve helping teens to talk about feelings or concerns rather than acting them out, as well as learning skills to self-soothe.

Physical exercises to relieve tension, breathing/relaxation, creative expressions such as journaling or artwork, and temporary distraction techniques may also be taught. Adolescents may be taught to identify triggers such as emotional reactions and cognitive distortions which may precipitate cutting so they can use skills to cope with these thoughts and feelings at an earlier point. Parents and clinicians should encourage positive peer group conformity and the development of feelings of control and self-efficacy through positive channels such as developing a skill or ability. Pharmacological treatment of co-occurring psychiatric disorders may also be helpful.

References

Nock MK, Prinstein MJ: A functional approach to the assessment of self-mutilative behavior. *J Consult Clin Psychol* 2004; 114: 140–146.

Lloyd-Richardson EE, Perrine N, Dierker L, Kelley ML: Characteristics and functions of non-suicidal self-injury in a community sample of adolescents. *Psychol Med* 2007; 37(9):1372.

Swenson LP, Spirito A, Dyl J, Kittler J, Hunt J: Psychological correlates of cutting behaviors in an adolescent inpatient sample. Under Review, *J Child Psychiatr Human Develop*.

DR. DYL is a staff psychologist at Bradley Hospital in the Adolescent Program and a clinical assistant professor in the Department of Psychiatry and Human Behavior at the Warren Alpert Medical School at Brown University.

Violence in Adolescent Dating Relationships

"The early-to mid-teenage years mark a time in which romantic relationships begin to emerge. From a developmental perspective, these relationships can serve a number of positive functions. However, for many adolescents, there is a darker side: dating violence."

ERNEST N. JOURILES, PHD, CORA PLATT, BA, AND RENEE MCDONALD, PHD

For many, the early- to mid-teenage years mark a time in which romantic relationships begin to emerge. From a developmental perspective, these relationships can serve a number of positive functions. However, for many adolescents, there is a darker side: dating violence. In this article, we discuss the definition and measurement of adolescent dating violence, review epidemiological findings regarding victimization, and describe correlates of victimization experiences. We end with a discussion of prevention and intervention programs designed to address adolescent dating violence and highlight important gaps in our knowledge.

Defining and Measuring Adolescent Dating and Dating Violence

"Dating" among adolescents is complicated to define and measure, in part because the nature of dating changes dramatically over the course of adolescence (Connolly et al., 1999; Feiring, 1996). In early adolescence, dating involves getting together with small groups of friends of both sexes to do things together as a group. From these group experiences, adolescents progress to going out with or dating a single individual. Initial single-dating relationships are typically casual and short-term; more serious, exclusive, and longer-lasting relationships emerge in mid- to late-adolescence.

"Dating" among adolescents is complicated to define and measure.

In research on adolescent dating violence, adolescents are often asked to respond to questions about a "boyfriend" or "girlfriend" or someone with whom they have "been on a date with or gone out with." However, what constitutes a boyfriend or girlfriend or a dating partner is not clear, and these judgments are likely to vary tremendously across adolescents. These judgments are probably also influenced by a number of factors including the amount of time spent with each other, the degree of emotional attachment, and the activities engaged in together (Allen, 2004). They are also likely to change over the course of adolescence, as youth mature and become more experienced with dating.

Most everyone has a general idea about what constitutes "violence" in adolescent dating relationships, but not everyone conceptualizes and defines it the same way. In the empirical literature, multiple types of dating violence have been studied, including physical, sexual, and psychological violence. Definitions for these different types of violence vary from study to study, but each is typically based on adolescents' reports of the occurrence of specific acts. For example, physical violence often refers to adolescents' reports of hits, slaps, or beatings; sexual violence refers to forced kissing, touching, or intercourse; and psychological violence to reports of insults, threats, or the use of control tactics. These different types of violence are sometimes further subdivided. For example, indirect aggression (also referred to as relational or social aggression), which includes spreading hurtful rumors or telling cruel stories about a dating partner, has recently begun to be conceptualized as a form of dating violence that may be distinct from more overt forms of psychological or emotional abuse (Wolfe, Scott, Reitzel-Jaffe et al., 2001). As another example, in a recent prevalence study, sexual assault was distinguished from drug- or alcohol-facilitated rape, with the latter defined as sexual assault that occurred while the victim was "high, drunk, or passed out from drinking or taking drugs" (Wolitzky-Taylor et al., 2008).

In the bulk of studies on adolescent dating violence, the youth are surveyed about the occurrence of specific acts of violence within a particular time period, for example, during the previous 12 months. These surveys are typically administered on a single occasion, in either a questionnaire or interview format. Some include only one or two questions about violence; others include comprehensive scales of relationship violence with excellent psychometric properties (e.g., Wolfe et al., 2001). A handful of investigators have attempted to study adolescent dating violence using other methods, such as laboratory observations (e.g., Capaldi, Kimm, & Shortt, 2007), and repeated interviews over a short, circumscribed period of time (e.g., Jouriles et al., 2005). However, studies using alternatives to one-time, self-report survey assessments are few and far between.

This first section highlights some of the complexities involved in conceptualizing adolescent dating violence and describes how different types of dating violence are often defined and measured, providing a backdrop for understanding and interpreting empirical findings in the literature. As illustrated in the section below, different conceptualizations and definitions of dating violence lead to different research findings and conclusions. Similarly, various data collection methods (such as using more questions and/or repeated questioning) also yield different results. At the present time, there is no gold standard with respect to defining or measuring adolescent dating violence; the field is still developing in this regard.

Prevalence of Adolescent Dating Violence

Over the past decade, data from several different national surveys have been used to estimate the prevalence of the various forms of adolescent dating violence. Surveys conducted by the Centers for Disease Control suggest that 9–10% of students in grades 9–12 indicate that a boyfriend or girlfriend has hit, slapped, or physically hurt them on purpose during the previous 12 months, and approximately 8% report having been physically forced to have sexual intercourse against their wishes (Howard, Wang, & Yan, 2007a, 2007b). The 2005 National Survey of Adolescents (NSA) indicates that 1.6% of adolescents between 12 and 17 years of age have experienced "serious dating violence" (Wolitzky-Taylor et al., 2008). Serious dating violence was defined as experiencing one or more of the following forms of violence from a dating partner: physical violence (badly injured, beaten up, or threatened with a knife or gun), sexual violence (forced anal, vaginal, or oral sex; forced penetration with a digit or an object; forced touching of genitalia), or drug/alcohol-facilitated rape.

Most studies in this area ask about male-to-female and female-to-male violence or include gender-neutral questions without assessing whether a respondent is in an opposite-sex or same-sex relationship. The National Longitudinal Study of Adolescent Health is unique in that it reports data on violence

Table 1 Prevalence of Dating Violence in Same-Sex and Opposite-Sex Romantic Relationships

Data from National Longitudinal Study of Adolescent Health		
In the previous 18 months partner had been:	Opposite-sex relationship	Same-sex relationship
Physically violent	12%	11%
Psychologically violent	29%	21%

Halpern, Oslak, Young, Martin, & Kupper, 2001; Halpern, Young, Waller, Martin, & Kupper, 2004.

in opposite-sex as well as same-sex romantic relationships. As can be seen in Table 1, prevalence rates for both physical and psychological violence are similar in opposite-sex and same-sex romantic relationships among adolescents in grades 7–12.

Prevalence rates for both physical and psychological violence are similar in opposite-sex and same-sex romantic relationships among adolescents in grades 7–12.

The prevalence of physical dating violence appears to be fairly similar across studies of national samples. Variation across estimates most likely reflects differences in how violence is defined, and perhaps differences in the samples from which the estimates were derived (e.g., different age ranges sampled). It should be noted that prevalence estimates based on smaller, less representative, localized samples tend to be higher than those based on national samples. In fact, a number of researchers have reported prevalence estimates for physical dating violence among adolescents (over a one-year period or less) to be over 40% (Hickman, Jaycox, & Aronoff, 2004). These elevated estimates might stem directly from sampling differences, but also perhaps from differences in the conceptualization and measurement of dating violence. For example, in many of the smaller samples, investigators assessed dating violence more extensively (such as using more questions and/or through repeated questioning), which might contribute to higher prevalence estimates.

Taken together, the results across studies yield some general conclusions about the nature and scope of adolescent dating violence. Regardless of how it is defined, it appears that a substantial number of United States youth are affected by dating violence. Even with very conservative definitions, such as the one used in the NSA, it was projected that approximately 400,000 adolescents have been victims, at some point in their lives, of serious dating violence (Wolitzky-Taylor et al., 2008).

Psychological violence appears to be much more common than either physical or sexual violence. Data are mixed on the relative prevalence of physical and sexual violence, but some of the national surveys suggest that they are approximately equal in prevalence.

Onset and Course

Dating violence appears to emerge well before high school. For example, cross-sex teasing and harassment, which involve behaviors often construed as either psychological or sexual violence, is evident among 6th graders and increases in prevalence over time (McMaster et al., 2002). One-third of a sample of 7th graders who indicated that they had started dating also reported that they had committed acts of aggression (physical, sexual, or psychological) toward a dating partner; in over half of these cases, physical or sexual aggression was involved (Sears et al., 2007). In the NSA, serious dating violence victimization was not reported by 12-year-olds, but it was by 13-year-olds (Wolitzky-Taylor et al., 2008).

Longitudinal data on the course of adolescent dating violence are scarce, but there is evidence that psychological aggression predicts subsequent physical aggression (O'Leary & Slep, 2003). In fact, different types of dating violence commonly co-occur within adolescent relationships, with the occurrence of one type of violence (physical, psychological, or sexual) associated with an increased likelihood of other types of violence (Sears, Byers, & Price, 2007). In research on interpersonal victimization in general, victims of violence are known to be at increased risk for subsequent victimization. This appears to be true for victims of adolescent dating violence as well (Smith, White, & Holland, 2003).

Demographics of Adolescent Dating Violence

Certain demographic variables including age, race and ethnicity, geographic location, and sex are associated with increased risk for victimization. Specifically, the risk for dating violence victimization increases with age, at least through the middle and high school years. This trend appears to be true for physical, psychological, and sexual violence (e.g., Halpern et al., 2001; Howard et al., 2007a, 2007b; Wolitzky-Taylor et al., 2008). This might be attributable to a number of things, including the changing nature of dating over the course of adolescence. Some evidence has emerged pointing to racial and ethnic differences in adolescents' experiences of dating violence, but other recent, large-scale studies call these findings into question. For example, a number of investigators have found Black adolescents to be more likely than their White counterparts to experience physical and sexual dating violence (e.g., Howard et al., 2007a, 2007b). However, these differences have sometimes disappeared when other variables, such as prior exposures to violence, are considered (Malik, Sorenson, & Aneshensel, 1997). Moreover, recent, well-designed studies of very large samples have found no evidence of racial or ethnic differences in adolescent victimization

(e.g., O'Leary et al., 2008; Wolitzky-Taylor et al., 2008). There do appear to be regional differences in dating violence, with adolescents in southern states at substantially greater risk for experiencing dating violence than adolescents in other regions of the U.S. (Marquart, et al., 2007). Although the reasons for regional differences are not known, it is interesting to note that the South has a higher prevalence rate of overall violence than other regions in the U.S. In short, there may be factors in the Southern U.S. that facilitate the promotion, acceptance, or tolerance of violent behavior.

When violence is defined broadly, prevalence rates for male and female victimization tend to be similar (e.g., Halpern et al., 2001). However, narrower definitions of violence point to some sex differences in the experience of violence. For example, female adolescents are more likely than males to experience severe physical violence (violent acts that are likely to result, or actually have resulted, in physical injuries) and sexual violence (e.g., Molidor & Tolman, 1998; Wolitzky-Taylor et al., 2008). Females are also more likely than males to experience fear, hurt, and the desire to leave the situation for self-protection (Molidor & Tolman, 1998; Jackson, Cram, & Seymour, 2000). In addition, females are more likely to report physical injuries and more harmful and persistent psychological distress after being victimized (O'Keefe, 1997).

Correlates of Adolescent Dating Violence

Most of the findings on the correlates of adolescent dating violence come from studies in which data were collected at a single point in time. Thus, it is difficult to discern if observed correlates are precursors or consequences of the violence, or if they are simply related to experiencing violence, but not in a cause-and-effect manner. Although it is tempting to interpret some of these associations in a causal, unidirectional manner, more often than not, alternative explanations can also be offered. For example, the documented association between dating violence and psychological distress is typically interpreted to mean that experiencing dating violence causes psychological distress (e.g., Howard et al., 2007a, 2007b; Molidor & Tolman, 1998). However, it is not too difficult to imagine how feelings of psychological distress might influence an adolescent's decision about whom to go out with (i.e., adolescents who are psychologically distressed, compared with those who are not, may make different choices about whom to date) and, perhaps, lead an adolescent to an abusive relationship.

Many adolescents engage in antisocial or illegal activities, but those who do so consistently and frequently are at increased risk of dating violence victimization (e.g., Howard et al., 2007a, 2007b). In addition, simply having antisocial friends increases risk for victimization. For example, females who associate with violent or victimized peers appear to be at increased risk for dating violence victimization (Gagne, Lavoie, & Hebert, 2005). Similarly, male and female adolescents exposed to peer-drinking activities within the past 30 days (e.g., "Hanging out with friends who drank") were victimized more often than their counterparts who were not exposed to such activities (Howard, Qiu, & Boekeloo, 2003).

Many other adolescent experiences have also been associated with dating violence victimization. For example, earlier exposures to violence, both within and outside of the family, are associated with victimization (e.g., Gagne et al., 2005; Malik et al., 1997). Negative parent-child interactions and parent-child boundary violations at age 13 predict victimization at age 21 (Linder & Collins, 2005). Trauma symptoms, which may result from violence exposure and untoward parent-child interactions, are posited to interfere with emotional and cognitive processes important in interpreting abusive behavior, and possibly to heighten tolerance for abuse (Capaldi & Gorman-Smith, 2003). Having had prior sexual relationships with peers increases adolescent females' risk for experiencing relationship violence (e.g., Howard et al., 2007a, 2007b). Also, the likelihood of victimization increases as the number of dating partners increases (Halpern et al., 2001).

Several different dimensions of adolescent relationships have been examined in relation to dating violence. For example, physical violence is often reciprocated within relationships, meaning that when dating violence is reported, both partners are typically violent toward one another (e.g., O'Leary, Slep, Avery-Leaf, Cascardi, 2008). Relationship violence is more likely to happen in serious or special romantic relationships, rather than more casual ones (O'Leary et al., 2008; Roberts, Auinger, & Klein, 2006). It is also more likely to occur in relationships with problems, conflict, and power struggles (Bentley et al., 2007; O'Keefe, 1997).

Relationship violence is more likely to happen in serious or special romantic relationships, rather than more casual ones.

Although there are many risk factors for adolescent dating violence, some protective factors have emerged as well. For instance, having high-quality friendships at age 16 is associated with reduced likelihood of experiencing dating violence in romantic relationships at age 21 (Linder & Collins, 2005). High-quality friendships are characterized by security, disclosure, closeness, low levels of conflict, and the effective resolution of conflict that does occur. Also, adolescents who do well in school and those who attend religious services are at decreased risk for experiencing dating violence (Halpern et al., 2001; Howard et al., 2003).

Prevention and Intervention

Much of the prevention research in this area is directed at an entire population (e.g., 9th grade at a school) with the goal of preventing violence from occurring. However, the prevalence data indicate that a sizable number of adolescents in high school, and even middle school, have already perpetrated and/or experienced dating violence. Thus, in most cases the research

is not technically universal prevention, from the standpoint of preventing violence before it ever occurs. Rather, it is an attempt to reduce dating violence, by preventing its initial occurrence as well as preventing its re-occurrence among those who have already experienced it.

A sizable number of adolescents in high school, and even middle school, have already perpetrated and/or experienced dating violence.

Many of the school-based prevention programs share a number of commonalities, in addition to the joint focus on prevention and intervention (Whitaker et al., 2006). Most are designed to address perpetration and victimization simultaneously. Many are incorporated into mandatory health classes in middle or high school. Most are based on a combination of feminist and social learning principles, and involve didactic methods to increase knowledge and change attitudes regarding dating violence. Despite these similarities, there are potentially important differences in the structure (e.g., duration) and content of these various programs. Unfortunately, most of these school-based programs have not undergone rigorous empirical evaluation to determine whether they actually reduce occurrences of violence.

A notable exception is Safe Dates, a program developed for 8th and 9th grade students (Foshee, Bauman, Arriaga et al., 1998) that has undergone a fairly rigorous evaluation. Safe Dates includes: (a) ten interactive classroom sessions covering topics such as dating violence norms, gender stereotyping, and conflict management skills, (b) group activities such as peer-performed theater productions and a poster contest, and (c) information about community resources for adolescents in abusive relationships. Evaluation results indicate that Safe Dates reduces psychological and physical violence perpetration, but not victimization, among the students who participated in the program. At first glance, this result might be puzzling: How can the perpetration of violence go down, without a commensurate reduction in victimization? This might be explained, in part, by the fact that not all individuals who participated in Safe Dates dated other Safe Date participants. Although the Safe Dates participants were less likely to commit acts of dating violence after completing the program, they were not necessarily less likely to date individuals who commit violent acts.

Evaluations of other school-based programs using techniques similar to those employed in Safe Dates have not had demonstrable effects on violence perpetration or victimization. Some of these evaluations simply did not include measures of perpetration or victimization as outcomes. Others, however, have attempted to measure intervention effects on violent behavior and victimization, but have found no effects (e.g., Avery-Leaf et al., 1997; Hilton et al., 1998). Many of these school-based programs, however, *have* achieved changes in knowledge or attitudes regarding dating violence (e.g., Avery-Leaf et al., 1997; Hilton et al., 1998; Krajewski et al., 1996; Weisz & Black, 2001).

Another program with demonstrated results is The Youth Relationships Project (YRP) (Wolfe et al., 2003). YRP is a community-based intervention designed for 14-16 year olds who were maltreated as children and were thus at increased risk of being in abusive relationships in the future. YRP is an 18-session, group-based program with three primary components: (a) education about abusive relationships and power dynamics within these relationships, (b) skills development, and (c) social action. The skills targeted in this program include communication skills and conflict resolution. The social action portion of the program includes, among other things, allowing program participants the opportunity to become familiar with and to practice utilizing resources for individuals in violent relationships, as well as the chance to develop a project to raise awareness of dating violence within the community. Sessions include skills practice, guest speakers, videos, and visits to relevant community agencies. Evaluation results indicate that YRP reduces physical dating violence perpetration and physical, emotional, and threatening abuse victimization.

It is encouraging that Safe Dates and the YRP have yielded promising results in reducing dating violence among adolescents. However, given the current state of the prevention literature in this area, it would be erroneous to suggest that we know how to prevent adolescent dating violence. Systematic reviews of this literature indicate that the vast majority of studies attempting to evaluate a dating violence prevention program have *not* found intervention effects on behavioral measures, and even though changes in knowledge and attitudes are often documented, it is not really clear if such changes lead to changes in either perpetration or victimization (Hickman et al., 2004; Whitaker et al., 2006). The promising findings of the Safe Dates and YRP programs require replication, and more information is needed on how these programs accomplished their positive effects. Researchers and practitioners can use these programs as a starting point in their own efforts at preventing relationship violence, but it is still important to continue exploring new ideas about prevention in this area.

Concluding Remarks

It is clear that violence in adolescent dating relationships is a prevalent problem with potentially devastating consequences. We also know a great deal about correlates of such violence. On the other hand, there are still important gaps in our knowledge. For example, longitudinal research on this topic is extremely scarce; thus, we know little about the emergence and unfolding of dating violence and victimization over time. This is particularly true for high-risk groups, such as children from violent homes and other groups potentially at risk. In addition, we know very little about how to address the problem of adolescent dating violence effectively. This might be due, in part, to the dearth of well-designed longitudinal studies on this topic, which are necessary to develop a solid knowledge base on the causes of relationship violence and targets for intervention. Although there are promising and notable efforts in the area of understanding and preventing violence in adolescent dating relationships, we still have much to learn.

> **Longitudinal research on this topic is extremely scarce; thus, we know little about the emergence and unfolding of dating violence and victimization over time.**

References

Allen, L. (2004). "Getting off" and "going out": Young people's conceptions of (hetero) sexual relationships. *Health & Sexuality, 6,* 463–481.

Avery-Leaf, S., Cascardi, M., O'Leary, K.D., & Cano, A. (1997). Efficacy of a dating violence prevention program on attitudes justifying aggression. *Journal of Adolescent Health, 21,* 11–17.

Bentley, C.G., Galliher, R.V., & Ferguson, T.J. (2007). Associations among aspects of interpersonal power and relationship functioning in adolescent romantic couples. *Sex Roles, 57,* 483–495.

Capaldi, D.M., & Gorman-Smith, D. (2003). The development of aggression in young male/female couples. In P. Florsheim (Ed.), *Adolescent Romantic Relations and Sexual Behavior: Theory, Research, and Practical implications* (pp. 243–278). Lawrence Erlbaum Associates, Publishers.

Capaldi, D.M., Kim, H.K., & Shortt, J.W. (2007). Observed initiation and reciprocity of physical aggression in young, at risk couples. *Journal of Family Violence, 22,* 101–111.

Connolly, J., Craig, W., Goldberg, A., & Pepler, D. (1999). Conceptions of cross-sex friendships and romantic relationships in early adolescence. *Journal of Youth and Adolescence, 28,* 481–494.

Feiring, C. (1996). Concept of romance in 15-year-old adolescents. *Journal of Research on Adolescence, 6,* 181–200.

Foshee, V., Bauman, K.E., Arriaga, X.B., Helms, R.W., Koch, G.G., & Linder, G.F. (1998). An evaluation of safe dates, an adolescent dating violence prevention program. *American Journal of Public Health, 88,* 45–50.

Gagne, M., Lavoie, F., & Hebert, M. (2005). Victimization during childhood and revictimization in dating relationships in adolescent girls. *Child Abuse & Neglect, 29,* 1,155–1,172.

Halpern, C.T., Oslak, S.G., Young, M.L., Martin, S.L., & Kupper, L.L. (2001). Partner violence among adolescents in opposite-sex romantic relationships: Findings from the national longitudinal study of adolescent health. *American Journal of Public Health, 91,* 1,679–1,685.

Halpern, C.T., Young, M.L., Wallet, M.W., Martin S.L., & Kupper, L.L. (2004). Prevalence of partner violence in same-sex romantic and sexual relationships in a national sample of adolescents. *Journal of Adolescent Health, 35,* 131.

Hickman, L.J., Jaycox, L.H., & Aranoff, J. (2004). Dating violence among adolescents: Prevalence, gender distribution, and prevention program effectiveness. *Trauma, Violence, and Abuse, 5,* 123–142.

Hilton, N.Z., Harris, G.T., Rice, M.E., Krans, T.S., & Lavigne, S.E. (1998). Antiviolence education in high schools: Implementation and evaluation. *Journal of interpersonal Violence, 13,* 726–742.

Howard, D.E., Qiu, Y., & Boekeloo, B. (2003). Personal and social contextual correlates of adolescent dating violence. *Journal of Adolescent Health, 33,* 9–17.

Howard, D.E., Wang, M. Q., & Yan, F. (2007a). Psychosocial factors associated with reports of physical dating violence among U.S. adolescent females. *Adolescence, 42,* 311–324.

Howard, D.E., Wang, M.Q., & Yan, F. (2007b). Prevalence and psychosocial correlates of forced sexual intercourse among U.S. high school adolescents. *Adolescence, 42,* 629–643.

Jackson, S.M., Cram, F., & Seymour, F.W. (2000). Violence and sexual coercion in high school students' dating relationships. *Journal of Family Violence, 15,* 23–36.

Jouriles, E.N., McDonald, R., Garrido, E., Rosenfield, D., & Brown, A.S. (2005). Assessing aggression in adolescent romantic relationships: Can we do it better? *Psychological Assessment, 17,* 469–475.

Krajewsky, S.S., Rybarik, M.F., Dosch, M.F., & Gilmore, G.D. (1996) Results of a curriculum intervention with seventh graders regarding violence in relationships. *Journal of Family Violence, 11,* 93–112.

Linder, J.R., & Collins, W.A. (2005). Parent and peer predictors of physical aggression and conflict management in romantic relationships in early adulthood. *Journal of Family Psychology, 19,* 252–262.

Malik, S., Sorenson, S.B., & Aneshensel, C.S. (1997). Community and dating violence among adolescents: Perpetration and victimization. *Journal of Adolescent Health, 21,* 291–302.

Marquart, B.S., Nannini, D.K., Edwards, R.W., Stanley, L.R., & Wayman, J.C. (2007). Prevalence of dating violence and victimization: Regional and gender differences. *Adolescence, 42,* 645–657.

McMaster, L.E., Connolly, J., Pepler, D., & Craig, W.M. (2002). Peer to peer sexual harassment in early adolescence: A developmental perspective. *Development and Psychopathology, 14,* 91–105.

Molidor, C., & Tolman, R.M. (1998). Gender and contextual factors in adolescent dating violence. *Violence Against Women, 4,* 180–194.

O'Keefe. M. (1997). Predictors of dating violence among high school students. *Journal of Interpersonal Violence, 12,* 546–568.

O'Leary, K.D., & Slep, A.M.S. (2003). A dyadic longitudinal model of adolescent dating aggression. *Journal of Clinical Child and Adolescent Psychology, 32,* 314–327.

O'Leary, K.D., Slep, A.M., Avery-Leaf, S., & Cascardi, M. (2008). Gender differences in dating aggression among multiethnic high school students. *Journal of Adolescent Health, 42,* 473–479.

Roberts, T.A., Auinger, M.S., & Klein, J.D. (2006). Predictors of partner abuse in a nationally representative sample of adolescents involved in heterosexual dating relationships. *Violence and Victims, 21,* 81–89.

Sears, H.A., Byers, E.S., & Price, E.L. (2007). The co-occurrence of adolescent boys' and girls' use of psychologically, physically, and sexually abusive behaviours in their dating relationships. *Journal of Adolescence, 30,* 487–504.

Smith, P.H., White, J.W., & Holland, L.J. (2003). A longitudinal perspective on dating violence among adolescent and college-age women. *American Journal of Public Health, 93,* 1,104–1,109.

Weisz, A.N., & Black, B.M. (2001). Evaluating a sexual assault and dating violence prevention program for urban youths. *Social Work Research, 25,* 89–102.

Whitaker, D.J., Morrison, S., Lindquist, C., Hawkins, S.R., O'Neil, J.A., Nesius, A.M., Mathew, A., & Reese, L. (2006). A critical review of interventions for the primary prevention of perpetration of partner violence. *Aggression and Violent Behavior, 11,* 151–166.

Wolfe, D.A., Scott, K., Reitzel-Jaffe, D., Wekerle, C., Grasley, C., & Straatman, A.-L. (2001). Development and validation of the conflict in adolescent dating relationships inventory. *Psychological Assessment, 13,* 277–293.

Wolfe, D.A., Wekerle, C., Scott, K., Straatman, A. L., Grasley, C., & Reitzel-Jaffe, D. (2003). Dating violence prevention with at-risk youth: A controlled outcome evaluation. *Journal of Consulting and Clinical Psychology, 71,* 279–291.

Wolitzky-Taylor, M.A., Ruggiero, K.J., Danielson, C.K., Resnick, H.S., Hanson, R.F., Smith, D.W., Saunders, B.E., & Kilpatrick, D.G. (2008). Prevalence and correlates of dating violence in a national sample of adolescents. *Journal of the American Academy of Child and Adolescent Psychiatry, 47,* 755–762.

ERNEST N. JOURILES, PHD is Professor in the Department of Psychology and Co-Director of the Family Research Center at Southern Methodist University. **CORA PLATT** is a doctoral student in the Department of Psychology at Southern Methodist University. **RENEE McDONALD, PHD** is Associate Professor in the Department of Psychology and Co-Director of the Family Research Center at Southern Methodist University.

Prevention of Domestic Violence during Adolescence

DAVID A. WOLFE, PHD AND PETER G. JAFFE, PHD

Some days it seems that little progress has been made in addressing the fundamental causes and consequences of domestic violence and its effects on children. The problem seems as serious as ever, and the major underlying causes, such as abuse of power, inequality, and modeling of violence in the home, have remained largely unchanged over the past three decades. The government response has been to manage adult domestic violence, which involves providing services on an individual basis only when absolutely necessary. Crisis management is a necessary part of the response to adult domestic violence, but more proactive strategies of prevention are also strongly needed.

The news is not all bad; in fact, encouraging progress has been made in less than two decades. Scientific, professional, and activist groups have played a prominent role in recognizing the links between domestic violence and child adjustment problems, among other issues. A growing interest by researchers and clinicians in the field of domestic violence has made it possible to establish a scientific foundation for implementing prevention and treatment initiatives and public policy to end domestic violence. The field is in the process of finding alternatives to violence that can be activated in each community in a manner that stimulates interest, informs choices, and promotes action to decrease violence and abuse in the lives of children, youth, and families.

In this article, key issues in the prevention of domestic violence are reviewed. Included are discussions of the goals of prevention programs and theories of the causality of domestic violence and abuse. Next, prevention efforts designed to address the needs of children and adults are viewed through a developmental, or life-span, lens. Critical issues for prevention programs are described for adolescents. Finally, research and policy implications are explored for violence prevention endeavors in a number of settings, from homes, schools, and neighborhoods to courts and the culture at large.

Emerging Goals of Prevention Efforts

Emerging changes in public policy, legislation, and service delivery illustrate a commitment to finding ways to reduce the prevalence and harmful effects of adult domestic violence. Still, strategies that address the issue at a broader level need to be developed and evaluated. Such strategies must take into account the many factors that influence the likelihood of adult domestic violence and those that promote nonviolence. There are established precedents for such an approach, such as public health campaigns to eliminate health risks among adolescents and health promotion campaigns to encourage healthy (low-risk) behaviors among segments of the population (Hamilton & Bhatti, 1996; Sherman et al., 1998). These approaches, adopted primarily for known health issues, hold considerable promise for behavioral issues as well because they recognize that change occurs through finding positive ways to communicate messages about healthy families and relationships.

One way to envision the goal of prevention is to promote attitudes and behaviors that are incompatible with violence and abuse, and that encourage the formation of healthy, nonviolent relationships. The implications of this paradigm are significant and far reaching if attention and resources are primarily focused on the occurrence of undesirable behavior, such as identified acts of violence, prevention efforts are usually directed toward identification, control, and punishment. However, if the goal of prevention is the promotion of healthy, nonviolent relationships, attention and resources are more likely to be directed toward establishing and building trust, respecting others' thoughts and expressions, and encouraging and supporting growth in relationships. This perspective implies a different list of intervention and educational possibilities, such as school-based curricula, neighborhood-based health and social services, and family-based child and health care.

Theories of Causality

The prevention of domestic violence at first glance seems impeded by a lack of theoretical consensus as to its fundamental causes. However, the foundation of prevention programs might include several important principles:

- Domestic violence has been ignored as a major health, criminal, and social problem until recently and remains poorly understood among the general population.
- Domestic violence is a complex problem that cannot be understood by a single variable. Explanations require a multifaceted approach that recognizes individual behavior within a familial and cultural context (Dutton, 1995).
- The significance of childhood trauma, including witnessing adult domestic violence, is common to all theories even though there is disagreement as to the processes involved. In general, these processes include learning maladaptive behaviors through modeling and reinforcement by people in the child's family, neighborhood, and cultural environment (Emery & Laumann-Billings, 1998). In turn, prevention efforts may include efforts to prevent children from ever experiencing such trauma as well as community readiness to respond as soon as possible to children in violent homes.
- As long as domestic violence is seen as acceptable behavior or tolerated by silence through public attitudes, institutions, and the media, there is little chance of changing individual behavior. In other words, the prevention of domestic violence is everyone's business and is each human services provider's responsibility.

Although far from realized, domestic violence prevention efforts have begun to organize around the principle of building on strengths and developing protective factors in an effort to deter violence and abuse. Learning to relate to others, especially intimates, in a respectful, nonviolent manner is a crucial foundation for building effective prevention strategies for related forms of violence and abuse between partners.

Prevention Efforts

Because violence in intimate relationships is deeply rooted in early family experiences and in broader cultural and social influences, deciding where to focus prevention efforts for greatest impact is a critical starting point. In principle, prevention efforts should involve every aspect of social ecology. Societal, community, and neighborhood forces; schools and peer groups; family processes; and individual strengths and weaknesses have all been linked to adult domestic violence. Therefore, all of these influences play a role in the prevention of violence and care should be taken to ensure that the interventions are appropriate and beneficial. The following discussion will focus exclusively on interventions aimed at adolescents (for discussion of the other age groups, see Wolfe & Jaffe, 2001).

Adolescence is a time of important cognitive and social development, during which teenagers learn to think more rationally and become capable of thinking hypothetically. At the same time, they must develop and use effective decision-making skills involving complex interpersonal relationships, including an awareness of possible risks and considerations of future consequences and balancing their own interests with those of their peers, family members, and dating partners. Conformity to parental opinions gradually decreases, and the tendency to be swayed by peers increases until late adolescence. By mid-adolescence, romantic partners increase in their importance as social support providers (Furman & Buhrmester, 1992). Thus, early to mid-adolescence offers a unique opportunity for learning healthy ways to form intimate relationships, and teenagers are often keen to explore this unfamiliar territory.

Youth, especially those who grew up experiencing violence in their homes, profit from education and skills that promote healthy relationships and provide useful alternatives to violence and abuse. Clear messages about personal responsibility and boundaries, delivered in a blame-free manner, are generally acceptable to this age group, whereas lectures and warnings are less helpful. By offering youth the opportunities to explore the richness and rewards of relationships, they become eager to learn about choices and responsibilities. The initiation phase of social dating is a prime opportunity to become aware of the ways in which violent and abusive behavior toward intimate partners may occur, often without purpose or intention. This premise holds true not only for individuals from violent and abusive family backgrounds where negative experiences were prominent but also for other adolescents (Gray & Foshee, 1997).

A discussion of choice and responsibility for one's own behavior and how abusiveness has different consequences and meanings for young men and women is a critical step in enhancing youth awareness and recognition of dating violence (Gray & Foshee, 1997). Moreover, facilitating discussions about the meaning of violent dynamics, violent acts, and woman abuse simultaneously raises awareness of these issues and provides an opportunity to deal directly with issues of blame, responsibility, and victim-victimizer dynamics within the context of teenage dating relationships. Programs delivered universally through the high school often involve activities aimed at increasing awareness and dispelling myths about relationship violence. These activities can include: a) school auditorium presentations involving videotapes, plays, or a survivor's speech; b) classroom discussions facilitated by teachers and community professionals involved in domestic violence intervention, such as shelter staff or law enforcement personnel; c) detailed lesson plans, programs, and curricula that encourage students to examine those attitudes and behaviors that promote or tolerate violence (these exercises serve as an introduction to nonviolent alternatives in relationships); and d) peer counseling and peer support groups to assist students in developing empowerment initiatives.

> **The prevention of domestic violence is everyone's business and is each human services provider's responsibility.**

Community-based programs for the prevention of relationship violence have goals similar to those of school-based programs, although they are intended for a more selective population, such as teenagers who are at greater risk of dating violence because of their early childhood experiences or similar risk factors. One example is the Youth Relationships Project (Wolfe et al., 2003), which was developed to help youth understand the critical importance of the abuse of power and control in relationship violence and relate these to their own social and dating relationships. The Youth Relationships Project involves adolescents referred from active caseloads of child protective service agencies who experienced violence and abuse in their families. They are informed of the program by their child protection caseworker, counselor, or other community agent. The program has an emphasis on building healthy, nonviolent relationships rather than attending treatment per se (which adolescents generally resist). Because the Youth Relationships Project is a secondary prevention program, participation does not require evidence of dating violence. Through group discussion and exercises, the youth learn how to select appropriate alternatives to abuse and violence with dating partners. This strategy builds on current strengths and identifies negative relationship factors at a time when teenagers are motivated to learn about intimate relationships.

Efforts to provide youth with such positive educational and cultural experiences in which power is understood, not abused, are very recent, and program evaluations are incomplete. Early findings, however, show that youth are responsive to such information, especially if they are involved in its design and delivery. Six dating violence prevention programs designed for high school teenagers have included evaluation components (Wekerle & Wolfe, 1999). Each program addressed specific skills and knowledge that oppose the use of violent and abusive behavior toward intimate partners. Positive changes were found across the studies in violence-related attitudes and knowledge as well as self-reported perpetration of dating violence. Although preliminary, such efforts indicate that adolescents are receptive to these learning opportunities.

Policy and Research Implications

Regardless of their attractiveness, prevention and health promotion efforts have not been popular strategies among professionals or the general public for addressing the problem of domestic violence. Prevention entails environmental and cultural explanations in addition to individual ones for causes of violence and necessitates a strong commitment to large-scale, proactive intervention using public resources rather than individually focused, private interests. Furthermore, prevention requires social and political action directed at achieving fundamental change. Nevertheless, we owe it to children, young people, and families to consider building other bridges that promote competency and adaptive behavior in an effort not only to prevent something unwanted but also to bolster potential and growth for individuals and society.

Although there is a paucity of evaluative data, there is general agreement that children and adolescents, especially those growing up in violent homes, are an important prevention focus. The following major prevention strategies and research issues stand out:

- Based on the collective wisdom of family court judges, child protection agencies, and domestic violence programs, there is a need to expand existing collaborative efforts by child protection and domestic violence agencies and staff to a more comprehensive primary prevention program (National Council of Juvenile and Family Court Judges, 1998).

- There is a growing recognition that crime prevention needs to focus on homes and communities to the extent that both are recognized as risk factors in violent behavior. Many children are exposed to violence not only in their homes but also in their neighborhoods and schools, which means there is a need for extensive collaboration among service systems. Thus, initial efforts may have to target high-risk neighborhoods and communities rather than assessing one client (potential victim) at a time (Earls, 1998).

- Primary prevention programs should be available in all schools and be developed as partnerships among students, teachers, parents, and community agents who have knowledge and expertise about domestic violence. For adolescents, the programs need to be relevant to their interests, such as dating violence, and actively involve counseling, such as peer support and peer models. A major challenge for the domestic violence field involves better collaboration with the more general crime prevention strategies that are being actively promoted in U.S. schools. There are overlapping strategies (e.g., clearly naming the problem), and domestic violence is often an underlying issue and concern for children. Although many parents and teachers are worried about violence in general, most children are more likely to witness and experience violence among people they know and trust. Therefore, the domestic violence issues are more relevant for them.

- Programs need to be planned according to both individual and institutional readiness for change. For example, boys and men may become defensive in discussions on violence against women and underlying issues of inequality until they have a better appreciation of the broader problems of violence in society. Therefore, programs have to acknowledge the stepping stones from awareness of a problem to a deeper understanding and ultimately an ongoing commitment for social change (for further discussion see Jaffe, Wolfe, Crooks, Hughes, & Baker, 2004).

In the prevention of adult domestic violence, a clear commitment is needed from all levels of government to address these issues comprehensively, with the goal of establishing a consistent, coordinated, and integrated approach for each community. Given the extensive nature of domestic violence and its accompanying human suffering, this commitment to prevention cannot be postponed.

References

Dutton, D.G. (1995). *The Domestic Assault of Women: Psychological and Criminal Justice Perspectives.* Vancouver, B.C., Canada: University of British Columbia Press.

Earls, F. (1998, September). *Linking Community Factors and Individual Development* [Research preview] (NIJ 170603). Washington DC: U.S. Department of Justice, National Institute of Justice.

Emery, R.E., & Laumann-Billings, L. (1998). An overview of the nature, causes, and consequences of abusive family relationships: Toward differentiating maltreatment and violence. *American Psychologist, 53,* 121–135.

Furman, W., & Buhrmester, D. (1992). Age and sex differences in perceptions of networks of personal relationships. *Child Development, 63,* 103–115.

Gray, H.M., & Foshee, V. (1997). Adolescent dating violence: Differences between one-sided and mutually violent profiles. *Journal of Interpersonal Violence, 12,* 126–141.

Hamilton, N., & Bhatti, T. (1996). *Population Health Promotion: An Integrated Model of Population Health and Health Promotion.* Ottawa, Ontario: Health Canada.

Jaffe, P., Wolfe, D.A., Crooks, C., Hughes, R., & Baker, L. (2004). The Fourth R: Developing healthy relationships through school-based interventions. In P. Jaffe, L. Baker, & A. Cunningham (Eds.), *Protecting Children From Domestic Violence: Strategies for Community Intervention* (pp. 200–218). New York: Guilford.

National Council of Juvenile and Family Court Judges. (1998). *Family Violence: Emerging Programs for Battered Mothers and Their Children.* Reno, NY: Author.

Sherman, L.W., Gottfredson, D.C, MacKenzie, D.L., Eck, J., Reuter, P., & Bushway, S.D. (1998, July). *Preventing Crime: What Works, What Doesn't, What's Promising* [Research in brief I (NIJ 171676)]. Washington DC: U.S. Department of Justice, National Institute of Justice.

Wekerle, C, & Wolfe, D.A. (1999). Dating violence in mid-adolescence: Theory, significance, and emerging prevention initiatives. *Clinical Psychology Review, 19,* 435–456.

Wolfe, D.A., & Jaffe, P.D. (2001). Prevention of domestic violence: Emerging initiatives. In S.A. Graham-Bermann & J.L. Edleson (Eds.), *Domestic Violence in the Lives of Children: The Future of Research, Intervention, and Social Policy* (pp. 283–298). Washington DC: American Psychological Association.

Wolfe, D.A., Wekerle, C, Scott, K., Straatman, A., Grasley, C, & Reitzel-Jaffe, D. (2003). Dating violence prevention with at-risk youth: A controlled outcome evaluation. *Journal of Consulting and Clinical Psychology, 71,* 279–291.

DAVID A. WOLFE, PhD, is with the Department of Psychiatry, Centre for Addiction and Mental Health, University of Toronto. **PETER G. JAFFE,** Ph.D, is with the Center for Children and Families in the Justice System, London Family Court Clinic, and is an Adjunct Professor in the Departments of Psychiatry and Psychology of the University of Western Ontario.

This article is adapted from David A. Wolfe and Peter G. Jaffe (2001). Prevention of domestic violence: Emerging initiatives. In S.A. Graham-Bermann & J.L. Edleson (Ed.,), *Domestic Violence in the Lives of Children: The Future of Research, Intervention, and Social Policy* (pp. 283–298). Washington DC: American Psychological Association. It appears here with permission from *The Future of Children,* a publication of the David and Lucile Packard Foundation.

Prescription for Disaster

BOB SMITHOUSER

The current enrollment at Fossil Ridge High School in Keller, Texas, stands at 2,147. It should be 2,148. That's because freshman Tyler Bailey, a promising athlete who dreamed of attending college on a football scholarship, died of a drug overdose and was buried in his black No. 86 jersey. The culprit wasn't cocaine or heroin. Tyler died from oxycodone intoxication after he and some friends raided a parent's stash of prescription drugs.

A growing number of families are discovering what that loss feels like.

"This is an entirely new category of substance abuse, and we're only seeing the tip of the iceberg," said Steve Pasierb, president and CEO of the Partnership for a Drug-Free America. "Ease of access is the number-one reason kids are abusing prescription drugs. They don't have to go to a scary street dealer, because the drugs are right there in Mom's or Grandma's medicine cabinet."

Illicit drug use among teens has dropped radically since 2001. There's also been a slight decline in alcohol and tobacco use. Yet several studies concur that the number of adolescents abusing prescription drugs has *tripled* since 1992. According to Columbia University's National Center on Addiction and Substance Abuse, 75 percent of them are "polysubstance abusers" who combine prescription meds with other drugs or alcohol. A Monitoring the Future study released in December found that 14 percent of high school seniors, 11 percent of 10th graders and 7 percent of 8th graders said they had used tranquilizers, barbiturates or sedatives for nonmedical purposes within the past year.

> ## "This is an entirely new category of substance abuse, and we're only seeing the tip of the iceberg."
>
> —Steve Pasierb, Partnership for a Drug-Free America

Donald Hauser serves as medical director with The Right Step, a drug and alcohol treatment clinic in Houston. He noted, "By far, the most common trend I think we're seeing are sedative hypnotics, particularly Xanax—'bars' is what they call 'em—and the opiates, the hydrocodone derivatives, the Vicodins, the Loracets. Almost every adolescent that comes in this program has used some of them."

Teenagers think that, because these products are FDA approved, popping pills from a pharmacy is safer than buying marijuana or Ecstasy from an unknown source. They don't realize the potential dangers and addictive qualities of depressants, antidepressants, stimulants, muscle relaxants, anti-anxiety medications, tranquilizers and opiate pain relievers—all modern drugs of choice. In fact, *USA Today* reported recently that only 48 percent of teens see "great risk" in experimenting with prescription medication.

Wendy is a 17-year-old who experimented mightily. One day she took Xanax and remembers nothing more than regaining consciousness in a garage, clearly a victim of sexual assault. "I don't even know who it was," said the young woman, now in a treatment program. "You have to hit your bottom. For me it was almost dying."

This problem is pervasive enough to have inspired *Rx*, a new teen novel by Tracy Lynn. Written from a teenager's point of view, it's the story of an overachieving 17-year-old who sneaks Ritalin to help her focus. Soon she finds herself trading and dealing a wide assortment of prescription drugs, both to fuel her own habit and to "help" peers facing similar challenges.

Pharm Country

How do teens score these drugs? They rummage through their parents' medicine cabinets or beat the system by phoning in prescriptions, forging signatures or duping the online questionnaires of Internet pharmacies. Ryan Haight got caught in that web. After faking his age and concocting an ailment to get drugs online, the 17-year-old died from an overdose of prescription pain meds.

Teens also purchase pills in school hallways (a single Vicodin tablet can fetch $4 or $5) and take advantage of relatives' existing prescriptions. "My mom was prescribed alprazolam, which is Xanax's generic name," a rehabbing teen told ABC's *Nightline*. "All I had to do was find the pill bottle and call CVS and type in the prescription number. And then maybe an hour later, you go pick it up and say, 'I'm picking up Blair's prescription.' That's how I got a lot of mine."

One of the trendiest, most social ways to get a pharmaceutical high is at "pharming parties," pot luck-style gatherings where teens contribute to a chemical "trail mix." Even those who would never do crack or cocaine think nothing of grabbing fistfuls of these diverse, colorful drugs and washing them down with alcohol. Ernest Patterson, a recovering addict, recalls,

Warning Signs

Parents should look for these common symptoms of prescription drug abuse in teenagers:

- missed prescription drugs
- slurred speech
- lack of concentration or coordination
- glassy eyes or frequent use of eye drops
- rapid weight loss
- secretiveness or dishonesty
- truancy or a drop in grades
- an unexplained change in eating or sleeping habits
- a constant need to borrow money
- less concern about hygiene or appearance
- waning interest in favorite sports or hobbies
- unusual emotional outbursts or a sudden change in friends

No Laughing Matter

Television sitcoms have a way of making light of heavy issues and ignoring consequences. Dr. David Crousman isn't amused. Specifically, he's upset about a running gag on *Will & Grace,* a recently retired, Emmy-winning series getting new life in syndication. Megan Mullally plays Karen Walker, a wealthy woman whose fondness for alcohol and prescription painkillers gets played for laughs.

"It's no joke at all," said Crousman, who runs an outpatient counseling facility in Beverly Hills. "It depicts a woman who's held hostage to her addiction. They're not showing her when she doesn't get her pain pill, when she doesn't have the alcohol. How she gets diarrhea, how she starts vomiting, how her skin will crawl, her legs will cramp. They don't show that because it's not cute."

It's the modern equivalent of the happy drunk. By downplaying the danger and cranking up the laugh track, the show's creators send a troubling message.

"They'll just reach their hands in there, take a handful and just take them. It could be anything."

Pharming parties also let users swap pills as if they were *Yu-Gi-Oh!* cards. "If I have something good, like OxyContin, it might be worth two or three Xanax," a girl told *Time.* "We rejoice when someone has a medical thing, like, gets their wisdom teeth out or has back pain, because we know we'll get pills. Last year I had surgery and I thought, Well, at least I'll get painkillers."

OxyContin seems to be the most popular . . . and deadly. Depending on the dose taken, OxyContin can slow or even halt breathing, especially when consumed with alcohol or other sedatives. Dubbed by one doctor "one of the strongest opiates and potentially addictive painkillers ever created," it was approved for round-the-clock pain, such as that experienced by patients with advanced stages of cancer. Its recreational use has increased 26 percent among 8th, 9th and 12th graders since 2002.

Dr. Nora Volkow, director of the National Institute on Drug Abuse, explained, "Some abusers bypass the time-release system by crushing or chewing the pills. That way, they get all of the drug their system at one time, and the body responds very differently. The risk of overdose then becomes huge. And an overdose of OxyContin can kill you."

That's precisely what happened to 17-year-old Julie Zdeblick. Julie's mother told *Family Circle,* "[Parents] are looking for alcohol and pot, not prescription drugs. It's like we got suited up for the game but were dressed for the wrong sport."

What Parents Can Do

With the medical community continuing to create stronger, more efficient drugs, the potential for this type of abuse will only get worse. Still, parents can take steps to keep teenagers from becoming statistics:

1. As part of an ongoing dialogue, give children a healthy respect for prescription medication. Express your strong disapproval of abuse. Silent or wishy-washy parents can be a teen's worst enemy.
2. Know which prescription drugs are in your home and keep them locked up. Even if your teens aren't tempted, guests could be. A New Jersey youth declared, "The best part about going to a new house was rifling through the medicine cabinet."
3. Be aware of how many pills remain in partially used prescriptions so you'll know if any are missing, and be sure to discard medications you're no longer taking.
4. Know which drugs are prone to be abused, including over-the-counter cough medicines containing dextromethorphan (or DXM), such as Robitussin DM and three of the four forms of Coricidin HPB.
5. Familiarize yourself with the warning signs of abuse *(see above)* so you can intervene before it's too late.
6. Explain the diminishing returns of drug abuse, which releases unnaturally large amounts of dopamine into the brain. Over time the brain gets used to it, and the addict ceases to enjoy life's normal pleasures without the dopamine flood that only the drugs can deliver.

Our overmedicated culture has a pill for just about everything. Ads for prescription drugs outnumber toothpaste commercials. So for many young people it's second nature to manage moods and stimulate performance with capsules that come in amber-colored plastic bottles. Members of Generation Rx need to know that, if not taken as intended, prescription drugs could land them in the emergency room . . . or the morgue.

Youth's Reactions to Disasters and the Factors That Influence Their Response

While most individuals are resilient even in the face of catastrophe, the chaos, confusion, and destruction as well as the human morbidity and mortality associated with disasters can create collective trauma.

BETTY PFEFFERBAUM, MD, JD, ET AL.

An apparent increase in disasters in recent years has garnered the attention of both professionals and the public resulting in an expanded knowledge base about these events and their effects. Disasters can damage and overwhelm the infrastructure needed for response. As we saw with Hurricane Katrina, inadequacies in response can engender enduring mistrust, demoralization, and social disarray. While most individuals are resilient even in the face of catastrophe, the chaos, confusion, and destruction as well as the human morbidity and mortality associated with disasters can create collective trauma (McFarlane & Norris, 2006). Youth are especially vulnerable to the effects of disasters. Their reactions span the continuum from distress and transient emotional and behavioral changes to impaired functioning and enduring psychopathology (Norris et al., 2002).

Disaster mental health is a burgeoning field with opportunities for general practitioners as well as specialists. In fact, disaster management encourages, and indeed depends on, professional and lay volunteers from the community where an event occurs. Fortunately, events do not occur often, but they are commonly unpredictable. Thus, some level of professional readiness is essential. This article addresses the need for preparedness by providing a basic primer on youth's disaster reactions and the factors that influence their reactions. Rather than providing a comprehensive critique of the literature, we review exemplary research to summarize pertinent findings and also present additional studies to highlight other issues of interest.

Disaster management encourages, and indeed depends on, professional and lay volunteers from the community where an event occurs.

Outcomes Associated with Disasters

Numerous studies have contributed to the knowledge base about child disaster mental health. The outcomes most commonly examined in relation to disasters are posttraumatic stress disorder (PTSD) and stress symptoms, depressive and anxiety disorders, disturbed behavior, grief, and impaired functioning.

In a comprehensive study of youth's reactions to disasters, William Yule and colleagues (2000) assessed a survivor group of over 200 young adults five to eight years after being exposed to a shipping disaster during their adolescence. This sample was compared to a group of sex- and age-matched friends and acquaintances attending the same school. Approximately one-half of the survivors developed incident-related PTSD, which endured for over five years in one-fourth of the survivors who developed the disorder (Yule et al., 2000). Rates of any new post-disaster anxiety or mood disorder among survivors who developed PTSD were higher than rates of these disorders among the unexposed participants. Survivors who did not develop PTSD did not have higher rates of anxiety and mood disorders than unexposed participants (Bolton et al., 2000). This suggests that the occurrence of other post-disaster disorders was more tied to vulnerability to PTSD rather than comprising an independent response to disaster exposure per se.

Some studies have investigated outcomes in terms of emotional and behavioral responses rather than diagnoses. For example, Shaw and colleagues (1995; 1996) examined a host of internalizing and externalizing symptoms in a longitudinal study of elementary school children (6–11 years of age) exposed to Hurricane Andrew. Participants in this study were enrolled in both high- and low-impact schools. The high impact school was directly in the path of the hurricane, while the low-impact school was north of Miami and not in the hurricane's direct path. Most children in both high- and low-impact schools exhibited at least moderate levels of symptoms. Two months after the event, children in the high-impact school had significantly higher posttraumatic symptom frequency scores than those in the low-impact school (Shaw et al., 1995). Posttraumatic stress symptoms decreased over time. At 21 months, 70% of all of the children from the high-impact school still exhibited moderate to severe symptoms (Shaw et al., 1996).

The findings related to externalizing behaviors are of particular interest. There was an initial marked decrease in school-reported externalizing behaviors in children in the high-impact school during the first two grading periods post-hurricane which was followed by a return to levels of the previous year. By contrast, in the low-impact school, there was a temporary increase in disruptive behavior, which the authors suggested may have resulted from increased demand and limited resources in the low-impact school due to the influx of students transferring from directly affected areas coupled with a shift of resources to directly affected areas (Shaw et al., 1995).

Traumatic grief, which may occur with loss of a loved one in traumatic events such as disasters, is conceptualized as intrusion of trauma symptoms into the bereavement process. Youth do not typically experience persistent trauma symptoms as part of the grief process even if the loss is traumatic (Cohen et al., 2002). With traumatic grief, thoughts and images can be so terrifying and anxiety-provoking that the child avoids or suppresses other thoughts and images of the deceased that might serve as comforting reminders of the person (Brown & Goodman, 2005). Preliminary evidence suggests that traumatic grief can be distinguished from normal grief. Brown and Goodman (2005) studied children (8–18 years of age) of uniformed service personnel killed in the 2001 World Trade Center attack. Factor analysis identified three distinct child response factors. The first, a traumatic grief factor, included PTSD symptoms (intrusive reexperiencing, avoidance/ numbing, hyperarousal), revenge, yearning, and impaired functioning. Two other factors, positive memory and ongoing presence, delineated normal grief responses. Positive memory appeared to capture the process of memory construction needed for the child to maintain an inner representation of the deceased. Ongoing presence of the deceased may provide comfort to the bereaved child.

Factors Affecting Outcome

Many factors can influence how youth respond to disasters. These can include the characteristics of the disaster and youth's exposure to it, individual characteristics, family factors, and the social environment—both pre- and post-disaster. See Table 1.

Disaster Characteristics and Exposure

The literature identifies disaster characteristics, and characteristics of the environment in which the disaster occurs, as predictors of outcome. These characteristics include, for example, predictability, duration, morbidity and mortality, property loss and destruction, disruption and chaos, and later secondary disaster-related adversities (e.g., unemployment and lost income) (Institute of Medicine, 2004). Predictability of a disaster is likely to influence preparedness activities. Duration may influence

Table 1 Factors Affecting Outcomes in Youth Exposed to Disasters

Disaster Characteristics
- Predictability of the disaster
- Duration of the disaster
- Morbidity and morality caused by the disaster
- Property loss and destruction due to the disaster
- Disruption and chaos created by the disaster
- Secondary adversities

Exposure
- Physical presence
- Close relationship to victims and survivors
- Subjective appraisal of danger and life threat
- Media coverage

Individual Characteristics
- Demographics (age, gender, ethnicity, socioeconomic status)
- Preexisting conditions

Family Factors
- Parental reactions
- Family interactions

Social Factors
- Social support

perceived life threat, loss, and secondary adversities. The extent of victimization and property damage may determine response and recovery efforts.

Youth may be exposed to disasters in many ways. For example, they may be physically present at the disaster site or their close family members and/or friends may be directly exposed. We know little about the relative importance of these exposures or about confounding effects among them. While not representing disaster exposure per se, youth may also lose cherished possessions in disasters, and they may watch extensive and graphic television coverage of the event, which can also be distressing and further confound exposure effects. Secondary adversities in the recovery environment may further stress children by creating hardship that precipitates, maintains, or increases negative reactions. Shaw and colleagues (1996) attributed increased psychopathology and high levels of enduring posttraumatic stress and behavioral disruption 21 months after Hurricane Andrew to experiences of persistent secondary adversities, ongoing traumatic reminders, and pervasive demoralization.

The youth's subjective appraisal of danger and life threat in association with an event is a key aspect of the traumatic experience. The diagnosis of PTSD requires a subjective reaction of "intense fear, helplessness, or horror" as part of exposure (American Psychiatric Association, 2000, p. 463). Numerous studies document the association between subjective appraisal of danger and life threat with adverse outcomes (Silverman & La Greca, 2002).

The youth's subjective appraisal of danger and life threat in association with an event is a key aspect of the traumatic experience.

For example, with the young adults exposed to the shipping disaster, subjective appraisal of life threat, along with the degree of exposure and level of anxiety measured five months post-disaster, were the best predictors of PTSD (Udwin et al., 2000).

Individual Characteristics

A number of individual characteristics have been linked to disaster outcomes. These include demographic features such as age, gender, and racial/ethnic heritage; preexisting disorders; and exposure to prior trauma.

Demographics: Of the demographic factors thought to be important in youth outcomes, only gender has been well studied and the results are inconsistent. The influence of age on trauma is complex (Silverman & La Greca, 2002). Immature cognitive and verbal ability may limit or alter the expression of distress in very young children, but that does not mean young children are unaffected. Greater cognitive capacities of older children and adolescents enable them to conceptualize the dangers that accompany disasters. Older children and adolescents also should have better developed coping skills to deal with these events. Studies suggest that ethnic minority youth may be at greater risk for maladaptation in the context of disasters than youth from the majority population (Silverman & La Greca, 2002). It is unclear, however, to what extent poorer outcome reflects differences in socioeconomic status, different disaster experiences, exposure to other traumatic events, and/or family or other social influences rather than ethnicity.

Greater cognitive capacities of older children and adolescents enable them to conceptualize the dangers that accompany disasters.

In the final analysis, demographic characteristics of youth exposed to disasters may prove less important than exposure and other variables in predicting disaster outcome. These other variables include preexisting conditions, exposure to other trauma, and family and social variables, as described in more detail below.

Preexisting Conditions: Disaster studies have identified the importance of preexisting conditions, especially anxiety symptoms and disorders, in disaster outcomes. For example, preexisting anxiety symptoms, attention problems, and academic difficulties predicted PTSD symptoms associated with Hurricane Andrew three months after the disaster while preexisting anxiety symptoms predicted PTSD symptoms seven months after the disaster (La Greca et al., 1998). Similarly, one year after the Northridge earthquake, youth (8–18 years of age)

with pre-event anxiety disorders had significantly more post-traumatic stress symptoms than did those without pre-event anxiety disorders. Neither pre-event depressive disorders nor disruptive behavior disorder were associated with PTSD symptoms (Asarnow et al., 1999).

Other Trauma: Exposure to other trauma also contributes to disaster outcome. In a study of children six months after Hurricane Andrew, lifetime trauma and post-hurricane events were among a number of variables that predicted PTSD (Garrison et al., 1995). Pfefferbaum and colleagues (2003) found that posttraumatic stress reactions related to other trauma contributed significantly to disaster-related posttraumatic stress in Nairobi school children (9–17 years of age) 8 to 14 months after the 1998 bombing of the U.S. Embassy.

Family Factors

While children's disaster reactions reflect their developmental status and thus may differ from those of adults, children's reactions generally parallel those of their parents in degree (Silverman & La Greca, 2002). Children may respond to parental distress, and they take cues from their parents about danger and safety. Decreasing strength in the relationship between parent and child reactions as children age may reflect increasing autonomy as youth develop and mature (Laor et al., 2001).

Children's reactions generally parallel those of their parents in degree.

The quality of interactions within the family also influences the child's adjustment (Laor et al., 2001; McFarlane, 1987). For example, McFarlane (1987) found emotional and behavioral problems in children from families characterized by parental irritable distress, over-involvement or enmeshment, and overprotection. Neither parental overprotection nor irritable distress alone was a problem, but together they did constitute problems for children, perhaps because parents in these families conveyed the potential for danger. High involvement and high parental irritable distress also created problems (McFarlane, 1987). A five-year longitudinal study of Israeli families displaced because of damage to their homes by SCUD missile attacks during the first Persian Gulf War found that family cohesion—the emotional bonds among family members—was a predictor of preschool-aged child adjustment. Both disengaged and enmeshed families created risk for displaced children. Disengaged families may not help the child process traumatic experiences while enmeshed families may spread unmodified negative emotions from one family member to another (Laor et al., 2001).

Social Factors

Social factors have not been well examined as predictors of child adjustment to disasters. Udwin and colleagues (2000) found that self-reported perceived and received social support just after a shipping disaster and at follow-up were associated with the development and duration of PTSD. Among adolescents with PTSD, those who reported receiving little or no help from their schools following the disaster had more PTSD symptoms (Udwin et al., 2000). Similarly, La Greca and colleagues (1996) found that children reporting high levels of social support from significant others during the three months immediately after Hurricane Andrew had fewer posttraumatic stress symptoms at ten months.

Among adolescents with PTSD, those who reported receiving little or no help from their schools following the disaster had more PTSD symptoms.

Conclusions and Implications for Providers

Research has documented stress reactions, PTSD, and comorbid conditions in youth exposed to disasters. As many as one-half of those directly exposed to severe events may develop diagnosable psychopathology which may endure for years. PTSD appears to be the most prevalent post-disaster disorder and to be associated with vulnerability to other disorders. Thus, providers working with youth in post-disaster environments should anticipate PTSD symptoms but must not be so focused on PTSD that they miss other treatable symptoms and conditions. In some youth, preexisting externalizing behavior problems may decrease initially, but these behaviors appear to resume later. Follow-up is essential to understanding the full course of youth's reactions and recovery.

Research has also elucidated a number of factors that contribute to youth outcomes including event characteristics and exposure, and individual, family, and social predictors. These factors help providers identify high-risk groups and they suggest service delivery strategies. For example, youth with the greatest exposure and those with preexisting conditions are likely to suffer the most. In addition, since youth in the disaster setting tend to respond to parental distress, interventions aimed at helping parents should benefit youth as well.

Additional research is essential to address numerous gaps in our knowledge. For example, more precision is necessary in exploring trauma exposure and its differential effects on outcome. Further research is also necessary to clarify the potential interactive risks created by socioeconomic disadvantage, preexisting conditions, and exposure to other trauma as well as to better delineate the contributions of family and various social factors. Moreover, our appreciation of outcomes and the factors that predispose and protect youth would be enhanced by systematic exploration of resilience, coping, and the factors that promote healthy adaptation.

While many youth are resilient in the face of disaster, distress in many and suffering in some requires professional attention. Disasters are often unpredictable, and they have the capacity to damage social and professional infrastructures, sometimes overwhelming response systems. The disaster mental health field is advancing, with apparent increased interest in the field. Providers who serve youth must prepare for disasters by learning about the effects of these events and about the factors that influence their effects.

References

American Psychiatric Association (2000). *Diagnostic and Statistical Manual of Mental Disorders* (4th ed., text rev.). Washington, DC: Author.

Asarnow, J., Glynn, S., Pynoos, R.S., Nahum, J., Guthrie, D., Cantwell, D.P., & Franklin, B. (1999). When the Earth stops shaking: Earthquake sequelae among children diagnosed for pre-earthquake psychopathology. *Journal of the American Academy of Child and Adolescent Psychiatry, 38*(8), 1,016–1,023.

Bolton, D., O'Ryan, D., Udwin, O., Boyle, S., & Yule, W. (2000). The long-term psychological effects of a disaster experienced in adolescence: II: General psychopathology. *Journal of Child Psychology and Psychiatry, 41*(4), 513–523.

Brown, E.J., & Goodman, R.F. (2005). Childhood traumatic grief: An exploration of the construct in children bereaved on September 11. *Journal of Clinical Child and Adolescent Psychology, 34*(2), 248–259.

Cohen, J.A., Mannarino, A.P., Greenberg, T., Padlo, S., & Shipley, C. (2002). Childhood traumatic grief: Concepts and controversies. *Trauma, Violence, & Abuse, 3*(4), 307–327.

Garrison, C.Z., Bryant, E.S., Addy, C.L., Spurrier, P.G., Freedy, J.R., & Kilpatrick, D.G. (1995). Posttraumatic stress disorder in adolescents after Hurricane Andrew. *Journal of the American Academy of Child and Adolescent Psychiatry, 34*(9), 1,193–1,201.

Institute of Medicine (2004). *Preparing for the Psychological Consequences of Terrorism: A Public Health Strategy.* Washington, DC: The National Academies Press.

La Greca, A.M., Silverman, W.K., Vernberg, E.M., & Prinstein, M.J. (1996). Symptoms of posttraumatic stress in children after Hurricane Andrew: A prospective study. *Journal of Consulting and Clinical Psychology, 64*(4), 712–723.

La Greca, A.M., Silverman, W.K., & Wasserstein, S.B. (1998). Children's predisaster functioning as a predictor of posttraumatic stress following Hurricane Andrew. *Journal of Consulting and Clinical Psychology, 66*(6), 883–892.

Laor, N., Wolmer, L., & Cohen, D.J. (2001). Mothers' functioning and children's symptoms 5 years after a SCUD missile attack. *American Journal of Psychiatry, 158*(7), 1,020–1,026.

McFarlane, A.C. (1987). The relationship between patterns of family interaction and psychiatric disorder in children. *Australian and New Zealand Journal of Psychiatry, 21,* 383–390.

McFarlane, A.C., & Norris, F.H. (2006). Definitions and concepts in disaster research. In F.H. Norris, S. Galea, M.J. Friedman, & P.J. Watson (Eds.), *Methods for disaster mental health research* (pp. 3–19). New York: Guilford Press.

Norris, F.H., Friedman, M.J., Watson, P.J., Byrne, C.M., Diaz, E., & Kaniasty, K. (2002). 60,000 disaster victims speak: Part I. An empirical review of the empirical literature, 1981–2001. *Psychiatry, 65*(3), 207–239.

Pfefferbaum, B., & North, C.S. (in press). Children and families in the context of disasters: Implications for preparedness and response. *The Family Psychologist.*

Pfefferbaum, B., North, C.S., Doughty, D.E., Gurwitch, R.H., Fullerton, C.S., & Kyula, J. (2003). Posttraumatic stress and functional impairment in Kenyan children following the 1998 American Embassy bombing. *American Journal of Orthopsychiatry, 73*(2), 133–140.

Shaw, J.A., Applegate, B., & Schorr, C. (1996). Twenty-one-month follow-up study of school-age children exposed to Hurricane Andrew. *Journal of the American Academy of Child and Adolescent Psychiatry, 35*(3), 359–364.

Shaw, J.A., Applegate, B., Tanner, S., Perez, D., Rothe, E., Campo-Bowen, A.E., & Lahey, B.L. (1995). Psychological effects of Hurricane Andrew on an elementary school population. *Journal of the American Academy of Child and Adolescent Psychiatry, 34*(9), 1,185–1,192.

Silverman, W.K., & La Greca, A.M. (2002). Children experiencing disasters: Definitions, reactions, and predictors of outcomes. In A.M. La Greca, W.K. Silverman, E.M. Vernberg, & M.C. Roberts (Eds.), *Helping children cope with disasters and terrorism* (pp. 11–33). Washington, DC: American Psychological Association.

Udwin, O., Boyle, S., Yule, W., Bolton, D., & O'Ryan, D. (2000). Risk factors for long-term psychological effects of a disaster experienced in adolescence: Predictors of post traumatic stress disorder. *Journal of Child Psychology and Psychiatry, 41*(8), 969–979.

Yule, W., Bolton, D., Udwin, O., Boyle, S., O'Ryan, D., & Nurrish, J. (2000). The long-term psychological effects of a disaster experienced in adolescence: I: The incidence and course of PTSD. *Journal of Child Psychology and Psychiatry, 41*(4), 503–511.

BETTY PFEFFERBAUM, MD, JD, (betty-pfefferbaum@ouhsc.edu) is the Paul and Ruth Jonas Chair in the Department of Psychiatry and Behavioral Sciences at the University of Oklahoma Health Sciences Center, Oklahoma City, Oklahoma. **J. BRIAN HOUSTON, PhD,** is Assistant Professor of Research in the Department of Psychiatry and Behavioral Sciences at the University of Oklahoma Health Sciences Center, Oklahoma City, Oklahoma. **CAROL S. NORTH, MD, MPE,** is the **NANCY** and **RAY L. HUNT CHAIR** in Crisis Psychiatry and Professor of Psychiatry and Surgery at the University of Texas Southwestern Medical Center, Dallas, Texas. **JAMES L. REGENS, PhD,** is Presidential Professor and Director of the Center for Biosecurity Research at the University of Oklahoma Health Sciences Center, Oklahoma City, Oklahoma.

Acknowledgement—This work was supported in part by the Substance Abuse and Mental Health Services Administration (SAMHSA) grant 5 U79 SM057278-03 and the National Institute of Mental Health (NIMH), National Institute of Nursing Research (NINR), and SAMHSA grant 5 R25 MH070569-04 to Betty Pfefferbaum; the NIMH grant RO1 MH068853-06 to Carol S. North; and the Defense Threat Reduction Agency (DTRA) and the Air Force Research Laboratory under Cooperative Agreement FA8650-05-2-6523 to James L. Regens. Points of view expressed in this article are those of the authors and do not represent the official position of SAMHSA, NIMH, NINR, DTRA, or the Air Force Research Laboratory.

Test-Your-Knowledge Form

We encourage you to photocopy and use this page as a tool to assess how the articles in *Annual Editions* expand on the information in your textbook. By reflecting on the articles you will gain enhanced text information. You can also access this useful form on a product's book support website at *http://www.mhcls.com*.

NAME: DATE:

_____

TITLE AND NUMBER OF ARTICLE:

_____

BRIEFLY STATE THE MAIN IDEA OF THIS ARTICLE:

_____

LIST THREE IMPORTANT FACTS THAT THE AUTHOR USES TO SUPPORT THE MAIN IDEA:

_____

WHAT INFORMATION OR IDEAS DISCUSSED IN THIS ARTICLE ARE ALSO DISCUSSED IN YOUR TEXTBOOK OR OTHER READINGS THAT YOU HAVE DONE? LIST THE TEXTBOOK CHAPTERS AND PAGE NUMBERS:

_____

LIST ANY EXAMPLES OF BIAS OR FAULTY REASONING THAT YOU FOUND IN THE ARTICLE:

_____

LIST ANY NEW TERMS/CONCEPTS THAT WERE DISCUSSED IN THE ARTICLE, AND WRITE A SHORT DEFINITION:

We Want Your Advice

ANNUAL EDITIONS revisions depend on two major opinion sources: one is our Advisory Board, listed in the front of this volume, which works with us in scanning the thousands of articles published in the public press each year; the other is you—the person actually using the book. Please help us and the users of the next edition by completing the prepaid article rating form on this page and returning it to us. Thank you for your help!

ANNUAL EDITIONS: Adolescent Psychology 7/e

ARTICLE RATING FORM

Here is an opportunity for you to have direct input into the next revision of this volume.
We would like you to rate each of the articles listed below, using the following scale:

1. **Excellent: should definitely be retained**
2. **Above average: should probably be retained**
3. **Below average: should probably be deleted**
4. **Poor: should definitely be deleted**

Your ratings will play a vital part in the next revision.
Please mail this prepaid form to us as soon as possible.
Thanks for your help!

RATING	ARTICLE
	1. Trashing Teens
	2. Profile in Caring
	3. A Peaceful Adolescence
	4. Something to Talk About
	5. Youth Participation: From Myths to Effective Practice
	6. Healthier Students, Better Learners
	7. Mental Assessment Test
	8. Body Dissatisfaction in Adolescent Females and Males: Risk and Resilience
	9. Goodbye to Girlhood
	10. Influence of Music on Youth Behaviors
	11. Researchers Examine the Impact of Early Experiences on Development
	12. Adolescent Stress
	13. Coping with Stress
	14. ADHD and the SUD in Adolescents
	15. Supporting Youth during Parental Deployment: Strategies for Professionals and Families
	16. When Play Turns to Trouble
	17. Aggression in Adolescent Dating Relationships: Predictors and Prevention
	18. A Host of Trouble
	19. Great Expectations
	20. Reclaiming 'Abstinence' in Comprehensive Sex Education
	21. Give Students the Knowledge to Make Wise Choices about Sex
	22. The Perils of Playing House

RATING	ARTICLE
	23. The Dropout Problem: Losing Ground
	24. My Year as a High School Student
	25. School's New Rule for Pupils in Trouble: No Fun
	26. In an Era of School Shootings, Lockdowns Are the New Drill
	27. Effects of After-School Employment on Academic Performance
	28. Immigrant Youth in U.S. Schools: Opportunities for Prevention
	29. Reducing School Violence: School-Based Curricular Programs and School Climate
	30. The Cultural Plunge
	31. Character and Academics: What Good Schools Do
	32. High School with a College Twist
	33. Video Game Violence
	34. The Overdominance of Computers
	35. Bullying at School among Older Adolescents
	36. Underage Drinking Debate: Zero Tolerance vs. Teaching Responsibility
	37. Problem Gambling in Youth—A Hidden Addiction
	38. Understanding Cutting in Adolescents: Prevalence, Prevention, and Intervention
	39. Violence in Adolescent Dating Relationships
	40. Prevention of Domestic Violence during Adolescence
	41. Prescription for Disaster
	42. Youth's Reactions to Disasters and the Factors That Influence Their Response

BUSINESS REPLY MAIL
FIRST CLASS MAIL PERMIT NO. 551 DUBUQUE IA

POSTAGE WILL BE PAID BY ADDRESSEE

McGraw-Hill Contemporary Learning Series
501 BELL STREET
DUBUQUE, IA 52001

ABOUT YOU

Name

Date

_____

Are you a teacher? ☐ A student? ☐
Your school's name

_____

Department

_____

Address   City   State   Zip

_____

School telephone #

_____

YOUR COMMENTS ARE IMPORTANT TO US!

Please fill in the following information:
For which course did you use this book?

_____

Did you use a text with this ANNUAL EDITION? ☐ yes ☐ no
What was the title of the text?

_____

What are your general reactions to the Annual Editions concept?

_____

Have you read any pertinent articles recently that you think should be included in the next edition? Explain.

_____

Are there any articles that you feel should be replaced in the next edition? Why?

_____

Are there any World Wide Websites that you feel should be included in the next edition? Please annotate.

_____

May we contact you for editorial input? ☐ yes ☐ no
May we quote your comments? ☐ yes ☐ no

NOTES

NOTES

NOTES

NOTES

NOTES

NOTES

NOTES

NOTES